Human–Computer Interaction INTERACT '99

IFIP TC.13 International Conference
on Human–Computer Interaction,
30th August – 3rd September 1999, Edinburgh, UK.

Volume II

Edited by

Stephen Brewster
University of Glasgow
UK

Alison Cawsey
Heriot-Watt University
UK

Gilbert Cockton
University of Sunderland
UK

Published by the British Computer Society on behalf of the
International Federation for Information Processing (IFIP)

ISBN 1-902505-19-0 (British Computer Society)

Publisher
British Computer Society
1 Sanford Street
Swindon,
Wiltshire,
SN1 1HJ
UK

Distributer
Digital Media Network
The Informatics Centre
University of Sunderland,
PO Box 299,
Sunderland, SR6 0YN,
UK
Email: dmn@dmn.org.uk

Printed in the United Kingdom by The Edinburgh Press.

Human-Computer Interaction

INTERACT '99

(Volume II)

IFIP — The International Federation for Information Processing

IFIP was founded in 1960 under the auspices of UNESCO, following the First World Computer Congress held in Paris the previous year. An umbrella organization for societies working in information processing, IFIP's aim is two-fold: to support information processing within its member countries and to encourage technology transfer to developing nations. As its mission statement clearly states:

> IFIP's mission is to be the leading, truly international, apolitical organization which encourages and assists in the development, exploitation and application of information technology for the benefit of all people.

IFIP is a non-profitmaking organization, run almost solely by 2500 volunteers. It operates through a number of technical committees, which organize events and publications. IFIP's events range from an international congress to local seminars, but the most important are:

- the IFIP World Computer Congress, held every second year;
- open conferences;
- working conferences.

The flagship event is the IFIP World Computer Congress, at which both invited and contributed papers are presented. Contributed papers are rigorously refereed and the rejection rate is high.

As with the Congress, participation in open conferences is open to all and papers may be invited or submitted. Again, submitted papers are stringently refereed.

The working conferences are structured differently. They are usually run by a working group and attendance is small and by invitation only. Their purpose is to create an atmosphere conducive to innovation and development. Refereeing is less rigorous and papers are subjected to extensive group discussion.

Publications arising from IFIP events vary. The papers presented at the IFIP World Computer Congress and at open conferences are published as conference proceedings, while the results of the working conferences are often published as collections of selected and edited papers.

Any national society whose primary activity is in information may apply to become a full member of IFIP, although full membership is restricted to one society per country. Full members are entitled to vote at the Annual General Assembly. National societies preferring a less committed involvement may apply for associate or corresponding membership. Associate members enjoy the same benefits as full members, but without voting rights. Corresponding members are not represented in IFIP bodies. Affiliated membership is open to non-national societies, and individual and honorary membership schemes are also offered.

Contents

Part One **Keynote Speakers**

Part Two **Technical Sessions**

Part Three **Doctoral Consortium**

The first three parts appear in Volume I of the INTERACT '99 Proceedings Published by IOS Press.

IFIP TC.13 Preface xi

Editors' Preface xiii

IFIP TC.13 xiv

IFIP TC.13 Members xv

International Programme Committee xvii

Volume II Additional Reviewers xviii

INTERACT '99 Committees xix

Part Four **Posters** 1

Influences of Software Design on Formal Reasoning 3
J. Aczel, P. Fung, R. Bornat, M. Oliver, T. O'Shea and B. Sufrin

Demonstrating the Concept of Physical Hyperspace for an Art Gallery 5
Chris Baber, Toby Harris and Bob Harrison

Multimodal Eye-Based Interaction for Zoomed Target Selection on a Standard Graphical User Interface 7
Richard Bates

PUMA: Bridging Disciplinary Gulfs in HCI 9
Ann Blandford, Richard Butterworth and Jason Good

How do we Build Web Sites Fit for Purpose? 11
George Buchanan, Gil Marsden, Harold Thimbleby and Yin Leng Theng

Enhancing Interaction Scenarios with Domain-Oriented Visualizations 13
Tom Carey, Kevin Harrigan and Simon Holland

Integrating 'Hard' and 'Soft' Approaches to Modelling Intuition in Retail Site Assessment 15
Ian Clarke, William Mackaness and Masahide Horita

Inside the Consumer's Wallet: An Ethnographic Inquiry 17
Lee Cooper, Graham Johnson and Chris Baber

Scope for Progress – Monitoring Background Tasks with Sound 19
Murray Crease and Stephen Brewster

Resource Sensitive Multi-Modal Widgets 21
Murray Crease, Philip Gray and Stephen Brewster

Spatial Data Management Systems: Human Factors Perspectives 23
T. Cribbin and S. Westerman

Costs Matrix: Systematic Comparison of Competing Design Solutions 25
Stephen Cummaford and John Long

Virtual Actors in Collaborative Virtual Environments for Museum Education 27
Daphne Economou, William Mitchell and Tom Boyle

Workplace Groups, Status Differences and Multimedia Communications Technology 29
Emma France

Improving Understanding Using Video Technology 31
David Grayson

PRIDE: Task-Related Principles for User Interface Design 33
Fraser Hamilton, Hilary Johnson and Peter Johnson

Assembly Training with Augmented Reality and Virtual Reality 35
David Haniff, Andy Boud and Chris Baber

A Support System for the Visually Impaired Using a Windows PC and Multimedia 37
Satoshi Ina

Speechreading-Phone for the Hearing Impaired 39
Christian Martyn Jones and Satnam Singh Dlay

The Impact of Computer Mediated Communication (CMC) on Conflict Resolution 41
L.Katz, A. Thatcher and D. Trepess

Who Are Qualified for Usability Evaluation? 43
Masaaki Kurosu and Sachiyo Matsuura

Improving the Design of Telephone-Based Interfaces 45
Grégory Leplâtre and Stephen Brewster

Using Computing Science Principles in Interface Design 47
Gary Marsden, P. Gillary, M. Jones and H. Thimbleby

Choosing the UI Tool Which Best Suits Your Needs 49
Joanna McKirdy

A Laser Pen for a Virtual Wallpaper 51
G. Ménier and F. Poirier

Dynamic Training Feedback: A Test-Bed for Naval Training 53
Amanda O'Shea and Catherine Cook

A Pragmatic Evaluation Methodology for an Assessment of Learning Effectiveness of Instructional Systems 55
Clark Quinn, Leila Alem and John Eklund

A State Transition Model Representing Pen-based Selection Strategies 57
Xiangshi Ren and Shinji Moriya

Human Factors and the WWW: Making sense of URLs 59
Dominic Stanyer and Rob Procter

An Investigation of the Properties of Information as the Common Object of Cooperative Work 61
Ros Strens, Susan Turner and Phil Turner

Fear Reduction for Seniors 63
Richard C. Thomas

Syndetic Modelling of Engaging Electronic Lifeforms 65
Mark Treglown

Trading Space for Time in Interface Design 67
Ashley Walker and Stephen Brewster

Do CTA Findings Influence Design? 69
B.L. William Wong

Part Five Videos 71

Meeting in the Magic Lounge 73
Bryan Cleal, Masood Masoodian, Niels Ole Bernsen and Laila Dybkjær

Part Six Interactive Experience 75

HyperMask: Projection onto 3D Moving Surfaces 77
Kim Binsted, Shigeo Morishima, Frank Nielsen, Claudio Pinhanez and Tatsuo Yotsukura

'Dissemination': Indexing Peers' Learning Experiences as a Multimedia Discourse Database 79
F. Dineen and J.T. Mayes

Providing Critiquing Support for Web Page Design 81
Pete Faraday

Interactions with a Three-Dimensional Sound World 83
Frederic Foveau and Jean-Claude Tarby

Semantic Highlighting: Enhancing Search Engine Display and Web Document Interactivity 85
Ali Hussam, Terry Anderson, Nathan Jacobs, Damon Eckhoff, Ali Meryyan and Yunhai Yang

Joovin8 - Narrative Interactions 87
Andrew Hutchison

Explorers of the Ancient World: Egypt 89
Sarah Jensen, Jennifer Kelley and Allison O'Mahony

Haptic Visualization of Spatial Structures by Low-cost Force-Feedback Devices 91
Anders Johansson and Joakim Linde

Adding Tactile Feedback to the Trackpoint: A Demonstration of Tractile 93
Paul Maglio, Shumin Zhai, Christopher Campbell, Kim May and Barton Smith

Designing for Navigation in Virtual Reality 95
David Modjeska

Haptic Visualisation 97
Ian Oakley, Stephen Brewster, Aidan Glendye and Michelle M. Masters

How a Professional Firm Uses an Interactive Internet Game to Talk to Students 99
Cathrine Strand, Tone Pettersen and Helge Storøy

Mutator for the Blind Musician 101
Stephen Todd

Part Seven Tutorials 103

Designing Movement in Interactive Multimedia: Making it Meaningful 105
Michelle Bacigalupi

Industry Standard Usability Tests 107
Nigel Bevan

Planning and Implementing User-Centred Design 109
Nigel Bevan

Solution Engineering Techniques 111
Anthony Crawford

Producing Usable Artefacts with Java 2.0 113
Fintan Culwin

From Components to JavaBeans 115
Fintan Culwin

Human-Centred Processes, Their Maturity and Their Improvement 117
Jonathan Earthy, Brian Sherwood-Jones and Jenny Weston

Computing Outside the Box 119
Chris Esposito

Programming Collaborative Applications for the Web 121
Andreas Girgensohn and Alison Lee

Cognitive Factors in Design: Basic Phenomena in Human Memory and Problem Solving 123
Thomas Hewett

Contextual Inquiry: Gathering and Using Customer Data 125
Karen Holtzblatt and Hugh Beyer

Designing Speech-driven User Interfaces 127
Tony Rose and Elisa del Galdo

Designing Multimedia Presentations 129
Alistair Sutcliffe and Stephanie Wilson

Part Eight Workshops 131

Second Workshop on Human-Computer Interaction with Mobile Devices 133
Stephen Brewster and Mark Dunlop

HCI - Theory or Practice in Education 134
Margaret Cox, Lars Oestreicher, Clark Quinn, Matthias Rauterberg and Markus Stoltze

Usability Pattern Language: Creating a community 135
Richard N. Griffiths, Lyn Pemberton and Jan Borchers

How to Make User Centred Design Usable 136
Jan Gulliksen, Ann Lantz and Inger Boivie

Workshop on the Organisational Aspects of Human Error and Systems Failure 137
Chris Johnson

Methodology for Design: CUI, GUI or Web 138
Joseph Kramer and Eugenie Bertus

Making Designers Aware of Existing Guidelines for Accessibility 139
Monique Noirhomme-Fraiture, Julio Gonzalez-Abascal and Colette Nicolle

Representational Support for User-Developer Communication in Systems Development 140
Eamonn O'Neill, Hilary Johnson, Peter Johnson and Pat Healey

Is Cognitive Engineering the Way Forward for HCI? 141
Adam Stork, John Long and Tony Lambie

Part Nine Professional Practice and Experience 143

Human Factors and the Design of an Enhanced GUI to Support Post-Production Tasks 145
Clare Borras and Richard Foster

More Than Meets the Eye! Usability and Iris Verification at the ATM Interface 151
Lynne Coventry and Graham Johnson

Turbo-Prototyping: Ultra Rapid User Centred Web Development 157
Gautam Ghosh

Usability Designers Improve the User-Centred Design Process 163
Bengt Göransson and Torsten Sandbäck

Measuring the Usability of WWW Sites: Lessons Learned in a Commercial Development Environment 168
Karen Gunn

Using Quantitative Usability Goals in the Design of a User Interface for a Cellular Phone 174
Timo Jokela and Jani Pirkola

Microwave Bank: Consumers in Context 179
Paula Lynch and Alexandra Trabak

Supporting Collaboration in Multimedia Design 185
Marianne Graves Petersen and Kim Halskov Madsen

Scenario-Based System Validation by Users 191
Barbara Schmidt-Belz, Dietmar Fleischhauer and Oliver Märker

Experiences (Painful and Good) Developing HCI Standards 196
Tom Stewart

No Pain, No Gain - Applying User-Centered Design in Product Concept Development 201
Tiina Hynninen, Tea Liukkonen-Olmiala and Timo Kinnunen

Part Ten Panels 207

Story and the Design of Participatory Media 209
Ivor Benjamin, Kim Binsted, Lydia Plowman, Sharon Springel and John Thomas

'Artificial Morality': Representations of Trust in Interactive Systems 211
Elisabeth Davenport, Harold Thimbleby, Steve Marsh and Mark Dibben

Gender and Human-Computer Interaction 213
D. Ramanee Peiris, Alison Crerar, Peter Gregor, Britta Schinzel and indigo V

Interfaces with an Attitude 215
Govert de Vries and Paula Lynch

From Analysis to Design: Do Different Analytical Methods Make a Difference? 217
Catherine G. Wolf, Christine Halverson, Victor Kaptelinin, Andrew Shepherd and John Karat

Part Eleven Laboratory Overviews 219

E.S.R.C. Cognitive Engineering Programme 221
Anne Anderson, Rose Luckin, Andrew Monk, Jean McKendree and Tom Ormerod

Designing the Human Experience at Nortel Networks 223
Mike Atyeo, Judith Ramsay and Judith Rattle

Applied Computing at the University of Dundee 225
Peter Gregor and Alan F. Newell

Laboratory Overview: Human Communication Research Centre, University of Edinburgh 227
HCRC

NCR Knowledge Lab 229
P. Lynch, S. Emmott and G. Johnson

Many Irons in the Fire: A Strategic Usability Programme in Lucent Technologies Network Management 231
Rod Moyse

The Centre for HCI Design - City University 233
Alistair Sutcliffe

Author Index 235

IFIP TC.13 Preface

Fifteen years ago the first INTERACT Conference was held in the United Kingdom. It set out the main areas of study which made up the discipline at that time. One hundred and fifty two papers addressed issues under the headings: user aspects, hardware interface, software interface, cognitive aspects, design and implementation, wider issues and application. Additional components of the conference focussed on an application emphasis devoted to behavioural issues in the system life cycle and usage aspects of electronic mail, conferencing and journals.

Professor Brian Shackel, the conference chair, drew attention to four general aspects of HCI research. He considered that hardware ergonomics was well covered and did not need to be enlarged; that software human factors and cognitive ergonomics were important areas needing growth; that the basic issue of human cognitive characteristics and performance when interacting with computing and IT systems needed to become better known and a sound theoretical basis established; that the inter-relationship of computing and IT systems with job and organisational structure and functioning was a large and complex gap in HCI research.

He concluded that "at last we are beginning to recognise and understand just how much we do not know and how much still needs to be studied" and made a plea for larger funds to allow the reduction of ".. the extent to which our knowledge about computer technology exceeds our knowledge about human usage of that technology."

In the intervening years technological development has been exponential. Technologies have come and gone, some have persisted. The social and work environment has changed dramatically. Most applications developed today pay little heed of HCI and the need to integrate it into the development life cycle. Has Shackel's prediction been realised ?

INTERACT '99 provides an opportunity for some response to these issues. It can be seen that learning, design and evaluation tools and techniques, organisation issues and social psychology are still active fields of research. It is also clear that new phenomena such as the web and its applications, 3-dimensional and virtual environments, mobile systems, and emerging forms of applications, such as electronic commerce, are current, vibrant grounds for the application of HCI research.

Today, one of the most written and spoken about impacts of computing and IT is communication and the easy accessibility to information. Geography is no longer a constraint. With these advances in first and second world nations, and slower introduction to the third world, an enlarging proportion of the world population is encountering computer based systems. This brings a changing basis of approach, as issues such as cultural, political and economic differences must be accommodated in ways that have not existed before.

HCI researchers and practitioners have a responsibility to propose scientifically, socially and environmentally sustainable solutions that will help ease the burden that current new technologies impose on people and organisations. The goal must be to achieve benefit from technological advances, for it should match the skills, needs and expectations of users of those technologies.

This volume of proceedings is a permanent record of the panels, posters, videos, interactive experiences, tutorials and workshops, laboratory and organisational overviews and professional practice and experience components that were part of INTERACT '99. The paper presentations and the doctoral consortium are recorded in Volume 1 of the INTERACT '99 Proceedings, published by the IOS Press and available from them. The sum reveals the growth of international HCI in terms of facets and the depth of examination that has occurred since the 1984 INTERACT.

Its internationality is reflected by the number of countries represented by presenters and by IFIP's determination, through the Developing Countries Support Committee scheme, to support HCI scientists from Africa, China, India and South America so that they can participate in this INTERACT conference.

IFIP TC.13 provides quality activities and publications that promote and advance HCI in all regions of the world associated with IFIP. INTERACT '99 is a major part of this undertaking and I thank the British Computer Society, through the British HCI Group, for inviting the conference to Edinburgh. The Group has incorporated its annual conference within INTERACT '99 - a gesture that is warmly acknowledged by TC.13. This joint activity will refresh the HCI community nationally as well as internationally.

TC.13 thanks most sincerely the conference chair, Professor Alistair Kilgour, and all the members making up the INTERACT '99 committees for their substantial efforts in creating this conference. Dedication is the facilitator of a conference such as INTERACT '99. This conference organisation has once again shown that spirit. It is reflected in the work of the various professional societies which are co-operating societies whose active support brings the international theme to the fore. Corporate sponsors have also played a significant role in making the conference possible. IFIP TC.13 is strengthened through these alliances which demonstrate a common goal - the advancement of HCI around the world.

Special recognition goes to those who helped in the creation of the technical programme and proceedings, particularly the Editors, the International Programme Committee and those undertaking organisational aspects that are integral to covering the diversity and complexity of such a conference. Their names are recorded in this volume.

The International Conference Committee has provided unstinting support and advice to the INTERACT '99 committee during the long period of planning. Their involvement is much appreciated, especially that of the INTERACT Conference Advisor, Professor Brian Shackel, whose substantial knowledge and experience of all preceding INTERACT conferences has been invaluable.

With members of committees being geographically disbursed, the organisation of this conference has been made possible by technology. Email and the World-Wide Web were employed at all stages and for most processes - something that could not have been done in earlier conferences in the series.

Achieving a high standard is the continuing goal of TC.13. This publication is a component of that goal. We are indebted to the editors of this volume for their efforts to create this book in the style of volume 1 by collaborating over many weeks (by email with attachments) with Professor Brian Shackel and me, the conference chair and others involved in the production of the whole INTERACT Proceedings.

Unfortunately it is not possible, at the time of publication, to identify the paper which has been awarded the initial Brian Shackel Award for the most outstanding contribution in the form of a refereed paper submitted to and delivered at each INTERACT conference. Reference to the IFIP TC.13 web site will do that, as the paper will be mounted there. The Award marks the contribution of Professor Brian Shackel to the establishment of HCI as an international discipline, and is intended to draw attention to the need for a comprehensive human-centred approach in the design and use of information technology in which the human and social implications have been taken into account.

Without the submission of papers, a conference cannot occur. TC.13 sincerely thanks all those who spent much effort in developing their papers and making their presentations. The role of the world-wide reviewers is also acknowledged as their judgements made possible the assembly of a diverse set of papers and so have enabled the sharing of HCI knowledge and advances both at the conference and in the Proceedings.

Judy Hammond
IFIP TC.13 Chair
University of Technology, Sydney, Australia

Editors' Preface: Sparks and Seeds

Volume 1 covers three of the ages of an HCI researcher (don't ask us what the other four are!) It descends from the crowns of distinguished researchers and practitioners at the peak of their careers, via the substantial body of mature HCI research, to the first steps of the doctoral consortium candidates. These papers capture, in written form, the state of the art in the discipline.

However, as Sasse and Johnson acknowledge in their preface to volume 1, there are real difficulties in getting the high quality research in this area to have an impact on current practice. One way that this is addressed at INTERACT conferences is by providing a range of tracks that provide a more immediate demonstration and experience of innovations. HCI is too visual and tangible to leave all communication to the written form. We need to see (and sometimes hear and feel) it "happening" and argue with fellow practitioners.

This volume is thus in some ways a tease. It contains two page summaries of the most interactive activities at INTERACT '99. It thus resorts to the written form for those aspects of the conference that require a more interactive presentation. It begins with the Posters, which were displayed throughout the main part of the conference, with attendance by their authors to allow discussion of the reported research. It continues with the Video and Interactive Experience tracks. Both videos and direct demonstration can communicate the realities of interaction with a fidelity that must evade the written form. In parts eight and ten, there are previews of the debates and discussions from the Workshops and Panels. The remaining sections summarise more conventional presentations: summaries of Tutorials (part seven), the Professional Practice and Experience track (part nine); and the Laboratory Overviews (part eleven).

Although the balance of submissions reported in this volume had a critical interactive component at the conference, what actually unites these accepted submissions is their timeliness. All accepted submissions were received by an early May deadline, and therefore provide a current and we hope fresh and vital perspective on the field. However, this has not been achieved at the expense of reviewing standards.

Every submission in this volume has received at least three reviews, from track chairs, the International Programme Committee, and from additional reviewers recruited because of their particular expertise. Thus every submission published in this volume has been refereed to the standards required by an international conference of INTERACT's standing. We are grateful to all those who have contributed in producing what we believe is a high quality publication, but particularly to all the track chairs, and to our reviewers, all of whom have given generously of their time without thought of renumeration. We would also like to thank the PhD students who helped in the production of the volume, and the Engineering and Physical Sciences Research Council (EPSRC), which provided special financial support allowing projects funded by them to be presented here. (Such projects are marked with the EPSRC logo).

The diversity of contributions in this volume defies summary. We leave you to enjoy this diversity and its implications for future directions in HCI. They are the sparks of innovation and the seeds of future achievements in HCI.

Stephen Brewster
University of Glasgow, UK

Alison Cawsey
Heriot-Watt University, UK

Gilbert Cockton
University of Sunderland, UK

IFIP TC.13

Established in 1989, the International Federation for Information Processing Technical Committee on Human–Computer Interaction (IFIP TC.13) is an international committee of 23 member national societies and 5 Working Groups, representing specialists in human factors, ergonomics, cognitive science, computer science, design and related disciplines.

IFIP TC.13 aims to develop a science and technology of human–computer interaction by encouraging empirical research, promoting the use of knowledge and methods from the human sciences in design and evaluation of computer systems; promoting better understanding of the relation between formal design methods and system usability and acceptability; developing guidelines, models and methods by which designers may provide better human-oriented computer systems; and, co-operating with other groups, inside and outside IFIP, to promote user-orientation and 'humanization' in system design. Thus, TC.13 seeks to improve interactions between people and computers, encourage the growth of HCI research and disseminate these benefits world-wide.

The main orientation is towards users, especially the non-computer professional users, and how to improve human–computer relations between them. Areas of study include: the problems people have with computers; the impact on people in individual and organizational contexts; the determinants of utility, usability and acceptability; the appropriate allocation of tasks between computers and users; modelling the user to aid better system design; and harmonizing the computer to user characteristics and needs.

While the scope is thus set wide, with a tendency towards general principles rather than particular systems, it is recognized that progress will only be achieved through both general studies to advance theoretical understanding and specific studies on practical issues (e.g. interface design standards, software system consistency, documentation, appropriateness of alternative communication media, human factors guidelines for dialogue design, the problems of integrating multimedia systems to match system needs and organizational practices, etc.).

IFIP TC.13 stimulates working events and activities through its Working Groups. WGs consist of HCI experts from many countries, who seek to expand knowledge and find solutions to HCI issues and concerns within their domains, as outlined below:

WG13.1 (***Education in HCI and HCI Curricula***) aims to improve HCI education at all levels of higher education, coordinate and unite efforts to develop HCI curricula and promote HCI teaching.

WG13.2 (***Methodology for User-centred System Design***) aims to foster research, dissemination of information and good practice in the methodical application of HCI to software engineering.

WG13.3 (***HCI and People with Special Needs***) aims to make HCI designers aware of the special needs of disabled and elderly people and encourage development of systems, hardware and software tools permitting adaptation of interfaces to individual users.

WG13.4 (also WG2.7) (***User Interface Engineering***) investigates the nature, concepts and construction of user interfaces for software systems, using a framework for reasoning about interactive systems and an engineering model for developing user interfaces.

WG13.5 (***Human Error, Safety and System Development***) seeks a framework for studying human factors relating to systems failure, develops leading edge techniques in hazard analysis and safety engineering of computer-based systems, and guides international accreditation activities for safety-critical systems.

New Working Groups are formed as areas of significance to HCI arise. Further information is available at the IFIP TC.13 website: http://www.csd.uu.se/ifip_tc13/

IFIP TC.13 Members

Australia
Judy Hammond (IFIP TC.13 Chair)
Australian Computer Society

Austria
Michael Tauber
Austrian Computer Society

Belgium
Monique Noirhomme-Fraiture
Federation des Associations Informatiques de Belgique

Canada
Mary Frances Laughton
Canadian Information Processing Society

China
Liu Zhengjie
Chinese Institute of Electronics

Czech Republic
Vaclav Matousek
Czech Society for Cybernetics & Informatics

Denmark
Leif Lovborg
Danish Federation for Information Processing

Finland
Pekka Lehtio
Finnish Information Processing Association

Germany
Peter Gorny
Gesellschaft für Informatik eV

Greece
John Darzentas
Greek Computer Society

Italy
Fabio Paternò
Italian Computer Society

Japan
Masaaki Kurosu
Information Processing Society of Japan

The Netherlands
Gerrit van der Veer
Nederlands Genootschap voor Informatica

Norway
Svein Arnesen
Norwegian Computer Society

Poland
Julius Kulikowski
Polish Academy of Sciences

Portugal
Mário Rui Gomes
Associacão Portuguesa de Informática

Spain
Julio Abascal
Federacion Española de Sociedades de Informática

Sweden
Lars Oestreicher (IFIP TC.13 Vice-chair)
Swedish Interdisciplinary Society for Human–Computer Interaction

Switzerland
Matthias Rauterberg
Swiss Federation of Information Processing Societies

UK
Brian Shackel (IFIP TC.13 Secretary)
British Computer Society

USA
John Karat (IFIP TC.13 Vice-chair)
Association for Computing Machinery

Affiliate Member
Andrew Westlake
International Association for Statistical Computing

Corresponding Member
José A. Pino
Centro Latinoamericano de Estudios Informatica

Working Group Chairmen

WG 13.1
(Education in HCI and HCI Curriculum)
Matthias Rauterberg

WG 13.2
(Methodology for User-Centred System Design)
Alistair Sutcliffe

WG 13.3
(HCI and People with Special Needs)
Geoff Busby

WG 2.7/13.4
(User Interface Engineering)
Rick Kazman

WG 13.5
(Human Error, Safety, and System Development)
Chris Johnson

Cooperating Societies

All IFIP Member Societies
British Psychological Society (BPS)
Institution of Electrical Engineers (IEE)
British HCI Group
The Ergonomics Society
AFIHM
Association for Artificial Intelligence of Russia (RAAI)
CEPIS
CHISIG
ACM SIGCHI
EUROGRAPHICS
IMAS

International Programme Committee

Co-chairs

M. Angela Sasse, *UK*
Michael Tauber, *Germany*

Members

J. Abascal, *Spain*
A. Adams, *Australia*
C. Allwood, *Sweden*
J. Alty, *UK*
G. Andrienko, *Germany*
N. Andrienko, *Germany*
M. Apperley, *New Zealand*
W. Ark, *USA*
S. Arnesen, *Norway*
M. Atyeo, *USA*
C. Baber, *UK*
S. Balakrishan, *USA*
S. Balbo, *Australia*
M. Beaudouin-Lafon, *France*
D. Benyon, *UK*
J. Bonner, *UK*
S. Brewster, *UK*
D. Busse, *UK*
J. Carroll, *USA*
A. Cawsey, *UK*
J. Cañas, *Spain*
L. Clark, *UK*
G. Cockton, *UK*
I. Connell, *UK*
M. Costabile, *Italy*
J. Coutaz, *France*
J. Darzentas, *Greece*
F. Détienne, *France*
D. Diaper, *UK*
A. Dix, *UK*
C. Dormann, *Denmark*
P. Dourish, *USA*
J. Dowell, *UK*
S. Dray, *USA*
J. Earthy, *UK*
D. England, *UK*
P. Faraday, *USA*
M. Gomes, *Portugal*
D. Gorgan, *Romania*
P. Gorny, *Germany*
P. Gray, *UK*
S. Greenberg, *Canada*
T. Gross, *Austria*
J. Grundy, *New Zealand*
S. Guest, *USA*
K. Gunn, *USA*
J. Hammond, *Australia*
M. Harrison, *UK*
H. Hasan, *Australia*
T. Hewett, *USA*
P. Holt, *UK*
J. Horton, *UK*
I. Ismail, *UK*
N. Iwayama, *Japan*
R. Jacob, *USA*
C. Johnson, *UK*
L. Johnston, *Australia*
S. Jones, *Australia*
J. Jorge, *USA*
A. Jorgensen, *Denmark*
V. Kaptelinin, *Sweden*
J. Karat, *USA*
J. Kay, *Australia*
R. Kazman, *USA*
R. Keil-Slawik, *Germany*
A. Kilgour, *UK*
M. Kurosu, *Japan*
E. Kuwana, *Japan*
A. Lantz, *Sweden*
L. Larsen, *Denmark*
M. Laughton, *Canada*
D. Lavery, *UK*
A. Lee, *USA*
P. Lehtiö, *Finland*
H. Lowe, *UK*
L. Loevborg, *Denmark*
A. MacLean, *France*
V. Matousek, *Czech Republic*
I. McClelland, *The Netherlands*
A. Monk, *UK*
M. Montgomery Masters, *UK*
M. Muller, *USA*
J. Newman, *UK*
L. Nigay, *France*
J. Noble, *USA*
M. Noirhomme-Fraiture, *Belgium*
L. Oestreicher, *Sweden*
N. Ozkan, *Australia*
P. Palanque, *France*
F. Paternò, *Italy*
J. Pino, *Chile*
R. Procter, *UK*
H. Reiterer, *Germany*
D. Rigas, *UK*
C. Roast, *UK*
M. Rosson, *USA*
V. Ruvinskaia, *Ukraine*
D. Scapin, *France*
A. Sears, *USA*
B. Shackel, *UK*
M. Sikorski, *Poland*
C. Stary, *Austria*
A. Sutcliffe, *UK*
G. Szwillus, *Germany*
A. Takeuchi, *Japan*
J. Tanaka, *Japan*
J. Tang, *USA*
B. Thomas, *Australia*
R. Thomas, *Australia*
M. Tscheligi, *Austria*
S. Turner, *UK*
C. Unger, *Germany*
C. van der Mast, *The Netherlands*
G. van der Veer, *The Netherlands*
J. Vanderdonckt, *Belgium*
A. Watson, *UK*
J. Whittle, *UK*
P. Wild, *UK*
C. Wolf, *USA*
W. Wong, *New Zealand*
V. Wulf, *Germany*
J. Ziegler, *Germany*
N. Zin, *UK*

Volume II Additional Reviewers

S. Allison, *UK*
I. Benest, *UK*
S. Bhachu, *UK*
R. Blyth, *UK*
C. Brotherton, *UK*
C. Chen, *UK*
A. Clark, *USA*
L. Coventry, *UK*
I. Curson, *UK*
A. Doswell, *UK*
J. Finlay, *UK*
J. Galliers, *UK*
M. Hartswood, *UK*
D. Hawdale, *UK*
R. Heath, *UK*
G. Johnson, *UK*
P. Jordan, *The Netherlands*
C. Jones, *UK*
M. Kirby, *UK*
J. Lee, *UK*
A. McKinlay, *UK*
L. Mackinnon, *UK*
N. Maiden, *UK*
D. Murray, *UK*
A. Newell, *UK*
E. O'Neil, *UK*
R. Rajani, *UK*
P. Sergeant, *UK*
H. Sharp, *UK*
M. Smyth, *UK*
R. Stepney, *UK*
T. Stewart, *UK*
M. Treglown, *UK*
J. Wilkinson, *UK*
R. Williams, *UK*
A. Wrightson, *UK*

INTERACT '99 Committees

International Conference Committee

INTERACT '99 Conference Chair
Alistair Kilgour, *Heriot-Watt University, UK*

INTERACT Conference Adviser
Brian Shackel, *HUSAT Research Institute, UK*

Members
David Gilmore (IPC Chair, INTERACT '95), *IDEO Product Development, USA*
Judy Hammond (Conference Chair, INTERACT '97), *University of Technology, Sydney, Australia*
Masaaki Kurosu (Conference Chair, INTERACT 2001), *Shizuoka University, Japan*

Technical Programme Committee

Chair
Chris Johnson, *University of Glasgow, UK*

Papers
M. Angela Sasse, *University College London, UK*
Michael Tauber, *University of Paderborn, Germany*

Tutorials
Janet Finlay, *University of Huddersfield, UK*

Workshops
Alistair Sutcliffe, *City University, UK*
Alan Newell, *University of Dundee, UK*

Doctoral Consortium
James Alty, *Loughborough University, UK*
John Karat, *IBM, USA*

Panels
David Benyon, *Napier University, UK*
Dianne Murray, *King's College London, UK*

Posters
Gilbert Cockton, *University of Sunderland, UK*
Alison Cawsey, *Heriot-Watt University, UK*

Professional Practice and Experience
Graham Johnson, *NCR, UK*
Alistair Kilgour, *Heriot-Watt University, UK*

Interactive Experience
Julian Newman, *Glasgow Caledonian University, UK*
Stephen Brewster, *University of Glasgow, UK*

Laboratory and Organisational Overviews
Rob Procter, *University of Edinburgh, UK*

Videos
Richard Coyne, *University of Edinburgh, UK*

Organizing Committee

Press
Tom McEwan, *Napier University, UK*

Publicity
Phil Gray, *University of Glasgow, UK*

Treasurer
Ian Benest, *University of York, UK*

Sponsorship
Alistair Kilgour, *Heriot-Watt University, UK*
Brian Shackel, *HUSAT Research Institute, UK*
Richard Wilson, *University of Glasgow, UK*

Exhibition
Richard Wilson, *University of Glasgow, UK*

Social Programme
Lachlan Mackinnon, *Heriot-Watt University, UK*

Student Volunteers
Alison Cawsey, *Heriot-Watt University, UK*

Web
Mark Dunlop, *University of Glasgow, UK*

Conference Manager
Christian Jones, *Heriot-Watt University, UK*

Internet Access
Patrick McAndrew, *Heriot-Watt University, UK*

Invited Speakers
Chris Brotherton, *Heriot-Watt University, UK*
Patrik Holt, *Heriot-Watt University, UK*

Proceedings
Brian Shackel, *HUSAT Research Institute, UK*

British HCI Group Adviser
Chris Roast, *Sheffield Hallam University, UK*

Asia-Pacific Liaison
Richard Thomas, *University of Western Australia, Australia*

Scholarships
Fabio Paternò, *CNUCE, Italy*

Reviewing Support
Ismail Ismail, *University College London, UK*
Nadav Zin, *University College London, UK*
Louise Clark, *University College London, UK*
Ann Watson, *University College London, UK*

Secretariat
Vicki Grant, *Meeting Makers Ltd, UK*
Elaine King, *Meeting Makers Ltd, UK*
Yvonne Prager, *Meeting Makers Ltd, UK*

Part Four

Posters

Human-Computer Interaction - INTERACT'99 (Volume II)
S. Brewster, A. Cawsey & G. Cockton (Editors)
Published by The British Computer Society © IFIP TC.13, 1999

EPSRC
Engineering and Physical Sciences Research Council

Influences of Software Design on Formal Reasoning

J. C. Aczel

The Open University
Milton Keynes, UK
Email:j.c.aczel@open.ac.uk

P. Fung

The Open University,
Milton Keynes, UK
Email:p.fung@open.ac.uk

R. Bornat

Queen Mary & Westfield College,
London, UK
Email: richard@dcs.qmw.ac.uk

M. Oliver

University of North London
London, UK
Email: M.Oliver@unl.ac.uk

T. O'Shea

Birkbeck College,
London, UK
Email: master@bbk.ac.uk

B. Sufrin

University of Oxford
Oxford, UK
Email:
Bernard.Sufrin@comlab.ox.ac.uk

Abstract: Evaluation of software for learning symbolic logic has indicated that students' formal reasoning strategies can be influenced by interface design. It is also possible that perceptions of the nature of logical proof itself can be altered by design choices. These results arise out of an EPRSC-funded project that aims to increase understanding of the effectiveness of visualisation tools in supporting the learning of formal reasoning for software engineering. The particular program discussed here has a tactic language that allows an educator to bind actions to mouse clicks, menu items and keystrokes, and to control the display of proofs and the syntax of logical formulae. In addition, there is flexibility as to the permitted inference rules. The project is exploring the benefits of the program - and possible refinements to the interface - by videotaping program usage in order to contrast conjectured cognitive processes with those in operation during pencil-and-paper episodes.

Keywords: cognition, symbolic logic, visualisation, evaluation methods, interface design

1 The Project

The findings presented here are from an EPSRC-funded project examining the effectiveness of a particular visualisation tool in supporting the learning of formal reasoning for software development.

The program Jape allows interactive, step-by-step construction of proofs for a variety of logics (Bornat & Sufrin, 1996). The program allows an instructor to control the syntax of formulae, to dictate the way the proof is displayed on-screen, and to assign actions to mouse clicks, menu items and keystrokes. Proofs can therefore be directly manipulated simply by clicking on a formula with the mouse.

2 The Research

The fieldwork involved about 170 first-year computer science undergraduates following a course in introductory first order logic in London. The particular implementation of Jape being investigated ("ItL Jape") was pre-loaded with a "natural deduction" style of reasoning:

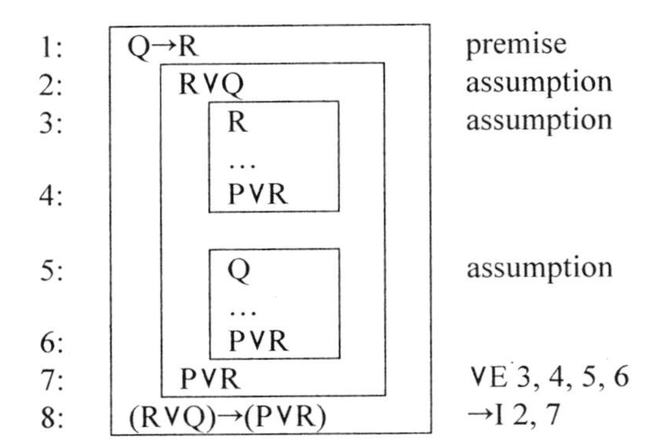

Table 1: A partially-completed natural deduction proof.

Research methods included naturalistic observation, tests of logic, mathematics and informal reasoning, questionnaires, logs of program usage and videotaped, task-based interviews. The aim was to explore the benefits of the program by contrasting conjectured cognitive processes when students used the program with those in operation during pencil-and-paper episodes.

3 Findings

We give three findings here that suggest an impact of interface design on cognition.

Firstly, the videotape study enabled the identification of a number of strategies that students might be using to help them construct proofs; for example, strategies akin to «Break down conjunctions in the premises.», «VE has precedence over most rules.», and «When reasoning backwards from the conclusion, check if the lines produced are provable from the premises.». A distinctive feature of Jape users was that a strategy akin to «Break up implications in the conclusion.» typically became almost automatic very quickly; whereas when using pencil-and-paper prior to Jape, the less reliable strategy «Make an assumption.» tended to predominate.

What aspects of ItL Jape's interface encourage the development of robust strategies? It must clearly help when starting to use the program that it adopts familiar gestures, commands and visual cues from commonplace graphical user interfaces, and that its proof display is just like that in the course notes. In addition, many students praised the opportunity for experimentation provided by the guarantee of accuracy in applying chosen rules and by the "undo" facility for when poor choices became apparent. It is not clear yet why some students seemed more prone than others to fruitless pattern-matching trial-and-error. However, strategy-development seemed most successful when the visible effects of an action were not only sufficient to allow students to make an informed decision about the utility of the action, but were also subtle enough to place the onus of strategy-development on the student. One crucial factor would also appear to be students' *initial expectations* of the effects of a rule.

A second finding was that deferring a decision to provide references for *labelled* unknowns in Jape may be less comfortable than leaving unknown formulae unwritten on paper until they *are* known. What may complicate the issue is that the appearance of unknowns is used by some students as an indicator of a poor choice of rule, rather than as a withholding of appropriate parameters; and that students can be unconfident about what each rule's parameters are, and about whether the rule is applied forwards from premises or backwards from conclusions.

Thirdly, the typical pencil-and-paper perception of a proof as a written, linear sequence of logical formulae that have to be "justified" in some sense contrasts with the perception encouraged by Jape that a proof is a set of simplifications of the conclusion and premises, out of which justifications are automatically generated. One effect of this difference in perception is whether students focus on complicated formulae or on missing justifications when deciding how to proceed. One student suggested that she would prefer to type in successive lines, much as she would write them on paper, rather than have Jape generate the lines in response to simple clicks. On the other hand, other students have reported "hunches" about fruitful proof avenues when using Jape. Certainly there is a feeling of completion that Jape provides when a proof is done that is absent from pencil-and-paper.

References

Bornat, R. & Sufrin, B. (1996) "Jape's quiet interface", paper presented at UITP96, also available from Department of Computer Science, Queen Mary & Westfield College, University of London, ftp://ftp.dcs.qmw.ac.uk/jape/papers/

Human-Computer Interaction - INTERACT'99 (Volume II)
S. Brewster, A. Cawsey & G. Cockton (Editors)
Published by The British Computer Society © IFIP TC.13, 1999

Demonstrating the Concept of Physical Hyperspace for an Art Gallery

Chris Baber, Toby Harris and Bob Harrison

Industrial Ergonomics Group, School of Man & Mech Eng
The University of Birmingham,
Birmingham, B15 2TT

1 Introduction

The notion of hyperspace has been the subject of much research in the human-computer interaction (HCI) community. The concept has been developed to the extent that there are commercially available hypermedia products which allow users to browse and search quite complex information spaces. In recent years there has been extensive development in the concept of augmented reality, i.e., technology which allows computer-generated images to be projected onto real world objects (typically through head-mounted displays). Assume that one could combine the physical media-space of an art gallery with the information-space of a hypermedia system. Such a combination could allow access to interesting and useful information at salient points during the tour of the gallery. We term this concept physical hyperspace.

1.1 Development of Concept

In this section, the discussion will focus on the particular user requirements which might be needed in order to develop the concept. The technology required for this concept, i.e., belt-mounted computer, spectacle-mounted display, sensors to fit into badges etc., are sufficiently well advanced to be commercially. Consequently, there is a wealth of human factors questions associated with the design, implementation and use of the technology which require addressing.

2 Development of Prototype

In order to consider physical hyperspace, we have built a simple demonstrator system using a Personal Computer (InterVision 486 belt-mounted computer and Pentium II PC) and projecting displays (head-mounted, i.e., Seattle Sight monocular, monochrome display; and VGA projector). In order to support remote operation of the computer, a simple infra-red link was built using a transmitter which could be mounted on the person and a single button to change the displayed image. Figure one shows a sketch of the configuration for the PC and projector version of the prototype.

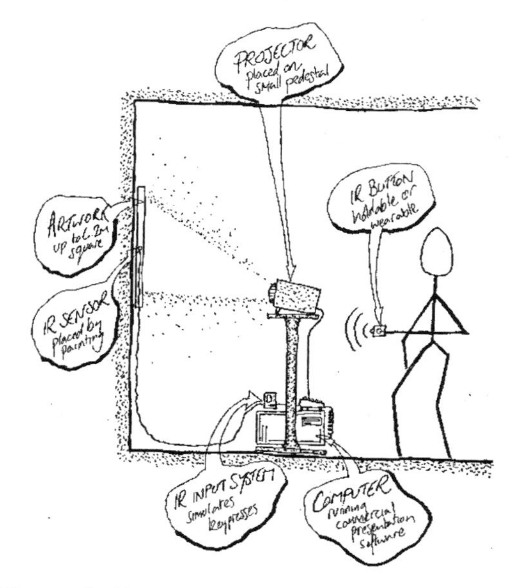

Figure 1: Sketch of equipment layout.

A slide show, developed using PowerPoint 97, is projected over a painting mounted on the gallery wall. The use of commercially available software led to rapid development. It is important to note that the painting remains a physical artifact; we could simply have scanned the painting and had to slide show annotate the computer image, but this defeats the whole point of the exercise. The slide show combines text, animation and graphics to highlight or occlude sections of the painting. Combining projected images with the painting can not only draw the viewers' attention to specific areas of interest, but also help to produce a 'guided tour' of the painting. This can increase the viewer's appreciation and enjoyment of a work of art. Having a projected slide show, of course, offers the opportunity of not using this information. The slide show is advanced using an infra-red transmitter (the receiver is mounted near the painting). Each time the transmitter button is pressed, the next slide in a sequence is displayed.

3 Initial User Trials

In order to test the concept, a user trial was conducted. Twelve undergraduate students were shown a print of Escher's *Persistence of Memory*. The participants were also presented with either a paper booklet describing the painting or a projected display. All participants experienced both paper and projected conditions. Various time-based measures were recorded, but we will concentrate on the comments elicited from participants for this poster.

Comments were elicited through semi-structured interviews during the sessions, and these comments were subjected to simple content analysis. There were six main categories of comment which were found. These are illustrated with quotations from participants (the letters in [ ] indicate the specific participant making the comment).

1. *The projected display keeps the viewer's focus on the art work.* "If you get a handout, you look at the handout not the painting, and I wouldn't want to look at a painting holding a handout. With a projector the words are by where you want to look, you're not flicking between them." [MR]
2. *The projected display is more appealing and more fun than the paper booklet.* "You can play with it, much more fun...People are drawn to it, moving things." [ZP]
3. *The projected display has a clearer presentation of complex ideas.* "Animation build up, going at your own pace to figure it out takes you with it instead of presenting the conclusion." [LG]
4. *The projected display forces deeper consideration of the concepts presented.* "I'm used to scanning text whatever but the projector draws to everything, the details." [LM]
5. *The projected display forces wider appreciation of concepts.* "With the paper guide the main thing you pay attention to is the water, but because the AAG can highlight bits it draws your attention much more than a text mention...Wasn't fully aware of bits until highlighted." [MR]
6. *Paper gives more control* "Paper more flexible as back and forwards, and you know what's coming; with the projector version we didn't know whether it would be an animation or a new slide." [LG]

4 Extensions and Developments

The user trials were intended to determine the viability of the concept. However, they have produced some concerns which had not previously been considered. In particular, the question of navigating the 'information space' requires further investigation. Clearly, a paper document supports a range of navigation which are well-practised by the participants in the trials. The computer condition only allowed the person to turn to the next page. Developments in hypertext have led to a wide range of interface designs to support different browsing and navigation styles. The next version of the system ought to consider the implementation of designs to support browsing. However, it is an intention in this work to minimise the amount of activity that the user is required to perform in order to interact with the computer. As category 1 indicates, the projected display is designed to maintain the viewers' focus on the art work not on the computer. Thus, the question of how to support remote interaction with a computer while simultaneously viewing an art work requires further investigation.

One further observation that we feel is worthy of report is how readily the participants in this trial adapted to the use of the technology. Initially, participants advanced slides in rapid succession, skimming over the content. One participant observed that she was using the projector like a book and only stopping when something interesting came up. However, within two or three slides, participants began to slow their slide advancing. It became evident from participant behaviour that the richness and detail of the slides, and the superimposition of slide onto painting became a source of enjoyment (and on at least two occasions, participants spontaneously requested to see to whole show for a second time). This suggests that for our user population, the concept has proved to be a success. Obviously, one cannot extrapolate from this trial to the population at large, and will be interesting and beneficial to investigate the responses of a broader range of potential users prior to drawing firm conclusion.

Human-Computer Interaction - INTERACT'99 (Volume II)
S. Brewster, A. Cawsey & G. Cockton (Editors)
Published by The British Computer Society © IFIP TC.13, 1999

Multimodal Eye-Based Interaction for Zoomed Target Selection on a Standard Graphical User Interface

Richard Bates

Imaging and Displays Research Group, Department of Computing Science
De Montfort University, The Gateway, Leicester, UK
Email: rbates@dmu.ac.uk

Abstract: This paper compares the performance of monomodal and multimodal eye-based interaction techniques when selecting screen targets using eye gaze position. It shows that the inherent inaccuracies of eye-based target selection can be overcome with the addition of a supporting modality to increase effective target sizes by screen zoom at the gaze position. It also shows that the addition of such modalities causes an increase in user workload.

Keywords: Eye gaze, eye tracking, multimodal interaction, evaluation, assistive technology

1 Introduction

Eye-based interaction in the field of assistive technology has given disabled users access to computer technology (Hutchinson 1989), but many of these systems have problems interacting with a standard GUI due to eye-tracking inaccuracies. One solution is to provide indirect interaction via an intermediate soft device such as a visual keyboard (Instance 1996). This paper proposes an alternative solution enabling direct interaction through the addition of a 'zoom' soft device to a standard GUI that will allow the user to enlarge a portion of the screen when selecting smaller targets. The paper presents some preliminary results of the author's PhD research into multimodal eye-based interaction for users with high-level motor disabilities.

2 Multimodal Interaction

In this system the zoom magnification of the screen is controlled by a second input modality of small body movements measured using a 6 DOF spatial tracker. This second modality was chosen as it is separable from eye movement and can be operated simultaneously with eye movement, offering the potential of an increased interaction bandwidth for users with motor disabilities.

3 A Comparison of Interaction Techniques

An experiment was conducted with 8 experienced computer users to compare the advantages and disadvantages of using eye-only monomodal and eye with zoom multimodal interaction in a target acquisition test. Screen zoom magnification was controlled by left shoulder elevation recorded by a Polhemus InsideTrack with a control to zoom mapping of 2mm vertical elevation incrementing the screen zoom by one on a linear scale where 2mm=x2, 4mm=x3, 6mm=x4 and 8mm=x5 magnification of the original screen size. Gaze position was recorded by a SensoMotoric Instruments R.E.D infrared eye tracker positioned 60cm from the user with the cursor position recorded every 50ms. Target sizes were chosen to be representative of standard Microsoft Windows™ objects as shown in table 1.

Target Object	Equivalent Size (mm)	Visual Angle (°) at 60cm
Desktop Icon	13	1.2
Toolbar Button	9	0.9
Scrollbar Button	6	0.6
Spin Control	4	0.4

Table 1: Target sizes.

(17" Monitor, 2.5 pixels/mm, 800x600 resolution) The equivalent sizes of the targets are the length of the sides of a square of equivalent area to the Windows™ target object.

Target selection was accomplished by a gaze dwell time of 750ms within 10mm (1° visual angle) of a 10 sample rolling average position. Targets were presented 64 times in random order and distance from the screen centre. To assess user workload a raw 0-20 NASA-tlx score (Byers 1989) was recorded after each test sequence. Test subjects also rated which system they preferred on a 0 (eye-only) to 20 (eye and zoom) scale. Each user was given a 15 minute practice period before the tests.

3.1 Test Results

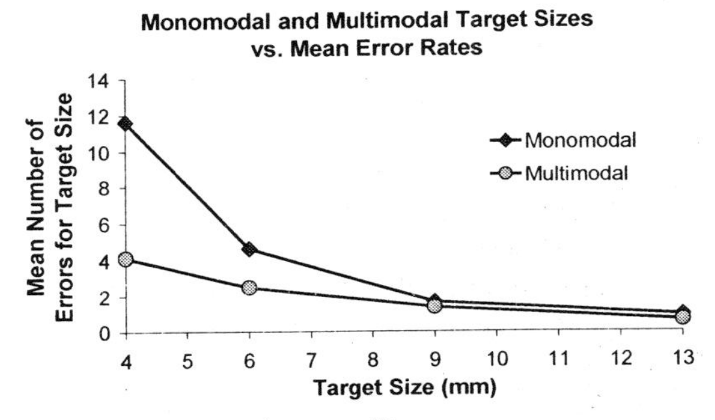

Figure 1: Target sizes vs. Error rates.

The mean error rates for the smaller targets, figure 1, reduced significantly when using zoom from 4.6 without zoom to 2.5 with zoom (45% reduction) ($t=2.7$, $p<0.03$) for the 6mm target and from 11.6 to 4.1 (65% reduction) ($t=4.2$, $p<0.003$) for the 4mm target. There were no significant differences in selection times for any target sizes between the two techniques. The cursor had a SD accuracy of 2.23mm x and 5.03mm y across the users. The relationship between target size and zoom level used to hit the target, figure 2, shows that zoom was not used on the 13mm target but was then progressively increased with decreasing target size. The curve can be modelled by a regression $y=13.314x^{-1.0348}$ R=0.98. The product of this curve and the hit zoom level used gives a near constant of 12.38mm (SD

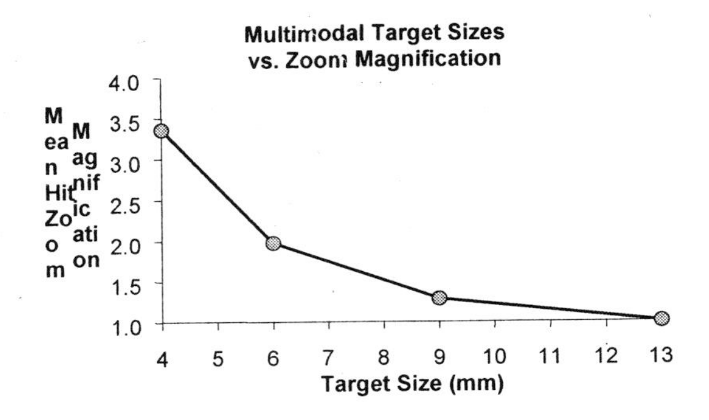

Figure 2: Target size vs. Zoom magnification.

0.38mm) for the zoomed target size hit by the user.

The NASA-tlx questionnaire results showed a 37% increase in mental workload ($t=1.66$, $p<0.14$), a 32% increase in physical workload ($t=1.64$, $p<0.14$) and an 18% reduction in frustration ($t=1.26$, $p<0.23$) for the multimodal system. Other ratings had insignificant differences between the systems. The users preferred the multimodal system, which scored a mean of 13.13 (SD 2.62).

3.2 Conclusions

This paper shows that eye gaze can be used to interact with standard GUI's if supporting modalities are added to enable interaction. Using an additional supporting modality to control zoom gives the benefits of direct manipulation of the interface, considerably reduced error rates, removal of the need for intermediate soft devices and a reduction in user frustration but has the cost of increased user workload. Further work will be carried out to investigate the cost-benefit of performance vs. workload when adding supporting modalities to eye-based interaction.

References

Byers, J. C., Bittner, A. C., Hill, S. G. (1989). "Traditional and raw task load index (tlx) correlations: are paired comparisons necessary?". In Mital, A. (Ed.) *Advances in Industrial. Ergonomics,* 481-485. Taylor & Francis.

Hutchinson, T. E., White, K. P. Martin, W. N., Reichert, K. C. and Frey, L. A. (1989). "Human-computer interaction using eye-gaze input". *IEEE Trans. Syst. Man Cybern.*, **19**(6), 1527-1534.

Instance, H. O., Spinner, C., and Howarth, P. (1996) "Eye-based control of standard GUI software" *Proceedings of HCI'96: People and Computers XI,* 141-158 Springer-Verlag.

Human-Computer Interaction - INTERACT'99 (Volume II)
S. Brewster, A. Cawsey & G. Cockton (Editors)
Published by The British Computer Society © IFIP TC.13, 1999

EPSRC
Engineering and Physical Sciences Research Council

PUMA: Bridging Disciplinary Gulfs in HCI

Ann Blandford, Richard Butterworth and Jason Good

Middlesex University
Bounds Green Road
London, N11 2NQ, UK
Email: a.blandford@mdx.ac.uk

Abstract: One aim of the PUMA project is to investigate ways in which findings from cognitive science can be exploited in reasoning about the design of interactive systems – by finding common ground between cognitive and computer scientists and between theoreticians and practitioners. In both cases, the common ground has been found through abstraction. The price that is paid is that some of the power of the original technique is lost.

Keywords: Cognitive models, PUM, software engineering, usability evaluation.

1 Introduction

The Human-Computer Interaction (HCI) community comprises a number of different traditions. The cultural boundaries within HCI can often prove difficult to surmount. One objective of the PUMA (Programmable User Modelling Applications) project is to investigate particular approaches to bridging gulfs between cognitive and computer scientists, and between theoreticians and practitioners.

The original motivation for PUM was that a simple problem-solving architecture, which could be 'programmed' with knowledge, should be provided (Young, Green & Simon, 1989). A designer could use the PUM to reason about likely interactive behaviours, and hence about possible design improvements. While this approach has delivered an improved understanding of cognition in an interactive setting, as an approach for delivering short-term benefits within HCI, it has limitations:

1. when implementing an architecture, it is generally necessary to add in local assumptions simply so that a model can be run. If these assumptions are poorly understood, properties of a behaviour might be incorrectly attributed to the architecture.
2. where there are a large number of possible behaviours, the model may have to be run an indefinite number of times to ensure that all possible behaviours have been considered.
3. constructing and running a model is very time-consuming; this activity is incompatible with the timescales that typify industrial practice.
4. model construction requires substantial expertise in cognitive modelling (Blandford, Buckingham Shum & Young 1998).

To address the first two of these difficulties, the approach taken was to investigate the use of mathematical proof techniques. To address the remaining two, we worked closely with design practitioners, to 'craft' a PUM-based technique that could sit comfortably within their existing practice.

2 Rigorous Reasoning

To support reasoning about interactive behaviour, taking into account the properties of a cognitive architecture (rather than an implementation) and those of a computer system, the work sought to bridge between cognitive and computer science. The guiding question was: Does mathematics provide a way of reasoning clearly about interactive behaviour, taking account of user cognition, device design and the role of the environment in the interaction?

Two distinct approaches have been developed and compared. The first, described by Blandford *et al* (1998), is to express basic axioms of user cognition mathematically, then to describe both user knowledge and device design using the same formalism. This approach has the advantage of inspectability: the underlying assumptions are open to inspection and criticism. However, the style of reasoning is simulation-based, and involves exhaustive search of a state space. The second approach involves abstracting away from the details of the modelled problem, to represent and reason about patterns of interaction, as illustrated by Butterworth, Blandford and Duke (1998). By simplifying, it is possible to generate models that are amenable to proof techniques, so that the analyst can reason about all possible behaviours.

Simulation models are suited to design scenarios where the user is likely to engage in planning behaviour, rather than simply responding to the current state of the device, and where there is a large repertoire of possible actions but only a few are rational at any given moment. Abstract proof models are better suited to analysis of cases where the user is likely to adopt a particular policy for behaviour and to react to the current state of the device.

3 Applying Theory in Practice

To address the problems of time constraints and level of expertise – bridging between theoreticians and practitioners – the guiding question is: How can a technique such as PUM, that demands an extensive background in cognitive science and is costly to apply, be adapted to fit within design practice?

Two studies have been conducted. The first was a fairly standard PUM analysis on a completed design; this involved taking the design documentation (which was prepared to ISO9001 standard, and was therefore extensive) and identifying issues that concerned the interaction with a human operator. In later discussions with the design team, it transpired that most of the difficulties identified through PUM had, in the meantime, also been identified through safety analysis, and the interface modified accordingly. The second study involved a PUM specialist working as a member of a safety engineering team, preparing a safety case to tight timescales. In this case, the PUM approach was represented by asking the most important questions that an analyst has to ask when preparing a model: that is, 'what does the user need to know?', 'how will the user know X?', and 'what are the likely consequences of the user not knowing X?' (Good & Blandford 1999).

Both studies demonstrate that user concerns can be accommodated systematically in the design process; the second study, in particular, demonstrated how the use of focused questions can allow an important class of user concerns to be considered explicitly very early on in the design process.

4 Discussion

There are necessarily trade-offs to be made when establishing common ground between different disciplines: each has to avoid imposing excessive details on the other. Bridging between cognitive and computing sciences involved focusing on behaviour rather than knowledge or architectural details, while bridging between theoreticians and practitioners involved focusing on knowledge questions, regardless of the underlying details.

Acknowledgements

Funded by EPSRC grant GR/L00391. Other project team members are David Duke (University of York), Sue Milner (Praxis Critical Systems Limited) and Richard M. Young (University of Hertfordshire).

References

Blandford, A. E., Buckingham Shum, S. & Young, R. M. (1998) Training software engineers in a novel usability evaluation technique. *International Journal of Human-Computer Studies*, **45**, 245-279.

Butterworth, R. J., Blandford, A. E. & Duke, D. J. (1998) The role of formal proof in modelling interactive behaviour. In P. Markopulos & P. Johnson (Eds.) *Design, Specification & Verification of Interactive Systems*. 87-101. Wien: Springer.

Good, J. & Blandford, A. (1999) Integrating HCI concerns into the design of safety-critical interactive systems: a case study. In *Proc. IEE Colloquium Digest 99/010.*

Young, R.M., Green, T.R.G. & Simon, T. (1989) Programmable user models for predictive evaluation of interface designs. In Bice, K. & Lewis, C. (Eds.) *Proc. CHI '89*, 15-19, New York : ACM.

Human-Computer Interaction - INTERACT'99 (Volume II)
S. Brewster, A. Cawsey & G. Cockton (Editors)
Published by The British Computer Society © IFIP TC.13, 1999

How do we Build Web Sites Fit for Purpose?

George Buchanan, Gil Marsden, Harold Thimbleby and Yin Leng Theng

School of Computing Science
Middlesex University
Bounds Green Road
London N11 2NQ, UK
Email: {g.buchanan, g.e.marsden, h.thimbleby, y.theng}@mdx.ac.uk

Abstract: As an EPSRC research project, Design and Evaluation of Tools and Guidelines for Hypermedia, GR/K79376, we have been working with the Royal Society of Arts (http://www.rsa.org.uk) and the Friends of Benjamin Franklin House (http://www.rsa.org.uk/franklin) to develop tools and methods to support quality web site design. Providing quality web sites is costly, especially as web sites often try to satisfy many aims, which makes achieving quality harder still. This poster introduces the concept of providing parallel views of web sites - for designers, authors and users. We also describe DocMan, a tool we have designed which demonstrates the advantages of parallel views by enhancing communication between web site authors, editors, designers and users. We also show how DocMan and parallel views can help improve usability strategies.

Keywords: quality web site design, parallel web views, DocMan.

1 Introduction

Web sites come in a huge variety, of size, sophistication, and of task supported. Many sites are designed to represent organisations, and organisations are complex, with many facets that can be represented to the world in conflicting ways. Thus, organisations often have large sites that reflect a multitude of design styles. Parts are time-critical and get attention, other parts become obsolete and 'dangle' on once sensible links. The complexity of managing a non-linear medium further make maintenance of the site harder than conventional print media. It follows that organisations often under-resource their web designers. Given that the web technology itself is continuously evolving, and simply staying up to date with a working site is hard enough, radical approaches are required to create — and keep — quality web sites.

2 Parallel Web Views

We define *parallel web views* as alternative views of a web site which are sufficiently related to the 'actual' web site not to require significant extra work for designers (possibly none at all), but they provide considerable additional value to users

To the extent that parallel web sites expand the range of uses a single site supports, they greatly extend the value of sites to users. Typically organisational web sites are designed on a hierarchy principle, and this makes life easy for designers but rarely meets user requirements very well. Parallel web views can provide alternative structures for sites that better fit users' requirements.

Simple examples of one-to-one parallel views are sites that provide options to be viewed with or without images. A slightly more complex parallel view is of a site that can be viewed with or without frames. Or consider the example of a linearised site — this is a flat structure that better suits certain tasks, such as printing, whereas the hyper-linked structure it is induced from might better suit interactive navigation.

3 Docman

DocMan is a tool that creates a parallel view of a core web site, with each page viewed with an additional set of commentary fields. A simple use of a DocMan view of a site is to allow users to add commentary to pages, but as we shall see, the idea is far more useful, and can be used very effectively for authors and site usability analysis. An example of a DocMan view is shown below in Figure 1. The top frame is commentary, the bottom frame is the RSA site page being referred to. In this example, the commentary text is referring to an issue over page linkage.

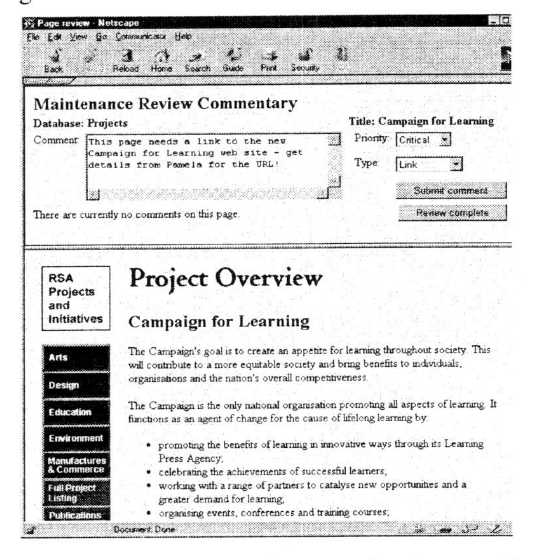

Figure 1: Docman screen shot (running in a standard web browser, which is not shown).

Notice that the Figure shows a web page with two frames, and with images. Clearly, the DocMan view of a site can itself be re-presented, with or without images. DocMan is a tool that can be provided on the core site's server, but the choices of viewing it with or without images is a browser option. This makes a nice and simple example of combining web views together.

DocMan allows designers, authors and others to jointly communicate together requirements and ideas for change in the web site. Being parallel it is properly integrated with the site structure. DocMan itself is specifically designed to cater for multiple authoring, and for a hierarchy of authors (e.g., a manager can comment to authors). DocMan relates each comment or to do item to a specific object (page, design template or to database content). Thus it is possible to undertake a formal review of usability commentary on the site, and to create more formal metrics automatically. Patterns of error can be used for taxonomic reasons and to help investigate patterns of author or design error.

4 Working Towards Usability

Few authors of a large site wish to evaluate the entire site, and indeed it is not realistic to do so. Instead, by working closely with designers and performing conventional usability studies, one may continuously improve the quality of the site after it is released to wide use.

An approach based on Docman allows usability tests to be correctly integrated into site development, with no burden imposed on designers.

How can we make use of usability categories? One approach is to provide Docman-like views with means of assessing pages (and sets of pages) in a site so that essentially the site itself (through the Docman view) directly supports its own evaluation.

Another usability application of Docman is to annotate pages with usability issues, such as there being catastrophic problems with a page. Since our implementation of Docman is extensible, it is easy to add new categories of commentary. One might envisage emailing usability concerns to the relevant authors (or to their managers).

Docman's categories and comments can be searched (e.g., by using a standard web search engine), and thus provide a very easy way for site managers to find specific features that they are interested in. For example, they can search for usability or legal problems.

5 Conclusion

Parallel views represent a clean separation of design issues away from the core site. Thus, the core site becomes easier to design, because it can be envisaged as a more specialised and more focused product. As a special case of parallel views, we pointed out that designers themselves may wish to work with a view of a site that suits their purposes, but from which the user's normal view of the site is automatically constructed. Doing so provides further guarantees that a site is well-designed and fit for purpose.

References

For further references, see:

http://www.cs.mdx.ac.uk/wrt/

Human-Computer Interaction - INTERACT'99 (Volume II)
S. Brewster, A. Cawsey & G. Cockton (Editors)
Published by The British Computer Society © IFIP TC.13, 1999

Enhancing Interaction Scenarios with Domain-Oriented Visualizations

Tom Carey[1], Kevin Harrigan[1] and Simon Holland[2]

[1]HCI and TeleLearning Lab
University of Waterloo, Waterloo
Ontario, N2L 3G1, Canada
{tcarey,kevinh}@uwaterloo.ca

[2]Department of Computer Science
Open University, Milton Keynes
MK7 6AA, England
Email: s.holland@open.ac.uk

Abstract: We have developed a visual representation for enhancing interaction scenarios in the design domain of computer-mediated learning. We have applied the visualization within the Cognitive Apprenticeship model of learning. Each diagram is a visual abstraction for a learning activity design, complementing traditional storyboards and textual scenarios which are used by Instructional Designers. This has been valuable in focusing attention on high-level design properties and as a communication aid for collaborative design review.

Keywords: Interaction design, domain-oriented tools, visualization, scenario-based, learning environment.

1 Introduction

We have developed a visual representation, called MCCA diagrams, for enhancing user interaction scenarios in the domain of designing computer-mediated learning (Carey, Harrigan, & Palmer, 1998). The diagrams are used by Instructional Designers in an early stage in the design process. Our representation is based on an existing model in Education called the Conversational Model (Laurillard, 1993). Four iterations of these diagrams have been used by novice and expert Instructional Designers (48 designers) who have found MCCA diagrams useful:

- to convey the different interaction which they could build into their designs
- to document instructional design decisions
- to act as a resource for team communication.

The MCCA Diagrams are incorporated into a Design Kit (not shown) for which we are designing several alternative and complementary diagrams, each of which highlights some particular aspect of the interaction.

2 MCCA Diagrams

User interaction scenarios are recognized as a useful tool for requirements exploration and conceptual design for interactive systems. Scenarios are "narrative descriptions of what people do and experience as they try to make use of computer systems" (Carroll, 1995). Despite the proven benefits of scenario-based design, there are significant high level patterns in learning interactions (discussed below) that are not easily revealed or analysed using text based representations. MCCA diagrams use the Conversational Model to complement scenarios by allowing the Instructional Designer to visualize key elements relating to the scenario.

The original model by Laurillard (1993, p. 103) is the basis for the MCCA diagram shown in Figure 1. It categorizes user–system interactions into four classes, represented by the four large boxes in the diagram. These reflect who is taking the initiative [expert or learner] and what kind of operations are employed [working with concepts or working on their application]. This leads to four types of operational processes:

- *Upper left* process box: expert building concepts

- *Upper right process box*: learner building concepts
- *Lower left process box*: expert applying concepts
- *Lower right process box:* learner applying concepts

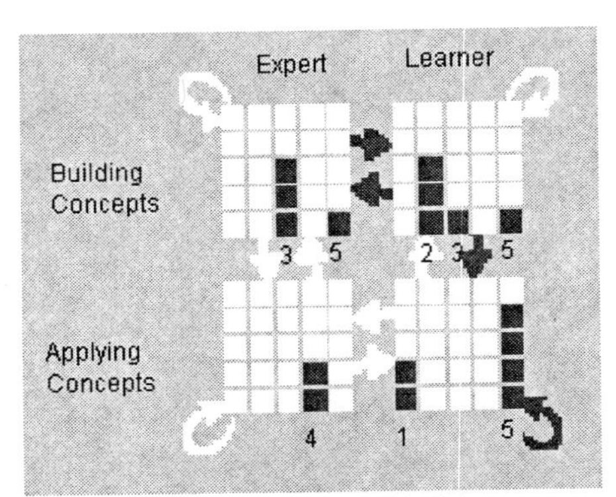

Figure 1: An example MCCA Diagrams.

Since the computer-mediated learning is intended to be highly interactive, *conversational* processes are also represented in the model with arrows.

The example MCCA diagram in Figure 1 represents a scenario (not shown) from a multimedia application that we have developed for a module on Critical Analysis. The major tasks corresponding to the scenario are:

- absorb cover story [10 minutes]
- review knowledge [15 minutes]
- ask expert [15 minutes]
- observe expert [10 minutes]
- *analyze article [20 minutes].*

In the diagrams, each of the 25 grid squares within a quadrant represents one unit of time that the learner engages in that interaction – typically 5 minutes. The diagrams incorporate the temporal dimension by representing each task in the interaction by one column within a temporal grid in each activity box. The digits (1,2,3,4,5) in Figure 2 correspond to the five tasks within our sample scenario. Following these digits in sequence allows the designer to see the temporal nature of the interactions within the scenario. Note that the digits do not actually appear in the diagrams but are included here to make the temporal information more explicit. In general, everything in the four column 1's happens first, then everything in the four column 2's happens next, and so on.

3 Alternative Representation

Our alternative representations of the MCCA diagrams are designed to highlight some particular aspect of the interactions. For example, Figure 2 is used to show the same information as the MCCA diagram but it displays the temporal nature of the interaction much more effectively, but loses the intuitive division into the four quadrants. We are experimenting with versions of our diagrams that can be used as Pattern Languages (Alexander, 1979) to represent different models. One such pattern is shown in Figure 3.

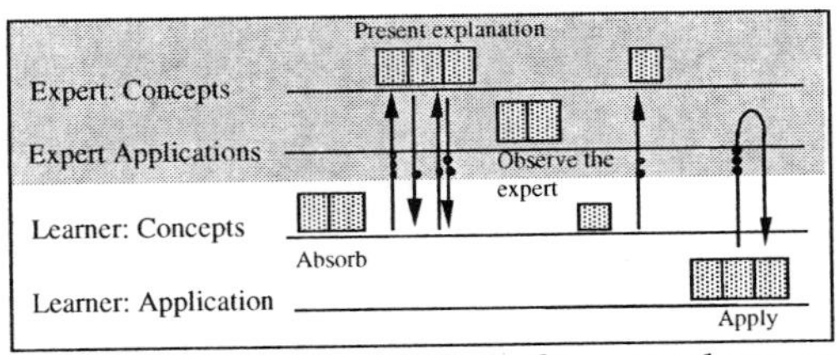

Figure 2: Good representation of temporal aspect.

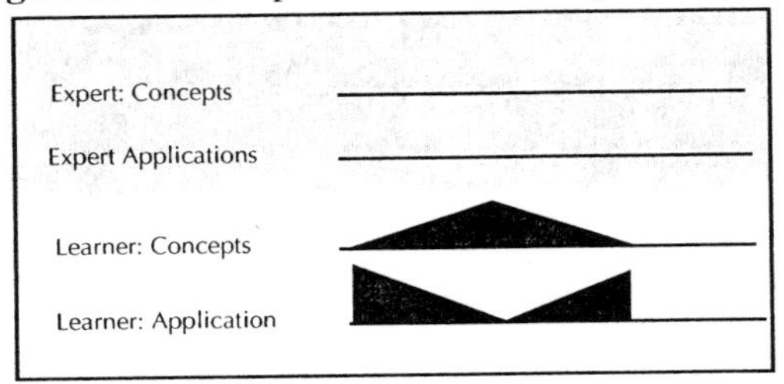

Figure 3: Possible pattern.

One key design issue is the overall balance amongst the processes during the learner's interaction with the system. Figure 4 shows the highest level of our diagrams that we have user tested, which is a summary of 80 minutes of user interaction.

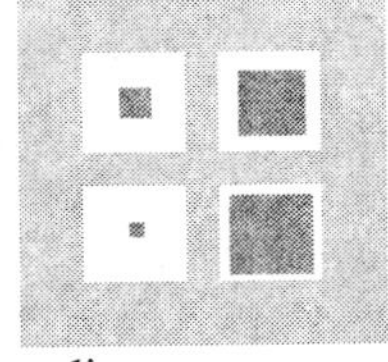

Figure 4: Summary diagram.

References

Alexander, C. (1979). The Timeless Way of Building. New York: Oxford University Press.

Carey, T.T., K. Harrigan, and A. Palmer, Mediated Conversations for Cognitive Apprenticeship: A Visual Tool for Instructional Designers. In Proceedings International Conference on the Learning Sciences. AACE, Charlottesville: VA, pp. 299-301.

Carroll, J.M. (1995). The Scenario Perspective on System Development. In J.M. Carroll (ed.), *Scenario-Based Design*. New York: John Wiley & Sons, Inc.

Laurillard, D. (1993). Rethinking university teaching: A framework for the effective use of educational technology. London: Routledge.

Human-Computer Interaction - INTERACT'99 (Volume II)
S. Brewster, A. Cawsey & G. Cockton (Editors)
Published by The British Computer Society © IFIP TC.13, 1999

EPSRC
Engineering and Physical Sciences Research Council

Integrating 'Hard' and 'Soft' Approaches to Modelling Intuition in Retail Site Assessment[1]

Ian Clarke[†], William Mackaness[‡] and Masahide Horita[†]

†University of Durham and ‡University of Edinburgh
Durham University Business School, Mill Hill Lane, Durham City, DH1 3LB,
Email: I.M.Clarke@durham.ac.uk

Abstract: This study presents an alternative methodology for modelling the cognitive structure of retail site assessment. Arguing that the absence of qualitative insights in existing methods have undermined their potential utility, this paper outlines a methodology to integrate 'soft' and 'hard' modelling approaches. The methodology incorporates cognitive mapping and neuro-fuzzy networks within a Geographical Information Systems (GIS) environment, to form a spatial decision support system for use in retail site assessment decision making. An illustration is given using preliminary results from interviews with the UK retailing industry.

Keywords: retail site assessment, intuition, GIS, cognitive mapping, neuro-fuzzy networks

1 Introduction

This study explores an alternative approach to modelling the cognitive structure of retail site assessment. The UK retailing and distribution industry utilises a variety of computer-assisted quantitative methods to assess the trading potential of sites. A gulf remains, however, between those quantitative analyses carried out in site research departments and the qualitative insights of senior retail executives.

The objective of this study is to fill this gap by proposing a methodology that establishes the 'hard' representation of a site assessment process through 'soft' problem structuring methods. The new methodology is designed to produce a better weave between computer-based systems and intuitive-led group decision-making. The following sections describe relevant theories, procedures for constructing such a reasoning model and its possible use as a basis of decision support systems. It should, therefore, be of wider conceptual and practical relevance.

2 Review of Previous Approaches

Various approaches have been proposed in retail site assessment, including: rule-based methods, game theory, analogue approaches, fuzzy logic, knowledge-based systems, artificial intelligence, and machine-learning. These models have often been incorporated into Geographical Information Systems (GIS), to provide a platform for rigorous scientific analysis of potential retail sites. Nevertheless, GIS in retailing are perceived as being inflexible, insufficiently integrated, misused and under-utilised (Miller, 1996).

The problem with the 'hard' approach has been voiced in the management science community, which resulted in a range of 'soft' methods. The soft approach primarily aims at broadening the scope of problem description towards that held by 'real'

[1] We gratefully acknowledge support of the Engineering and Physical Sciences Research Council (EPSRC) for the three year project ('Modelling Group Intuitive Spatial Reasoning in Retail Site Assessment'; Grant Ref. M07694) on which this work is based.

decision-makers. An example includes Eden's (1988) cognitive mapping technique, which aims to produce a model of one's own 'subjective world,' consisting of conceptual constructs and arrows linking them based on their causal relationship. The main advantage of this technique is that varied perceptions stemming from the different experiences of individuals match the variety inherent in the real situation.

In order to utilise the intuitive knowledge elicited by such a soft method along with the rational framework set out in the existing theoretical models, there is a need for an effective interface between the two ends. Among possible approaches for this purpose is fuzzy theory. For example, Kuo and Xue (1998) demonstrate how a sales forecasting model can be enhanced by explicitly modelling imprecision, ambiguity and uncertainty that inherently reside in the soft representation of a problem.

Thus, the following section proposes an alternative methodology for integrating the hard and soft approaches to modelling the retail site assessment process using GIS, cognitive mapping and fuzzy theory.

3 Outline of the New Methodology

This section describes the outline of the proposed methodology through an illustration of its possible use in the retailing industry. The example presented below is based our preliminary interviews with retail decision-makers, though results of more comprehensive empirical work will be presented in the conference.

3.1 Cognitive Mapping

First, cognitive mapping is carried out with retail decision-makers involved in the site assessment process within a certain organisation. Such stakeholders include: senior executives; property development managers; and site research personnel. A typical cognitive map might look like Figure 1, which identifies what makes a desirable retail site as well as its causal explanations. A map could include those qualitative concepts such as 'brand strength' and 'visibility' as key issues.

3.2 Constructing Neuro-fuzzy Network

Resulting cognitive maps are merged into a single composite map based on the common constructs among individual maps. The composite map is then transformed into a neuro-fuzzy network (see, for example, Lin and Lee, 1996), to form a spatial reasoning model for site assessment. Each link in a cognitive map can be translated into fuzzy logic statement. For example, a positive causal link between 'visibility' and 'proximity to a major road'

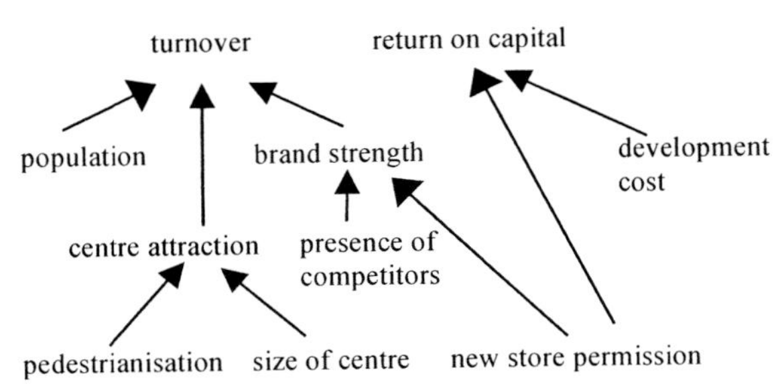

Figure 1: An example of a cognitive map.

could be defined as: "if a site is *very close* to a major road, then its visibility is *very high*," *etc*. With each construct associated with its membership function and each link with its fuzzy knowledge base, a cognitive map becomes a traditional neuro-fuzzy network.

Network training can be conducted by assigning objectively measurable scales to the network's 'heads' (*i.e.* constructs with no arrows *from* themselves) and 'tails' (*i.e.* constructs with no arrows *to* themselves). Less quantifiable constructs may be placed in-between. Existing store profiles constitute training inputs and targets to the system.

In a subsequent stage of the research programme a resulting spatial reasoning model will be used to predict the performance of new stores built on a given site. It will also be possible to cluster potential sites based on constructs in a composite map, and to associate them with similar analogue profiles of existing stores.

4 Conclusion

The new methodology proposed here forms the basis of a spatial decision support system that incorporates intuitive- and experience-based insights of senior decision-makers into retail site assessment. It is argued that such a computer-assisted system will open up a 'black box' that has deprived the industry of potential synthesis between 'everyday-life' judgement and rational scientific inquiry.

References

Eden, C. (1988) Cognitive mapping. *European Journal of Operational Research*, **36**, 1-13.

Kuo, R. J. and Xue, K. C. (1998) A decision support system for sales forecasting through fuzzyneural networks with asymmetric fuzzy weights. *Decision Support Systems*, **24**, 105-126.

Lin, C. T. and Lee, G. (1996) *Neural Fuzzy Systems: A Neuro-Fuzzy Synergism to Intelligent Systems*. Prentice Hall, New Jersey.

Miller, H. J. (1996) GIS and geometric representation in facility location problems. *International Journal of Geographical Information Systems*. **10**, 791-816.

Human-Computer Interaction - INTERACT'99 (Volume II)
S. Brewster, A. Cawsey & G. Cockton (Editors)
Published by The British Computer Society © IFIP TC.13, 1999

Inside the Consumer's Wallet: An Ethnographic Inquiry

Lee Cooper

Industrial Ergonomics Group
University of Birmingham
l.cooper@bham.ac.uk

Graham Johnson

The Knowledge Lab
206 Marylebone Road
London
gjohn@exchange.scotland.ncr.com

Chris Baber

Industrial Ergonomics Group
University of Birmingham
c.baber@bham.ac.uk

1 Introduction

A number of organizations are currently engaged in the creation of electronic wallets, which combine the traditional wallet with computer and, in some instances, communication technology. Their rationale is that the wallet is inherently associated with personal finance. Thus, it is argued that their wallets will provide a natural platform for electronic commerce and banking.

Typically electronic wallets intend to replace the traditional wallet within some form of 'smart card' based system. Smart cards are credit card-sized cards with an embedded computer chip. Some smart cards, such as the Mondex card, are designed to store monetary value. AT&T's electronic wallet, for example, allows Mondex users to view balance and transaction information stored on their card, as well as facilitating on-line transactions. Although the development of these electronic wallets may be motivated more by technological innovation than consumer desire, the history of the wallet has shown that it has always been influenced by technology. As a container of the necessities of everyday life both the wallets content *and* form have evolved to accommodate a society's technological developments. Be it the introduction of the paper money or the development of the credit card, the wallet has adapted. Therefore in an age of electronic commerce and banking it is hardly surprising that the wallet is currently 'Being Digital'.

In acknowledging the technological requirements that have motivated the wallet to change, however, we should not neglect consumers' non-technical needs. In the past these have included, for example, space to put military documentation, during the World Wars when a large portion of the population were in uniform. In order to develop an acceptable electronic wallet it is thus essential that an understanding both consumers technical and non-technical requirements are gained.

This poster summarizes research intent upon exploring the non-technical consumer requirements' associated with electronic wallets. To achieve this goal the research adopted an ethnographic approach. The term ethnography refers to the practice of conducting field research. Central to this practice, however, is an emphasis on understanding the world as experienced by those who live in it. Due to the fact that this experience is often (if not always) influenced by an individual's tacit knowledge, it is not enough to simply talk to people. In addition to interviews it is also necessary to observe how people behave.

This study is part of the NCR Knowledge Lab's research in the financial consumer field.

2 Method

Participants in the research were 55 adults, aged 17-75 years, from various socio-economic backgrounds. A series of semi-structured interviews was carried out, addressing the content of the people's wallets and how the wallet and its contents are used in everyday life. The interviews were augmented with observations of how wallets were used. Specifically, numerous photographs were taken, recording the contents of participant's wallets. As well as providing a record of exactly how participants used their wallets, the process of emptying the wallet's contents for documentation served as a prompt for discussion itself.

3 Results

Participants perceived the wallet primarily as a financial artifact. Despite the fact that the participants were observed to store a multitude of objects, including plasters, textile samples, teeth and pocket battleships, when asked why they carried a wallet the vast majority replied that it was "to keep my cards and money".

Typically, participants possessed several 'wallets' in the form of coin purses, cardholders, Filofaxes, etc. Indeed, many of participants used more than one wallet simultaneously (see Figure 1) the contents of each being constantly exchanged. For instance, 'phone numbers were transferred from pieces of paper stuffed in the wallet to the Filofax; bankcards were switched from the purse, to the jacket pocket and back again. However, far from this complex system proving problematic, it was considered by many people to be extremely useful, for example because of the flexibility offered and as a means of "keeping on top of things."

Interestingly, the amount of financial 'stuff' that participants carried around in their wallets was found to be related to their attitude towards electronic-banking and -commerce. Those participants who actively accepted electronic transactions subsequently found themselves loaded down with multiple bank cards, credit cards, debit cards and store cards (see Figure 2). Furthermore, the enormous numbers of receipts that are a by-product of electronic transactions are packed into the wallet along with the cash and coins necessary for 'micro-transactions'. Micro-transactions are those transactions under five pounds that typically include the purchase of "bus tickets", "newspapers" and "sandwiches". In contrast, those participants who have chosen to reject electronic-banking and -commerce are far less encumbered.

What was common to almost all wallets, however, was the presence of some form of emotive objects. Indeed, even in the most sparsely populated wallet, there could be found an old football match ticket or a picture of a child. Indeed, the wallet itself often held great sentimental value. As much as the wallet is a financial artifact it is equally an emotional one.

Figure 2: Multi-wallet user / Electronic commerce and banking acceptor.

4 Conclusions

The ethnographic approach adopted here revealed many hidden facets to the wallet, its contents and use. Of particular note is the presumption of the wallet only as a financial object, yet the reality being that it has many roles and exists as part of a highly modularized storage system. This demonstrates a need to address this system within future wallets. Future digital wallet designs must also be able to deal with the large amount of objects typically carried by the very people who are most likely to want to use them. Furthermore, and most importantly future electronic wallets must also the status of 'emotional artifact'. Existing electronic wallets seem to fail the consumers in these three areas.

This research also, however, underlines the value of the ethnographic approach in highlighting these issues which would probably not have emerged from a standard, interview only approach.

The next phase of this research will attempt to model consumers' acceptance of technologies such as the digital wallet, relying on a multi-method approach, and extending the literature on technology acceptance.

Human-Computer Interaction - INTERACT'99 (Volume II)
S. Brewster, A. Cawsey & G. Cockton (Editors)
Published by The British Computer Society © IFIP TC.13, 1999

EPSRC
Engineering and Physical Sciences Research Council

Scope for Progress – Monitoring Background Tasks with Sound

Murray Crease and Stephen Brewster

Glasgow Interactive Systems Group,
Department of Computing Science, University Of Glasgow,
Glasgow G12 8RZ, UK
Email: <murray/stephen>@dcs.gla.ac.uk

Abstract: This paper describes an evaluation of the effectiveness of adding sound to progress indicators. Standard progress indicators have usability problems because they present temporal information graphically, and if the user wants to keep abreast of this information, he or she must constantly visually scan the progress indicator. Non-speech sounds called *earcons* were used to indicate the scope of the task before it started, and the state of the task whilst it was under way. Results showed that the users were better able to monitor a background task using the audio progress indicator than a standard visual one, whilst typing in text as a foreground task.

Keywords: earcons, audio interfaces, progress indicators.

1 Introduction

Progress indicators are a common feature of most modern graphical user interfaces. They are used to track the state of a time consuming task as it progresses. Myers (1985) showed that users preferred systems with progress indicators as they allowed experts to predict the approximate time of completion for the task, whilst novices were given confidence the task had been accepted and was progressing.

For a progress indicator to be effective there are several items of information that it should convey. Conn (1995) described eight pieces of information that users need to be aware of if they are to monitor the progress of a task successfully: *Acceptance* - that the task can be done, *scope* of the task, *initiation* - that the task has started, *progress* of the task, *heartbeat* - that the task is still alive, *exception* - a problem with the task has occurred, amount *remaining* and *completion* of the task.

Progress indicators often provide all these pieces of information, but purely visually. If a task takes too long, users will often push the progress bar to one side of the screen, or perhaps cover it with a document upon which they are working whilst the task completes. In this instance, to monitor the progress of the task the user will have to move his/her visual focus from the primary task. To reduce the user's visual load, it was decided to present the progress indicator's information sonically, using abstract, structured non-speech sounds, *earcons* (Blattner *et al*, 1989). It has been previously shown that earcons are effective at alerting users to the completion of a task (Crease & Brewster, 1998), but there was no objective evidence that the users were using the sounds to monitor the progress of the tasks and this inspired the work described here.

The SonicFinder (Gaver, 1989) used auditory icons to present the information given by a progress indicator. The analogy of a jug being filled with water was used to indicate progress. Although the sounds did not provide all the information required by Conn and no formal evaluation was conducted, users anecdotally reported the system to be useful.

2 Experimental Evaluation

Five sounds were used to fulfil the requirements laid out by Conn: A scope sound to indicate the size of the task about to begin, an end point sound to indicate the target for completion, a progress sound for the percentage completed (the difference in pitch between the end point and progress sounds was proportional to the remainder), a rate of progress sound giving the absolute rate at which the task was progressing (proportional to the number of notes played per second), and a completion sound to indicate task termination (three brief chords played in succession).

To evaluate the effectiveness of these sounds an experiment was run. Sixteen participants were used (postgraduate students and researchers from the University of Glasgow). The participants were asked to download a series of files whilst typing in a set of texts. If a download stalled or was progressing too slowly, the participant could stop it and start the next one. Their task was to type in as many of the texts in the time it took to download a fixed amount, in bytes, of completed files. The experiment was a counter-balanced, two condition, within-groups design. One condition used an audio only progress bar (with no visual component) to indicate the progress of the downloads, the other a standard visual only progress bar. At the end of each condition the participants were asked to complete NASA TLX workload tests. Users were also asked to rate the annoyance felt during the task and to give an overall preference. Time taken to stop a download and begin the next was also collected. The main hypotheses were that the overall workload felt by the users would be reduced as the additional information provided by the sounds would be useful. The time taken to stop a download that had stalled would decrease as the sounds would allow the participant to monitor the state of a download and know when it was too slow.

Overall subjective workload was significantly reduced from 11.36 in the visual condition to 9.13 in the audio (T_5=6.22,p=0.0008), confirming the first hypothesis. Additionally, overall preference was increased in the audio condition, from 10.9 to 15 (T_{15}=3.95,p=0.002). The annoyance and frustration felt by the participants were unchanged between conditions. This suggests that the purely audio progress bar was effective at communicating progress in a form users were easily able to understand.

The time taken to stop a download after it had stalled was significantly decreased in the audio condition, from 9.00 sec. to 6.32 sec. (T_{15}=2.31, p=0.02). Additionally, the time to start the next download following a completed one was reduced from 3.7 sec. to 2.4 sec. (T_{15}=5.13, p=0.0003). These show that users were able to monitor the progress of downloads whilst doing the visual typing task. They were able to tell when a download should be stopped as it had stalled, or when a download had finished and the next be initiated. There was no difference in the amount typed between the conditions so the sounds did not reduce the amount of work users could do on their primary task.

3 Conclusions

In this paper, we have shown that sounds were effective in enabling users to monitor a background activity without hindering their primary (visual) task. This means that ongoing background tasks such as downloads, file copies or print jobs can be monitored using sound, freeing the visual channel for other tasks which rely on vision (such as typing or drawing). This has many benefits and shows that mapping tasks to the appropriate sensory channel can significantly improve performance in a multi-modal human-computer interface.

This work was funded by EPSRC grant GR/L79212

4 References

Blattner, M. & Sumikawa, D. & Greenberg, R. "Earcons and Icons: Their Structure And Common Design Principles". *Human Computer Interaction 1989,* **4**, 11-44.

Conn, A.P. "Time Affordances: The Time Factor In Diagnostic Usability Heuristics". *Proceedings of CHI'95 (Denver),* ACM Press, Addison Wesley, 1995, 186-193.

Crease, M.G. & Brewster, S.A. "Making Progress With Sound – The Design And Evaluation Of An Audio Progress Bar". *Proceedings of ICAD'98 (Glasgow),* British Computer Society, 1998, 15.

Gaver, W.W. "The Sonic Finder: An Interface That Uses Auditory Icons". *Human-Computer Interaction, 1989,* **4**, 67-94.

Myers, B.A. "The Importance Of Percent-Done Progress Indicators For Human-Computer Interaction". *Proceedings of CHI'85,* ACM Press, Addison Wesley, 1985, 11-17.

Human-Computer Interaction - INTERACT'99 (Volume II)
S. Brewster, A. Cawsey & G. Cockton (Editors)
Published by The British Computer Society © IFIP TC.13, 1999

EPSRC
Engineering and Physical Sciences Research Council

Resource Sensitive Multi-Modal Widgets

Murray Crease, Philip Gray and Stephen Brewster

Glasgow Interactive Systems Group,
Department of Computing Science, University Of Glasgow,
Glasgow G12 8RZ, UK
Email: <murray/pdg/stephen>@dcs.gla.ac.uk

Abstract: Visual feedback is still the predominant and often sole output modality used by many interactive applications. Other modalities such as sound or touch are often under-used in human computer interfaces or not used at all. In this paper we describe the design and initial implementation of a toolkit of resource sensitive multi-modal widgets. In this toolkit, each modality is treated as an equal, with the behaviour of the widget defined separately from the feedback the widget generates.

Keywords: Widgets, toolkits, multi-modal interaction

1 Introduction

Most modern computers are capable of producing high quality graphics, and this can be seen in the graphical quality of the interfaces seen on our computers. Similarly, most modern computers are capable of producing high quality sounds, but this has not been translated into high quality audio being used in computer interfaces. This, in part, may be because the designers of human-computer interfaces do not have the necessary skills to incorporate sounds into the interface. Whilst this is often also the case for graphics, toolkits of interface interaction objects - or widgets - are available which allow interface designers to incorporate graphical objects without needing any knowledge about how they have been produced. For interfaces to incorporate audio, toolkits which encapsulate the knowledge of audio designers are required.

Designers cannot expect that applications will always run in environments with the same presentational resources. Mobile platforms may limit both audio and graphical output. Workstations in open-plan offices cannot use the full range of sound system volume. These environments motivate the search for interactive systems sensitive to the perceptual context in which they are embedded and that can dynamically change the way they offer feedback.

Currently, building such systems is difficult because of limitations in the software resource programmers have to work with. Widget presentation is still organised around graphical parameters and graphical output methods; other modalities are not usually directly supported. One could add auditory presentation by creating an "auditory context" object, by analogy with a graphics context object, with appropriate methods for auditory output Nevertheless, this would still result in widgets with their modalities "hard-coded" in their presentation methods.

We introduce a new level of abstraction in the widget architecture, to accommodate the mapping from modality independent ("highlight") to modality dependent ("shade shape", "play button press sound") descriptions of output and to provide a level of external control over this mapping (e.g., to reflect the presence or absence of certain resources, such as CD quality sound or to allow for configuration of the mapping).

We do this by an approach similar to that taken in the ENO system (Beaudoin-Lafon & Gaver, 1994), in which auditory feedback is generated by high-level requests (in terms of non-audio descriptions of the feedback, e.g., the size and virtual material composition of the interaction object) to an audio server which converts requests into a form suitable for rendering via an audio device. Our architecture goes beyond ENO in offering general, modality-independent tailoring to reflect the requirements of the interaction and the resources available to meet those requirements. Our toolkit supports dynamic adjustment of feedback based on the current state of user settings and presentational resources. For example, should an application request multiple sounds that may interfere with each other, the widgets' run-time environment can adjust the feedback to minimise inter-sound interference.

2 Toolkit Design

The toolkit has two parts: classes defining each widget type and a set of classes defining the objects used for run-time presentation management. A widget is modelled as four subcomponents: a behaviour controller, a feedback controller, an audio mapper and a graphics mapper. These four components serve to translate external events affecting the widget into internal requests for feedback. The **Behaviour Controller** (BC) accepts external events and, based on the current state of the widget, filters and converts these events into internal events which are passed to the **Feedback Controller** (FC) for modification and routing to the **Audio Mapper** (AM) and **Graphics Mapper** (GM), as appropriate. Feedback controller modifications can include blocking the event or changing its attributes, as instructed by the **Resource Manager** (RM) component. For example, the event's weighting can be adjusted for each modality. This weighting enables the user to "turn up" or "turn down" the graphics or audio. Each of the mappers embellish these events with additional modality dependent parameters set by the user in a **Control Panel** (CP). Events are finally passed to a **Rendering Manager** (RM) responsible for co-ordinating all rendering operations carried out by its constituent **Output Modules** (OM). Figure 1 shows how all these objects interact.

An initial version of the toolkit has been implemented, consisting of a button class, a progress bar class and a simple control panel for configuring modalities. The visual components for the widgets consist of Java Swing objects. The audio components are based upon previous designs for audio buttons (Brewster *et al,* 1995) and progress bars (Crease & Brewster, 1998). In this initial simple version the feedback weighting corresponds to size in the visual modality and volume in the auditory modality. The mechanism is, however, capable of handling more sophisticated mapping rules.

3 Conclusions

Our modality independent toolkit offers support for the construction of more context sensitive user interfaces able to reconfigure themselves dynamically as presentation conditions change. The first prototype, although simple, proves the concept is implementable. We are now investigating the modelling and implementation of a rich set of presentation mapping rules for a complete toolkit.

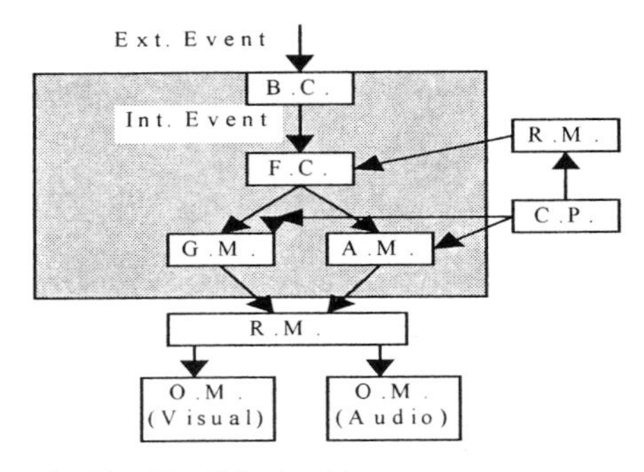

Figure 1: The Toolkit Architecture.

This work was funded by EPSRC grant GR/L79212

References

Beaudouin-Lafon, M. and Gaver, W.W (1994) "ENO: Synthesising Structured Sound Spaces" Proceedings of UIST'94 (Marina del Rey), pp49-57

Brewster, S.A., Wright, P.C., Dix, A.J. & Edwards, A.D.N. (1995). "The sonic enhancement of graphical buttons." In Proceedings of Interact'95, Lillehammer, Norway: Chapman & Hall, pp.43-48.

Crease, M.G., Brewster, S.A. (1998). Making Progress With Sounds - The Design and Evaluation Of An Audio Progress Bar. In Proceedings of ICAD'98 (Glasgow, UK), British Computer Society.

Human-Computer Interaction - INTERACT'99 (Volume II)
S. Brewster, A. Cawsey & G. Cockton (Editors)
Published by The British Computer Society © IFIP TC.13, 1999

EPSRC
Engineering and Physical Sciences Research Council

Spatial Data Management Systems: Human Factors Perspectives

T. Cribbin and S.J. Westerman

Psychology Institute
Aston University
Birmingham
United Kingdom
Email: t.cribbin@aston.ac.uk

Abstract: This presents an overview of an EPSRC funded project examining human factors issues as they relate to virtual environment representations of computer-based information.

1 Introduction

The volume of available electronic information continues to increase at exponential rates (e.g. the internet). This has the potential to transform the way that people work and manage their lives. However, in reality the benefits are not fully realised due to difficulties of access. Currently, perhaps the most common method of locating computer-based information is to use a simple keyword search. This method relies on the user being able to define, with precision, suitable query terms. Unfortunately many words have multiple meanings and concepts can be described by many words. Consequently, search results will frequently contain large quantities of marginally relevant, or irrelevant, information.

The question that must be addressed, therefore, is how can the user gain fast, easy access to the information they need? One promising technique that has recently come to the forefront involves representing the semantic associations between items of information in three-dimensional virtual environments. Items of information (nodes) are represented as objects. Node location is dependent on semantic content. Semantically similar nodes are positioned so that they are spatially proximate and/or share clear, visual, links. In order to achieve this, the semantic relationships between nodes must be quantified using computer algorithms. Such spatial data management systems (SDMSs) capitalise on real world navigational skills. In order to locate information the user travels within the virtual environment and is able to form a cognitive map of the information space. Many impressive systems of this type are already in existence. However, there has been little scientific research into the human factors issues associated with this genre of interface. Two issues are of particular importance. The first concerns the 'goodness-of-fit' between a computer-generated semantic model of an information space and the cognitive model that will be applied by the user. It seems reasonable to expect that if the match between these models is poor then information retrieval performance will also be poor. The second concerns the additional spatial demands that are placed on the users of such systems. It is not clear how much increased semantic information must be conveyed in order to compensate for the associated additional cognitive demands. Supported by an EPSRC grant, we are currently conducting a series of experiments designed to address these issues.

2 Evaluating Techniques for Automatic Text Analysis

Two sets of journal abstracts (documents) were analysed, using a vector space procedure that incorporated a variety of common similarity/distance algorithms. We also acquired similarity ratings for all possible pair-wise combinations of documents from a sample of human raters. The degree of concurrence between the various computer and human solutions was examined. Key results were:

- Correlations between the mean of participant (P) ratings and the computer-generated ratings ranged from moderate to strong. Particular ATA algorithms were identified as achieving a better match in this respect.
- Human inter-rater agreement was quite poor. Following from this, although the conceptual model of some Ps matched the computer model fairly well, for other Ps this was not the case.

In further experiments we are beginning to establish how discrepancies between the computer-generated and the human user's model will affect the usability of an SDMS.

3 Exploring Spatial Navigational Issues

A virtual reality interface was programmed to allow investigation of spatial navigational issues. This software (to be demonstrated during the conference poster session) was not designed as an end user product but as a functional experimental tool. Nodes are represented as primitive objects (spheres or cubes), with facet colour also being definable via an input file.

The first experimental paradigm that we used involved a simple search task, in which Ps were required to locate target nodes. Ps completed a number of trials, and various performance measures were captured within the program. These included the length of time taken to locate the target, the total distance travelled, the shortest possible distance to the target, the total number of nodes visited, and the number of different nodes visited. Ps also completed various psychometric tests of cognitive ability. This approach was used to examine the cognitive demands associated with navigating 2D vs 3D representations of the same database. A database of 64 animal names was generated. Each was associated with a randomly positioned object in the virtual environment. The 2D condition used an 8 x 8 configuration and the 3D condition used a 4 x 4 x 4 configuration. We found that:

- Navigational efficiency improved over time. However, interactive effects indicated that low spatial ability Ps performed more poorly than high spatial ability Ps during the early stages of task performance. A relatively steeper acquisition slope, for low spatials, meant that eventual performance was comparable.
- There was a significant interaction between spatial ability and the number of database dimensions for self-report workload. Ps with high spatial ability experienced comparatively lower workload when using the 2D configuration, but this pattern was reversed for low spatials.

A further study examined the effects of node configuration ('cube' vs 'real distance') on performance. Initially, a sample of Ps rated all pairs of items in the animals database for similarity. This produced a similarity matrix that was scaled to three dimensions using the ALSCAL procedure. In one experiment, these co-ordinates were used as the basis for ordinal positioning of objects within a 4 x 4 x 4 ('cube') configuration, whereby neighbouring objects were equidistant. This arrangement involved some compromises in terms of node location and therefore was less semantically consistent than that used in a second experiment where the configuration was based on the original co-ordinates ('real distance'). Users, in both experiments, performed the same search task as outlined above, completing a number of trials distributed equally across five levels of object density (manipulated using a scaling factor). The key findings were:

- Generally, low spatials performed more poorly than high spatials.
- Ps with high associative memory ability performed more poorly than low associative memory Ps when the constrained ('cube') configuration was used. However, this pattern was reversed, in the second experiment, when the 'real distance' configuration was used.

We hypothesise that congruence between the user's cognitive model and the actual organisation of the information space is of greater importance to Ps with high associative memory ability.

Our current work involves an examination of the nature of the potential trade-off between the cognitive demands of navigating higher dimensional virtual spaces, on the one hand, and the greater semantic information that can be conveyed, with respect to the contents of a database, on the other.

Human-Computer Interaction - INTERACT'99 (Volume II)
S. Brewster, A. Cawsey & G. Cockton (Editors)
Published by The British Computer Society © IFIP TC.13, 1999

Costs Matrix: Systematic Comparison of Competing Design Solutions

Stephen Cummaford and John Long

Ergonomics & HCI Unit
University College London
26 Bedford Way, London, UK
Email: {s.cummaford; j.long}@ucl.ac.uk

Abstract: There is a need for a systematic means of evaluating competing solutions to a design problem, in terms of their relative performance. This poster presents the 'costs matrix', a design representation to support the evaluation of physical and cognitive costs incurred by users whilst interacting with computers to perform work. The costs matrix is illustrated with reference to the evaluation of existing internet shops. Such explicit representation of costs supports the systematic evaluation of competing solutions to a design problem in terms of performance.

Keywords: cognitive engineering, domain models, user models, user costs, performance

1 Introduction

There is a need for a systematic means of evaluating the costs incurred by users, whilst interacting with computers to perform work effectively, to support comparison of competing solutions to a design problem in terms of their relative performance.

This poster presents the 'costs matrix', a design representation, which has proved useful in establishing relative performance in a systematic manner. The matrix, it is argued, provides a systematic means of representing the relationship between the work and how well it is achieved by a human-computer worksystem, and the costs which are consequently incurred by the user. Specification of this relationship facilitates the comparison of competing solutions to a design problem in a systematic manner.

The costs matrix was operationalised during a recent study evaluating the performance of users transacting with online shops (e-shops) to order and to buy goods. The costs matrix relates concepts contained in the HCIE (Human-Computer Interaction Engineering) general design problem (Dowell & Long, 1989). This problem is summarised later, illustrated by examples from the e-shop study.

2 HCIE General Design Problem

The expression of the HCIE general design problem comprises a domain model, a user model, a computer model and statement of inequality between actual and desired performance. These concepts are summarised here to inform the presentation of the costs matrix.

A domain model comprises objects which have attributes having particular values, for example, in the e-shop domain, products (e.g. books) have an attribute 'owner'. The work to be performed is expressed as domain object attribute transformations, collectively termed the product goal. In the e-shop design problem, the product goal includes transforming attribute 'ownership' from value 'vendor' to value 'customer'.

The human-computer worksystem is represented as a user model and a computer model, each of which comprises structures which support behaviours. User structures in the e-shop design problem included 'items ordered' and an evaluation process, which supported user behaviours, e.g. 'write to representation'. The evaluated e-shops comprised different structures, e.g. on screen versus separate screen shopping cart. These differences in structure resulted in the product goal being achieved, but with different performance.

The behaviours effected by the worksystem to achieve the product goal are expressed as the task goal structure. The effectiveness with which the task goal structure achieves the product goal is expressed as performance, evaluated as the task quality achieved, and the costs incurred by the user (Dowell & Long, 1989) (the costs incurred by the computer are not addressed here).

3 Costs Matrix Specification

The costs matrix is constructed by listing the user physical and cognitive structures on the y axis and the domain transformations, specified in the product goal, on the x axis. The cells of the matrix are instantiated by analysis of user data, informed by the user model and product goal. This instantiation is illustrated later.

The utility of the costs matrix depends on the validity of both the product goal and the user model. The assumption that activation of any structure in the user model will result in an equal cost to the user is dependent on the specification of the user model, which must reflect this assumption in the partitioning of structures. The cumulative physical costs and cognitive costs are represented separately.

The costs matrix supports the evaluation of user costs as numerical values, thus facilitating comparison between competing design solutions. However, such comparisons are only valid if the elements on both axes are the same for each analysed design solution.

4 E-Shop Case Study

User trials were conducted to evaluate performance using existing e-shops. Users were asked to complete a series of tasks, including ordering, evaluating the collated order and completing the transaction. These tasks were the same across shops, to support valid comparison of performance. The users produced a verbal protocol, which was recorded on video. An additional interview was then conducted and videotaped to gather further data about the users' behaviour and reflections during task performance.

The user costs were then represented in the form of the costs matrix. The costs matrix for one user is shown on the poster. The video recording and verbal protocol for each user were interpreted to populate the matrix. The videotapes were analysed to diagnose directly observable physical behaviours, and so costs, e.g. keystrokes, and indirectly observable cognitive behaviours, and so costs, e.g. calculation of the total order price on the basis of the subtotal and knowledge of shipping rates. Cognitive costs were diagnosed when a listed structure was activated, as inferred from the verbal protocol or analytically from the domain transformations effected by the user. Structure activation supported any of four behaviours: 'evaluate', 'calculate', 'read from mental structure' (e.g. 'subtotal for goods') or 'write to mental structure' (e.g. increment 'items ordered list'). Each user trial was analysed in this manner, and the matrices collated to give an expression of performance for the task goal structure of each of the e-shops evaluated. The use of a common representation for data from user trials facilitated direct comparison between alternative design solutions, both generally and at each stage of the task.

The total costs incurred during each trial was then used to evaluate and compare the overall effectiveness of the existing systems. The representation of costs incurred at each stage of the task informed the specification of a design solution, by indicating stages which resulted in high costs.

Thus, the costs matrix supports the systematic specification of physical and cognitive costs for users interacting with computers, here, existing internet shops. The comparison of numerical expressions of costs is valid between solutions, if the axes of the costs matrix are the same in each case. Systematic evaluation of costs supports comparison of competing solutions to a design problem in terms of their relative performance.

References

Cummaford, S.J.O. and Long, J.B. (1998). Towards a conception of HCI engineering design principles. *Proc. ECCE-9*, ed. Green et al; Limerick, Eire.

Dowell, J. and Long, J.B. (1989). Towards a conception for an engineering discipline of human factors. *Ergonomics 32*, 1513-1536

Virtual Actors in Collaborative Virtual Environments for Museum Education

Daphne Economou, William L. Mitchell and *Tom Boyle

Manchester Metropolitan University,
Department of Computing and Mathematics,
Chester Street, Manchester, M1 5GD,
England

*University of North London,
School of Informatics and Multimedia Technology,
166-220 Holloway Road London N7 8DB,
England

Email: D.Economou@doc.mmu.ac.uk, B.Mitchell@doc.mmu.ac.uk

1 Aims of the Research

This research is developing a set of design factors relating to the use of virtual actors in Collaborative Virtual Environments (CVEs) for learning. These factors address issues of pedagogy, communication and interactional needs in such environments, and consider how these impact upon CVE system design.

2 Problems

One problem is the vast amount of factors to be considered. (Kaur, 1997) has identified 46 properties relating to usability in VEs. The number of factors increases dramatically when considering communication and collaboration issues introduced in CVEs. This makes it difficult to isolate which design decisions are responsible for the overall effectiveness of the environment. It is also difficult to identify the inter-play between various factors.

The second problem faced is that the immaturity of the technology means that many applications developed so far have been of a prototypical nature.

3 Approach

The research approach is primarily exploratory in nature. The studies being carried out are observations rather than evaluations. (Roussos, 1998) supports the need for such exploratory work which involves building novel learning applications and carrying out informal evaluations of them. To determine the requirements of a CVE it is necessary to study a "real world" situation.

A typical exemplar is the work of the Manchester Museum Education Service (Mitchell, 1999). The CVE is based on *senet*, an ancient Egyptian board game. The game allows both co-operation (in learning) and competition (in trying to win) to be studied. The CVE is aimed at Key Stage Level 2 (~9-10 years old) of the National Curriculum for education in England.

A model of CVE use in education was synthesised from existing models of VEs, CVEs and the classroom. This was then used to develop a preliminary framework of design factors concerning virtual actors.

The framework is being progressively refined by structuring the studies into three distinct phases.

4 First Two Phases

The first phase prototypes were developed using 2-D multi-media technology (Macromedia Director) and are examples of single display groupware (Stewart, 1999). Interactions take place face-to-face in the real world external to the VE.

The prototypes were observed in use by the general public during an open week at Manchester Museum. Observations of school children were also conducted under more controlled conditions.

The purpose of the first phase was primarily to study what went on in the real world game-playing situation. Several situations were identified (1 child and an adult expert, 2 children, 1 naive and 1 "expert" child, 1 child and a parent). What stood out was how important it was for an expert to be aware of and to be able to control even such a seemingly well structured activity as game playing.

For the second phase, the prototypes took the form of multi-user groupware where the users are located remotely from each other. The second phase focused on issues surrounding the internalisation of the interactions and the effects on the behaviour of participants.

The groupware element was provided by NetMeeting. Three prototypes were developed. One of the prototypes was semi-populated (the participant can see other actors present) and the other two fully-populated (the participant can represent themselves via an actor).

Studies took place at a local school. These were video recorded and are currently being transcribed.

The results so far from the second phase indicate that problems arise because the established 2D collaborative technology limits the access of the expert to information about the situation. A comparison of the video of the expert and a video of the remotely located child shows the discrepancies. Turn taking was particularly difficult. The expert was often unsure whether the child had completed their turn or was thinking over their actions. Technical problems (such as system lag) made this problem worse. To overcome these problems an informal protocol arose whereby a participant would place the mouse pointer in a particular area of the screen to signify turn completion.

5 Future Work

In the third phase of work the design factors identified previously will be used to guide the design of a 3D fully-populated prototype. The technology that is being used is the DEVA 3D CVE tool developed by Manchester University (Pettifer, 1997).

User studies of this CVE will allow the validity of the design factors identified in previous phases to be tested. In this way the results can be used to guide the development of the underlying technology itself so that it reflects the needs of real users in real educational situations.

References

Work from the project can be found at:
www.doc.mmu.ac.uk/RESEARCH/virtual-museum

Kaur, K. (1997). Designing Virtual Environments for Usability. *Proceedings of Human-Computer Interaction: INTERACT'97*, S. Howard, J. Hammond and G. Lindgaard (eds.), Chapman & Hall, 1997, pp. 636-639.

Mitchell, W. L. (1999). Moving the Museum onto the Internet: The use of Virtual Environments in Education about Ancient Egypt. *Virtual Worlds on the Internet*, J.A. Vince and R.A. Earnshaw (eds.), IEEE Computer Society Press, 1999, pp. 263-278.

Pettifer, S.R. and West, A.J. (1997) Deva: A Coherent Operating Environment for Large Scale Virtual Reality Applications. *Proceedings of Virtual Reality Universe '97*, M. Kruger, G. Burdea, H. Fuchs and M. Zyda (eds.), April 1997.

Roussos, M., Johnson, A., Moher, T., Leigh, J., Vasilakis, C. and Barnes, C. (1999). Learning and Building Together in an Immersive Virtual World, to appear in *Presence*, Vol. 8, No. 3, June 1999, MIT Press.

Stewart, J., Bederson, B.B. and Druin, A. (1999) Single Display Groupware: A Model for Co-operative Collaboration, to appear in *Proceedings of CHI'99, Conference on Human Factors in Computing Systems*. ACM Press.

Human-Computer Interaction - INTERACT'99 (Volume II)
S. Brewster, A. Cawsey & G. Cockton (Editors)
Published by The British Computer Society © IFIP TC.13, 1999

Workplace Groups, Status Differences and Multimedia Communications Technology

Emma France

University of Glasgow,
52 Hillhead Street,
Glasgow G12 8QB, Scotland

Abstract: Increasingly, organisations are utilising multimedia communications technologies such as video and audio conferencing. Yet little is known about how the communication of *groups*, especially groups with organisational status differences, is affected by such technology. This field research compares mixed- and same-status workplace groups audio conferencing and communicating face-to-face to reveal that high-status group members dominate interactions and that the technology seems to exaggerate this inequality of participation. This has implications for meeting effectiveness and development of communications technology.

Keywords: multimedia, communication, audio conferencing, video conferencing, status.

1 Introduction

Increasingly, organisations are utilising multimedia communications technologies such as video and audio conferencing. Most studies of their impact focus on dyadic interaction, despite their use for *group* communication.

One neglected factor is the effect of status differences on multimedia supported group communication. High-status group members have more influence and dominate face-to-face interaction in workplace and lab groups (e.g. Carletta, Garrod & Fraser-Krauss 1998), while text-based computer-mediated communication (CMC) in the lab tends to equalise participation and influence in mixed-status groups (e.g. Dubrovsky et al. 1991) but only when participants are unaware of status differences (Weisband et al. 1995).

Participating equally is considered of great importance in workplace groups since if low status prevents group members from contributing important information, the group may perform sub-optimally (Carletta et al. 1998).

This research addresses the question: what is the effect of organisational status differences on equality of participation in workplace groups and how does multimedia communications technology influence this?

2 Field Data

12 collaborative business meetings using 3 different media - face-to-face meetings, telephone audio conferencing and audiographic PC conferencing (BT's Conference Call Presence™) - have been analysed. Audio conferences used an open channel audio link via the telephone network. Conference Call Presence™ includes file transfer, shared whiteboard and application sharing capabilities. For further details see:

http://presence.conferencing.bt.com/presence/index.html

Meetings include team progress reviews, writing of a research proposal, and preparing a presentation, last from 1 to 3 hours, have 3 to 7 participants and consist of mixed- and same-status groups. Mixed-status groups are ones in which a leader was responsible for decision-making.

3 Communication Analyses

All meetings were audio recorded and transcribed. Detailed communication analysis was carried out including counts of words spoken. This allows computation of an equality of participation score based on a measurement of the distance between actual number of words spoken by each participant and the number expected had they all participated equally (Carletta et al. 1998).

This analysis differs from previous mediated group research as *patterns* of interaction are focused on. Furthermore, detailed communication analysis can uncover subtle effects of the technology of which users may be unconscious, something which subjective data, from questionnaires for example, may not do.

4 Results

This research is in progress and more meetings are currently being analysed. With this caveat in mind, the main characteristics of group multi-mediated communication are: there is a tendency for less equal participation in all types of mixed-status group meetings - senior members dominate; multimedia communications technology seems to exaggerate this inequality of participation.

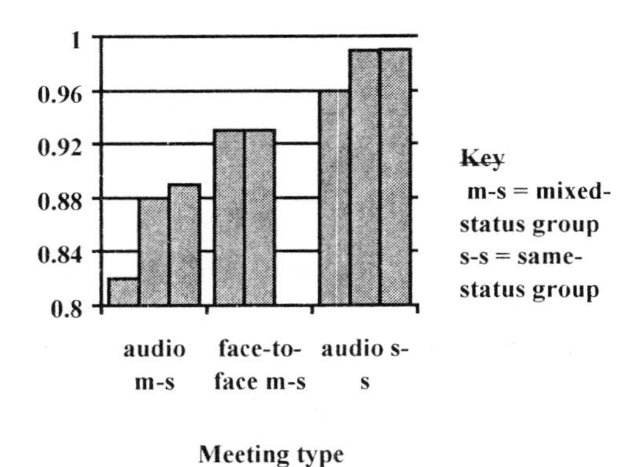

Figure 1: Equality of participation scores.

Interpretation of equality of participation scores: 1 - all participants say the same amount; 0 - only one person speaks.

Figure 1 shows equality of participation scores for 8 meetings. When a series of meetings was analysed the score from the first meeting is given. Type of audio conference is not differentiated.

Although this field research is incomplete, a controlled lab study also shows multi-mediated group communication using video has significantly less equal participation than face-to-face communication (France, in preparation).

5 Discussion

Carletta, Garrod and Fraser-Krauss (1998) and others highlight the importance of equal participation for better and more innovative decisions in company meetings but warn that status differences are a barrier to this. Initial studies of communications technologies suggest that these can reduce the negative impact of status on participation rates when status cues are unavailable (Dubrovsky et al. 1991, Weisband et al. 1995).

This research confirms that high-status group members tend to dominate discussions in meetings while also indicating that rich multimedia communications technology can exaggerate this effect. It is therefore a challenge to the design of such technology to support mixed-status groups.

Possible solutions include adapting the technology, perhaps to capture an element of the anonymity of text-based CMC which reduces status effects, or training users to overcome status constraints on equal participation (Carletta et al. 1998).

In sum, it is important to combine research in the field with controlled lab experiments and detailed communication analysis to gain an understanding of the subtleties of mediated multiparty interaction. This will facilitate innovative solutions to its constraints and help us to better support it with new communications technologies.

References

Carletta, J., Garrod, S., & Fraser-Krauss, H. (1998) Communication and Placement of Authority in Workplace Groups -The Consequences for Innovation. *Small Group Research*, 29(5), 531-559.

Dubrovsky, V. J., Kiesler, S., & Sethna, B. N. (1991) The equalization phenomenon: status effects in computer-mediated and face-to-face decision-making groups. *Human-Computer Interaction*, 6(2), 119-146.

France, E. (in preparation) A comparison of small group face-to-face and video-mediated communication.

Weisband, S. P., Schneider, S. K. & Connolly, T. (1995) Computer-mediated communication and social information: status salience and status differences. *Academy of Management Journal*, 38 (4), 1124-1151.

Human-Computer Interaction - INTERACT'99 (Volume II)
S. Brewster, A. Cawsey & G. Cockton (Editors)
Published by The British Computer Society © IFIP TC.13, 1999

Improving Understanding Using Video Technology

David Grayson

University of Glasgow
52 Hillhead Street, Glasgow, Scotland.
Email: david@mcg.gla.ac.uk

Abstract: When an individual engages in a video-mediated interaction with a stranger, it is known that they are likely to be more interactive if the image of their partner appears very close (zoomed in). An experiment was run to investigate whether or not this difference in conversational style had any subsequent effect on individuals understanding of the topics discussed. Participants discussed financial advice with a remote financial advisor who appeared either close or far away. After discussing 4 investment options, participants stated which they would choose. After the experiment, a surprise recall interview was used to measure participants understanding of the options. The results showed a trend towards participants being more interactive in the zoomed in conditions. When split into groups of interactivity, results clearly showed that participants who were more interactive had a significantly greater understanding of the options discussed. It is concluded that being more interactive in a conversation leads to better understanding. One way to improve understanding when using video-mediated technology is to alter the zoom on a camera so that the information giver appears closer than usual.

Keywords: Video-Mediated Communication, Zoom, Proximity, Interactivity, Understanding

1 Video-Mediated Communication (VMC)

To improve the design of remote communication technologies, it is essential to understand the impact of technology on human communication processes, evolved for face-to-face interaction. One technology which can affect communication depending how it is configured is video (eg. Doherty-Sneddon, Anderson, O'Malley, Langton, Garrod & Bruce, 1994).

Although tempting to consider a video-mediated communication system as a singular entity, there are actually many variables within a video system that could affect the communication style of individuals using it (image size, quality, position, task purpose, camera view etc). Knowledge of exactly how these variables affect individuals both psychologically and behaviourally will aid design for specific purposes.

2 Perceived Distance

One variable shown to affect communicative style across video is perceived distance. Altering the level of camera zoom used can manipulate the perceived distance of ones conversational partner. It has been shown that when a stranger appears very close (zoomed in), people engage in a more interactive conversational style, in terms of more speaking turns, more words spoken, and more interruptions of the other speaker (Grayson & Coventry, 1998).

Apart from a trend showing that the more interactive dialogues took longer to complete, it is unknown if there are any knock-on effects of this increase in interactivity. Work by Schober & Clark (1989) showed that taking part in a conversation led to better understanding of topics discussed than simply overhearing a conversation. It was therefore hypothesised that understanding may be affected not only by whether or not interactivity was possible but also by the level of interactivity an individual actually engaged in.

To test this hypothesis, an experiment was conducted which involved participants discussing with a financial advisor 4 methods of investing money. At the end of the task, there was a surprise recall interview to measure individuals' subsequent understanding of the options they had discussed.

3 Method

60 participants role-played the part of a young person who had inherited £5000 and was seeking investment advice from the financial advisor of their local bank, who was available via a video link. They sat in front of a screen with a video window and whiteboard with textual information on it.

There were 2 independent variables (2x2 design), both relating to perceived distance. Image size was either life size (projector screen) or small (monitor), and camera zoom was either close (zoomed in) or far (zoomed out). Thus there were 4 conditions.

Understanding was assessed by way of a surprise recall interview of 23 questions. All questions related to information available on the whiteboard about the 4 possible options. A total score was computed offering 2 points for a correct answer and 1 for a partially correct answer.

4 Results

Dialogues in each condition were analysed for interactivity in terms of the total number of participant turns, and the number of times the participant interrupted the financial advisor. Results showed that participants interrupted significantly more often in the close conditions than in the far conditions [$F(1,54) = 6.46$; $p < 0.05$].

Analysis of the number of participant turns fell short of significance but did show a tendency towards there being more speaking turns in the close conditions than the far. On average there were 12% more participant turns in the projector close condition (54.8) compared to the monitor far condition (48.7).

To study the effect of interactivity on understanding, data was split into thirds, based on the number of participant turns spoken. The highly interactive group consisted of the one-third of participants who spoke the most turns, and was compared against the one-third who spoke the fewest turns. This scale most accurately separated "lecture-style" dialogues from highly interactive ones.

Results showed that highly interactive participants scored significantly more highly than those in the non-interactive group [$t(38) = 3.40$, $p < .01$]. The mean scores for the interactive and non-interactive groups are graphed in Figure 1.

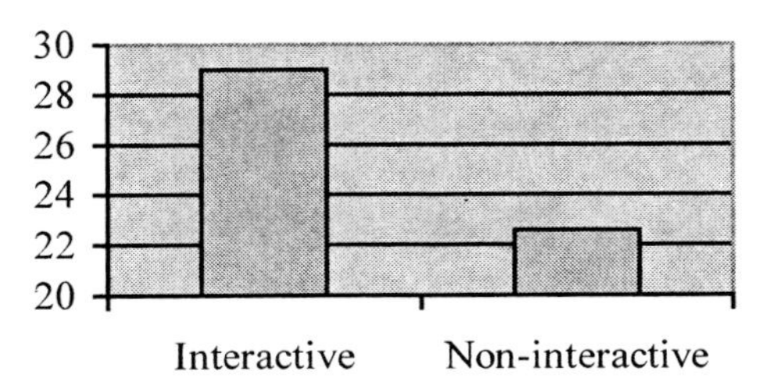

Figure 1: Mean Score.

5 Discussion

The results show that being more interactive leads to a better understanding of concepts discussed. This extends the research of Schober & Clark (1989) by showing that not only is the opportunity to be interactive important for understanding but the level of interactivity within an interactive conversation can lead to differences in the quality of understanding.

The results have also partially replicated the results of Grayson & Coventry (1998) showing that altering the zoom on the video camera can lead to greater interactivity in terms of turns and interruptions.

The implications of this research apply to all using video-mediated communication to pass on information. Users understanding will be improved if they are more interactive, something which can be affected subconsciously by changing the zoom of the camera so that only the head of the information giver is visible. Appearing closer will lead to an improvement in one's dissemination of information.

References

Doherty-Sneddon, G., Anderson, A.H., O'Malley, C., Langton, S., Garrod, S. & Bruce, V. (1997). Face-to-face communication and VMC: A comparison of dialogue structure and task performance. *Journal of Experimental Psychology: Applied*, **3**, 105-125.

Grayson, D. & Coventry, L. (1998). The effects of visual proxemic information in video mediated communication. *SIGCHI Bulletin*, **30**.

Schober, M.F. & Clark, H.H. (1989). Understanding by addressees and overhearers. *Cognitive Psychology*, **21**, 211-232.

Human-Computer Interaction - INTERACT'99 (Volume II)
S. Brewster, A. Cawsey & G. Cockton (Editors)
Published by The British Computer Society © IFIP TC.13, 1999

EPSRC
Engineering and Physical Sciences Research Council

PRIDE: Task-Related Principles for User Interface Design

Fraser Hamilton, Hilary Johnson and Peter Johnson

Department of Computer Science
Queen Mary & Westfield College
University of London
London, E1 4NS
United Kingdom
Email: fraser@dcs.qmw.ac.uk

Abstract: One aim of HCI as a discipline is to develop prescriptive and predictive principles to assist design teams in making informed design decisions. One source of these principles is from an understanding of users' task knowledge and task structures. An understanding of how users acquire, organise and utilise their task knowledge when interacting with computers, can provide the basis for developing operationalised, validated and general principles for user interface design. This paper provides an overview of our approach in PRIDE, a research project which is developing such principles. Two principles are briefly described and the contribution of task-related principles to the discipline of HCI and to HCI design is discussed.

Keywords: Principles, task knowledge, user interface design.

1 Introduction

HCI research and design practice has long recognised that interactive systems are useless if they do not support users in performing their work tasks. To this end a number of task analysis approaches have been developed that model users' task knowledge, or that seek to evaluate designs based on task specifications. However, a progression from predominantly descriptive and evaluative approaches to design to a more prescriptive and predictive form of HCI design is desirable.

The Task Knowledge Structures (TKS) approach to design provided a theory, a method and an environment for task-based design (Johnson, Johnson and Hamilton 1999). Additionally, task-related guidelines were developed to provide prescriptions about how best to support users' work tasks. However, the TKS approach was still not offering sufficiently predictive guidance. To this extent, we are extending TKS by developing task-related principles to enable designers to be guided in making design decisions and predicting the consequences of these decisions on the subsequent usability of their designs. The benefit of developing HCI principles is greater understanding and education about why some designs work well, why users make particular errors, and also enhanced support for design practice. The research objectives include developing the principles, empirically assessing their utility, demonstrating how they can be supported by interface features, and subsequently applied by design teams.

2 Task-Related Principles

Designers can be guided in making design decisions through personal experience, UI guidelines, and empirical/analytic evaluations. Operationalised, tested, and generalised principles add a powerful, complementary set of resources for assisting decision making. The principles should be prescriptive in that they guide design teams towards effective and efficient design solutions. Moreover, the principles should be predictive in that their application, or violation, will have known usability consequences for a specified scope of HCI design scenarios.

2.1 Examples of principles

We are currently investigating a number of potential task-related principles. An illustration of two principles are provided here, although the reader is referred to Hamilton (1999), Hamilton, Johnson and Johnson (1998) and Johnson, Johnson and Hamilton (1999) for a fuller account.

We believe that an understanding of how people structure their tasks – the *principles* of structuring tasks – is fundamental to designing systems with beneficial usability consequences. In developing our principles, then, one focus is to understand the relations that enforce structure on tasks. Two principles recently investigated, arising from Hamilton (1999), are *taxonomic categorisation* and *sequential dependency*:

Taxonomic categorisation. Actions related to similar or different instances of the same object will be performed together, and will form the basis for developing a subgoal comprising these actions. When reified in a user interface design these actions should cohere as a group through the use of spatial proximity, closure, colour, etc. Supporting the principle will improve task performance, through users being able to recall and perform the constituent actions of the subgoal more quickly than if the principles are not supported or even violated.

Sequential dependency: Actions that are sequentially related will be performed together, and will underpin the development of a subgoal comprising these actions. The application of the principle groups together actions that are procedurally related by sequential constraints. These actions can be grouped together at the user interface again by using spatial proximity, closure, greying-out and arrows. Supporting the principle leads to more rapid subgoal formation and hence more accurate recall and execution of user tasks.

Application of these two principles has been demonstrated in experiments to have beneficial impacts on usability across a range of usability metrics (see Hamilton *et al* 1998 and Hamilton 1999). A key finding was that users can and do structure their knowledge as predicted by the principles. Where user interfaces violated the principles users still attempted to develop taxonomic and sequential relations. However, because they had to reconcile the unprincipled display with their emerging task knowledge, their performance was detrimentally affected compared to users whose display *did* follow the principles.

3 Conclusions

Our development of task-based principles seeks to contribute to HCI as a discipline and as a design activity. Theoretically, we are developing an understanding of task knowledge, task structures and their relationship to user interface features. Empirically, we are validating and assessing the utility of the principles to improve usability and demonstrating that the principles can be supported by specific interface features. From a practical perspective we aim to demonstrate the principles through exemplar user interfaces, and develop techniques by which the principles can be applied by design teams.

Acknowledgements

PRIDE: EPSRC grant reference GR/L93874.

References

Hamilton, F. (1999). *Task-related principles for user interface design.* PhD Thesis, University of London.

Hamilton, F., Johnson, P. and Johnson H. (1998). Task related principles for user interface design. In G. van der Veer (ed), *Proceedings of the Schaerding workshop on task analysis, June 1998.*

Johnson, P., Johnson, H. and Hamilton, F. (1998). Getting the knowledge into HCI: Theoretical and practical aspects of Task Knowledge Structures. In S. Chipman, V. Shalin and J. Schraagen (eds), *Cognitive Task Analysis*, LEA Publications.

Human-Computer Interaction - INTERACT'99 (Volume II)
S. Brewster, A. Cawsey & G. Cockton (Editors)
Published by The British Computer Society © IFIP TC.13, 1999

Assembly Training with Augmented Reality and Virtual Reality

David J. Haniff, Andy Boud and Chris Baber

School Manufacturing and Mechanical Engineering
University of Birmingham
UK
Email: d.j.haniff@bham.ac.uk

1 Background

Augmented Reality (AR) is the enhancement of the real world by a virtual world which provides additional information (Feiner, 1993). This can be achieved by overlaying virtual information onto the user's senses (commonly the visual system). Virtual Reality (VR) simulates the real world within a virtual environment. Both can be described in terms of a *scale of interaction*. AR *supplements* the real world, the level of real world interaction is therefore high and the level of virtual world interaction can be relatively low. VR can *immerse* the user in a virtual environment, real world interaction is therefore low and virtual world interaction is high.

AR can also be categorised into two main types: context-aware and context-free. Context-aware AR systems are computationally aware of external objects, and can therefore display information in relation to those objects. Context-free systems are not aware of their surroundings. The user attends to the virtual world and the real world by switching between the two (Baber et al., 1998). These systems are implemented using see-though head-mounted displays (HMDs). A context-free AR system has been used in the study described.

Assembly tasks require the manipulation of real world objects to form a product. As the assembler becomes skilled their performance improves in terms of speed and accuracy. It is therefore important to provide training that will enable the worker to become skilled at the task. The following study examines the use of AR and VR to train individuals for a simple assembly task.

2 Experiment

2.1 Introduction

The study examines the use of virtual technology for training in assembly tasks. VR has been used for training in various areas such as flight simulation. AR has not been seen as a training device due to its ability to supplement the user's abilities as they are performing the task. However, the AR system will provide additional information to a point where it is no longer useful to the user. The same situation applies for training. AR should consequently be examined for training purposes.

2.2 Participants

Three groups of five participants from the University of Birmingham were asked to construct a water pump consisting of eight parts.

2.3 Method

The participants were given a maximum of eight minutes training in each of the conditions before they actually performed the task.

The conditions for the experiment described in this poster were as follows:

- Conventional;
- Context-free AR;
- Immersed VR.

The conventional condition consisted of studying a

2D engineering drawing. The AR system displayed a 2D engineering drawing (see figure 1) with a black background (to allow the user to clearly see though the display) on a see-though head-mounted display (HMD) developed by Seattle Sight and running on a Pentium 200Mhz PC. The virtual reality condition used a Silicon Graphics Indigo^2 Maximum Impact workstation Virtual Research 'Vr4' HMD, a Polhemus Fastrak tracking system and a '3D' mouse (see figure 2).

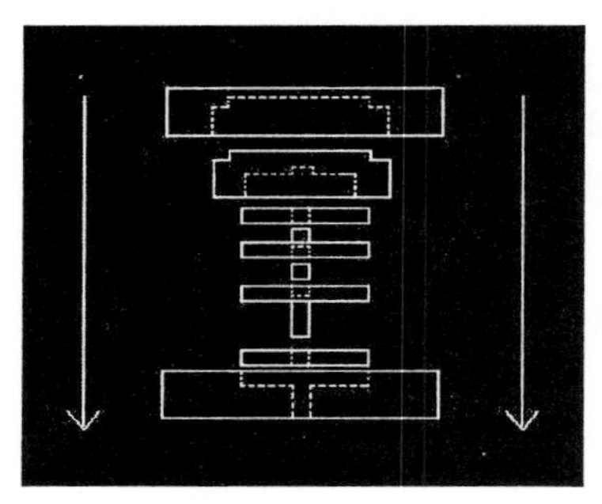

Figure 1.

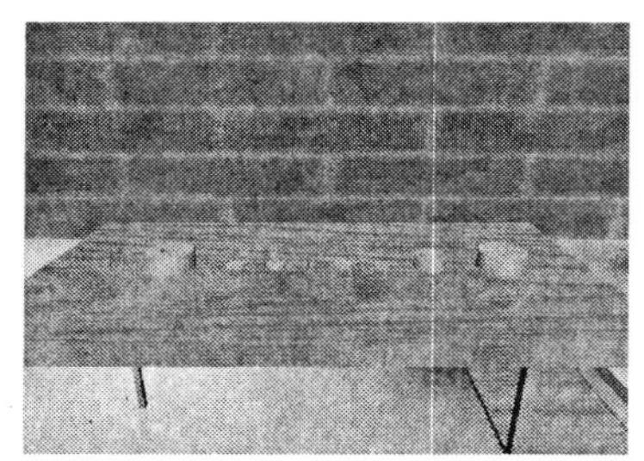

Figure 2.

2.4 Results

The mean completion times for each of the conditions are presented in figure 3. Both of the virtual technologies out performed the conventional 2D drawing condition.

Student t-tests were performed on the data due to the sample size. There was a significant difference between the conventional condition and the VR condition (t=2.776, df=4, $p < 0.05$). There was also a significant difference between the AR and the VR condition (t=2.132, df=4, $p < 0.01$).

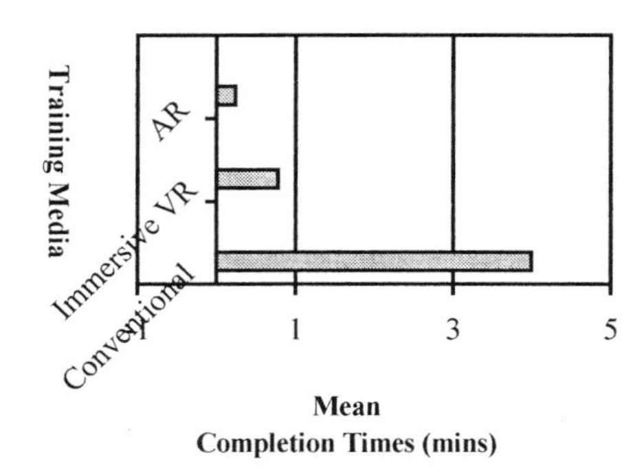

Figure 3.

2.5 Conclusions

Both the AR and VR conditions performed better than the conventional method of learning to construct a water pump. There was a significant difference between the AR and VR conditions due to the scale of interaction. The AR condition allowed the user to interact with the real objects to a greater extent than the VR conditions. However, due to the high interaction with virtual objects VR can be used in situations where the use of real objects is undesirable.

Nevertheless, the study described demonstrates the usefulness of both VR and AR for training purposes.

2.6 Further Work

The scale of interaction is convenient in terms of virtual technology. However, further studies are needed to ascertain the reason for this real world preference and how this can be compensated for within VR.

References

Baber, C., Haniff, D., Knight, J., Cooper, L. Mellor, B. A. (1998) Preliminary Investigations into Wearable Computers, *Proceedings of HCI '98.*

Feiner, S., MacIntyre, B., Seligmann, D. (1993) Knowledge-based Augmented Reality, *Communications of theACM*, 36, 7, 53-62.

Human-Computer Interaction - INTERACT'99 (Volume II)
S. Brewster, A. Cawsey & G. Cockton (Editors)
Published by The British Computer Society © IFIP TC.13, 1999

A Support System for the Visually Impaired Using a Windows PC and Multimedia

Satoshi Ina

Tsukuba College of Technology
4-12-7,Kasuga,Tsukuba, IBARAKI, Japan
Email: ina@cs.k.tsukuba-tech.ac.jp

Abstract: We show two types of a new human interface for the visually impaired using a Windows PC (Personal Computer) and multimedia. One is "Direct access interface to the Windows PC screen". We developed a new ActiveX type driver software for a touch panel (known as the Nomad Pad in the world of DOS systems) working under Windows95/98/NT, allowing for direct access to the PC screen for the visually impaired instead of requiring the use of a mouse. The other type of interface is what we call a "Hearing Picture". This "hearing picture" presents graphics for the blind using non-verbal sounds. Simply said the hearing picture is "figures observed by finger and ear" formed by the cooperative perception of non-verbal sound and fingertip position. At the end of the current paper, we show some applications of these interfaces.

Keywords: visual impairment, direct access, Nomad, hearing picture, tactile picture

1 Direct Access to the Windows Screen

We propose a new utilization of the Nomad Pad (Quantum Technology,1994) under a Windows PC (Personal Computer) system. The Nomad Pad was originally developed in Australia to present map and graphic information for the visually impaired. It was epoch-making equipment in those days in its combination of synthetic voice and a tactile picture. By putting a tactile picture on a pad, tactile operations for the fingers and palms of both hands are possible, and the Nomad Pad detects input only when fingertip pressure is applied on the surface. The problem with the Pad, however, is that a new device driver that will work under the Windows system has not been offered from the development agent; in addition, the pad's development has not progressed beyond conventional usage related to static maps and graphic presentation. We therefore propose a new use of the Nomad Pad for a direct access interface to the PC's GUI (Graphical User Interface) screen. We made an ActiveX device driver called PadX for the Nomad Pad to work under Windows 95/98/NT and Visual Basic/C++ language system. PadX reports an absolute coordinate value with one of the Pad's three depression modes. Here, the depression mode refers to the length of time the Pad is depressed.

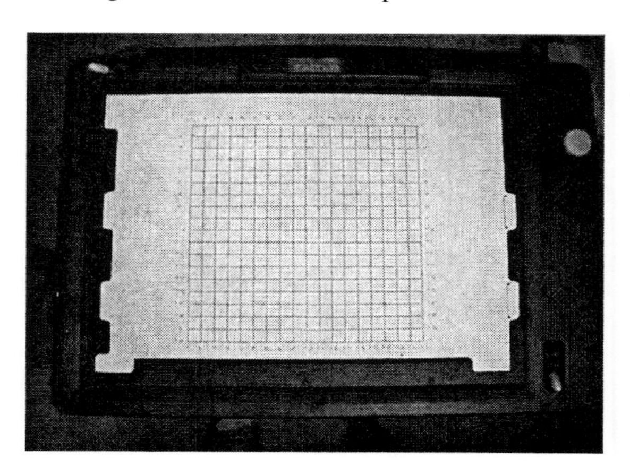

Figure 1: Nomad Pad with tactile checkerboard.

We applied the PadX to a kind of IGO game called RENJYU. We also created GomokuOcx (ActiveX), which has PadX built in, as shown in Figure 2, as well as a Client/Server program with built-in GomokuOcx. The visually impaired are able to play the game with the visually impaired or a sighted person in a distant location connected through the Internet. The execution screen is shown in Figure 3. By placing a tactile picture on the Pad that shows as a checkerboard, as shown in Figure 1, direct access to the screen image becomes possible. Throughout the game, a synthetic voice guide is available.

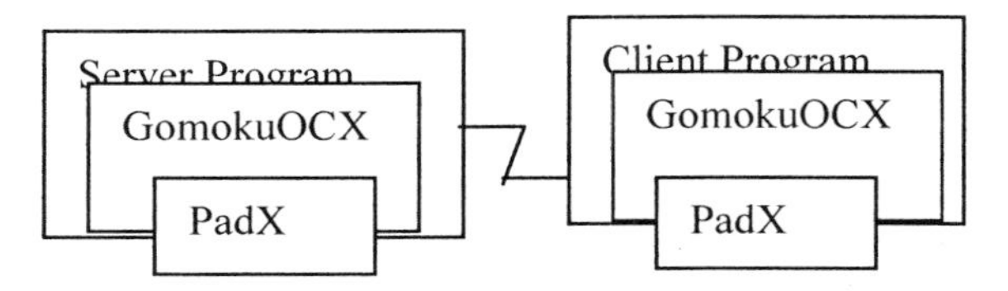

Figure 2: The structure of the remote IGO program.

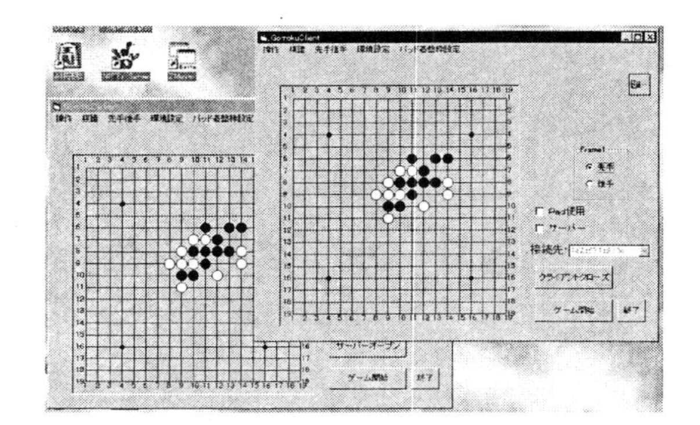

Figure 3: Execution screen of the remote IGO game.

2 Hearing Picture

We suggest here a new concept that we call a "hearing picture". It enables the visually impaired to have access to the screen and to recognize the colors, shapes, and sizes of figures or images displayed on the PC screen. A "Hearing picture" is a picture in which feedback of non-verbal sounds corresponds to the pixel color at the finger position. We adopted a touch panel as a pointing device.

The hearing picture has three features. One is real-time responsibility, the second is portability, and the third is color discrimination. We substituted three kinds of sounds into three primary colors (RGB) as follows. Red : the sound of a bell, Green : the sound

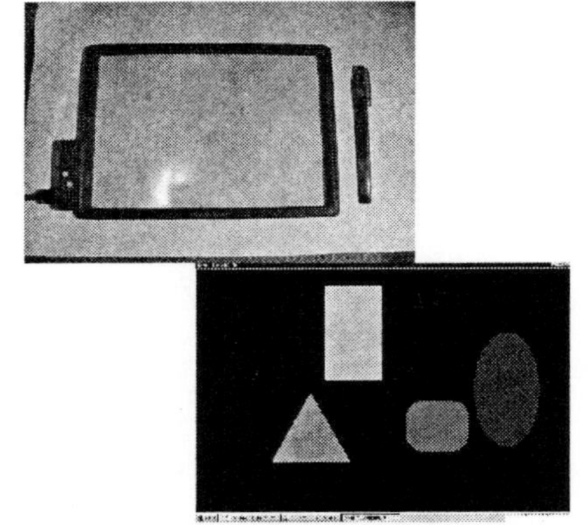

Figure 4: Touch panel and Hearing picture.

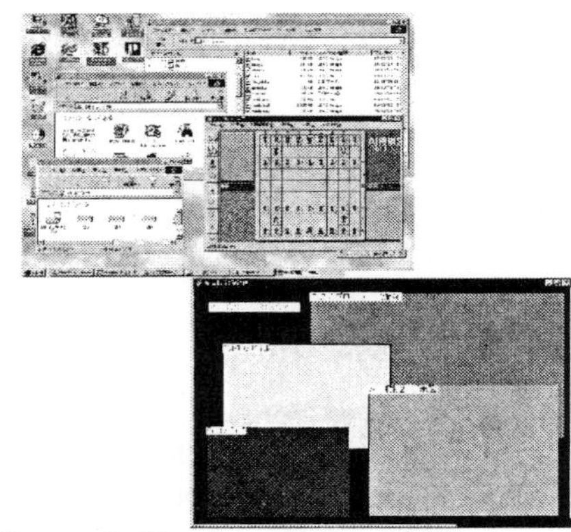

Figure 5: Hearing picture of Windows layout.

of a xylophone, and Blue : the sound of spring water. These primary sounds are simultaneously mixed in proportion to the intensity of each pixel's RGB components, and output through the Microsoft DirectSound framework. We experimented with our learning and experimental system (see Figure 4), and found that a tactile guide attached on the panel improved the results. In the end, we applied the hearing picture into Windows GUI. Figure 5 shows the Windows screen and its hearing picture indicating the top windows' overlay, position, size, and shape, except for desktop icons. These hearing pictures, which present the current windows' layout in real time using Windows API libraries, may help blind programmers, who intend to develop a visual GUI program himself or herself, design and check Windows' layout.

References

Quantum Technology, Pty.Ltd.(1994) Touch Blaster Nomad Installation and User Guide for NOMAD pad and TouchBlaster software.

Human-Computer Interaction - INTERACT'99 (Volume II)
S. Brewster, A. Cawsey & G. Cockton (Editors)
Published by The British Computer Society © IFIP TC.13, 1999

Speechreading-Phone for the Hearing Impaired

Christian Martyn Jones and Satnam Singh Dlay

Department of Computing and Electrical Engineering,
Heriot-Watt University, Riccarton,
Edinburgh, EH14 4AS, United Kingdom.
Email: cmj@cee.hw.ac.uk

Abstract: Multimodal interfacing is used extensively in everyday life. Not only do we use speech as a means of communication, but also speechreading and interpretation of body gestures. In particular, the visual information extracted from lip reading can significantly enhance communication that would otherwise be degraded by background noise. In normal hearing individuals this ability to utilise information from both audio and visual cues appears to be a talent we develop very early in life, even as young as four and five months. Hence, how much more important is visual-based communication for persons with a hearing loss? The research presents a 'speechreading-phone', providing facial cues to aid telephone communication for users with hearing impairment. The system automatically extracts the phonetic content of the transmitted speech soundtrack and recreates the facial articulation on a three-dimensional model. These initial results show that the system is capable of assisting persons with hearing loss to use telephone networks.

Keywords: lip reading, speech recognition, visemes, facial models, talking heads, deaf studies, telephony

1 Introduction

The study is interested in the addition of visual information to speech in order to improve communication for the hearing impaired during telephone conversations. The visual content consists of a computer generated synthetic face which automatically articulates in synchrony with the speech soundtrack. The research is based on latest developments in speechreading, and uses the speech recognition engine of the already internationally recognised MARTI project (Jones 1997[a]). The results presented represent the initial findings of the project.

A feasibility study to simulate the effect of hearing loss concluded that the addition of a synthetic face could substantially improves the intelligibility of speech (Beskow 1997). With marked improvements observed with normal-hearing individuals it was considered that similar results could be achieved with persons suffering from hearing loss. Taking the results of the feasibility study to be true, the research presented here addresses the implementation of a fully automated speechreading-phone.

2 The Speechreading-Phone

The development of the speechreading-phone has been based on our general purpose MARTI (man-machine animation real-time interface) system. The speech soundtrack is first recognised phonetically, then the phonetic transcription is translated into visually distinct articulations (visemes) which are used to drive the motion of the facial model. The speechreading-phone front-end comprises of a newly developed hybrid multi-layered perceptron / hidden Markov Model speech recogniser, trained (using the American-English DARPA TIMIT database) to recognise 60 distinct phonemes with time-signatures from continuous, speaker independent speech.

The study into speechreading considered firstly, the motion of facial muscles during speech, in order to develop a novel set of visual distinct facial articulations (visemes) for general American

English. Secondly a novel technique for mapping the acoustic information into facial articulation was developed termed 'viseme mapping'. The mapping not only provides the required facial motion for accurate lip sync. but also eliminates many of the errors in the recognition transcription.

Finally the viseme transcription was used to control a computer generated, three dimensional, parameterised model of a human head (a derivative of Parke's Fascia) in time with the speech soundtrack.

3 System Results

The initial results compiled use a range of speechreading studies (Fisher, Jeffers, and Auer and Bernstein) together with our novel work into everyday American English (Jones 1997[b]).

Viseme groupings have been devised based on the speechreading studies, and used by the new viseme mapping algorithms to translate the acoustically recognised transcription (obtained automatically from speech recognition system) into the required facial articulation for the synthetic head. The performance results presented show the level of accuracy achieved in terms of determining the facial position (% correct recognition) and time-alignment of the lip sync. with the speech soundtrack. There exists a trade-off between the number of distinct facial positions (the number of visemes, i.e. the visual realism) against the recognition performance. By reducing the number of viseme groups the recognition 'accuracy' can be improved, however this is associated with a reduction in the number of facial positions and fewer visual cues for the speechreader. In finding a balance (using MARTI viseme set), the speechreading-phone can correctly recognise 68.8 % of the speech soundtrack, determine the required articulation, and lip synchronising 90.8 % of the synthesised facial motion to within ±20 milliseconds, Table 1. The performance of the additional visual information for the receiver is sufficiently accurate, in terms of articulation and timing, such that it can be used to aid the hearing impaired converse via speechreading.

4 Conclusions

The addition of a face to communication, especially when involving persons with hearing loss, can significantly help the conveyance of the message. To assist hearing impaired users of telephony, this paper has proposed the implementation of the 'speechreading-phone'. The system is capable of automatically recognising the phonetic information contained in the speech soundtrack and recreating the facial articulation using a synthetic model displayed at the receiver. The subject can then use the additional visual information to aid their understanding of the spoken signal.

The system is in it's infancy, however initial findings are presented in relation to the level of accuracy achieved with the synthesised facial images. The next stage of the work will consider field testing with users and further optimisation of the system. However, performance levels already attained are considered to be sufficient to assist subjects with hearing loss to effectively use telephone networks.

References

Beskow, J. et. al. (1997) "The teleface project multi-modal speech-communication for the hearing impaired", *European Conf. Speech Communication and Technology (EuroSpeech)*, **4** , 2003-2006.

Jones, C.M. and Dlay, S.S. (1997[a]) "Automated lip synchronisation for human-computer interaction and special effect animation", *European Conf. Speech Communication and Technology (EuroSpeech)*, **2** , 891-894.

Jones, C.M. and Dlay, S.S. (1997[b]) "Human-computer interaction and animation system for simple interfacing to virtual environments", *IEEE Int. Conf. Systems, Man, and Cybernetics (SMC)*, **5**, 4242-424.

Speechreading research instigator	Groupings	No. of phone groups	No. of viseme groups	Lip sync. accuracy (% correct recognition)	Lip sync. timing accuracy (to within ±20 ms)
MARTI viseme set	American English	23	16	68.8 %	90.8 %
Fisher	Initial position	25	10	67.6 %	90.2 %
Fisher	Final position	24	10	67.8 %	90.4 %

Table 1: Articulation performance achieved using a range of viseme mappings for the speechreading-phone.

The Impact of Computer Mediated Communication (CMC) on Conflict Resolution

L.A. Katz*, A. Thatcher* and D.W. Trepess^

*University of the Witwatersrand
Psychology Department
Wits 2050 South Africa
Email: 018ajt@muse.wits.ac.za

^Staffordshire University
Computing Department
Stafford, UK

Abstract: The impact of computer-mediated communication on conflict resolution was explored using a sample of university students. Using TeamWave groupware, participants engaged in a two hour synchronous discussion on a contentious issue aimed at evoking a conflict situation. Conflict resolution tactics were required as participants attempted to reach consensus. A focus group and the logged discussions were thematically analysed. Four themes that emerged were emotional responses to the conflict, cognitive processing, social interaction, and practical considerations. The implications of this, given the increased use of the computer as a communication medium, are discussed.

Keywords: conflict, conflict resolution, communication, computer-mediated communication

1 Introduction

The rapid increase in the range and scope of information technology has resulted in the computer becoming a widely used means of communication. E-mail, chat rooms, and video conferencing are just some of the more popular, emergent methods. The extensive body of literature and research on computer-mediated communication (CMC) and computer-supported co-operative work (CSCW) in recent years is testimony to the importance of understanding how technology influences communication (eg. Daly-Jones, Monk & Watts, 1998). Conflict arises as a normal course of action during communication. Bendix and Graham (1987, p4.) describe conflict as " ...the competition between different parties for scarce resources such as money and benefits, or for less tangible resources such as power and influence." It can also be seen to include perceived incompatibilities or discrepant views between participants (Boulding, 1993 cited in Jehn, 1995). It is argued that conflict is a natural and inherent part of any relationship, but where there is a shared interest or investment in the outcome, conflict resolution is necessary. Conflict resolution requires compromise and a willingness to move from ones' position. This process can be aided by formal procedures, or it can occur informally, through the continuous exchange of ideas, concerns, and concessions. Conflict resolution is not always possible, and is also not always constructive. Aside from the attitudes and personalities of the participants, the manner in which information, ideas, and opinions are communicated will impact on how successful the resolution process will be.

2 Methodology

The sample for consisted of nine postgraduate students, four male participants and five female participants, ranging from 24 to 33 years old. TeamWave workplace groupware was used to engage in real time synchronous discussion through the medium of a computer. In the experimental session participants were required to log onto TeamWave simultaneously, and were assigned to one of two virtual discussion rooms, forming groups of five and four respectively. In each room, they were asked to discuss and reach consensus on the topic:

"The death penalty is an appropriate way of punishing violent crimes." An administrator was present in each room to ensure that the discussion remained on track. After two hours of discussion the conversations were ended, whether the participants had reached consensus or not. This was followed by a face to face session, where participants where asked to reach consensus on the same issue. A focus group was held a day later to elicit information from the participants. The logged transcripts of the conversations were also used as part of the analysis.

3 Results

At an **emotional** level using the computer to express themselves during the arguments mediated their emotional responses to the conflict. The time it took to type, read and enter a message, coupled with an inability to interrupt others resulted in a less emotionally heightened responses to what was being said to others. In addition, the lack of facial expressions, hand gestures, and tone of voice meant that the emotional content of what was being said was not always passed on. It was found that it was easier to maintain emotional distance and hence control.

Cognitive differences were experienced in rationalising and expressing arguments. Seeing their thoughts in hard type made them reconsider expressing things they would normally have willingly expressed verbally. In addition the wording and form of expression used was reported to be more formal and structured. Consideration had to be given to spelling and typing errors, and this detracted from processing other more pertinent information.

The manner in which the participants initiated, sustained and concluded **social contact** within the conflict situation differed from face-to-face interaction. Participants reported not always being aware of who was in their room at any given time. They also felt that they needed to remind people that they were present or had returned to the room. New social norms (such as the acceptability of typing errors) also had to be established.

Practical matters refer to environmental and practical inhibitors or facilitators, such as typing skill and speed, and the physical network time lag. Participants with better typing skills were able to express themselves quicker and more often than those participants who were less adept. The long time lag (in screen updates) meant that participants had more time to think about their responses, but also had to wait for other participants to respond to their comments.

4 Discussion & Conclusions

With the increased use of CMC potentially more conflict situations will arise. This research has shown that the computer makes a significant impact on conflict resolution processes. The time lag and the emotional distancing that the computer provides will potentially mean that conflict will take longer to resolve. Participants were unable to express the full weight of their beliefs and statements through access to non-verbal expression (such as physical presence, facial expressions, etc) to add to their written content. Computer-mediated conflict resolution also allows those participants who are less vocal in face-to-face discussions to express themselves. These participants are able to make their points without being interrupted or "shouted down" by more vocal participants. It is quite possible that more recent developments in computer technology will alleviate some of the problems encountered in this study (i.e. the incorporation of sound and video). Also, as CMC becomes more widely available people will adapt to the narrow bandwidth of physical and emotional expression by creating new social norms and expectations.

References

Bendix, D. & Graham, A. (1987). Strike Activity in South Africa. Industrial Relations Journal of South Africa, 1st Quarter, 4-32.

Daly-Jones, O., Monk, A., and Watts, L. (1998). Some advantages of video conferencing over high-quality audio conferencing: fluency and awareness of attentional focus. International Journal of Human-Computer Studies, 49: pp. 21-58.

Jehn, K. (1995). A Multi method Examination of the Benefits and Detriments of Intragroup Conflicts. Administrative Sciences Quarterly, 40, pp. 256-282.

Who Are Qualified for Usability Evaluation?

Masaaki Kurosu[1] and Sachiyo Matsuura[2]

[1]Faculty of Information, Shizuoka University
Email: PFD00343@nifty.ne.jp
[2]Yamaha Motors Co. Ltd.
Email: Matsuura_sachiyo@ccgw.yamaha-motor.co.jp

Abstract: The personality traits of the people who are qualified for the usability evaluation were investigated by taking the correlation between the personality test scores and the number of problems they detected in terms of the heuristic evaluation method.

Keywords: usability evaluation, inspection method, personality

1 Introduction

It is empirically recognized that there are individual differences in the ability for the usability evaluation. Even if situated in the same evaluation settings after the equal amount of training, some people can detect enough number of important usability problems while others cannot. It is necessary to assign qualified people to the usability engineering activity in order to make it more efficient and effective. But it is not yet well known what type of people are qualified for the usability engineering jobs.

In this research, we tried to investigate this problem from the viewpoint of the personality traits. If we could identify the personality traits which are strongly related to the ability to detect the usability problems, we can use them for screening the personnel for the usability evaluation.

2 Method

An experiment was conducted to investigate the relationship between the ability to detect the usability problems and the personality traits.

Subjects were 253 undergraduate students and the experiment was done for all the students at the same place as a group experiment.

They were first instructed the usability guidelines which Nielsen (1993) proposed for the heuristic evaluation method (Nielsen and Molich 1990). They then inspected the usability of the digital watch in terms of its specification and the video which shows its basic operations. They were allowed 30 minutes to write down the usability problems.

Personality traits were estimated by applying two personality tests, i.e. YG test or Yatabe-Guilford test (Yatabe et al. 1951, 1965) and CPI or California Psychological Inventory (Agatsuma et al. 1967). Because it took 50 minutes and 80 minutes respectively, the personality tests were done on different days.

3 Results

By summarizing the number of usability problems, the distribution shown as Fig. 1 was obtained. The average number was 2.37 and the range was from 0 to 7. By this result, we could confirm that there is certainly individual differences regarding the ability to detect the usability problems.

We then calculated the correlation coefficients between the number of problems and the personality traits. The correlation with YG-test is shown in Table 1 and the correlation with CPI is shown in Table 2.

D (Depression)	-0.034	
C (Cyclic Tendency)	0.027	
I (Inferiority feeling)	-0.025	
N (Nervousness)	-0.043	
O (Lack of Objectivity)	-0.112	
Co (Lack of Cooperativeness)	-0.063	
Ag (Lack of Agreeableness)	0.058	
G (General Activity)	0.090	
R (Rhathynia)	0.174	*
T (Thinking Extraversion)	0.105	
A (Ascendance)	0.214	**
S (Social extraversion)	0.078	

Table 1: The correlation between the number of usability problems and the YG-test personality traits. (N=153).

Although the absolute values of the correlation are relatively low, some were significant at 5 % level (*) and 1 % level (**) because of the large number of samples.

The direct interpretation of this result will give us some hints on the characteristics of qualified person for the usability evaluation that they are ...

(1) likely to hold the coltrol (S of YG-test)

(2) not satisfied and are eager for something (Wb of CPI)

(3) not tolerant for the current situation (To of CPI)

(4) less motivated for self expression (Gi of CPI)

But for some personality traits (R of YG-test, Ai and Fx of CPI), it was difficult to interpret the correlation results.

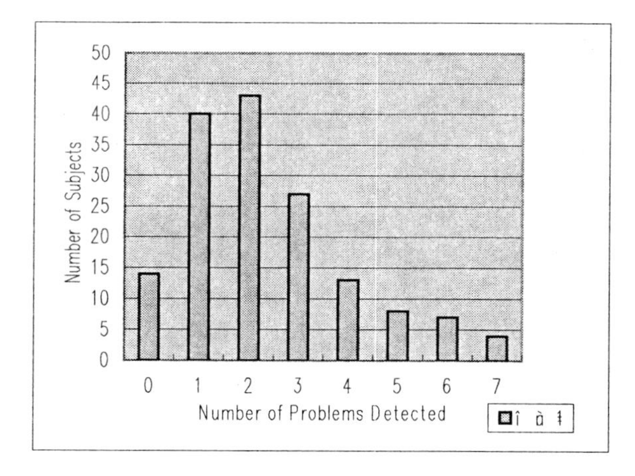

Figure 1: The distribution of the number of usability problems detected by the subjects.

Do (Dominance)	0.135	
Cs (Capacity for Status)	0.024	
Sy (Sociability)	0.035	
Sp (Social Presence)	0.057	
Sa (Self-acceptance)	-0.017	
Wb (Sence of Well Being)	-0.176	*
Re (Responsibility)	0.043	
So (Socialization)	0.067	
Sc (Self-control)	-0.156	
To (Tolerance)	-0.165	*
Gi (Good Impression)	-0.167	*
Cm (Communality)	0.082	
c (Achievement via Conformance	0.048	
i (Achievement via Independence	-0.156	*
Ie (Intellectual Efficiency)	-0.082	
Py (Psychological-mindedness)	0.055	
Fx (Flexibility)	-0.173	*
Fe (Feminity)	-0.015	

Table 2: The correlation between the number of usability problems and the CPI personality traits. (N=206).

4 Conclusion

By applying the personality tests, we could find a perspective on the qualified characteristics of the people for the usability evaluation.

References

Agatsuma, H. et al. (1967) "CPI – Japanese Version", Seishin Shobou

Nielsen, J (1993) Usability Engineering AP Professional

Nielsen, J. and Molich, R. (1990) Heuristic evaluation of user interface Proc. ACM CHI'90•PP.249-256

Yatabe, T. et al. (1951,1965) "Yatabe Guilford Personality Test", Japan Psychological Test Institute.

Human–Computer Interaction — INTERACT '99 (Volume II)
S. Brewster, A. Cawsey & G. Cockton (Editors)
Published by the British Computer Society © IFIP TC.13, 1999

EPSRC
Engineering and Physical Sciences
Research Council

Improving the Design of Telephone-Based Interfaces

Grégory Leplâtre and Stephen A. Brewster

Department of Computing Science, University of Glasgow
Glasgow, UK

Tel: (+44) 141 330 4966
Fax: (+44) 141 330 4913
Email: {gregory,stephen}@dcs.gla.ac.uk
URL: http://www.dcs.gla.ac.uk/~{gregory,stephen}

Abstract: Creating usable telephone-based interfaces (TBIs) requires designers to make the best use of the interface modality and to conform their design to general human factors principles. In this paper, we outline the stages of our research that led us to the development of a computer-based tool that aims at supporting TBI designers in accomplishing their task.

Keywords: Telephone-Based Interfaces, Non-Speech Sounds, Computer-Aided Design of Interfaces

1 Introduction

In the process of designing usable TBIs, we aim to make the best use of the audio modality, which is dominant in this type of interface. In particular, we intend to use non-speech sounds to support tasks or provide users with beneficial feedback. However, before considering the use of non-speech sound in TBIs, the first part of our work has consisted of applying existing guidelines to the design of this kind of interface. We could then work on a firm basis to enhance interaction by means of non-speech sounds. Practically, we have undertaken the development of a tool that supports the interface designer in his/her task. The system allows the designer to specify the attributes of the interface he/she is developing, and comes up with suggestions concerning both:

- Structure of the interface, according to human factors principles
- Audio materials to support the interaction

We believe that this method and the tool we develop can be useful for a number of sonification or audiation problems. In the following sections, we present the issues raised by this research, the main questions we are concerned about being: why, where and how to use non-speech sound in telephone-based interfaces?

2 Supporting the Development of TBIs

The telephone is an ubiquitous device and is many people's primary method of entering information infrastructures. However, a lot of effort is still to be put in improving the design of TBIs. The first step in trying and improve interaction with a TBI is to conform to general human factors principles (Schumacher et al., 1995). However the generality of these guidelines raises concerns about their application in specific situations. Schumacher *et al.* begin their guidelines with a warning: "No claim is made as to the appropriateness of these guidelines in a given situation. They are a rules of thumb." (Schumacher et al., 1995). Similarly, Maguire claims that: "It is recognised that in order to improve the usability of telephones, attention needs to be focused on 'families' of products that belong together serving similar users, for similar purposes, in similar context of use" (Maguire, 1996). Therefore it seems beneficial to support the design of interfaces taking into account their specificities, rather than addressing the design from a general point of view towards TBIs. We are currently investigating means for designers to specify interfaces in terms of the interaction medium as well as the tasks performed by users. Offering designers the possibility to describe the interaction they are aiming at, allows them to get the most relevant support from our tool.

3 Enhancing the Interaction with Non-Speech Sounds

In the second stage of our approach, we intend to enhance the interaction by means of using non-speech sounds. There are numerous reasons why sounds can be beneficial in a non-visual interface like a TBI (Brewster, 1997). Among the issues raised by the use of non-speech sound in this context, the following are particularly important.

3.1 Psychological Basis

In using non-speech sounds to convey information, looking at psychoacoustics and cognitive science issues helps finding the right approach to the design of non-speech sounds. Psychoacoustics and cognition have traditionally put the emphasis on perception and cognition of psychophysical parameters of sounds or musical attributes. This is for both historical and theoretical reasons, as Gaver explains (Gaver, 1993). On the other hand, an ecological approach to auditory event perception focuses on what makes sense in everyday listening: what causes the sounds we hear (Gaver, 1993). There is no such thing as a musical sound, but there is a musical audition of sounds. *Music Concrete* seems to be a perfect illustration of this point. Therefore there is no contradiction between the two previous approaches of audition. It is though essential to know when sound design should be undertaken upon one or the other of these approaches. The question that arises is: what kind of audition of the sounds we create can we expect from the user.

In previous research, 'musical' audition of hierarchical sets of sounds have been proved helpful for users to navigate in hierarchical menus (Leplâtre & Brewster, 1998). We are know considering the effectiveness of sounds within an everyday listening framework. As a simple example, we have looked over the two most appropriate sounds for the 'play' and 'delete' command in a voice-mail system.

3.2 Supporting the Sonification

As well as wishing to help designers get the structure of the interface right, we hope to assist them in using non-speech sounds profitably. As sound design requires a specific knowledge that designers may not have, providing this kind of support is a bit more challenging. One of the main functions of the tool we are developing is to come up with automatic sonification solutions, with easy sound editing and customisation facilities. Whether the designer deals with beeps or more complex sounds, we are trying to give him/her meaningful control over the generation of sounds. Indeed, sound generation can be controlled in relation to the interface specification itself, rather than in terms of sound synthesis techniques, for example. Practically, sound synthesis is operated by the synthesis software Csound, but this is transparent from the designer's point of view. From his/her point of view, sound design is related to user actions or tasks, e.g. to general interface design elements.

4 Conclusion

Designing TBIs in conformance with general human factors principles and making the best use of the interface (audio) modality have been shown to be the key points of our research. We have undertaken the development of a tool that will support TBI designers to effectively fullfill their aims. Moreover, we believe that the general interface design method implemented in the software will make it useful in a larger range of design situations where sound enhancement is beneficial.

5 Acknowledgement

This research was founded by EPSRC grant number GR/L66373.

References

Brewster, S. (1997), Navigating telephone-based interfaces with earcons, *in* H. Thimbleby, B. O'Conaill & P. Thomas (eds.), *Proceedings of BCS HCI'97*, Springer, Bristol, UK, pp.39–56.

Gaver, W. W. (1993), "What in the world do we hear? An ecological approach to auditory source perception", *Ecological Psychology* **5**(1), 1–29.

Leplâtre, G. & Brewster, S. A. (1998), An investigation of using music to provide navigation cues, *in Proceedings of ICAD'98*, Glasgow, UK.

Maguire, M. (1996), "A human-factors study of telephone developments and convergence", pp.446–451.

Schumacher, R., Hardzinski, M. & Schwartz, A. (1995), "Increasing the usability of interactive voice response systems", **37**(2), 251–264.

Human-Computer Interaction - INTERACT'99 (Volume II)
S. Brewster, A. Cawsey & G. Cockton (Editors)
Published by The British Computer Society © IFIP TC.13, 1999

EPSRC
Engineering and Physical Sciences Research Council

Using Computing Science Principles in Interface Design

Gary Marsden
Department of Computer Science
University of Cape Town
Private Bag RONDEBOSCH
7701 South Africa.
Email: gaz@acm.org

P. Gillary, M. Jones and H. Thimbleby
School of Computing Science
Middlesex University
Bounds Green Road
London, N11 2NQ

Abstract: In this paper, we describe how computing science algorithms can be successfully applied to user interface design – in this instance, the interface of cellular telephone handsets.

Keywords: Mobile telephone, design rules, algorithms

1 Introduction

This work was instigated by a cellular telephone service provider which had become concerned by the difficulties experienced by their clients when trying to use their cellular handsets. In an effort to reduce the amount being spent on customer support lines, the service provider wondered if it would be possible to design a handset which would not be so confusing to use.

In response to this request, we have undertaken an analysis of current handsets and produced a novel solution with which we are currently conducting usability trials.

2 Finding Functions

2.1 Current Handset Design

To understand the difficulties in using cellular telephone handsets, products from three different manufacturers were examined. Each of these handsets provided access to their functionality by means of hierarchical menus. Whilst menus may work well on computers capable of displaying all options simultaneously, they are less effective on devices which can only show one option at a time. The use of nested menus also means that it is necessary for a novice user to guess how functions have been classified by an expert designer. Although conventional, it is not clear that menus are the optimal interface design heuristic for mobile cellular handsets.

2.2 Computing Science Solution

At the Interaction Design Centre, one of the guiding philosophies is that any interface design should be sufficiently simple to let a computer program manipulate it [3]. Following this philosophy should produce an interface that is consistent and requires a much shorter manual than would otherwise be needed [4]. It is clear that no such program could easily be written for current handset interfaces based on a designer's intuition.

One algorithmic solution would be to have the user directly type the name of the function they wished to access using the letters printed on each of the numeric keys. This would require no menus, but would be tedious for the user as, for example, typing the single letter 'C' would require three key presses. In fact, this is a solution used by IBM's Speech Filing System [1]. However, as a handset interface is used to retrieve existing commands, rather than enter new text, it is possible to use a hashing algorithm to reduce the number of key strokes.

Hashing is used to map between the alphanumeric keys and the list of functions provided by the handset. So to access, for example, the "Call Divert" function, the user would start by typing the keys 2-2-5-5 to enter the word "Call" (the key 2 has the letters

"ABC" and key 5 has letters "JKL"). The handset processor searches the list of function names for any that start with the letter 'A' or 'B' or 'C', whose second letter is 'A' or 'B' or 'C' whose third letter is 'J' or 'K' or 'L' etc. Our analysis of the function list of typical handsets concluded that the correct function could be uniquely selected, on average, after only 1.9 key presses.

3 Benefits of New Approach

One of the most obvious benefits of using hashing to drive the interface is the reduction on the number of keystrokes needed to access any given function. For one of the handsets in our initial study, this average was 5.86 keystrokes. Not only can this approach be used to retrieve functions, but can also be used to access the address list (in fact, it is possible to remove these two modes and merge the address list and function list in one).

3.1 Current Experimentation

The solution we describe was arrived at by making the assumption that users would prefer an interface based on a computer algorithm. This may not turn out to be the case.

So, whilst there are strong quantitative reasons why this is a "good" solution, we are currently embarked on user testing which will help us understand how users react to interfaces which require them to employ a computing science algorithm.

Initial prototypes have been well received, but were not robust enough to conduct full usability testing. We have now completed a full Java implementation of two handsets (one using a traditional menu interface, and the other using a hashing based interface) which can be found at [2]. These simulations can be used in two ways:

- To conduct local usability tests, where the user is fully monitored and all their actions recorded.
- To conduct usability tests over the Internet, where the user response is recorded on a Web server.

In both sets of experiments, the subjects will be asked to complete a set of tasks using each of the two simulations. Times, and keystrokes used in completing each task will be recorded. Before using either simulation, the subject will be provided with a brief description of how each handset works. Full manuals for each system will also be made available, and access to these will also be recorded – studies have shown that the need to refer to a cellular handset manual almost guarantees that the user will fail to achieve the task [5]. Finally, we will record qualitative data to determine if users are comfortable using an interface based on a computing science algorithm.

From initial investigations with the early prototypes and expert users, we expect that time and keystrokes to complete tasks will be greatly reduced. Also, users of the new interface should not need to access the manual as frequently as before. However, there remain concerns over naïve users being able to express their needs in a vocabulary from a domain of which they have no experience.

3.2 Commercial Viability

The approach described in this paper is similar to that taken by Tegic's T9 software which is used for text entry on devices with a reduced keyboard – such as cellular telephone handsets. Rather than restrict the domain to function names, the T9 software disambiguates user input to generate relatively unrestricted natural language. It would seem logical to apply this technology to drive the interface as well.

Acknowledgements

This work is currently being funded by EPSRC grant GR/M14548.

References

1. Gould J.D. and Boies, S.J. Speech Filing – An office system for principals. *Readings in Human Computer*), 8-24.
2. Marsden, G. Java Handset implementation. Available at http://www.cs.mdx.ac.uk/gadget/
3. Thimbleby, H. User Interface Design. Addison Wesley 1990.
4. Thimbleby, H. Combining Systems and Manuals, in *People and Computers* VIII, (HCI 1993), Cambridge University Press , 479-488.
5. Youngs, E. Evaluating the Impact of Application, Ergonomic and Process design on Handset Success in *Proceedings of Euro-forum* (London, UK September 1998.

Human-Computer Interaction - INTERACT'99 (Volume II)
S. Brewster, A. Cawsey & G. Cockton (Editors)
Published by The British Computer Society © IFIP TC.13, 1999

Choosing the UI Tool Which Best Suits Your Needs

Joanna McKirdy

Department of Computing Science
University of Glasgow
Glasgow
Scotland
Email: jo@dcs.gla.ac.uk

Abstract: The large number and power of user interface development tools (UIDTs) has answered the question of *how* designers can construct user interfaces which meet increasing consumer demands. It has, however, raised a new question – *which tool should they choose?* Previously, little work has been done to provide an effective and systematic mechanism to enable designers to select the most appropriate UIDT given their design requirements and levels of knowledge and experience. A recent industrial survey of the use of UIDTs found that this lack of evaluative support led to the selection of unsatisfactory tools and highlighted the need to provide developers with a mechanism to help them confidently select the tool which is right for them (McKirdy 1998). S.U.I.T. is a framework and methodology for the **s**election of **u**ser **i**nterface development **t**ools which meets this need. This paper presents S.U.I.T. and discusses a recent empirical study conducted to evaluate its practical use.

Keywords: user interface development tool, context sensitive, evaluation, selection, fitness-criteria

1 Introduction

S.U.I.T. – a framework and methodology for the **s**election of **u**ser **i**nterface development **t**ools – was developed in response to the evaluative needs of user interface developers (McKirdy 1998). It provides a context sensitive, extensible, systematic, and effective means by which developers can select the user interface development tool (UIDT) which best fits their needs. This paper provides an overview of S.U.I.T. and discusses a recent empirical study which was conducted to investigate its practical application.

2 S.U.I.T.

S.U.I.T. adopts a reference model-based approach to tool selection, and can be used in three different ways: (1) to select a tool based on a generic comparison of tools; (2) to select the best-fit tool for an unprecedented project (within the context of an organisation) based on the specific context and requirements of that project; and (3) to identify an appropriate tool for a specific project based on comparisons with previous projects.

The applicability of each approach has three determining factors: the stage of design/development; the novelty of the project; and the intended specificity of the outcome of using S.U.I.T. Each approach dictates the appropriate route through the methodology and hence the manner in which the framework is manipulated.

The S.U.I.T. framework is essentially a reference model of all functionality and support features that might be found in a UIDT. Guided by the appropriate methodological setting, the framework is tailored to provide a structure for data collection and thereafter, a context for interpretation of that data.

S.U.I.T. is based on the hypothesis that an accurate and effective tool selection for a specific project *must* consider: the purpose for which the tool is being selected – the functional requirements; and the context in which the tool will be used – including the institutional development process, technical resources, and human resources.

Following the S.U.I.T. methodology, the framework is manipulated to produce a project specific tailored framework for data collection such that only data of relevance to the given project is considered during the evaluation. A copy of the tailored framework is further manipulated to integrate the contextual information with the functional requirements and thus generate a profile of the *ideal* tool for that project. It is against this profile that the data concerning *real* tools is compared in order to determine which tool best matches the ideal.

3 An Empirical Study of S.U.I.T.

S.U.I.T. was the subject of an empirical comparative study, the aims of which were to evaluate and compare the usability and outcome of using S.U.I.T. with that of the nearest alternative evaluation mechanism (Hix 1991).

3.1 The Study

Twenty seven final year undergraduate computing science students were divided into two groups – one using S.U.I.T. and the other, the alternative method. The subjects in each group were taught how to use their allocated method and were divided into pairs and given a problem scenario which outlined the requirements and context for a project. Each pair was given 30 man hours to complete an evaluation of two web authoring tools and make a recommendation for the selection of one. All subjects were required to submit an evaluation report, their evaluation forms, and a log sheet detailing their allocation of time to subtasks. They were also requested to complete a questionnaire based on the NASA TLX (NASA 1985).

3.2 Summary of Results

The results of the study were analysed in a number of ways. The evaluation reports were examined and a tally of references to specific terminology was created in order to compare the focus of consideration during the evaluation process for each group. Anecdotal evidence was collected to gauge subject response to the methods. The log sheets were considered to determine the time related breakdown of the overall evaluation task. Finally, the responses to the questionnaires were analysed to determine the workload experienced by the subjects in each group.

Analysis of results found that S.U.I.T. achieved its goal of increasing the evaluators' attention to detail and context of use compared to the other method. Further, amongst the subjects in the S.U.I.T. group there was greater consistency regarding consideration of issues than amongst the subjects in the other group. Despite increasing the complexity of issues requiring consideration during an evaluation and therefore increasing the preparation time, S.U.I.T. did not increase the average time taken to complete an evaluation and showed considerable potential for reduction of the time required for hands-on evaluative use of the tools and comparison of the results. Anecdotal evidence collected for S.U.I.T. proved positive and provided endorsement for its future use. Finally, although using S.U.I.T. was found to require greater mental effort, it was also found to instil a higher degree of user confidence in performance than the alternative method and to reduce levels of frustration.

4 Summary & Conclusions

S.U.I.T. has introduced the concept of contextually sensitive approaches to UIDT selection. Initial results of empirical evaluation suggest the method is practicable and effective. A software tool to assist and automate much of the S.U.I.T. evaluation mechanism is currently being designed and it is hoped this will greatly reduce the time required to complete a comprehensive tool selection.

References

Hix, D. (1991) An Evaluation Procedure for User Interface Development Tools - Version 2.0, Virginia Polytechnic Institute and State University

McKirdy, J. (1998) "An Empirical Study of the Relationships Between User Interface Development Tools & User Interface Development", Technical Report TR-1998-06, University of Glasgow, Department of Computing Science

NASA (1985) NASA Task Load Index (TLX) Version 1.0 Users Guide, Moffett Field, CA: NASA Ames Research Centre, http://cseriac.flight.wpafb.af.mil/products/tlx/toc.htm

Human-Computer Interaction - INTERACT'99 (Volume II)
S. Brewster, A. Cawsey & G. Cockton (Editors)
Published by The British Computer Society © IFIP TC.13, 1999

A Laser Pen for a Virtual Wallpaper

G. Ménier and F. Poirier

Equipage, Laboratoire VALORIA, Equipe Accueil 2593
Université de Bretagne Sud, 56000 Vannes, FRANCE
Email: gildas.menier@univ-ubs.fr

Abstract: This paper introduces a low-cost solution for the problem of interaction with projected information (slides or videos). The scheme proposed involves the use of a laser-based device for drawing and/or pointing. A mini camera is used to keep track of the laser spot on the screen. The gestural commands are then interpreted by a fast pattern-recognition system and a visual feedback is eventually provided. The interaction with the document is object-based: each graphical object can be activated by a specific pattern and can trigger an hypertextual link or a multimedia event (sound or video). The system is designed to perform well on common PC based system with a low-cost camera.

Keywords: Interaction, Visual Feedback, Video, Pattern Recognition, Laser Pointer

1 Introduction

The LCD projector is one of the simplest ways to display information on any available surface, simple screen (slide for presentation), whiteboard [1] or wall [2]. Despite of this output simplicity, the interaction scheme may involve technical solutions that could be difficult to manage for the user, regardless of the development cost. Remote controls have to provide many buttons and may allow poor pointing or drawing features. We propose in this paper an interaction scheme that is not only independent of the display surface used, but also based on a simple one-button laser pointer for only tool.

2 Overview

The graphical view of the document is displayed on a white screen using a LCD projector (Figure 1). A mini-camera (WebCam) provides a visual feedback to the computer. A real-time analysis scheme is used to track the laser spot on the white screen. The tracks are then related to the objects that compose the document and interpreted by fast pattern recognizers. The selected objet can trigger an action related to the gestural command, such as an hypertextual link or a multimedia event (sound or video playback). If no object is selected, the system provides a visual feedback - a set of strokes – enabling the user to point-out an important topic in the document or to sketch a drawing on this virtual whiteboard.

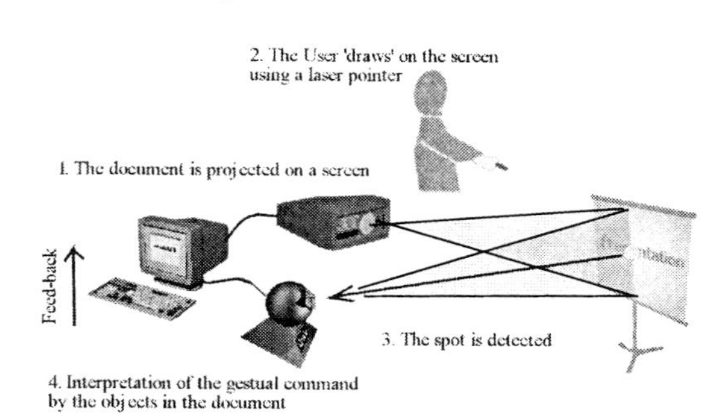

Figure 1: Overview.

Thanks to this system, the user does not need to stay near the display screen and can use the laser pointer both as a *one-switch* remote control and as a *virtual pen* to sketch on the screen. Since the document is hyperlink structured, the user is able to adapt the show taking into account public reactions or questions.

3 Interactions

Each page contains objects whose graphical representation is a text or an image. The interaction scheme is taken after the concept of an electronic paper: each object can inherit a predefined behavior and is associated to a pattern recognizer.

There are mainly two levels of gestural command:
-Object-based action (hyperlink, video, sound …)
-Document-based action (navigation in the document, parameters changes – as ink color, stroke width ...)

3.1 Object Interactions

This stroke is sent to the overlapping object as a message and interpreted by its pattern analyzer. If the system acknowledges the sign, then the object triggers its associated action. If not, then the system provides a visual feedback, drawing the stroke on the display. The possible actions include hypertextual jump to other pages, performance of video or sound and zoom (Figure 2) on images.

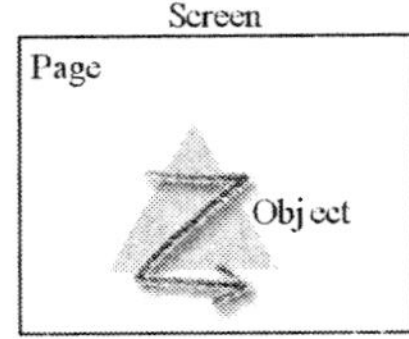

Figure 2: A Zoom Command on an Image.

The user draws a 'z'-shaped stroke on the screen (a Zoom command), overlapping the graphical view of the image. The related image-object can trigger a zoom on itself: a magnified view of the object is then presented on the full screen as a new page.

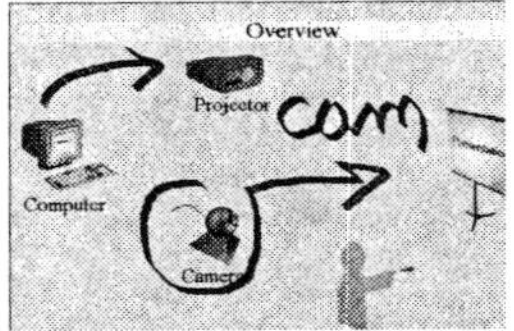

Figure 3: Sketching on a Page.

If the sign is not recognized, it is assumed to be a sketch and it is therefore displayed as a stroke (Figure 3).

3.2 Document Interactions

The document background is a special object that inherit recognition features aimed to control the navigation (Figure 4).

Figure 4: Some Basic Gestural Commands.

4 Laser Spot Analysis

4.1 Spot Tracking

A mini camera provides a real-time video sequence of the display screen to the computer. The frame sequence is analyzed and luminosity differences are computed. A fast classification algorithm (see [3]) provides a spot center approximation that is then related to the last position known. The track is then related to the document.

4.2 Pattern Recognition

The analyzer uses a simplified version of the recognizer described in [4]. The elastic matching scheme has been replaced by a customized editing distance (see [5]). This *stripped down* version is faster – allowing real time analysis – and provides an acceptable reliability due to the very limited number of different signs to recognize.

5 Experiment and Discussion

The main critics that users made are related to the blind aspect of the spot location: it is sometimes difficult to make the spot appears immediately at the right place, especially if the distance between the user and the screen exceeds 10-15 meters. It seems that this problem almost disappears after some use. Despite of a relative short adaptation time, all the users agree that the use of the laser/active document becomes very natural and intuitive. They appreciate the fact that is it possible to move, point and command the system without having to take care of a complicated or heavy remote control. The sketch feature is appealing too. One of the possible extensions is to provide character recognition to the system or drawing assistance to help the user sketch on the screen.

References

1. Elrod, S, and al. Liveboard. A Large Interactive Display supporting Group Meetings, Presentations and Remote Collaboration. In *CHI'92 Proc.* pp. 599-607, 1992.
2. Ishii, H. and al. AmbientROOM in CHI'98 Video, 1998.
3. Diday, E, Simon, J.C. Clustering Analysis. Chapter in *Digital Pattern Recognition.* K.S.Fu Ed. Springer Berlin 1976.
4. Ménier, G, Lorette, G, Gentric, P. A New Modeling Method for Handwriting Recognition. In *ICDAR'95 Proc*, Vol.I, pp. 499-503, 1995.
5. Levenstein, A. Binary Codes Capable of Correcting Deletions, Insertions and Reversal. In *Sov. Phy. Dohl.*, Vol.12, No.11, pp. 1080-1087, 1990.

Dynamic Training Feedback: A Test-Bed for Naval Training

Amanda O'Shea and Catherine Cook
DERA Centre for Human Sciences

Abstract: A test-bed has been developed and is being used to support an experimental investigation of the provision of dynamic training feedback for future Naval systems. Currently, shore-based simulators provide a substantial amount of Naval training, and feedback is largely delivered post-exercise. However, advances in training technologies mean that future systems may incorporate an enhanced embedded training capability. As a result, trainees could be provided with additional feedback relating to their performance in real-time, generated by the system itself. It is important that the principles for providing this additional information are well founded, and that learning is supported. A synthetic experimental role has been developed and an analysis of the necessary competencies and learning requirements conducted. The test-bed incorporates a Naval simulation, two primary task displays, head/eye tracking, keystroke capture, and a feedback delivery system. A programme of human factors experiments is currently being conducted, using the test-bed.

1 Background

The drive for manpower reduction in future military systems has led to an examination of current and predicted training practices. The provision of cost-effective training is a major concern for the Royal Navy, and while high fidelity shore-based trainers and simulators provide effective training for existing systems, they are very expensive to procure and maintain. One option for the future is for a greater proportion of operator and team training to be conducted at sea, provided by intelligent embedded training systems. Embedded training systems offer a number of advantages, namely: reduced cost through the reduction in additional equipment required; elimination of the gap between the training and working environment, thus accelerating transfer of training to on-the-job performance; and increased availability of training facilities, resulting in the provision of 'enough training, just in time'.

The ideal embedded training system would incorporate many features of human trainers: it would be intelligent, and therefore capable of interpreting, making decisions about and reacting immediately to trainee responses, whether in the form of provision of feedback or adaptation of the training scenario. It would also have additional features over and above the human instructor: it would be capable of monitoring *every* response the trainee makes, and providing the *optimum* training reaction according to contemporary training theory *reliably and systematically*. Such a system would take into account all variables that have been statistically proven to predict training performance in its derivation of a training solution (including trainee experience, trainee qualifications, the learning style of the trainee, attributes of team members, etc.). The aim would not necessarily be to replace the human instructor, but would allow him/her more time to concentrate on 'softer' issues relating to training 'teamwork' activities.

The focus of our research is to investigate the provision of training feedback in an ideal training system as described above. Currently in RN simulators, feedback is mostly delivered post-exercise, or is dependent upon an instructor observing and intervening at the appropriate time. An advanced embedded training system, however, offers an opportunity for providing enhanced, on-line feedback to the trainee. Although it is frequently documented that feedback is critical to learning (e.g. Broadbent, 1987; Patrick, 1992), this wealth of literature has been derived mostly from psycho-motor tasks. The focus of this research is a cognitive decision making task in the Naval Anti-Air Warfare domain, and the aim is to investigate any training benefits provided by the provision of on-line feedback.

2 Feedback Test-Bed

Augmented Reality is a maturing technology which, in future, might provide a means of providing additional or supplementary visual information to the user (Caudell, 1994), such as training feedback. This augmentation is usually presented via a see-through, head mounted display, and the user's visual field is tracked to ensure that the augmented image is projected in the correct position, relative to the real world. However, technological limitations relating to calibration and image registration are yet to be resolved. For the purposes of this research, an experimental test-bed has therefore been developed which facilitates the investigation of on-line feedback, provided in the trainee's line of sight.

The test-bed incorporates a number of components: a simulation of Naval Anti-Air Warfare (AAW); a scenario generator; two large screen task interfaces; head and eye tracking; keystroke capture; and a feedback generator. The simulation is based upon an abstraction of a Naval AAW task, and combines elements of several AAW roles into a single operator role. The detailed breakdown and identification of the skills and knowledge (competencies), and therefore the learning requirements, necessary to perform the experimental task was undertaken using hierarchical task analysis (HTA). The feedback generator is an 'expert model' which monitors trainees' performance as they make their way through the training scenario. Dependent upon particular actions made by the trainee, and an indication that critical information has been observed (derived from the eye tracking components), the system will generate a feedback message to assist the trainee. This feedback might relate to what the trainee should be looking at; what the trainee should do; what the trainee should have done; or provide data on the trainee's performance. This facility enables the experimenter to provide the appropriate feedback item at the required time, driven by the trainee's performance, and in the trainee's line of sight on the primary task display.

3 Experimental Programme

A series of experiments is currently being conducted which aim to investigate the provision of on-line training feedback for future RN systems. Firstly, the provision of on-line feedback will be compared with post-exercise feedback (and a control condition of no feedback). Secondly, the provision of this on-line feedback in the trainee's line of sight on the primary display will be compared with its provision via a side VDU, or verbally from an instructor.

4 Conclusions

A test-bed has been developed which facilitates an experimental investigation of the delivery of on-line feedback in future embedded training systems for the Royal Navy. This will result in the development of guidelines for future training systems. The test-bed offers potential for future experimental investigations of 'teamwork' related feedback, i.e. the provision of additional information to the operator regarding other team member's activities. However, the integration of keystroke capture, eye-tracking, performance measurement, and the sophisticated underlying simulation of Naval platforms, means that it could also support human factors studies of novel interfaces to derive the optimum means of displaying complex information to the human operator.

References

Broadbent, D.E. (1987) Structures and strategies: Where are we now? *Psychological Research*, 49, 73-79.

Caudell, T.P. (1994) Introduction to Augmented Reality. SPIE Proceedings Vol. 2351: Telemanipulator and Telepresence Technologies.

Patrick, J. (1992) *Training: Research and Practice*. Academic Press Ltd., London, UK.

This work was carried out as part of the Technology Group 5 of the MoD Corporate Research Programme.

Human-Computer Interaction - INTERACT'99 (Volume II)
S. Brewster, A. Cawsey & G. Cockton (Editors)
Published by The British Computer Society © IFIP TC.13, 1999

A Pragmatic Evaluation Methodology for an Assessment of Learning Effectiveness of Instructional Systems

Clark N. Quinn[1], Leila Alem[2] and John Eklund[3]

[1]Knowledge Universe Interactive Studio
Email: cnquinn@knowledgeu.com
[2]CSIRO Mathematical and Information Sciences
Email: leila.alem@cmis.csiro.au
[3]Access Australia Co-operative Multimedia Centre
Email: j.eklund@accesscmc.com

Abstract: The evaluation of instructional technology applications has been idiosyncratic at best. One of the obstacles is the time and expense involved in traditional evaluation methods. Instructional design offers some advice, but usability has more explicit experience in cost-effective evaluation; and has spawned a variety of applicable techniques. This source of inspiration has strongly influenced the development of the Learning Effectiveness Assessment (LEA) service, as used at Access' Testing Centre. LEA provides a set of evaluation instruments and methods for the pragmatic assessment of learning effectiveness. In this paper we describe the development process and constraints that shaped LEA, focussing on those aspects of the design process which draw together important issues from the HCI and educational communities and produce an effective solution for educational effectiveness evaluation.

Keywords: Evaluation, learning

1 Introduction

When learning with technology is designed, there is an educational outcome intended. The goal of learning effectiveness assessment (LEA) is to provide a means of measuring the attainment of outcomes against a set of both design and acceptance criteria. In the practical world of product development, evaluation must fit within pragmatic time and cost constraints. Here, we outline such a procedure which has been developed at Access Australia Co-operative Multimedia Centre (a consortium of leading Australian educational institutions, multimedia developers and corporations in New South Wales) and CMIS (CSIRO Mathematical and Information Science), for implementation at the Access Testing Centre. In particular, we focus on the design of instruments by which Learning Effectiveness may be assessed.

Evaluation methods can be classified in term of user/learner methods and expert review methods. User/learner methods are methods in which the evaluation data is collected from the users/learners directly (questionnaire, confidence log, interview, focus group) or is collected by observing the user using the system (observation, code sheet, log, test data analysis). Expert review methods are methods that involve experts going through the system to be evaluated (checklist, questionnaire). Some methods are easy to administer, others require a lot of data and others are difficult to assess their validity. Different types of evaluation methods are appropriate at different stages in the development of a computer based learning system.

2 LEA Methodology

We propose that the basis for evaluating the effectiveness of a learning environment is how well a number of key instructional features are supported by such an environment (design factors) and how much the learning environment has been accepted by the learner (acceptance factors). The design factors include: instructional goals; instructional content; learning tasks; learning aids; and assessment.

The acceptance factors include: level of motivation to use the product; level of active participation involved; quality of learning support; and level of user satisfaction. We do not evaluate the attainment of learning objectives or evaluate the domain content, as such evaluation requires content expertise. The aim of our framework is to provide a unified and principle-based theoretical basis within which learning effectiveness evaluation can take place, as well as to provide guidelines for conducting the evaluation. The process considers all steps from defining the evaluation objectives to writing the evaluation report via determining the criteria for evaluation, and choosing the right evaluation instrument.

The design of our evaluation framework involves three processes: developing a set of key learning effectiveness principles according to a set of instructional knowledge types; defining learning effectiveness key criteria and their classification to allow cross evaluation synthesis; and implementing the criteria into the evaluation instruments. Using an analogy to Nielsen's (1994) heuristic evaluation (Quinn, 1996), we designed a converging information evaluation mechanism. Similar to Nielsen, we have an expert review guided by principles, in this case principles for learning. We also are similar in our use of user participation. This analogy is deliberate in two ways. First, our interest is in creating a pragmatic model, which Nielsen's model accomplishes successfully. Second, the existing usability testing methods used at the Testing Centre are similarly modelled on Nielsen's heuristics, and the similarities would minimise implementation difficulties. The learning principles provided a platform upon which to specify evaluation instruments. Our principles include understanding the objective, intended pedagogical strategy, and the audience, which guides the design of a client information instrument. This briefing document is completed prior to any evaluation and guides the subsequent evaluation.

The expert review process is scaffolded by a questionnaire that instantiates the learning principles. Each question is grouped according to the principles, and the alternatives are designed to anticipate variances from good design. For each grouping there is a place to add comments which identify the point of the problem. The scaffolding is designed to minimise the likelihood that the expert misses any issues and maintains consistency. The user/learner method includes observing use from a small sample of the intended audience to identify any problems arriving from attitudinal issues or obstacles that the expert review did not find. The user/learners also complete a questionnaire that looks for their attitudes towards the product as well as collecting demographic data.

Each of these instruments has an associated method by which they are to be applied. The briefing document requires the participation of the developer, and is conducted in the form of an interview. The expert review document requires one pass through (at least) a representative sample of the product and then a second pass through while filling out the questionnaire. The user/learner method includes briefing the subject, use of a representative sample, observation by the expert and an observer, and a post-use questionnaire. The summary report has structural relations to the previous instruments that guide the presentation, and guidelines for the language used in the report.

3 Conclusion

In this paper we have outlined considerations which informed the design of a set of evaluation instruments for learning effectiveness assessment (LEA). We have outlined the LEA framework, and the instrument specification. The resulting LEA service provides a well-articulated set of instruments and methods for assessing learning technology. The service is aligned with learning principles, strikes the best balance between rigor and efficiency, and integrates into a successful testing enterprise.

References

Nielsen, J. (1994). Heuristic Evaluation. In J. Nielsen & R. L. Mack (Eds) *Usability Inspection Methods*. New York: John Wiley & Sons.

Quinn, C. N. (1996). Pragmatic evaluation: lessons from usability. In A. Christie, P. James & B. Vaughan (eds.) *Proceedings of ASCILITE 96*. Uni SA, Adelaide. p. 437-444.

Human-Computer Interaction - INTERACT'99 (Volume II)
S. Brewster, A. Cawsey & G. Cockton (Editors)
Published by The British Computer Society © IFIP TC.13, 1999

A State Transition Model Representing Pen-based Selection Strategies

Xiangshi Ren and Shinji Moriya

Department of Information and Communication Engineering,
Tokyo Denki University
2-2 Kanda-Nishikicho, Chiyoda-ku, Tokyo 101-8457, Japan
Email: ren, moriya@c.dendai.ac.jp

Abstract: A state transition diagram is shown describing target selection with a style pen. We show that selection strategies can be described using the state transition diagram.

Keywords: state transition modes, target selection strategies, pen-based systems

1 Introduction

State transition diagrams are very useful for describing pointing/selecting interactions. Buxton suggested a state transition model to help characterize graphical input (Buxton, 1990). However target selection has not been considered in detail. Chen proposed a state transition diagram for describing interaction with a target, but 3D targets have not been reported (Chen, 1993). In this short paper, we offer a state transition model for selecting a target with a pen, and then show that selection strategies can be described using the state transition diagram.

2 A State Transition Model for Selecting a Target with a Pen

Our model, shown in Figure 1, may expand and refine research (Buxton, 1990; Chen, 1993) on target selection using a pen.

It is a simple state transition model which elucidates a number of properties for selecting both 2D targets and 3D targets. It should be noted that an electromagnetic tablet allowed us to trial both 2D and 3D target selection strategies. When the pen-tip is above the tablet surface (within a height of 1 cm), the computer can recognize the coordinates (x, y) of the pen-tip. Thus, even though a target (e.g. a menu) on the screen is 2 dimensional (2D), it can be highlighted or selected when the pen is above the tablet surface (within 1cm). This means that the target can also be expressed as a 3 dimensional (3D) target.

The state transition diagram shows an interaction with a target. It consists of the target, and the status and position of the pen-tip. The oval with a solid line shown in Figure 1 illustrates 2D targets or bottom of 3D targets on the screen. The cylinder shows that the target is the body of a 3D target. Some responses will take place when the pen-tip is in the cylinder. The section of Figure 1 which is surrounded by a dotted line relates to the selection of 2D targets (in which case, there is no need to consider the cylinder). The dot (small dark circle) shows where the target selection is made by the pen. Although the illustration in Figure 1 shows oval/cylinder targets, the shape of the target has no definitive bearing on this discussion. States A and B represent the pen outside the target. States C and D represent the pen inside the target. States B and C represent the pen in contact with the tablet surface (the pen is dragged over the 2D plan). States A and D represent the pen as not in contact with the tablet surface (the pen is approaching or is above in the 3D space). Thus there are four states, State A: approach/removal, outside; B: contact, outside, C: contact, inside; and D: approach/removal, inside a 3D cylinder.

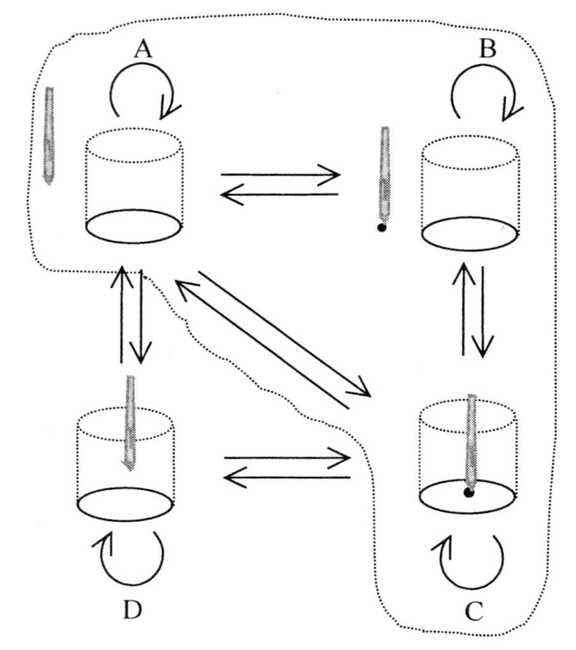

Figure 1: State transition diagram describing target selection with a style pen. States A: pen-tip outside target, pen-tip switched off; B: outside target, switched on; C: inside target, switched on; D: inside target, switched off. A, B and C (surrounded by a dotted line) are for 2D targets, in which case, there is no need to consider the cylinder.

3 Describing the Six Selection Strategies Using the State Transition Model

Selection strategies can be described using the state transition diagram in Figure 1. For example, assume A or B is an initial state, and C is a final state. The state transitions to select a target can be expressed as A→ B → C or A→ C. In other words, new strategies can be designed using this state transition diagram. The state transition diagram representing the manipulation of a pen from an arbitrary initial state to an arbitrary final state can become a strategy. Theoretically, an infinite range of selection strategies exists.

The states in Figure 1 are an adequate basis for 2D target (states A, B and C) and 3D target design (states A, B, C, and D).

Here, we show how the six selection strategies (Ren and Moriya, 1998) fit into the state transition diagrams shown in Figure 1. Assume I is a collection of initial states, described as I = { }, F is a collection of final states, described as F = { }. An arrow "→" means that a state changes to another state. "⇔" means there are changes between two states.

- Direct On strategy: I = {A}, F = {C}, A→ C.
- Slide Touch strategy: I = {A}, F = {C}, A→ C; A → B → C.
- Direct Off strategy: I = {A}, F = {A}, A→ B ⇔ C → A; A → C → A.
- Slide Off strategy: I = {A}, F = {A}, A → B ⇔ C → A; A → C → A; A → C → B → A.
- Space On strategy: I = {A}, F = {C}, A ⇔ D → C.
- Space Touch strategy: I = {A}, F = {B, C}, A ⇔ D → C; A ⇔ D → A → B.

4 Future Study

The state transition diagram (Figure 1) provides a new vocabulary in both reporting and modelling selection strategies with pen-based devices. However, it requires further development, for example, it does not deal with parameters such as, time (that the pen stays in a certain state etc.), the state of the switch on the side of the pen (side switch), pen-tip sensitivity (pressure of pen-tip), pen rotation, highlighting and sound output. Further research is required to expand it.

References

Buxton, W. (1990). A three state model of graphical input. In Human-Computer Interaction (Edited by D. Diaper et al.), - *INTERACT '90: IFIP TC13 International Conference on Human-Computer Interaction.* Elsevier Science B.V., pp.449-456.

Chen, M. (1993). A Framework for Describing Interactions with Graphical Widgets Using State-Transition Diagrams. *In Adjunct proceedings of the INTERCHI'93 Conference on Human Factors in Computing Systems.* Addison Wesley, pp.131-132.

Ren, X. & Moriya, S. (1998). The influence of target size, distance and direction on the design of selection strategies, *Proceedings of the HCI'98 (Sheffield Hallam University, UK, September 1-4, 1998)*, Springer, pp.67-82.

Human-Computer Interaction - INTERACT'99 (Volume II)
S. Brewster, A. Cawsey & G. Cockton (Editors)
Published by The British Computer Society © IFIP TC.13, 1999

EPSRC
Engineering and Physical Sciences Research Council

Human Factors and the WWW: Making sense of URLs

Dominic Stanyer and Rob Procter

Institute for Communicating and Collaborating Systems
Division of Informatics, University of Edinburgh
Scotland
Email: dsjs|rnp@dcs.ed.ac.uk

Abstract: We present a study of how WWW users 'make sense' of URLs. Experiments were used to investigate users' capacity to employ the URL as a surrogate for the resource to which it refers. The results show that users can infer useful information from URLs, but that such improvisation has shortcomings as a navigation aid.

Keywords: Universal Resource Locator (URL), usability, World Wide Web, navigation

1 Motivation

The typical user interface is an abstraction over the behaviour of the underlying system. The user interacts with system functionality through this abstraction which hides the complex realities of the underlying mechanisms (Dourish and Button 1998). We argue that the typical WWW browser hides too much. Users often find themselves having to navigate without a clear idea of either 'where' they are going, or of 'how long' it will take to get there.

Such deficiencies force users to improvise, to use any means to hand that might afford them a window onto a richer picture of the content, form and behaviour of the underlying system. As Nielsen (1999) observes, the Universal Resource Locator (URL) is one such window. In earlier experiments, we explored ways in which URLs may afford useful clues concerning referenced resource content, location and even the behaviour of the download process (Stanyer and Procter 1999). We report here preliminary results from a follow-up study. This is part of on-going research to develop an understanding of how users use the World Wide Web. The goal is to improve WWW usability through better browser interfaces.

2 The URL

Every WWW resource has a unique reference, or URL, by which it can be retrieved. The three major parts of a URL are `site`, `path` and `resource` name, where the latter two parts being optional. Breaking down the URL into its components may enable users to extract useful information about content, location and download behaviour of the referenced resource. An experiment was undertaken to explore users' ability to make sense of URLs in this way.

3 Experimental Method

The subjects were eighteen Edinburgh University students with varying degrees of WWW experience. Each was presented with ten URLs in random order. They consisted of either: `site` name (short), `site` and `path` name, or `site`, `path` and `resource` name (long), and were chosen to represent a range of inference affordability. Subjects were asked to rate their confidence in predicting content, location, and download time on a scale 1 to 6. Downloading was then initiated, and subjects asked to relate the observed behaviour to the URL. On download completion, subjects were asked to rate the accuracy of their predictions. Subjects' remarks were recorded.

www.dcs.shef.ac.uk/~wmlh/ipcat97book.htm
"It's at Sheffield University, and it's in someone's personal home directory because it has a tilde for a UNIX account, home directory, and there is some acronym 97 which presumably means that it's the proceedings or something to do with the year 1997, that's what I would assume, I don't know that it will be. Book indicates that it might be an on-line version of a document ... like a paper document maybe and htm indicates that it is hypertext. My intuition would say that book htm could be fairly fast because it could be a big text file representation of a book. Again ... it is just me implying that."

Figure 1: Extract from subject transcript.

4 Results and Discussion

Averages of subjects' confidence and accuracy in location, content and download time prediction are shown in Table 1. They suggest that subjects were more confident at inferring location (e.g., see Figure 1) than content or download time. Subjects also rated their accuracy of location prediction higher than content or download time. Accurarcy is rated quite highly for all predictions. We suspect that this may be an effect of self-assessment. Performance in both tasks was better for long URLs.

The transcripts showed that subjects made sense of URLs in ways that were broadly consistent with URL format and constituent parts, but that they were easily mislead. E.g.: location inferences might be driven by recognition of a site name sub-domain, rather than a 'parsing' of the whole name. E.g.: most subjects based their inference of the location of `uk.samba.org` on its first sub-domain. There was a correlation at the 0.95 level between location and download predictions, suggesting that subjects often based their estimate of the latter on the former. This was confirmed by the transcripts. Other bases for download time inference included inferences about site popularity. E.g.: "Microsoft is always slow because so many people use it". Once download had started, subjects were able to rationalise observed download behaviour by reference to the URL. Subjects' strategy for inferring content had to be that URL parts were meaningfully named. It may be that lower confidence in content predictions reflected awareness of the unreliability of such an assumption. Content inferences were often conditioned by 'common sense'. E.g.: subjects were very confident about `www.scottishpower.plc.uk`, but much less so about `uk.samba.org`.

	Confidence	Accuracy
Location	4.9	5.2
Content	4.2	4.6
Time	3.9	4.0

Table 1: Average subject prediction confidence and accuracy.

5 Summary and Conclusions

The URLs were chosen because they exemplified different forms, not because they were typical of what users may encounter 'in the wild'. Nevertheless, the results suggest that though users can make quite artful use of URLs as surrogates for WWW resources, such improvisation has its limitations. It would seem that users are best at inferring location, yet location may be less valuable for navigation than either content or download time (Johnson 1997).

We conclude that browsers should afford users better means for navigating and understanding WWW behaviour. In particular, techniques such as link traversal preview and download time affordances deserve investigation (Kopetzky and Mulhauser 1999, Stanyer and Procter 1999). Such techniques can provide with browsable levels of abstraction without making too much of a commitment as to how these abstractions may actually be used.

References

Dourish, P. and Button, G. (1998) On Technomethodology: Foundational Relationships Between Ethnomethodology and System Design. Human Computer Interaction, Vol 13, 395-432.

Johnson, C. (1997) What's the Web Worth? The Impact of Retrieval Delays on the Value of Distributed Information. Workshop on Time and the Web, Staffordshire University, June.

Kopetzky, T. and Mulhauser, M. (1999) Visual preview for link traversal on the WWW. Proc. 8th International WWW Conference, Toronto.

Nielsen, J. (1999) URL as UI, Jacob Nielsen's Alertbox, March. http://www.useit.com/alertbox/990321.html

Stanyer, D. and Procter, R. (1999) Improving Web Usability with the Link Lens. Proc. 8th International WWW Conference, Toronto.

Human-Computer Interaction - INTERACT'99 (Volume II)
S. Brewster, A. Cawsey & G. Cockton (Editors)
Published by The British Computer Society © IFIP TC.13, 1999

EPSRC
Engineering and Physical Sciences Research Council

An Investigation of the Properties of Information as the Common Object of Cooperative Work

Ros Strens, Susan Turner and Phil Turner

University of Northumbria at Newcastle
Department of Computing and Mathematics
Newcastle upon Tyne NE1 8ST
Email: susan.turner, phil.turner, ros.strenns@unn.ac.uk

Abstract: We propose that the properties of information as the common object of work should be addressed formally with a systematic approach to the elicitation and representation of the requirements that they generate on CSCW systems. An information properties matrix is being developed to provide a reference description of each property using an organising framework based on Activity Theory. This tool, which also identifies techniques for defining properties, will be used to reason about CSCW systems and will inform the requirements and design stages and ongoing evaluation.

Keywords: Information properties, Activity Theory, cooperative work

1 Information as an Object of Work

The properties of information have so far been a neglected dimension in the design of CSCW systems. Information properties such as timeliness, security, maturity and modality are implicit in the design itself, but are rarely treated explicitly in the requirements and analysis process. Moreover, as information is transformed, properties change both in terms of the values ascribed to them and their relative importance to stakeholders in the collaborative system. We therefore propose that information properties need to be addressed formally with a systematic approach to the elicitation and representation of the requirements that they generate.

The objectives of the 'Information Matters' project, which is in its early stages, are therefore:

- To define the properties of information as the common object of work which are relevant to requirements on, and the design, implementation and introduction of, CSCW systems;
- To create an information properties matrix which embodies these properties and identifies techniques for defining relevant properties in particular organisational settings.

2 Information Properties

Information can acquire properties at all stages from its generation to its use and in several ways. Values ascribed to properties may be intrinsic to the information item and unchanging (e.g. the originator of the information), they may be deliberately assigned and enduring but changeable (e.g. security status), or they may be perceived dynamically during the work process according to a person's viewpoint and responsibilities (e.g. timely).

Values of properties may change as a result of the work process itself (e.g. maturity) or as a result of changes in context, particularly when crossing a boundary into a different context (e.g. trust-worthiness).

Information properties can have as many levels of encapsulation as the information itself. For example in a monthly briefing paper the statistics cited may be public domain with long term validity, whereas the document itself may be confidential to the organisation with a lifespan of a month. This encapsulation of information items does not necessarily imply inheritance of properties although if, say, information contained in a document is confidential then that document should be too.

This brief introduction is intended to demonstrate the potentially complex, changing and subjective nature of information properties and thus the need for a means of investigating them systematically within the overall requirements and design process of CSCW systems.

3 The Information Properties Matrix

The approach that the project is taking consists of a number of steps. The first step is to identify a set of properties that can be important in a CSCW context. The second step is to produce a structured reference description of each property, based on a template which has been developed for this purpose.

Here we have found activity theory (Kuuti, 1996, Nardi, 1996) to be a useful organising framework for reasoning about information properties. In activity theoretic terms, information has a dual role as an artefact supporting the work activity (e.g. a note of recommended source references from a colleague) and as the common object itself which is transformed in that activity (e.g. a co-authored paper). Properties which are salient in the artefact role include such matters as reliability and trustworthiness, while issues of maturity, ownership and so forth surface in connection with information as the common object. Of course many properties belong to both aspects of information, but a consideration of the artefact/object distinction helps to identify what is most relevant for the part of the activity under consideration. Further, information commonly moves from one activity to another, so the common object of one activity may become an artefact for another - in fact, a boundary object. Finally information properties influence and are influenced by the rest of the activity system - the organisation of human tasks (community and division of labour in activity theory terms), prevailing rules and norms (praxis) and the technical aspects of the system (other artefacts).

Our matrix is structured to reflect these relationships. It lists technological, human and process issues for each property together with the techniques that could be used for their elicitation and representation.

Thirdly relational and impact matrices are being populated to show how the properties are related to one another and on which aspects of context each property is most likely to have a significant impact.

We envisage these descriptions and matrices being used as a reference tool for the investigation of information properties in a specific context. Such a tool will be of use at the requirements stage, to determine properties salient to the work process, and at the design phase to ensure that new systems preserve their value and visibility as appropriate - something that is particularly important for boundary objects. Ongoing evaluation using the tools will identify properties that are inadequately supported by the current version of the system.

4 In Conclusion

Each of the above steps is at an early stage of development. The poster shows current versions of the overall list of properties, the template for the individual property descriptions, an example of a structured property description, the structure of the relational and impact matrices and examples of use of chosen techniques.

The approach is being applied to a workflow case study. The poster shows examples from the case study of how properties change as documents pass from one workgroup to another, and how a new system could ensure that these properties are supported.

Acknowledgements

We gratefully acknowledge the support of EPSRC (GR/M12148) and the University of Northumbria.

References

Kuuti K (1996) Activity Theory as a Potential Framework for HCI Research, *in B.Nardi (Ed) Context and Consciousness,* MIT Press, Cambridge, Ma., pp.17-44.

Nardi B. (1996) Some reflections on the application of Activity Theory *in B.Nardi (Ed) Context and Consciousness,* MIT Press, Cambridge, Ma., pp235-246.

Fear Reduction for Seniors

Richard C. Thomas

Department of Computer Science
The University of Western Australia
Nedlands 6907
Australia
Email: richard@cs.uwa.edu.au

Abstract: The paper describes a research-driven course attended by mainly retired people who had difficulty mastering computers. The approach was active learning, no computers in the classroom, and review of personal learning objectives and experiences with peers and teacher. It was rather successful for most but little use for two people with pressing problems. Once the level of fear was reduced, enthusiasm grew and people set their own goals and devised solutions to their problems. Some ideas in this pilot project may prove to be especially beneficial for teaching older users - something not so far identified in the literature.

Keywords: older users, exploration, usability, active learning, strategies, observation, process dynamics

1 Introduction

It was argued in *New Scientist* recently (Chown 1999) that "...the older you are, the more you need to be on-line". Unfortunately in practice the elderly are excluded. Generally older users learn and perform tasks slower than their younger counterparts, but are not technophobic. No techniques have yet been identified as especially beneficial for teaching older people (Czaja 1997).

The techniques developed for the present pilot project focus on fear reduction and the belief that people take years to become expert users. Longitudinal research suggests that learning and system use may be constrained by major Process Dynamics (Thomas 1998):

- a continuous, low level rate of exploration
- a rather stationary level of vocabulary use
- sudden crossovers between methods
- performance improvement with experience

It was proposed to exploit these dynamics by teaching active learning and encouraging reflection. For example, if participants could appreciate just how long it takes to become skilled, then they might be more open to exploring patiently and systematically over the long run. Furthermore reflection may enhance exploration (Trudel and Payne 1995).

It was felt that validation of experiences was a crucial factor in reducing fear and ability to learn computers. Validation means sharing of concerns and understanding that reactions to a situation are reasonable. Usability concepts can explain why some things are awkward and might therefore help fearful people. Perhaps users could be empowered to critique the interface rather than criticise themselves.

2 The Course

"Learning to Learn About Computers" was offered to the public in February 1999 through the *UWA Extension* programme. It was not ideally targeted, with hindsight, and only 6 people signed up. Two were retired and one retired during the course. Two more were probably 50-something - an executive secretary and a retired senior administrator now in a less senior job. One person was 16. The last two dropped out, while the others thrived. It was obvious the course had to be adapted to fearful seniors. The course aims were:

- to validate the experiences of participants
- to understand the skill acquisition process
- to show how users explore
- to be empowered to critique applications
- to know why technology is as it is

There were 5 weekly sessions of 1.5 hours - a considerably longer time span than usual (Czaja 1997). Computers were not used. All sessions had a brief introduction, followed by participants sharing their experiences for up to an hour. Conceptual material was presented next, finishing with the week's *home-computer work.*

Wk	Concepts	Home work
1	Need for a long term view. Skill acquisition concepts	Eureka slips
2	Sources of information. Exploration skills and rates	Exploration plan
3	Minimise vocabulary. Multiple methods. Process Dynamics. Crossovers	Development plan
4	Usability: affordance, consistency, generalisation. Observation skills	Usability evaluation
5	Strategies. Tables	

In the first session everyone was surprised to discover others felt the same way, even the youngest. The Eureka slips recorded any explorations during the following week, based on Rieman (1993). Next week error-recoveries were reported - they were more prepared to try given their new motivation. Reliance on the help system was seen to be illusory - they learned it is one of many sources.

By week 3 they were setting their agendas according to their interests, e.g. customising menus, deciding on fonts, merging mail. This contrasts with merely devising exercises to assist learning in Guided Exploration (Wiedenbeck et al 1995). Skills to observe the display had to be taught during the usability part. Similarly Bhavnani et al (1999) have previously identified *Learning to See* as necessary while teaching strategies. Bhavnani and John's earlier work on strategies (1996) was adapted to demonstrate task-oriented skill - attendees were hungry for this by week 5.

3 Evaluation

The four who stayed the course were most enthusiastic. Two completed questionnaires had marks of 4 or 5 out of 5 for: "I have less fear than when I started", "I am more confident to explore" and "I am better able to use the help system". Both thought it "brilliant" not having computers in the classroom and enjoyed the interaction with the group. The senior administrator, in contrast, awarded 2, 2 and 3 respectively, liked a very short exercise with a computer, but also realised the need for self confidence. Tellingly he says an exploratory approach is too slow for a busy person.

It may be that retirees, particularly, do have time to explore. These techniques may suit them better than those in work. Cognitive loads may be lower as they only learn what they decide to learn and in their own time; and observation reduces memory load. Perhaps also it worked because it desensitised the fear first. Further investigation is required.

References

Bhavnani, S.K. and John, B.E. (1996) "Exploring the unrealized potential of Computer-Aided Drafting." *CHI 96,* 332-339.

Bhavnani, S.K., John, B.E. and Flemming, U. (1999) "The strategic use of CAD: an empirically inspired, theory-based course." *CHI 99.*

Chown, M. (1999) "World Wide Wrinklenet." *New Scientist* **161**(2174), 49, 20 February.

Czaja, S.J. (1997). "Computer Technology and Older Adults." In M. Helander *et al* (eds) *Handbook of Human-Computer Interaction* (2nd ed). Elsevier Science, Amsterdam, 797-812.

Rieman, J. (1993) "The diary study: a workplace-oriented research tool to guide laboratory efforts." *CHI '93,* 321-326.

Thomas, R.C. (1998) *Long Term Human-Computer Interaction.* Springer-Verlag, London.

Trudel, C.I. and Payne, S.J. (1995) "Reflection and goal management in exploratory learning." *Int J of Human-Computer Studies, 307-339.*

Wiedenbeck, S., Zila, P.L. and McConnell, D.S. (1995) "End-user training: an empirical study comparing on-line practice and methods." *CHI 95,* 74-81.

Human-Computer Interaction - INTERACT'99 (Volume II)
S. Brewster, A. Cawsey & G. Cockton (Editors)
Published by The British Computer Society © IFIP TC.13, 1999

Syndetic Modelling of Engaging Electronic Lifeforms

Mark Treglown

Computers and Learning Research Group, The Open University
Walton Hall, Milton Keynes, UK. MK7 6AA
Email: M.Treglown@open.ac.uk

Abstract: We introduce a project focussed on improving the usability of engaging embodied agents. While often marketed as toys, these mobile computing devices are also employed as interfaces to educational software with important learning outcomes, and so are deserving of research effort. We examine the applicability to this project of syndetic modelling, an integrated approach capturing both a system model and cognitive architecture, known to be able to support reasoning about gestural and multimodal interaction. We outline the project's aims and present intermediate results.

Keywords: embodied agents, usability, formal system modelling.

1 Introduction

A growing number of research directions in human-computer interaction (HCI) are focussed on mobile and ubiquitous computing systems, and on agent-based interfaces. As with much HCI research, new technology outpaces theory that can account for such technologies' usability and which can guide development of subsequent systems. The technology that we are currently investigating are those mobile computing devices that can be described as engaging agent-like electronic lifeforms. Examples of such devices include the Tamagotchi and Furby. The project addresses these devices as unsupported disparaging claims as to their usability have been made within the HCI community, and because other examples of such devices, such as ActiMates and the animatronic Barney the Dinosaur, are promoted and employed as engaging intermediaries to educational software, the usability of which is inextricably linked to the success of the child's learning tasks. Our current project is to derive methods for analysing the usability of existing engaging electronic lifeforms, and to suggest guidelines for improving the usability of future agent- and creature-based interfaces.

One might object that agent-based systems cannot be understood using conventional usability methods, Resnick (1988), for example, shows that children who build and program their own simple robots use both a design and a psychological level to explain the robot's behaviour. Laurel (1997), however, says that a key issue in an agent's design is the *accessibility* of its traits, and the ease with which tasks can be performed with the agent, which is a legitimate area of investigation.

2 Syndetic Modelling

Contrary to Laurel's (1997) demand for improved prototyping tools for developing embodied agents, of the sort devised by Kaminsky et al (1999), the project is concerned with a more 'scientific' approach to HCI, refining software from specifications, demonstrating usability properties, and generating revised and further requirements that future systems should satisfy from usability testing of the specifications. The syndetic (from the Greek for 'joined') modelling framework (Duce & Duke, 1996) is used to describe the behaviour of electronic lifeforms. Syndetic modelling combines interactor models of a computing system with an interactor version of Philip Barnard's Interacting Cognitive Subsystems (ICS) cognitive architecture - configured so that appropriate transformations of input stimuli into mental representations and physical actions can be performed. The combined (syndetic) model includes the system model, the ICS interactor, and a number of deontic logic axioms that describe the user's interaction with the system. While deontic logic is known to the formal computer science community as a notation for describing distributed systems, its original development was as a means of capturing legal and ethical frameworks. Because children's interaction and play with their toys and pets, and other children, is restricted by ethical frameworks, and by the obligations of caring for the object of their play, the syndetic modelling approach is deemed to be a useful choice of model. Our choice is also supported by the ability of syndetic modelling to capture, and reason about, multimodal and gesture-based interaction, as supported by Barney and Furby.

3 Finding Usability Faults

The project began by modelling simpler electronic lifeforms, the first case study being the Tamagotchi Angel. This device displays an animated dinosaur-like creature in a small LCD panel. Nurturing the creature from birth to adulthood is achieved by using three unlabelled buttons on the case to highlight and select operations, such as feeding, and to cancel modes, and, unlike similar devices, by tapping the LCD panel itself. The system model was built by exploratory learning while thinking aloud, the user consulting the manual only when display contents could not be understood, or no action sequence to perform a task could be generated by experimentation. The largest difficulty in constructing the model is coping with the large number of modes, over ten system attributes describe system modes and the majority of axioms describe changes of mode. The moral framework governing interaction with the creature was found to be bound with the details of switching between modes.

Generally, the number of usability failings is low, but some problems can be found. Among them, while the model can capture the constraints on the user's behaviour, some obligations such as:

`bat` in `display` $\Rightarrow$ **obl**(tapScreen) (when a bat tries to steal the angel's candy in the feeding time mode, then the user is obliged to scare the bat away by tapping the screen) cannot be assumed as being behaviours that would obviously occur to the user, they can only be learned from reading the manual. Also, the model reveals a weakening of the user's responsibilities in caring for the angel. The angel must be entertained by playing a game with it. In the model, however, playing the game can only be stated as a permission, the overloading of buttons in different contexts means that if playing the game were an obligation, the system would become non-normative, as modes can be left before obligations are discharged. The system design is found to be often inconsistent and design choices made often prohibit expected and moral actions by the user.

4 Further Work

We have found that syndetic modelling is capable of modelling aspects of the behaviour of an engaging electronic lifeform and of revealing usability failings of the system. The project that produced these results in on-going, the modelling technique will be applied to a number of other electronic lifeforms to reveal their usability failings which empirical testing will seek to verify. Our eventual aim is to produce guidelines for the behaviour of embodied agents that are intended to be useful interfaces to educational applications, syndetic modelling has demonstrated so far that it is a useful technique for this objective.

Acknowledgements

"Tamagotchi Angel" is a trademarks of Bandai. "Furby" is a trademark of Tiger Electronics Inc. "ActiMates" is a trademark of Microsoft Corp. "Barney" is a trademark of The Lyons Group, L.P.

References

Duce, D. A. & Duke, D. J. (1996) *Syndetic Modelling: A New Opportunity for Formal Methods.* AMODEUS 2 project (ESPRIT BRA7040) technical report ID/WP57.

Kaminsky, M., Dourish, P., Edwards, W. K., LaMarca, A., Salisbury, M. & Smith, I. (1999) SWEETPEA: Software Tools for Programmable Embodied Agents. In *Proceedings of CHI'99*, (15-20 May 1999, Pittsburgh PA), ACM.

Laurel, B. (1997). Interface Agents: Metaphors with Character. In J. M. Bradshaw (ed.) *Software Agents.* AAAI Press/MIT Press, 67-79.

Resnick, M. (1988) LEGO, Logo, and Life. In C. Langton (ed.) *Artificial Life.* Addison-Wesley, 397-406.

EPSRC
Engineering and Physical Sciences
Research Council

Trading space for time in interface design

Ashley Walker and Stephen Brewster

Department of Computing Science, University of Glasgow, Scotland G128QQ
Email: ashley,stephen@dcs.gla.ac.uk

Abstract: This work addresses problem of (visual) clutter in modern computer interfaces. The solution it proposes involves the translation of techniques — from the visual to the audio domain — for exploiting space in information representation. As an example, a spatialized audio progress bar is built using rapidly emerging 3D audio render tools. The usability of this progress bar is compared with that of a visual progress bar in multi-tasking interfacing scenario. The results show that users are able to perform a visually demanding foreground task significantly more efficiently when simultaneously monitoring a background task via a spatialized audio (vs. visual) progress bar. Moreover, task monitoring accuracy is significantly improved when spatialized audio vs. visual cues are provided.

Keywords: interface design, 3D audio, delay affordance, usability testing

1 Introduction

With the rapid growth of networked and integrated computing systems, human-computer interactions are becoming increasingly multi-tasking. While immersed in a foreground task, a user is typically engaged in monitoring multiple simultaneously running background tasks with widely varying response times. This interaction scenario challenges the ability of existing interface architectures to support efficient interactions. Moreover, as interactions become increasingly visual bandwidth limited (e.g., as populations turn to small screen devices), simply supplying the (visually overloaded) user with more windows and/or graphical representations of system state will not proportionally increase usability. (In fact, we are likely to see the opposite trend.) A key strategy for overcoming this (visual) information presentation bottleneck involves the creation of interaction tools which exploit other sensory and actuation modalities. This article provides a general and extensible example of this in the form of an audio progress bar which exploits a powerful GUI (graphical user interface) design principle.

Trading space for time in interface design: Much of the richness of the interactions supported by GUIs relies on a well-founded exploitation of space. One of the most simple and yet sophisticated examples of this is the *progress bar* which communicates task progress as the position of the end of a thick horizontal line along a spatial axis. The principle underlying this mapping is that a spatial representation of temporally extended information can afford a more natural interaction with a temporally extended task. This is generally true because search and recall can be more easily performed on spatial than temporal memory (Schulman, 1973). With the advent of inexpensive and reasonable quality spatial audio for the PC, the advantages of this space-time mapping can often be realized in the audio domain as effectively as in the visual.

A spatialized audio progress bar: The simplicity and clarity of the visual progress bar is derived from its use of two basic components: (i) a progress indicator which moves along (ii)a fixed reference axis. Similarly, a spatialized audio progress bar can be built using only two spatialized sound blips and allowing the spatial position and presentation rates of these two components to communicate the relevant delay affordances.

Percentage complete: The first blip (or 'lub' component of the of the progress 'heartbeat') provides the reference. It is played from a fixed target position located in front of the user. The 'dub' component is spatialized to indicate the percentage of the task complete by its angular position within a circular orbit centered on the user's head.

Rate: The overall rate of progress is perceived as the angular speed of the orbiting blip. The absolute (or size-independent rate) transfer rate is encoded as the time between the presentation of the two sounds. (This delay is determined via a transfer function running asymptotically to 500ms with increasing rate and to infinity in the extreme that the download is stalled).

Endpoints: When a task ends successfully, two identical — and therefore distinct — blips are played from in front of the user. By contrast to this uniquely symmetrical heartbeat, a stall is heard as a failed heartbeat (i.e., a lone lub sound followed by an infinite inter-blip delay).

2 Experimental Methods

To test the usability of the spatialized audio progress bar, users were set the (multi-tasking) task of creating a poetry archive on the local file server. This involved transferring files from 20 remote poetry archives while transcribing as much hard-copied poetry as possible in the time allotted. To force users to continually monitor the progress of the file transfers (as opposed to responding simply to endpoints), file transfers were periodically interrupted and users were then given the option of restarting the transfer or skipping to the next transfer. Users decided this based on whether the percentage of data transferred before the interruption exceeded the minimum percentage of data required from the present archive.

The experiment was a counterbalanced, two condition, within-groups design. Each of the sixteen participants performed the task using a conventional visual progress bar (Condition 1) and the spatialized audio progress bar (Condition 2) (with odd number participants performing the visual task first and *vice-versa*). In each condition, the number of words typed per minute and the number of errors in the 'Restart' vs. 'Skip to next' decision were measured. After each condition, users were asked to rate the subjective workload on a modified set of NASA TLX scales.

3 Results

Hypothesis I: The spatialized audio progress bar can be monitored more accurately. In the audio condition, users were significantly more aware of the internal state of task progress than in the visual condition. The mean error rate in the audio condition was 2.03 vs. 3.31 in the visual conditions ($T_{15} = 2.30$, $p = 1.82e-2$). The increased number of errors in the visual condition corresponds to an average of 21% more unnecessary data being downloaded.

Hypothesis II: The spatialized audio progress bar can facilitate a visually demanding foreground task. Users typed significantly more words per minute in Condition 2 (audio) as compared to Condition 1 (visual) ($T_{15} = 4.91$, $p = 9.3e-5$).

Hypothesis III: The spatialized audio progress bar will require less workload. Users reported that the audio condition required significantly less *effort* ($T_{15} = 2.73$, $p = 7.68e-3$) and *physically demand* ($T_{15} = 3.07$, $p = 3.85e-3$), and resulted in significantly lower levels of *frustration* ($T_{15} = 3.39$, $p = 2.03e-3$) and *annoyance* ($T_{15} = 2.93$, $p = 5.13e-3$). Users reported a higher sense of their own *performance* ($T_{15} = 2.83$, $p = 6.26e-3$) in the audio condition and a higher overall *preference* ($T_{15} = 5.60$, $p = 2.51e-5$) for the audio condition. (Users reported roughly similar *mental demand* and *time pressure* in both conditions.)

4 Discussion and Conclusion

The present work was motivated by the expectation that a spatialized audio progress bar would afford the same advantages over visual progress bars which have been demonstrated for existing (non-spatialized) audio progress bars (Gaver, 1989; Albers & Bregman, 1995; Crease & Brewster, 1998). Moreover, this study showed that the space-time trade-off exploited by a *spatialized* audio progress bar yields additional usability improvements in the form of (i) improved accuracy in a progress monitoring task and (ii) improved efficiency in a simultaneously conducted foreground task.

Spatialization may also prove to be a key ingredient in multi-tasking interface design, as spatialization facilitates segregation of multiple simultaneously playing sound streams (Cherry, 1953). The current article lays the ground work for a future study of the use of multiple audio progress bars.

References

Albers, M. & Bregman, E. (1995), The Audible Web: Auditory Enhancements for Mosaic, *in CHI Conference Champion*, ACM Press, pp.318–319.

Cherry, E. (1953), "Some experiments on the recognition of speech", *J. Acoust. Soc. Am.* **25**, 975–979.

Crease, M. & Brewster, S. (1998), Making progress with sounds — the design and evaluation of an audio progress bar, *in Proc. ICAD*.

Gaver, W. (1989), "The Sonic Finder: An auditory interface that uses auditory icons", *HCI* **4**, 67–94.

Schulman, A. (1973), "Recognition memory and the recall of spatial location", *Memory and Cognition* .

Human-Computer Interaction - INTERACT'99 (Volume II)
S. Brewster, A. Cawsey & G. Cockton (Editors)
Published by The British Computer Society © IFIP TC.13, 1999

Do CTA Findings Influence Design?

B.L. William Wong

Department of Information Science
University of Otago, Dunedin, New Zealand.
Email: william.wong@stonebow.otago.ac.nz

Abstract: This paper briefly describes an experiment to determine whether insights gained from a cognitive task analysis (CTA) of dynamic decision processes will result in designs that will enhance human performance. The experiment showed that knowledge of the CTA findings does lead to designs are directly supportive of the decision strategies identified in the CTA.

Keywords: cognitive task analysis, interface design, layout, information portrayal.

1 Introduction

This paper represents some of the work of an on-going investigation into how information may be portrayed to facilitate decision making in dynamic environments. A cognitive task analysis (CTA) using the Critical Decision Method (Klein et al., 1989), was conducted to elicit goals and decision strategies of emergency ambulance dispatchers. The goals and decision strategies were used to re-design the display of an operational ambulance dispatch management system. The re-designed display was evaluated and found to improve dispatch performance by about 40% (Wong et al., 1998; Wong et al., 1997). Following the evaluation, questions about the role of the CTA in the re-design process were raised. Was the design simply a good idea, or whether the insights about the decision process gained from the CTA influenced the manner in which the information display was designed?

To address this issue, a two-group experiment was conducted where participants were asked to re-design an ambulance status screen. The re-designed screens had to keep to the same data specified in the data model of the original screen. Both groups were given the same core information, but one group was given additional information about the 'focus and compare' decision strategy derived through the CTA interviews. The resulting design sketches were then assessed as either being able or not able to support this decision strategy. This paper will briefly report on this experiment.

2 Participants

51 students from a Human Factors in Information Systems course volunteered for this study. 35 of these students had computing backgrounds, while the remaining 16 were from non-computing disciplines like finance and education. Most had experience with designing simple information systems projects or had at least some experience designing simple interfaces during the course.

3 Task and Procedure

The participants were randomly assigned to two groups of 25 and 26 students. Both groups were given information about the old screen design, a map of the region, a data flow diagram and a supporting entity-relationship diagram of the process, and a design principle called the Proximity-Compatibility Principle. Additionally, participants in Group 1 were given the CTA outcome, referred to as the 'focus and compare' decision strategy (Wong, 1999). Any reference to this strategy was deliberately omitted from the information pack given to Group 2.

Participants were then provided with pencils and paper so that they could concentrate on the concept of the display rather than on the details of the layout. The participants were then instructed to sketch a new design for the old screen if they considered it necessary, describe the design concept, i.e. how it would work, and write the design rationale, i.e. a justification, for their design.

	Group 1 (exposed to CTA)			Group 2 (not exposed to CTA)		
	Computing	Others	Total	Computing	Others	Total
Yes, facilitates	88% (15/17)	75% (6/8)	**84%** (21/25)	22% (4/18)	38% (3/8)	**27%** (7/26)
No, does not facilitate	12% (2/7)	25% (2/8)	**16%** (4/25)	78% (14/18)	62% (5/8)	**73%** (19/26)

Table 1: The number of designs that facilitate or do not facilitate the decision strategy.

4 Analysis

The resulting design sketches were randomly evaluated to determine the basis of the design layout, i.e. table-and-list oriented, or spatially oriented, and whether or not, these layouts facilitated visual search for ambulance status information and comparison of such status information between neighbouring ambulance stations. Further evidence as to whether the design would or would not facilitate the decision strategy was obtained by examining each accompanying design concept and design rationale.

5 Results

Table 1 shows the percentages and proportions of designs that facilitated or did not facilitate the decision strategy. The results show that:

a. 84% of participants exposed to the CTA outcomes developed designs that facilitated visual search and comparison, while only 27% of those not exposed did.
b. A small proportion, 16%, of the participants exposed to the CTA outcomes, developed designs that did not facilitate comparisons. However when not exposed to the CTA outcomes, 73%, a much larger proportion of the sample, developed designs that were not supportive of the decision strategy.
c. Participants' backgrounds (computing vs. non-computing) showed a similar pattern. When exposed to the CTA outcomes, those with a computing background (88%) and those with a non-computing background (75%) developed designs that supported the decision strategy. Whereas only 22% and 38% of those not exposed to the CTA outcomes developed designs that supported the decision strategies.
d. Senior computing students (Year 3 and above) were more likely to develop designs supportive of the decision strategies even without exposure to the CTA outcomes.

6 Discussion

The results suggests three effects:

a. There is evidence of an exposure effect. Knowledge of the CTA outcome influenced design outcomes in general. Designer's background did not seem to influence design.
b. Design principles can help designers, but do not seem to play a major role in crafting the layout. Instead, the CTA seemed to play a larger role in guiding the design.
c. There is suggestion of a seniority effect. This is probably due to the senior students' familiarity and experience with alternative display types.

Standard systems analysis and data modelling provide knowledge of the processes and the data needed by the processes. Knowledge of the CTA outcomes, on the other hand, provide the designer with an understanding of the manner in which the data might be used or manipulated in a decision.

7 Conclusion

Knowledge of CTA outcomes specified in a manner useful for design can have a powerful influence on the nature of the resulting design. Further work is being planned to understand and formalise the CTA-to-design process.

References

Klein, G. A., Calderwood, R., and Macgregor, D. (1989). Critical decision method for eliciting knowledge. IEEE Transactions on Systems, Man and Cybernetics, 19(3), 462-472.

Wong, W. B. L. (1999). Information Portrayal in Dynamic Decision Making Environments. Unpublished PhD thesis, University of Otago, Dunedin, NZ.

Wong, W. B. L., O'Hare, D., and Sallis, P. J. (1998). The Effect of Display Location on Decision Making in Dispatch Management. In H. Johnson, L. Nigay, & C. Roast (Eds.) HCI '98 Conference (221-238). Sheffield, UK: Springer.

Wong, W. B. L., Sallis, P. J., and O'Hare, D. (1997). Eliciting information portrayal requirements: Experiences with the Critical Decision Method. In H. Thimbleby, B. O'Conaill, & P. Thomas (Eds.), HCI '97 Conference (397-415). University of West England, Bristol, UK: Springer.

Part Five

Videos

Human-Computer Interaction - INTERACT'99 (Volume II)
S. Brewster, A. Cawsey & G. Cockton (Editors)
Published by The British Computer Society © IFIP TC.13, 1999

Meeting in the Magic Lounge

Bryan Cleal, Masood Masoodian, Niels Ole Bernsen and Laila Dybkjær

Natural Interactive Systems Laboratory
Odense University, Forskerparken 10
Odense
Denmark
Email: {bryan, masood, nob, laila}@nis.sdu.dk

Abstract: Magic Lounge is a collaborative virtual meeting environment which facilitates interaction between physically remote people using heterogeneous communication devices. The aim of the Magic Lounge is to allow ordinary people, with little knowledge of technology, to use devices such as PCs, PDAs, and mobile telephones to participate in virtual meetings with intelligent services for information collection, summarisation, search and exchange. The design and implementation of the Magic Lounge is based on user-centred design methodology. This video presents a futuristic vision of the Magic Lounge as conceived by a number of individuals selected from the potential user population. The video combines the users' requirements and expectations from an ideal system, and shows the possibilities and advantages of performing a task in such a virtual meeting environment. The task scenario used as the basis for this video was selected from one of the user's current work practices, to provide a realistic story line.

Keywords: virtual environments, collaborative work, mobile computing, user-centred design, CSCW

1 Introduction

There are a number of virtual meeting environments which support interaction between physically remote people (Fitzpatrick 1995, Roseman 1996). The majority of these virtual meeting environments often rely on specific computer technology, such as PCs with audio and video input and output devices. However, as mobile computing and communication devices are becoming more widely available, there is a growing need for systems that can support the use of such devices in collaborative virtual meetings. There is also a need for systems that can allow interaction between people with different types of technology (for instance, someone with a mobile telephone interacting with someone with a PDA).

The aim of the Magic Lounge project (Bernsen 1998, Masoodian 1999) is to design and implement a virtual meeting environment which provides the necessary tools for communication and interaction needs of geographically separated individuals who want to collaborate with one another using heterogeneous devices such as PCs, PDAs, Palmtops, and mobile telephones. Magic Lounge is going to offer a range of services, some of which are:

- Intelligent multi-party communication management allowing recording and retrieving of the meeting communication history in a multi-media fashion.
- Content-based media conversion techniques coping with heterogeneous communication devices.
- Speech-operated information retrieval for embedding third-party information services, such as those provided on the Internet.
- Speech and gesture-based interrogation and navigation of information spaces.

Development of systems such as the Magic Lounge, which rely heavily on the involvement of the potential users, are often based on the user-centred design techniques, particularly participatory design. However, the success of the participatory design process depends very much on the effectiveness of the communication between the users, designers, and developers of the new technology. Unfortunately, in practice, there are often problems associated with this communication. The video described here, was created to facilitate the communication process between the users and designers of the Magic Lounge. This video combines the visions of the potential users of the Magic Lounge regarding its possible uses after the development, with their current everyday activities.

Figure 1: Three scenes from the video showing several people who are using heterogeneous communication devices to attend a meeting in the Magic Lounge.

2 Magic Lounge Software

Although this video presents a futuristic vision of the Magic Lounge, a prototype has been developed to provide some of the envisaged functionality of the final system. This prototype is currently being tested by the user group. The results of these tests will be used for improving the usability and functionality of the future prototypes (Masoodian 1999).

The current Magic Lounge prototype, which has been implemented in Java, utilises CORBA technology for its underlying client-server architecture, while the MBone technology has been used to provide the necessary means for multicast audio conferencing. This prototype includes a number of tools, among which are: an audio conferencing tool with a score-line graphical user interface for viewing the meeting history (Roy 1999), a textual chat tool with intelligent functions for tagging communicative acts, and a memory tool for accessing and interrogating the internal Magic Lounge meeting memory. At present, Magic Lounge can be accessed using a client program developed for either a PC, PDA, or a simulated telephone.

Future work will focus on improving and extending the tools for accessing and viewing the memory and meeting history using different communication devices, as well as, those tools used for audio and textual communication.

3 Acknowledgements

Magic Lounge is an Esprit Long-Term Research project (No. 25458), funded under the i^3 initiative. The authors would like to acknowledge the contributions of the other members of the Magic Lounge project.

References

Bernsen, N. O., Rist, T., Martin, J-C., Hauck, C., Boullier, D., Briffault, X., Dybkjær, L., Henry, C., Masoodian, M., Neel, F., Profitlich, H-J., Andre, E., Schweitzer, J., and Vapillon, J. (1998). "Magic Lounge: A Thematic Inhabited Information Space with "Intelligent" Communication Services." *Proceedings of Complex Systems, Intelligent Systems & Interfaces NIMES '98*, 188-192.

Fitzpatrick, G., Tolone, W., and Kaplan, S. (1995). "Work, Locales and Distributed Social Worlds." *Proceedings of ECSCW '95*, 1-16.

Masoodian, M., and Cleal, B. (1999). "User-Centred Design of a Virtual Meeting Environment for Ordinary People." *Proceedings of HCI International '99*, in print.

Roseman, M., and Greenberg, S. (1996). "TeamRooms: Network Places for Collaboration." *Proceedings of CSCW '96*, 325-333.

Roy, D. M., and Luz, S. (1999). "Audio Meeting History Tool: Interactive Graphical User-Support for Virtual Audio Meetings." *Proceedings of ESCA Workshop on Accessing Information in Spoken Audio*, 107-110.

Part Six

Interactive Experience

Human–Computer Interaction — INTERACT '99 (Volume II)
S. Brewster, A. Cawsey & G. Cockton (Editors)
Published by the British Computer Society © IFIP TC.13, 1999

HyperMask: Projection onto 3D Moving Surfaces

Kim Binsted, Shigeo Morishima, Frank Nielsen, Claudio Pinhanez and Tatsuo Yotsukura

Sony Computer Science Laboratories*
3-14-13 Higashi-Gotanda
Shinagawa-ku Tokyo
Japan 141
Tel: +81 3 5448 4380
Fax: +81 3 5448 4273
Email: kimb@csl.sony.co.jp
URL: http://www.csl.sony.co.jp

Abstract: HYPERMASK is a system which projects an animated face onto a physical mask, worn by an actor. As the mask moves within a prescribed area (the stage), its position and orientation are detected by a camera, and the projected image moves with it. Also, if the orientation of the mask changes, the projected image changes with respect to the viewpoint of the audience. The lips of the projected face are automatically synchronized in real time with the voice of the actor, who also controls the face's expressions.

Keywords: projection, entertainment, lip synchronization, face animation

1 System Overview

Our system consists of a camera which tracks marked surfaces on a stage, and a retro-projector which projects images onto the tracked surfaces (e.g. on the masks of the actors). Our first technical step is to implicitly calibrate the geometry implied by the camera and projector without explicitly calculating all intrinsic and extrinsic parameters (which is time-consuming and error-prone).

1.1 Calibration

The relationship between points observed on a plane surface from two different cameras is known to be a homography (Faugeras, 1993) (also called collineation). Note that the retro-projector can be considered as a camera whose direction of propagation of light is inverted. A homography is a 3x3 matrix defining a linear application in the projective space, thus preserving both incidence relationships and straightening of lines. In the static case, we need at least four marked points in the camera image (projection of four 3d points of the world) that coincide with the projector image. Practically, this means that we have to manually coincide a fixed projected known pattern (a model of our mask) onto the corresponding real pattern drawn on a planar object, i.e. the mask itself. Let $\mathbf{H}^{(i)}_{P\to C}$ denote the homography that relates the image of the projector image frame to the camera image frame. This means that a 2d image point p_1 in the projector image will match a 2d image point* p_2 in the camera image as follows:

$$p_2 = \begin{pmatrix} x_2 \\ y_2 \\ z_2 \end{pmatrix} = \mathbf{H}^{(i)}_{P\to C} p_1 = \begin{pmatrix} h_{11} & h_{12} & h_{13} \\ h_{21} & h_{22} & h_{23} \\ h_{31} & h_{32} & h_{33} \end{pmatrix} \begin{pmatrix} x_1 \\ y_1 \\ z_1 \end{pmatrix},$$

with $p_1 \sim (\frac{x_1}{z_1} \frac{y_1}{z_1})$ and $p_2 \sim (\frac{x_2}{z_2} \frac{y_2}{z_2})$ (homogeneous coordinates). This calibration step is numerically stable and can be done very quickly in practice.† If we have more than four pairs of corresponding features then we consider a homography that minimizes the least squares of matched points, etc.

*Shigeo Morishima and Tatsuo Yotsukura are at Seikei University, and Claudio Pinhanez is at the MIT Media Lab
*In practice, subpixels are used in order to give more reliable results.
†Automatic calibration of the geometry may also be considered for the future.

1.2 Tracking Features

During the performance, the actor moves freely on the stage; therefore, one task that has to be accomplished is the tracking of the mask. In order to avoid using complex feature detection algorithms that are highly sensitive to noise and to the continuity of the digitization process, we opted for markers. We put on the mask infrared LEDs[‡] that can be easily tracked by a camera with an infrared filter (removing any light other than infrared). The image collected by the camera is a set of cluster pixels (each cluster being a perceived image of a LED). Therefore, in the tracking algorithm, we first detect those clusters and identify for each cluster a central point, called "source" point. This can be done in real time without complex algorithmics since we have placed the LEDs such that clusters are pairwise disjoints for most reasonable movements (i.e. inclination of the actor's head). However, since the mask is allowed to rotate freely, we have also to label the source points (i.e., the clusters) so that we can eventually match them with the known reference pattern. Once again, we deliberately chose an unambiguous pattern that allows source points to be labelled straightforwardly.

1.3 Predicting Movements

As we slowly move the mask, we observe the following "shifting" effect: since we observe at discrete time t the camera image $C(t)$, we project our mask pattern through a homography at time $t + \Delta t$. Unfortunately, the features in the camera images $C(t)$ and $C(t + dt)$ are different because of this movement. Moreover, we have to deal with "gaussian" white noise. In order to reduce this "shifting" problem, we use a Kalman filter, which was proven very effective in practice.

1.4 Real-Time Talking Head

The projected image is the output of a talking head system (Morishima et al., 1995). A face texture is fitted to a 3d polygonal model, and a neural network is trained for predicting lip movements based on vowels. The system can then synchronize the lip movements of the face model with the voice of the actor (from a small microphone concealed in the mask) in real time. Facial expressions can also be manipulated by the actor.

2 Appearance

We will present a performance piece which uses a portable version of the HYPERMASK system. The equipment (camera, projector and computer) is loaded into a trolley, and the actor wheels the trolley around the performance area. The projector is set up to project images back towards the actor pushing the trolley. The actor tells stories and chats with the audience. The faces projected onto the mask reflects the tone and content of the various stories and interactions.

3 Conclusion

Here we have described HYPERMASK, a system for projecting images onto an actor's mask as that mask moves around in the performance area. The projected image is an animated face with real-time lip synchronization with the actor's voice. The face's expression is controlled by the actor to fit with the tone and content of the story being told.

References

Faugeras, O. (1993), *Three-Dimensional Computer Vision: A Geometric Viewpoint.* MIT Press, Cambridge, Massachusetts.

Morishima, S., Kawakami, F., Yamada, H., and Harashima, H. (1995) A modeling of facial expression and emotion for recognition and synthesis. In *Proceedings of the Sixth International Conference on Human-Computer Interaction*, volume I. Human and Future Computing of *I.8 Nonverbal Communication*, pages 251–256.

[‡]Infrared paint or other physical markers could also be used.

Human-Computer Interaction - INTERACT'99 (Volume II)
S. Brewster, A. Cawsey & G. Cockton (Editors)
Published by The British Computer Society © IFIP TC.13, 1999

'Dissemination': Indexing Peers' Learning Experiences as a Multimedia Discourse Database

F. Dineen and J.T. Mayes

Centre for Learning and Teaching Innovation
Glasgow Caledonian University
St. Andrew House, 141 West Nile Street
Glasgow, G1 2RN
United Kingdom
Email: fgdi@gcal.ac.uk

Abstract: The Vicarious Learner project at Glasgow Caledonian University and the University of Edinburgh has aimed at exploring the idea that learning can be facilitated by providing learners with access to the experiences of other learners. We believe it to be a paradigm that offers particular promise when seen as an innovative way of exploiting recent technical advances in multimedia and "distance learning" technologies. It will provide a real alternative to the building of intelligent tutors or to the direct support of live "dialogues". To achieve this aim we have developed a system (the "Dissemination" tutoring system) that contains a multimedia database of peer discussions. These are collected and structured according to a scheme of "Task-Directed Discussions" (TDDs), to provide a framework within which high-quality material can be elicited, stored, retrieved and re-used in a relatively efficient manner.

Keywords: Vicarious/Observational Learning, Educational Discourse, Multimedia Indexing and Retrieval.

1 Generating 'Mathemagenic' Discussions

The Vicarious Learner has been looking broadly at issues concerning the development of a multimedia database system to promote and enhance the role of dialogue in learning. A specific interest, and the origin of the project's name, is in the question of whether and how dialogue can be helpfully "re-used". What benefits can students gain from dialogue as observers, not just as participants?

Attempts to develop CMC environments that could support appropriate educational discourse has tended to simply result in designers repeatedly making the same mistakes (Graddol, 1989; Lee, Dineen and McKendree, in press). Centrally, one is faced with the problem of providing the conditions in which 'mathemagenic' ('that which gives birth to learning') discourse takes place (Laurillard, 1993).

One of the primary goals of the interactive demonstration will be to emphasise a model of vicarious learning in which the discursive competence and confidence of learners can be built-up through the use of an indexed multimedia database of Task Directed Discussions (TDDs), also see Mayes and Dineen (1999).

2 Capturing Learning Events

A set of eleven Task Directed Discussions were devised. The task basis for each discussion is the same, each having a defined and explicit goal. Also, the TDDs are used in a game like manner, were one student challenges another to describe or explain their understanding of the course notes in the way defined by the different discussion tasks. In each different TDD the idea is to focus attention onto an explicit and shared set of concepts that have been derived from the central course content (were the course content is, typically, a set of course notes, lectures and journal articles). Thus this material remains the target for each of the discussions, but the form and scope of each discussion is controlled through defined manipulations of the concepts. The Task Directed Discussions are an elicitation technique to aid the generation, control and flow of discussions. They are also used as a means to generate and contextualise discursive 'learning events', facilitating their indexing and retrieval by other learners (Dineen, Kilgour and Tobin, 1998).

We look at the problem of attempting to generate good educational discourse and consider the various roles of the environment, the participants and the decisions of the course organisers as some of the determinants of the kind of dialogue that results.

Motivated by our own experience in developing web-based CBL environments we describe and demonstrate the reasons for developing 'Dissemination', a multimedia database of discourse exchanges, as a means to promote better discussions.

3 Developing Tertiary Courseware

As stated, the development of the multimedia discourse database 'Dissemination' - including over 200 video, audio, graphic and text elements - has been driven by a wish to exploit technology as a means to promote patterns of discussion and enquiry that have proved difficult or problematic to initiate in traditional educational contexts.

The original motivation for the development of Dissemination was Mayes' (1995) model of educational courseware, the 'Groundhog Day' model, in which the roles and interaction between three types of learning technology are explained; these being Primary, Secondary and Tertiary Courseware. Primary Courseware is the technology to support the presentation of content, Secondary Courseware the technology that provides the support for the doing of learning tasks and, finally, Tertiary Courseware is the technology that supports and captures learning dialogues.

Participants will be given access to both the Dissemination system itself and an interactive multimedia presentation of the project using SMIL (the 'Synchronised Multimedia Integration Language'). The presentation and interactive systems will be of interest to a wide range of researchers, from those concerned with Computer Mediated Communication (CMC) properties to those involved with problems of Information Retrieval, but, more generally, to anyone developing or currently running a web-based distance learning course.

References

Dineen, F., Kilgour, J and Tobin, R (1998) "Some Pedagogical Characteristics of Information Retrieval Strategies." *Second Glasgow Workshop on IR and HCI*, 11 September.

Graddol, D. (1989). "Some CMC Discourse Properties and their Educational Significance." *Mindweave: Communication, Computers and Distance Education*, R. Mason and A Kaye, (Eds). Oxford: Pergamon Press.

Laurillard, D. (1993). *Rethinking University Education*, London: Routledge.

Lee, J., Dineen, F. and McKendree, J. (In press). "Supporting student discussions: it isn't just talk." To appear in *Education and Information Technology, IFIP TC3 Official Journal*, Kluwer Academic Publishers.

Mayes, J.T. (1995). "Learning Technology and Groundhog Day." Strong, W., Simpson, V.B., and Slater, D. (Eds.) Proceedings of *Hypermedia at Work: Practice and Theory in Higher Education*, Canterbury: University of Kent at Canterbury.

Mayes J.T., and Dineen, F., (accepted) "Developing Tertiary Courseware through capturing Task Directed Discussions." *Ed-Media '99*, June 19-24, Seattle, Washington USA.

Human-Computer Interaction - INTERACT'99 (Volume II)
S. Brewster, A. Cawsey & G. Cockton (Editors)
Published by The British Computer Society © IFIP TC.13, 1999

Providing Critiquing Support for Web Page Design

Pete Faraday

Microsoft
Redmond, WA 980058, USA
Email: peterfar@microsoft.com

Abstract: The paper explores how 'contact points' or co-references between text and visual media should be designed in web pages, via guidelines, to an authoring and critiquing tool.

Keywords: Web Page Design, Critiquing

1 Web Page Design

Our tool allows the designer to input a representation of the content to be presented, and then break it up into a number of 'contact points', each relating a particular visual sequence with part of the text. These are places within the text of a web page where the content needs to be coherently related with an image or animation eg for details of an object's appearance, or how to perform an action. The problem is how to help the designer decide where they should place these contact points, and which media they should use to reinforce the message in the text.

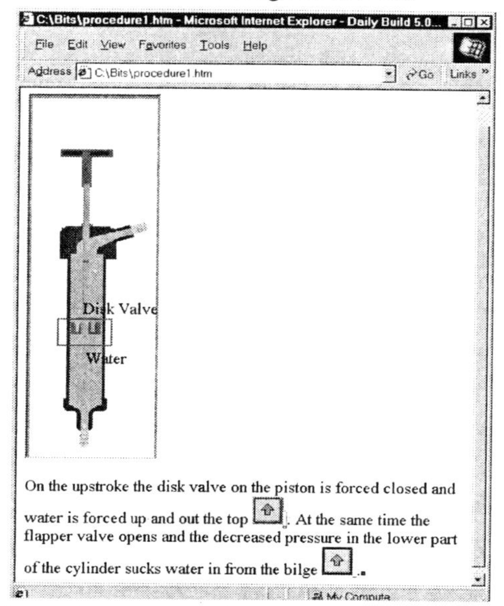

Figure 1: Contact Points in 'How a pump works'.

The tool provides the facilities of a simplified WYSIWYG word processor. When a contact point is created, a contact point 'button' (⇧) is embedded in the text. Referents, such as image components, highlights, labels, speech, and animation can then be added to the page which will be shown when the button is selected. It outputs web pages using dynamic HTML and Java Script. In figure 1, the user clicks the contact point button to reveal the animation of the handle being pulled up, with the inlet valve closing and outlet valve opening.

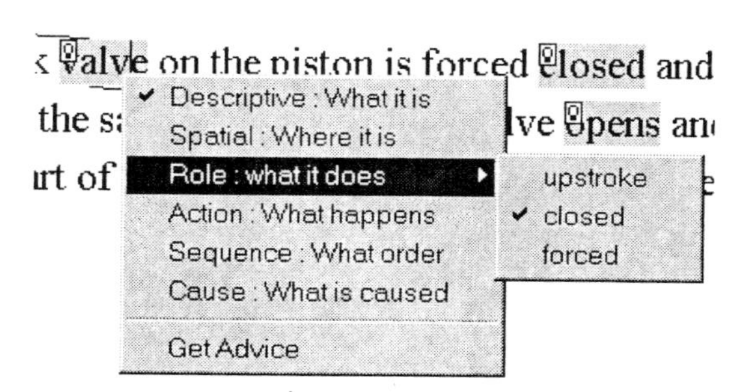

Figure 2: Marking up 'valve' with information types.

2 Critiquing the Design

How can the designer be sure that they have connected the right media to the contact point ? The tool uses Prolog to provide a critiquing facility. As

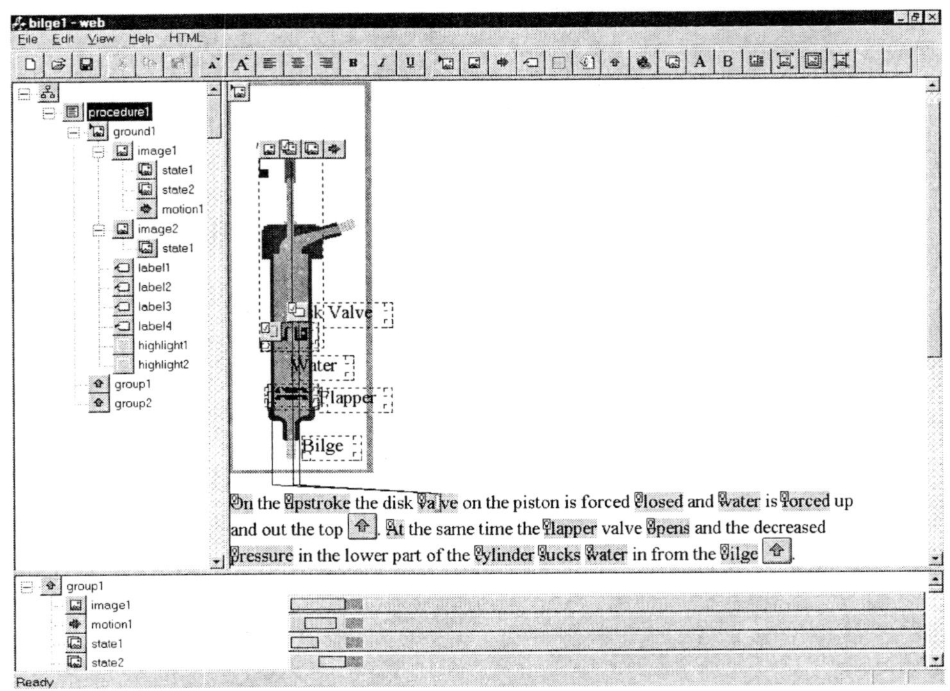

Figure 3: Screen shot of authoring tool showing design advice.

the designer sets contact points, they are able to mark up the text with the information types which they intend to communicate. The tool then provides design advice on the use of the media which the designer has entered.

The designer enters the information types which are to be communicated via a menu shown in figure 2. For the first sentence in the pump sequence, the designer marks ‘When’ as the beginning of a sequence, ‘pulled’, as an action with 'handle' as role.

The critiquer is activated when the designer sets an information type. It provides feedback on potential design problems via icons and a pop-up dialog.

a) *Critique the information type(s) associated with the contact point.* The tool analyses the information types the designer has set in the text. It scans the text from left to right and top to bottom, searching for information types and building a hierarchy from high level information giving cause & sequence, to action, role, descriptive and spatial types.

b) *Critique the contact points referents.* As each information type is placed in the hierarchy, a set of rules are applied which check the media with which it is associated. The rules provide advice for designing each media type based on Faraday & Sutcliffe (1996) :

i) For each information type the rules check that suitable media are used as referents. Eg for a role information type, the rules ensure that an image is shown and that it is labelled to provide identity; for an action they check that a change in state or location has been set.

ii) If the contact point has more than one referent the rules check that the referents can be located and identified. E.g. if a contact point refers to two or more descriptive types then a highlight should be given to separate the objects.

c) *Provide design advice.* When a problem is found icons are placed in the text and image to show that design advice is available.

Figure 3 shows an example of how the tools suggestions modify the presentation. Animation is suggested by the critique to show the process. Labels and highlights help distinguish and identify the referents.

3 Conclusion

The need for tool support is vital if guidelines are to be actually used by designers in the real world (Farday & Sutcliffe, 1996). Our current work is to allow the tool to support more diverse information types.

References

Faraday, P.M. & Sutcliffe, A.G. (1996) “An empirical study of attending and comprehending MM presentations.” *ACM Multimedia 96*, 265 - 277.

Interactions with a Three-Dimensional Sound World

Frederic Foveau and Jean-Claude Tarby

Laboratoire Trigone
Institut CUEEP
Universite des Sciences et Technologies de Lille
59655 Villeneuve d'Ascq cedex
France
Email: foveau@trigone.univ-lille1.fr, Jean-Claude.Tarby@univ-lille1.fr

Abstract: This paper presents a study about auditory metaphor benefits in computer applications. This computer science/psychology double competence research work is motivated by the fact that in real world human being extracts a lot of information from sounds, but computer environments do not exploit this ability. The main goal of the demo which is presented is to evaluate how people feel comfortable in a 3D sound interactive environment. A secondary goal is to use sounds to sensitise people to hearing, and show them how hearing process is powerful.

Keywords: three-dimensional sound, audio, interaction with sound, three-dimensional navigation.

1 Introduction

New user interfaces such CVEs[2] integrate 3D graphics and more rarely 3D sounds aiming to improve the users' work environment by recreating the real world. Research works in psychology demonstrated that sound is an efficient information support that can be applied in user interfaces (Gaver 1993). Unfortunately, those works restricted the experiences to the domain of perception (Pressing 1997) or visualisation (Tavera 1994, Bly 1994). Our work belongs to a double competence research work called MENSON[3] which merges both psychological and computer science domains. This project is an exploratory research which studies the benefits of auditory metaphors in computer applications. On the computer science side, our work fits in the use of 3D sound in domains such as CSCW[4], distance learning, and intelligent user interface, and is focused on three axes which are :

- Development of applications intending to validate concepts proposed by the psychological team;
- An object-oriented model for sound scenes (a scene may be 3D or not, and graphical or not);
- A framework which implements our object-oriented model and which is independent of the hardware.

2 3D Graphic and 3D Sound Environments

3D graphic environment like WWW3D (Snowdon 1996) became popular since a few years by software like 3D Studio or technologies such as VRML, Java 3D, or OpenGL. Only 2-3 years ago, manufacturers began to take an interest in sound with powerful sound cards integrating HRTF[5] and Dolby Prologic technologies for instance. It is too early yet to say whether 3D graphic is more interesting than 2D, and if 2D stereo sound is more efficient than 3D spatial sound. And what to say about use of 3D sound in 3D

[2] Collaborative Virtual Environment

[3] MENSON is in French "Métaphores pour ENvironnements SONores" (Metaphors for auditory environments).

[4] Computer Supported Cooperative Work

[5] Head Related Transfer Functions

environment such CVE, or in 2D environment such as Windows 98? Our object-oriented model for 3D sound scenes intends to answer to these two questions by providing all necessary parameters to reflect real world as realistic as possible. Our model focuses onto human interactions too that is how a user can interact into an auditory environment. The demo presented here is the first stage of this research.

3 Interactions in a 3D Sound Environment

The main goal of the demo is to evaluate how people feel comfortable in a 3D sound interactive environment. A secondary goal is to use sounds to sensitise people to hearing. By exploiting all natural properties of the human ear, the demo shows how hearing process is powerful in hard focusing task.

In the demo, the user is surrounded by musicians who play different instruments : drums, bass, piano, strings, keyboard. He/she can navigate between the different musicians with the numeric pad. A flat map which symbolises all the elements (sources and listener) of the scene may be displayed. The user is guided by a set of instructions which give a play aspect to the demo.

Human being extracts a lot of information from sounds, but everyone is more or less conscious of this faculty. Everybody is not able to focus on one particular sound on demand, although everybody can extract information from a global sound scene (e.g. a lively playground where children play soccer), or from a special sound immersed in a scene (e.g. a ticket machine delivering tickets in a station hall). Some people are used to focus on one sound on demand, e.g. the musicians when focusing on what is playing an instrument during a symphonic concert. Although we use this ability everyday (you can listen your wife/husband while TV is shrieking !), most of 3D audio computer environment limit to play sound and do not integrate the notion of audio focus. Therefore we propose this functionality in the demo. When pointing over a source, the corresponding sound becomes louder by applying a constant ratio.

A sub-goal of the demo is to enhance interface by providing interaction functionality. The user can change arbitrarily the place of every source of the scene, aiming to create its own disposition. So, the user plays the role of a conductor, what constitutes the main gaming task of this demo.

4 Conclusion

3D sound is the next stage in the user interfaces. "Sound should be approached as an integral thought in the design of every object" [IBM]. So, it is essential to study sound potentialities in both output (sound card's restitution power) and input (interaction level for the user). Until now we developed two test applications which intend to evaluate the users' mental image of environmental real life's sounds. Two demos are currently developed too. The demo presented aims to evaluate the user's ability to manipulate a 3D sound scene. The other demo will evaluate the user's navigation aptitude in 3D sound scenes. The results of those four experiences will be applied into CSCW, distance learning and e-business environments.

5 Acknowledgements

The study was supported by following institutions: National Center of Telecom Studies (CNET/CCETT) and the regional council of Nord-Pas-de-Calais (France) and the Science and Technology University of Lille.

References

Bly, S. "Multivariate data mapping." In *Kramer, G. (Eds.) Auditory Display : sonification, audification and auditory interfaces*. Proceedings Vol XVIII, Santa Fe Insitute, 405-416

Gaver, W. (1993) "How do we hear in the world ? Exploration of ecological acoustics." *Ecological Psychology* **5** (4), 285-313.

IBM: http://www.ibm.com/ibm/HCI/guidelines/ design/3d/ch7s5.html

Pressing, J. (1997) "Some Perspectives on Performed Sound and Music in Virtual Environments." *Presence* **6** (4), 482-503.

Snowdon, D., Fahlén, L. and Stenius M. (1996) "WWW3D: A 3D multi-user web browser", in *WebNet'96* October 16-19, San Francisco, CA, USA

Tavera, L. F. (1994) "Three dimensional sound for data presentation in a virtual reality environment." *PhD thesis*. Urbana, Illinois.

Semantic Highlighting: Enhancing Search Engine Display and Web Document Interactivity

Ali Hussam, Terry Anderson*, Nathan Jacobs, Damon Eckhoff, Ali Meryyan and Yunhai Yang

University of Missouri-Columbia
615 Locust St. Bldg.
Columbia, MO 65211 USA
Email: HussamA@missouri.edu

*School of Computing and Mathematics
University of Ulster
Co. Antrim BT37 0QB
United Kingdom
Email: TJ.Anderson@ulst.ac.uk

Abstract: Semantic Highlighting (SH) enhances the rate at which people can locate and understand web-based documents. By using visual metadata in the form of pie diagrams it allows rapid assessment of the relevance of documents located by a search engine. SH also supports highlighting and annotation of HTML pages by single or multiple users, providing a degree of web interaction not previously available.

Keywords: document, highlighting, search engine, metadata

1 Introduction

In this paper, we describe the inherent problems of locating and understanding web documents. We also discuss how SH addresses these issues.

SH mimics the paper-based practice of using highlighting pens and writing marginal notes. This form of marking is intended to convey meaning and is much more than mere presentational variation. In traditional highlighting, markings are discussed in terms of attributes, such as colour, and are used to draw attention to text or to indicate that it is important or 'clickable' (Marcus 1992 and Preece et. al. 1994). SH uses highlighting to attract the reader's attention to important text. SH, however, goes a step beyond this by attaching abstract meanings, such as 'main point', 'example', or 'repetition', to specific highlight colours.

Visual metadata in web documents is the major underpinning concept of SH. Historically, textually recorded and displayed metadata has been the dominant paradigm in document description. SH couples of the concept of presentational variation, provided by highlighting, and the information provided by metadata. Also SH allows for metadata that is not static and that may be created by the author or other users of the document.

2 Locating

Search engines often return a very large number of hits, making it difficult for users, especially novice users, to identify the most valuable URLs. The 'relevance' indications that are supposed to aid in this process are often of little assistance due to the users' lack of understanding of the relevancy ranking. This makes it difficult for the user to filter out unwanted data and focus on relevant items (Shneiderman, 1997). These relevance rankings do not provide the searcher with visual feedback to help them determine 'relevance'. In addition, since many search engines return a large number of documents it can take a long time to find the desired document. SH provides a method to quickly identify relevant documents by displaying a visual representation of the proportional distribution of hit terms within each document.

The SH Information Retrieval Engine (SHIRE) is a modified search engine, returning HTML page of hits to browsers in the usual way. SHIRE uses pie charts to provide the visual feedback stated above. For each document found, alongside a conventional text description, a pie chart is displayed in which the slices are divided to reflect the relative abundance of the search terms.

Highlighting can help emphasise and locate the important portions of text quickly and easily (Sanders, 1996). In order to deal with the difficulty of finding the location of terms within the document, SHIRE provides a legend of search terms. A colour is assigned to each term that is then used to colour the slices of the corresponding pie. SHIRE uses this colour to highlight the terms within the document to allow for rapid location of terms and concentrations of terms as the searcher is skimming the document. SHIRE uses visual metadata to aid the searcher in rapid location of web documents.

3 Understanding

Current web browsers enable users to read online or print documents. In the absence of annotation, marking and note-making tools for online documents, paper supports reading and writing tasks better (Adler et al, 98). The SH browser enhances upon traditional highlighting tools with several novel features. These features are overlapped highlighting, annotation, categorised highlights and highlight summary. This provides a degree of interaction with web documents not previously available. We see SH as an important tool for the reader as the obsolescence of books progresses (O'Hara, 97).

To support collaborative working SH provides the ability to view others' highlights and summarise them. This capability will support such scenarios as students viewing a document highlighted by their teacher. Because poor highlighting of text can override the benefits of good highlighting, such as focusing the users attention on relevant information (Baldonado and Winograd, 1998), designated experts can highlight a document for use by others. It will also allow group members to benefit from highlighting done by knowledgeable group members thereby considerably reducing time spent by the group.

4 Conclusion

Through the use of visual metadata, SH allows users to rapidly identify from pie diagrams relevant web documents, rapidly locate search terms inside an HTML document, benefit from views experts may have added to the original information, and allow users to add their own highlighting and comments to an HTML file. This form of highlighting and annotation mimics the familiar paper-based techniques but goes well beyond it. SH users can selectively view and compare contributions made by more than one "expert" or user.

References

Adler, A, *et al.* (1998) A Diary Study of Work-Related Reading: Design Implications for Digital Reading Devices, *CHI'98 Conference Proceedings on Human Factors in Computing Systems*, L.A., California, 241-248.

Baldonado, M. and Winograd, T., (1998) "Hi-Cites: Dynamically Created Citations with Active Highlighting." *CHI 98 Conference Proceedings*, ACM, L.A, U.S., 408-414.

Marcus, A. (1992) *Graphic Design for Electronic Documents and User Interfaces*, ACM Press, New York.

O'Hara, K. and Sellen, A. (1997) "A Comparison of Reading Paper and On-line Documents." *Proceedings of CHI 97, Human Factors in Computing Systems, March 22, Atlanta, Georgia*, 335-342.

Preece, J. *et al.*, (1994) *Human-Computer Interaction*, Wokingham, England: Addison-Wesley.

Sanders, S., (1996) *Highlighting and Underlining Written Textbooks* available at: http://bvsd.k12.co.us/~ssclass/highlight.html.

Shneiderman, B., (1997) "Visual Information Seeking: Advanced Interface and Web Page Design." *HCI International '97*, Tutorial, August 24, San Francisco, CA.

Examples of Semantic Highlighting are available at:

http://alih.iats.missouri.edu/sh.html

Human-Computer Interaction - INTERACT'99 (Volume II)
S. Brewster, A. Cawsey & G. Cockton (Editors)
Published by The British Computer Society © IFIP TC.13, 1999

Joovin8 - Narrative Interactions

Andrew Hutchison

The School of Design at Curtin University
GPO Box U 1987,
Perth, 6001, Western Australia
Email: thutchis@cc.curtin.edu.au

Abstract: This paper provides a background description of the 'Joovin8' project, a major interactive audio-visual narrative experience. In the 'Joovin8' experience, the user explores a 'virtual-reality' which is concerned with a difficult, emotional topic. A wide variety of developers from the media crafts have contributed to the development of the project, and significantly, none of them have a formal computer science/ HCI background. The project has many aspect of note, including the application of unconventional interaction modes for the user. In addition, the graphics, animations and sounds are unusual both in the mode of production, and their stylistic rendering. The project is an attempt to create a significant application of interactive audio-visual experience which is neither game/entertainment driven, nor productivity tool driven. It is concerned with emotional and intellectual exploration and expression. While this project has been developed to work within the existing standards for hardware and operating systems, it has ramifications for future application.

Keywords: Interaction, Interface, Virtual Reality, Virtual Environment, Expression, Multimedia Design

1 Overview

An audio-visually rich, analogue exploration, **Joovin8** is an intimate, interactive narrative that explores the fragility of existence and the opposing emotions of hope and despair, capturing sensations of rejuvenation and decay, joy and loss.

The interaction aspects of the project were born out of ideas formalised in Andrew Hutchison's Master of Design study, about alternative interaction modes for the application to narrative/expressive works. **Joovin8** has no apparent menus or buttons. Feedback is analogue, or incremental, not on/off, or 'digital'. In this way different elements are experienced, forcing scene changes and narrative development.

The expectation is that if non-productivity applications for computers are to develop beyond the level of the current state of games, then alternative modes of interaction and expression will be needed to attract different audiences. **Joovin8** is an attempt to provide an adult audience with challenging narrative experience, like a novel.

An early prototype of the **Joovin8** project was invited to exhibit in TECHNE, a national touring exhibition of new media art, (Jan 1997) and won "Winner of Best Animation" in the "Small Bytes" competition, held in association with the Summer Salon at the centre for Contemporary Photography, by Experimentia Media Arts, Melbourne. (Jan 1998)

The project has since received two separate funding grants from Arts funding organisations in Australia, both of which were won competitively. (ArtsWA- Feb 1998, Australian Film Commission- April 1998). The Australian Film Commission funding was to produce a published work of some 40 'scenes' by August 1999, representing a substantial interactive experience.

A 'beta' version of this was presented at the 'Interactive Frictions' conference at the University of Southern California (June 4-6 1999).

2 Narrative

Joovin8 is an imperative enquiry into the world of the sick, examining the catabolic process of a life that has contracted an unknown disease. It begins in a preternaturally fertile garden where a human contracts an infection. The infection spreads, eventually making the protagonist decrepit and bed ridden - death may soon follow.

Throughout the journey depravity and hope are juxtaposed against a backdrop of organic and inorganic objects, those which make up our everyday, domestic, intimate lives. How the user interacts with these objects decides how the narrative develops.

The user can weave a multitude of paths through **Joovin8's** many potential plot lines. Each level of descent to death offers the option to return to the beginning, rather than continuing down. Each of these return pathways explores the different myths about illness by evoking themes of childhood, food, reproduction, greed, care, isolation and love

Joovin8 was originally inspired by one of the artists own experience after being diagnosed with and treated for cancer. Consequently **Joovin8** is a very personal work. Everyone has, however, experienced illness to some degree, from being forced to stay home from school with a cold, to long-term hospitalisation. We become supremely aware of our mortality when we are ill, no matter how young or how unwell.

3 Style

Joovin8 employs an intentionally evocative and unusual audio/visual style. It is heavily textured with supersaturated colours and amplified sounds, conveying an enhanced reality that the ill can often experience. Imagery is constructed from real objects, but the users perception is exaggerated. Plants grow, infection visibly spreads, food decays, deliberately challenging the user toward investigation and inquiry.

It seemed wise to employ an audio-visual 'language' which is culturally non-specific. Dialogue has been avoided making **Joovin8** a work that can cross cultural boundaries, hopefully touching on concerns that are universal.

Joovin8 has no menus or buttons, challenging the existing and artificially evolved conventions of computer interaction. While precise mouse pointing and clicking may be appropriate for navigating technical information in a productivity tool such as a word processor or graphical imaging software, it seems inappropriate for a naturalistic, emotional experience, particularly involving a narrative.

4 Technical

While the audio-visual style of the Joovin8 project has reacted strongly against the 'look and feel' of most of our computer interface experiences, the technical implementation has been fully within existing software and hardware schemes. 'Multimedia' software packages such as Macromedia Director and Adobe Photoshop were used to produce an interactive which runs in common operating systems using only existing hardware, in order to ensure that the project is immediately accessible, delivered by the ubiquitous CD-ROM.

5 Conclusion

What can be learned from this project, about interactive media design and its application to narrative experience? Hopefully, the answers to this question will be forthcoming.

Explorers of the Ancient World: Egypt

Sarah Jensen, Jennifer Kelley and Allison O'Mahony

New York University
Interactive Telecommunications Program
721 Broadway, 4th floor
New York, NY 10003
USA
Email: aao202@is7.nyu.edu, jk266@is7.nyu.edu, sqj6538@is8.nyu.edu

Abstract: "Explorers of the Ancient World: Egypt" is a prototype of a collaborative educational environment exploring ancient Egyptian civilization and the crafts of archaeology and museum curation. "Explorers" is intended as a model for a series of educational simulations for use by late grade school students in the classroom environment, and will be developed in conjunction with teachers and museum educators. "Explorers of the Ancient World: Egypt" will be implemented using Microsoft's Virtual Worlds platform, currently under development at Microsoft Research, and VRML. The project will feature multi-user interaction in a 3D virtual environment with rich 2D textures. The prototype will be a simulation of the excavation of a New Kingdom royal tomb in the Valley of the Kings. The tomb will feature a wide range of objects and artifacts representative of the late 18th to early 19th dynasties in ancient Egypt.

Keywords: virtual world, education, exploration, archaeology, grade school

1 Audience

"Explorers of the Ancient World: Egypt" is intended for use by 3rd to 6th grade students (ages 9 to 12) in the classroom environment, with the assistance and supervision of an instructor. "Explorers" should serve as the interactive cornerstone of a broader, interdisciplinary unit covering the history and culture of ancient Egypt.

"Explorers" is also designed to be flexible and inclusive of educators' curriculum needs and wishes. The educator will be encouraged to adopt the role of the Field Director, overseeing the activities in the virtual world, and coordinating the way observations about artifacts are collected and shared among class members. "Explorers" collateral materials will include specific sets of artifacts with complete descriptions and background information, as well as suggested discussion topics and research exercises to help the educator implement "Explorers" in the class room.

2 Interaction in the World

Users are expected and encouraged to interact extensively with the environment, locating objects and information, and also with one another's avatars, collaborating to share observations, identify objects, put pieces of broken artifacts together, decode an important hieroglyphic text, and curate their objects into a coherent exhibit. Some of the areas that these objects/artifacts will encompass include: Commerce/ Mercantile activity, Warfare/Conquest, Science/ Engineering, Musical instruments, Agriculture, Art/ Symbolism and Religion/Ritual.

3 Construction of Identity / Avatar Selection

When the user first logs onto the Virtual Worlds program, she will select an Archaeologist Avatar, which will represent her on the dig. The basic avatars will all resemble 9-to-12 year-old kids. The user will have the opportunity to select gender, skin and hair color, and will also be able to choose from a limited assortment of other features in a kit of parts. However, since these avatars will function as archaeologists on assignment, all of the Avatars will be issued a common uniform of khaki garments and head coverings. The students will be expected to enter their own names for the Avatars, and all will be given the appellation of Doctor on the dig.

4 Explorers Headquarters

Upon completing the Avatar selection process, the users enter the Explorers HeadQuarters. Here, they will receive their assignment, instructions, and an assortment of tools to assist them with the excavation. The toolkit assigned to each group includes a Trowel, a Screen, a Brush and a Journal for recording observations. The young archaeologists will be expected to share and rotate the use of the tools to succeed at the excavation process.

An Excavation Leader Bot will greet the group in the HeadQuarters and present the group with their assignment: to join an excavation of a New Kingdom era tomb in the Valley of the Kings. The archaeologists will be told how to search for artifacts that they are expected to identify and bring back.

The young archaeologists will then be sent out on their dig. Upon completing their exploration of the excavation, and after observing and collecting objects and solving some puzzles, the archaeologists will return with their group to the Explorers HeadQuarters. They will be able to present and discuss the artifacts they have located, as well as see maps and other background information on the historical dig that uncovered the treasures of the royal tomb.

5 Excavation Site

Site: New Kingdom Tomb in the Valley of the Kings near Giza. The excavation site will simulate and be modeled after actual archaeological digs of late 18th and early 19th Dynasty tombs. Participants will be able to access a map and background information on the site at any time.

5.1 Specific Stages

1. Excavation of Buried Objects - In the first chamber of the tomb, the student archaeologists will have to unearth partially buried artifacts. If an object is improperly excavated, it will shatter and/or disappear. Students will be required to enter information and observations about the find in an online Journal before continuing.

2. Excavation and uniting of artifact fragments - Upon successful excavation of the first artifact, the student archaeologists will be granted access to a doorway that opens the route to the second chamber. In this second chamber, the archaeologists will have to locate several fragments of an artifact and unite them.

3. Location and decoding of Hieroglyph - Upon successful completion of Stage 2, the archaeologists will be granted access to a third doorway (the King's chamber chamber). In this third chamber, the archaeologists will have to find and decode a hieroglyphic message in order to open a tomb and view the mummy inside. All the archaeologists must be present in the chamber at once so their torches illuminate the walls and the hieroglyph is visible.

6 Curation of Artifacts into Exhibit

After a thorough exploration of the ancient civilization, the groups will return to the Explorers HeadQuarters and their original archaeologist avatars. Under the guidance of the teacher/Field Director, they will be expected to work together to present the artifacts in the display cases. They will be expected to work together, consult one another's archaeological journals and investigate outside sources recommended by the teacher in order to curate the artifacts in a coherent manner. In this exercise, they are encouraged to analyze findings and consider the relationship between objects.

7 Further Information

Further documentation may be found at

http://fargo.itp.tsoa.nyu.edu/~egypt

Human-Computer Interaction - INTERACT'99 (Volume II)
S. Brewster, A. Cawsey & G. Cockton (Editors)
Published by The British Computer Society © IFIP TC.13, 1999

Haptic Visualization of Spatial Structures by Low-cost Force-Feedback Devices

Anders J. Johansson and Joakim Linde

Teiresias Research Group
Lilla Södergatan 20c, 223 53
Lund
Sweden
Email: teiresias@bigfoot.com

Abstract: The potential of using force feedback technology as computer displays for blind people is big. One of the problems today is that the cost of the devices are prohibitive. We have investigated the use of low cost devices, primarily designed for games, as haptic visualization tools. We have designed applications around a framework, which take advantage of the layered architecture of the low cost devices, making it possible to run the applications on an ordinary home computer. We have tested two kinds of applications, one being a simple computer game with only a haptic interface, and the other a haptic representation of floorplans and maps. Results of the tests have shown that the simpler devices are useful for these tasks. This despite the lower maximum force capability and the reduced number of degrees of freedom in comparison with available high end systems.

Keywords: Force Feedback, Haptic Interface, Visualization, Tactile Map

1 Introduction

The use of force feed back (FF) devices for interfacing computers with visually handicapped people is a fairly new, but active research area (Sjöström et. al. 1999). Computerized tactile interfaces for blind people have traditionally consisted of pin-arrays which have been capable of presenting symbols according to the Braille system. Today's graphical user interfaces makes it more difficult to use text-based systems for translating the information presented by the system to a form understandable by a person lacking sight. The traditional applications for force feedback technology is, among others, medical training in virtual reality environments, design systems and in the entertainment business (Burdea 1997). But it has also been used as an added dimension to graphical displays, designated as computer haptics (Srinivasan et. al. 1997). We have investigated the use of commercial low-cost force feedback devices, designed for entertainment use, in the more complex application of presenting spatial relationships and properties of objects.

2 The Labyrinth Application

We have designed a couple of research applications in order to test the use of the low-cost FF devices in visualization of spatial objects. We have mainly been evaluating two kinds of applications: simple computer games with purely haptic interfaces, and representation of maps and floorplans. The applications are all running on a standard PC with Windows 95. No high demands are put on either processor speed, memory or additional hardware. The only necessary additional equipment is a sound card and the FF joystick. The programming interface makes use of haptic objects, described by their type and coordinates. It is therefore easy to translate a description of a scene to a representation readable by our applications. This representation is then used by the application to look up which objects are affecting the user according to the current position of the handle. The relevant objects are then sent to the FF device, which calculates the exact instantaneous forces and steer the actuators coupled to the handle accordingly.

2.1 Labyrinth

The labyrinth application is a simple game, played with a purely haptic interface. The objective of the game is to find your way from the start to the goal in a maze. All interaction with the program is done true the FF joystick. By pressing a button on the joystick a maze is chosen. Gripping the handle starts the game, and you find your way out by feeling the walls around you with the joystick. All output of information to the player is done by FF. When the player grips the handle, this is detected by the application by an optical detector, and the handle is pushed by the actuators to the correct start position for the maze. The maze is then enforced by applying forces to the handle if the player is trying to go through a wall. The maze is drawn in the absolute space of the joystick. For example, one maze have the start position in the middle down position, and your objective is to find the exit in the upper left position of the joysticks movement range. You have to feel your way around the maze by following the walls. When the goal is found, a vibration is applied to the handle as a signal to the player. The program exists in two versions, one with and one without a real-time graphical representation of the maze traversed. The mazes that you can chose between are a mix between simple custom drawn mazes and depictions of historical mazes, for instance the well known maze of Troy, found as stone circles at numerous locations around the Baltic sea.

2.2 Map

The Map application is implemented in the same framework as the labyrinth game. It gives a spatial representation of the indoor layout of a building, or the map of a town. By enforcing the walls, the user can wander around inside a house, and find out the layout of rooms and hallways. In the same way he can get an understanding of the layout of a town. The big advantage of using this compared with classical tactile maps are that the information is digital, and maps are thus easily stored and distributed.

3 Conclusion

The simple force feedback devises are useful not only in game applications but also as tools for visualization. Tests both with games and map applications have shown good results. This is especially interesting in the context of visually impaired people, for whom a cheap visualization system coupled to a computer would greatly enhance the usability of the computer. It is a good complement to the Braille displays and screen readers in use today. The big advantage over the research grade systems is the price of the devices, and the architecture of the systems which use a co-processor in the device. This as it makes it possible to use a simpler, and thus cheaper, host computer, which makes the whole system possible to be bought by individuals already today.

4 Acknowledgements

We would like to thank Microsoft and Logitech for supplying us with the hardware necessary for our experiments, and Certec, Lund University, of kindly lending us space, support and computer resources.

References

Burdea G. C. (1996) Force and Touch Feedback for Virtual Reality, Jogn Wiley and sons.

Sjöström, C., Rassmus-Gröhn, K."The sense of touch provides new computer interaction techniques for disabled people", Technology and Disability, Elsevier Science (in press)

Srinivasan M. A., Basdogan (1997) C."Haptics in Vrtual Environments: Taxanomy, Research Status and Challenges", Comput. & Graphics, Vol. 21,No. 4, pp. 393-404.

Human-Computer Interaction - INTERACT'99 (Volume II)
S. Brewster, A. Cawsey & G. Cockton (Editors)
Published by The British Computer Society © IFIP TC.13, 1999

Adding Tactile Feedback to the Trackpoint: A Demonstration of Tractile

Paul P. Maglio, Shumin Zhai, Christopher S. Campbell
Kim W. May and Barton A. Smith

IBM Almaden Research Center
650 Harry Rd.
San Jose, California, USA
Email: {pmaglio, zhai, ccampbel, kim, basmith} @almaden.ibm.com

1 Introduction

This demonstration supplements our companion paper "What you feel must be what you see: Adding tactile feedback to the Trackpoint" (Campbell, Zhai, Kim, Maglio, 1999). We intend to give conference attendees first hand experience with tactile feedback provided through the IBM Trackpoint, which a small in-keyboard isometric input device. We call our tactilely enhanced Trackpoint, *Tractile*. Though, various force feedback or tactile devices have recently been developed, Tractile is unique in that it is very small yet can provide useful tactile information.

In addition to the tractile device itself, we demonstrate two applications of tactile feedback. One is steering through tunnels, which is similar to menu selection, and the other is "Press-to-Select", which enables users to press the Trackpoint cap as a button.

2 Tractile Device

The design goal for the Tractile device is to maintain the very compact size and low power consumption of the IBM Trackpoint while adding tactile vibration. The result is a device that appears as a normal Trackpoint (Figure 1) and is suitable for laptop computers but that contains several internal modifications. One modification is the inclusion of a cylindrical coil at the base of the actuator. When current is passed though the coil, the resulting magnetic field forces a ferromagnetic slug upward toward the actuator tip. The movement of the slug

Figure 1: IBM Trackpoint with tactile feedback.

hitting the actuator tip feels like a tap even through the plastic cap that covers the actuator post. As shown in Figure 2, the plastic cap is attached to the post of the pointing device. The coil wrapped around the bottom of the sensor has a resistance of 70 ohms. The ferromagnetic slug is inserted into the cylinder with the correct polarity. A rubber cap is attached to the top of the cylinder to retain the ferromagnetic slug. The coil is excited by external electronics to apply a 10ms pulse at 5volts/100ma. Thus, a magnetic field repels the slug from the coil in an upward motion, striking the underside of the top rubber cap, which is what the user feels as tactile feedback. The maximum pulse rate of the device without significant loss of amplitude is 30Hz.

Movements in the actuator post are registered by the force sensor and communicated through the PS/2 port. Tactile events are monitored by a program and communicated to the device through the serial port. Thus, when the pointer hits a "bump" on the screen, the program can send a signal to the Tractile device. In this way a program can control both when to pulse and how often.

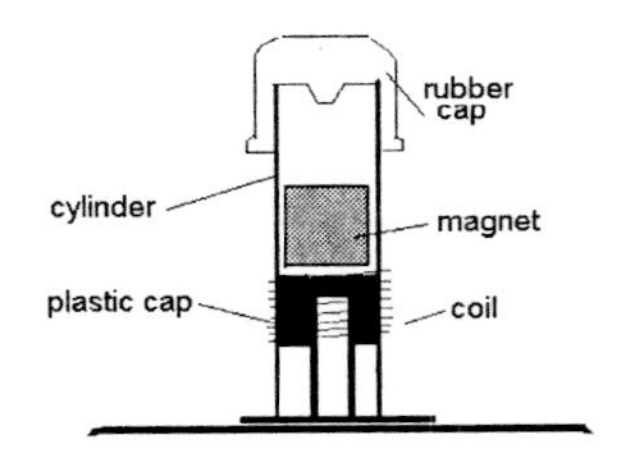

Figure 2: Schematic of the Tractile device.

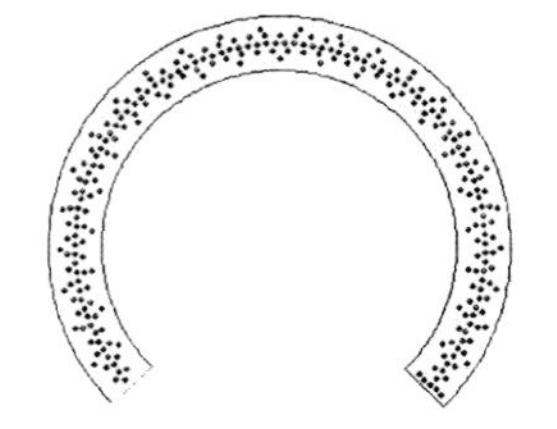

Figure 3: Tunnel Steering Task

3 Steering Demonstration

Being able to feel the "texture" of a GUI interface should enrich user experience and improve interaction performance, as an additional source of information about the location of the pointer can be provided. However, determining where and how textures can be effectively applied present a challenge. We have studied just this issue in steering tasks. Participants can steer the mouse cursor through a tunnel (Figure 3), which is similar to navigating through menus.

There are many ways to provide texture in the tunnel to help users. In our demonstration, participants will experience four feedback conditions. First is no tactile feedback, as a control condition. Second, as shown in Figure 3, the participant sees and feels more bumps toward the center of the tunnel. The user can see and feel the cursor deviation from the center of the tunnel by the frequency of bumps. Third, the user can both see and feel the deviation from the tunnel center, but what is felt is different from what is seen. Fourth, a solid line of bumps is placed on each side of the tunnel, similar to Botts dots on California freeways.

The rational and experimental results of these conditions can be found in our companion paper. The central conclusion, however, can be simply summarized as "What you feel must be what you see". The tactile information is most powerful when it is in concert with the visual information.

4 Selection Demonstration

When using the Trackpoint, many novice users attempt to press on the Trackpoint cap itself, rather than the buttons, to select a GUI object. To enable this, the *Press-to-Select* feature has been added to the Trackpoint in recent IBM Thinkpad models, such as the 600 and 770. With Press-to-Select, icons, windows, and files can be selected, picked-up, dragged, dropped, and double clicked by pressing down on the Trackpoint cap. However, the lack of feeling that the button has been pressed – as is provided by a normal mouse button – makes the Press-to-Select feature seem less appealing. This demonstration shows the effect of adding tactile feedback to Press-to-Select. In this case, the Tractile device provides tactile feedback for button-down and button-up events when the user makes selections through Press-to-Select.

Overall, our demonstrations enable participants to examine how tactile feedback can be added to the existing Windows visual interface, for instance, by adding tactile feedback operations for selecting and releasing desktop objects. They also enable users to experience the benefit of consonant visual and tactile information, and to consider how visual interfaces might be designed to better incorporate tactile feedback.

References

Campbell, C. S., Zhai, S., May, K. W., & Maglio, P. P. (1999). What you feel must be what you see: Adding tactile feedback to the Trackpoint. In *Proceedings of INTERACT '99*.

Human-Computer Interaction - INTERACT'99 (Volume II)
S. Brewster, A. Cawsey & G. Cockton (Editors)
Published by The British Computer Society © IFIP TC.13, 1999

Designing for Navigation in Virtual Reality

David Modjeska

Department of Informatics
Umeå University
901 87 Umeå
Sweden
Email: dmjeska@informatik.umu.se

Abstract: Navigational interaction is central to information exploration in electronic worlds. Three new virtual worlds were developed to evaluate spatial and textual representations of information structure. These interfaces explore strategies for interaction design in large-scale virtual environments. Participants will interactively experience one or more of these interfaces, navigating in a textual world, an object world, and a hybrid world.

Keywords: virtual reality, wayfinding, multimodality, design

1 Introduction

Navigation in virtual worlds is a relatively new phenomenon. Related real-world research comes from anthropology, psychology, and urban design (Lynch, 1960; Passini, 1984); related electronic-world research comes mainly from hypermedia (McKnight *et al.*, 1991). Since information domains are abstract, a tension arises between semantic and physical structures, when the latter serve to represent the former. Thus designers of virtual worlds should understand the tradeoffs between types of structure, particularly for the important task of user navigation.

In assessing design tradeoffs between textual and spatial representations of information structure, a key issue is the perceptions of users and designers. It is important for research to establish some reference points in the design space, where people can agree on the relative importance of specific representations. Interactive experience in virtual environments is a prerequisite for resolving these issues. Such experience can be both instructive and enjoyable. (Related research includes Darken & Sibert, 1996; Dieberger, 1995; and Rennison, 1994.).

2 Current Research

Research is being conducted in this area by the Department of Informatics at Umeå University (Waterworth, 1996). This work explores tradeoffs between textual and spatial representations of information structure in virtual worlds. Specifically, how do users perceive and learn such representations in VR? What are the implications for navigation and browsing, as well as design in general? An HCI experiment was recently conducted on these issues.

The experiment was designed for desktop VR. Three worlds were developed, reflecting key points on a design continuum between textual and spatial representations. All worlds present the same data, which has general interest, rich details, and computational tractability. 1500 items are included. The designs range from a virtual city landscape to a textual hierarchy browser. Each world engages the user in a unique way, as reflected in judgements of presence, ease of use, preference, and world size, but not by success rates in finding hidden items. Almost all subjects reported strong interest and engagement, during complex tasks in information exploration.

3 The Interactive Experience

Participants will experience these interfaces, navigating around one or more of the textual, object, and hybrid worlds. The object world is an urbanized landscape, with strong spatial and weak textual features (Fig. 1). Like a noon landscape, this world has strong color and lighting cues. The hybrid world is similar, but with weaker spatial and stronger textual elements (Fig. 2). Like a dusk landscape, this world offers weak color and lighting cues. The textual world has weak spatial and strong textual features (Fig. 3). Like a night city, this world has abstract space, with relative but not absolute position.

The virtual worlds were constructed in VRML 2.0, on the basis of a filtered subset of WWW structure. Worlds were algorithmically generated by C++ software, with input from ASCII data in a hierarchical format. The worlds are best viewed with the CosmoPlayer 2.1 plug-in to a Web browser on Windows NT or an SGI system. A good 3D graphics card facilitates efficient and enjoyable navigation.

Figure 1: A view of Color World.

Figure 2: A view of Gray World.

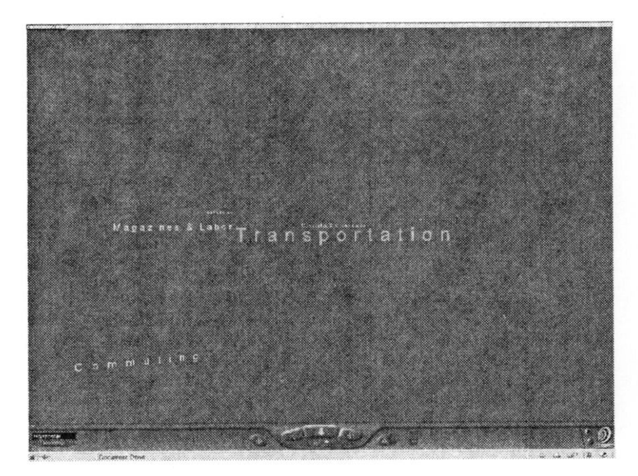

Figure 3: A view of Text World.

References

Darken, R. P. and Sibert, J. L. (1996). "Wayfinding Strategies and Behaviors in Large Virtual Worlds." *Human Factors in Computing Systems: CHI '96 Conference*. ACM, New York..

Dieberger, A. (1995). "Providing Spatial Navigation for the World Wide Web." *Spatial Information Theory: COSIT '95 Conference*. Springer, Berlin.

Lynch, K. (1960). *The Image of the City*. MIT Press, Cambridge, Massachusetts.

McKnight, C., Dillon, A., and Richardson, J. (1991). *Hypertext in Context*. Cambridge University Press, Cambridge, England.

Passini, R. *Wayfinding in Architecture (1984)*. Van Nostrand Reinhold, New York.

Rennison, E. (1994). "Galaxy of News: An Approach to Visualizing and Understanding Expansive News Landscapes." *User Interface Software & Technology: UIST '94 Symposium*. ACM Press, New York.

Waterworth, J. A. (1996). "A pattern of islands: exploring public information space in a private vehicle." *Multimedia, Hypermedia and Virtual Reality: Models, Systems, and Applications*. Springer-Verlag, Berlin.

Human-Computer Interaction - INTERACT'99 (Volume II)
S. Brewster, A. Cawsey & G. Cockton (Editors)
Published by The British Computer Society © IFIP TC.13, 1999

Haptic Visualisation

Ian Oakley, Stephen Brewster, Aidan Glendye and Michelle M. Masters

Glasgow Interactive Systems Group
Department of Computing Science
University of Glasgow, Glasgow, UK
Email: stephen@dcs.gla.ac.uk

Abstract: This paper describes two exploratory and ongoing projects in haptic, or tactile, visualisation. The first is a study evaluating the performance of vet students exposed to virtual reality (VR) training materials. The second details work investigating the haptic rendering of mathematical data in the form of graphs to facilitate access by blind users. Both of these areas stand to benefit greatly through VR. If vet students can be trained virtually then the inherent dangers to the animals reserved for training purposes can be radically reduced; with a sufficiently advanced rendering engine a blind user could gain access to graphically presented information previously unavailable to them.

Keywords: Haptic, touch, blind users, vets, multi-modal interaction, visualization, virtual reality, training.

1 Haptic Technology

The technology to feel virtual objects at a high fidelity is just becoming available. In the work described here a PHANToM (figure 1) is used to instantiate virtual objects. This is a very high resolution, 6 degrees of freedom device, consisting of a motor controlled jointed arm. Users operate the device by placing their finger in a thimble at the tip of the device. This affords a very natural interaction with the objects.

Figure 1: The PHANToM from SensAble Technologies.

2 Veterinary Training

The most significant problems with training vets are the risks conferred to their initial patients. Trauma, stress and injury can all be caused by unskilled internal examinations. Furthermore, in the course of training vets there is no guarantee that they will be exposed to all relevant diseases or symptoms – suitable animals may not be available. Finally, there are financial constraints as to the number of animals that can be maintained for training purposes. This can lead to students receiving very limited practical training and also to animals being subjected to significant numbers of examinations. These problems can all be solved through the use of VR and haptics. If haptic training can augment a large percentage of the practical work then the danger to animals can be diminished, many symptoms can be simulated in software and the amount of available practical work can be increased.

To provide these solutions we, in conjunction with the Glasgow Veterinary School, have produced models that simulate equine examinations (Brewster et al, 1999). Figure 2 shows a model of two horse ovaries. These haptic models have been developed using an iterative, participatory approach. Prototypes were built and then subject to continual refinement via evaluation by expert vet users. Evaluation of these models is now taking place through the comparison of subjects exposed to them with subjects exposed to more traditional, animal based, training mechanisms.

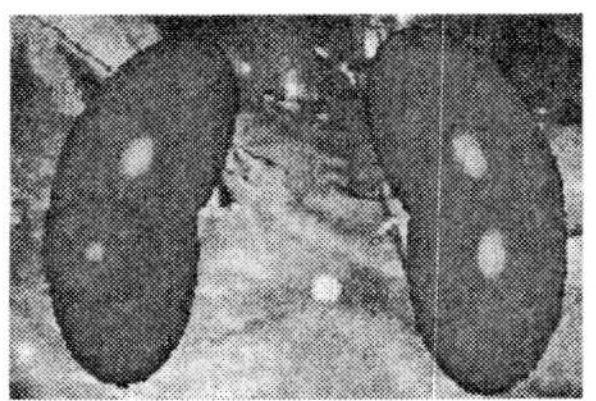

Figure 2: Horse ovaries.

3 Visualisation

Visualisation is the art of presenting complex information in such a way that it is simple to understand. A simple example is a graph. It is a very basic construct, yet contains a large quantity of information that is difficult to describe otherwise.

Computer based visualization techniques are now becoming highly advanced but they primarily rely on very high-resolution displays to present detailed graphical information. Visually impaired users have little access to the information presented in these systems (Edwards, 1995). Current visualization techniques for displaying information non-visually rely on synthetic speech and Braille. In both cases words or digits are presented sequentially. This is a poor mechanism for visualization. Consider a sighted person reading a matrix of numbers. He/she could immediately make certain inferences about the data, for instance that larger numbers were present at the right hand side. However a blind user experiencing this information sequentially would find it hard to make these same inferences. The situation becomes worse with any visualization techniques that rely on graphically represented data. For instance graphs, or complex three-dimensional plots.

Haptic technology has the potential to solve some of these problems. Our current work (Brewster & Pengelly, 1998) is investigating the haptic rendering of graphs. An example is pictured in Figure 3. In this model the user is confined to a small haptic workspace which restricts movements to the interesting areas of the graph. The information pertaining to the graph is presented by extruding it from a flat wall at the back of the workspace. The grid lines of the graph are raised slightly so that they can be felt but not enough to provide any significant resistance. The axes of the graph are large quarter cylinders. The lines of the graph itself are half cylinders.

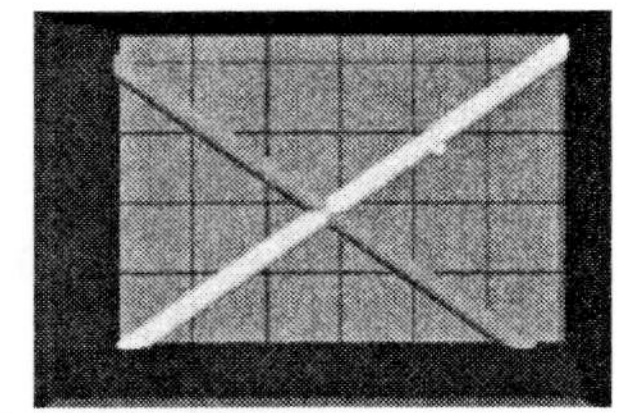

Figure 3: Haptic graph.

Initial evaluation of haptic graphs and bar charts has taken place. Subjects in this evaluation were sighted but could not see the graphical representation. Sighted users were used because our supply of blind users is limited. It is hoped that we can resolve the main problems with the models in these tests. Future evaluations will involve blind subjects.

Assessment of these models came in the form of questionnaires. Questions asked ranged from high level queries about the location of the maximum point on a graph to very low level. For instance questions were asked about whether gaps should be present in between the bars in a bar chart, or on the helpfulness of the grid lines presented.

This information has proven invaluable to our research effort. We are now incorporating these results into the next generation of haptic models. Work on these revised models will use more quantitative measures to fully evaluate our designs.

References

Brewster, S.A. and Pengelly, H. (1998) "Visual impairment, virtual reality and visualisation." *Proceedings of the First International Workshop on Usability Evaluation for Virtual Environments*, British Computer Society, 24-28.

Brewster, S.A., Montgomery Masters, M., Glendye, A., Kritz, N. and Reid, S. (1999) "Haptic feedback in the training of veterinary students." Accepted for *EdMedia'99*.

Edwards, A.D.N., Ed. (1995) *Extra-Ordinary Human-Computer Interaction.* Cambridge University Press, Cambridge, UK.

Human-Computer Interaction - INTERACT'99 (Volume II)
S. Brewster, A. Cawsey & G. Cockton (Editors)
Published by The British Computer Society © IFIP TC.13, 1999

How a Professional Firm Uses an Interactive Internet Game to Talk to Students

Cathrine Strand, Tone Pettersen and Helge Storøy

Andersen Consulting
Drammensveien 165, P.O. Box 228 Skøyen
0212 Oslo
Norway
Email: cathrine.strand@ac.com

Abstract: An interactive Internet game has been used by a professional firm for technical profiling and recruiting. Shockwave, ASP, and HTML created a consistent interface with documented student appeal.

Keywords: Interactive game, Usability, Graphical User Interface, Shockwave

1 Introduction

In March 1999, Andersen Consulting, Norway, launched an Internet game, "Mindstars". The game was directed at students at technological studies. The purpose of the game was to present Andersen Consulting as a potential future place of employment. By using a game that is consistent and has a functional graphic user interface, the students were left with a positive impression of the company. Moreover, this is a new and different way to get in contact with students. "Mindstars" is a proficiency game, consisting of tasks presented through text and visual presentations. The tasks of the game were divided into eight categories, which deal with a variety of themes, - from eCommerce and Star Wars, to games such as "Asteroids". The overall goal of the game is to identify a figure among the stars in the large control seen in Figure 1.

2 Communication Channels

Although we wanted to address one specific target group, we chose to place the game on the Internet. One of the things that distinguish "Mindstars" from other Internet games, is the limited time it was available. The game was marketed for the target group, and then removed from the Internet after a month. This gave the players something new and exciting, which was removed before they lost interest. Furthermore, the players could see the finals and distribution of prizes draw nearer, and the limited time therefore made the game more appealing.

In order to play the game, one must register at a login page using an e-mail address and some demographic data. The interaction with the players (such as password for the game, information about Andersen Consulting career opportunities, feedback from players etc.) was based on this e-mail channel, and messages were adapted for different segments of the players. This possibility for tailoring messages to different segments is a large benefit of this kind of interaction with students, both for profiling and recruiting.

3 Technology

"Mindstars" has been produced by means of Macromedia Shockwave and Java applets, and these have been linked through HTML and Active Server Pages. Macromedia Shockwave is a well-adapted tool for making graphic applications. Files containing complex vector based animation are easily made. These files are small, and thereby easy to load from the Internet. Moreover, Shockwave can, by using Macromedia Generator, interact with other programs. Text can be fetched from for example an ASP-file and added to the graphic. This means that both text and pictures are presented graphically. This gave the different pages in the game a similar graphic profile, even though different technology has been used.

4 User Interface

For the game to present Andersen Consulting in a positive way, the graphic user interface had to be made in a professional manner. To do this, we tried to give the game a consistent profile – it has for example only a limited number of game pages. The game has only two main pages - one for logging in and one for playing. When choosing a category, a new window will appear. This window will, by using similar colours and structure, indicate that it belongs to the master window. Thus, the player will not feel as if he is entering an entirely new page every time he opens a new category. Also, we saw it as important to present a clear and simple graphic presentation, which would make the player want to proceed with the game.

5 Results

As the game was launched, we hoped to attract the interest of about 1000 players. After two weeks, this goal had already been fulfilled. In total, 1600 people registered as players. This suggests that we have managed to produce an application, which appeals to the target group. We have today a database consisting of several potential candidates for positions in Andersen Consulting. A user survey showed positive feedback regarding this way of profiling a company. It is important to adopt new methods that can arouse the interest of young people, and we believe this game is a good alternative to the traditional methods of marketing, such as brochures and advertising.

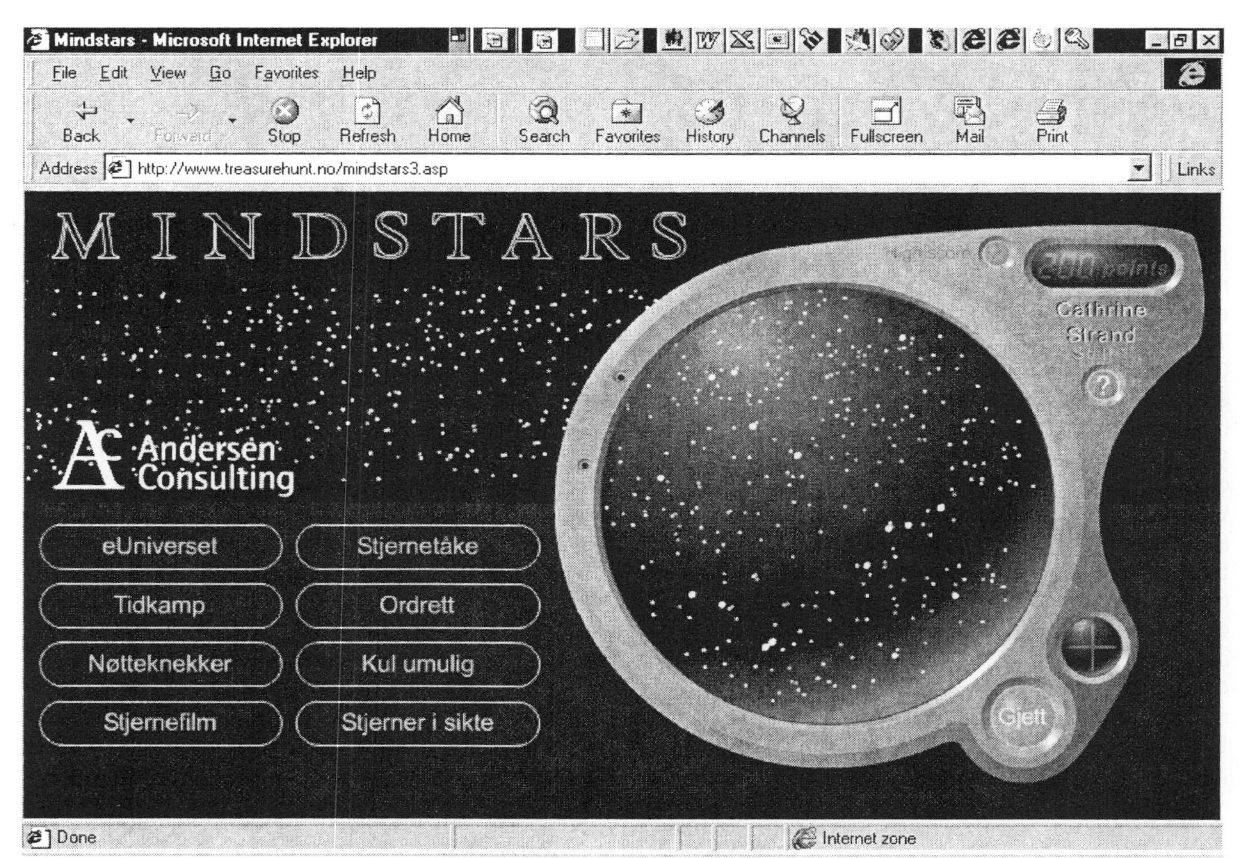

Figure 1: The main game page of "Mindstars" showing the main control in which a star sign is to be identified, and the eight categories with "sub-games" that, when solved, gradually reveals the star sign.

Mutator for the Blind Musician

Stephen Todd

IBM United Kingdom Laboratories
Hursley Park
Winchester
Hants
Email: stephen_todd@uk.ibm.com

Abstract: This note describes a variant on the Mutator evolutionary user interface suitable for musical applications. The interaction uses simple keystrokes for judgement of sounds controlled by Mutator. It does not require the user to look at a computer screen, thus removing the artistically confusing mind switch between looking and listening.

Keywords: HCI, music, non-GUI, evolution

1 Introduction

Mutator (Todd and Latham 1990) (Todd and Latham 1992) was the first of several programs, including (Sims 1991), that apply user controlled evolution as a human computer interaction technique. The concepts were derived from *The Blind Watchmaker* (Dawkins 1986). The principal is to present the user with a set of alternatives. The user selects the best, which are used by Mutator to breed a further set of alternatives. Thus the user guides Mutator to a final 'best' solution.

The important feature of Mutator is that the user makes subjective judgements. Many of the technical aspects of using a computer are removed, so a computer artist concentrates on art, not technology. Mutator can be applied in many areas from what if spreadsheets to massage machines: wherever an end user makes judgements that lead to a subject 'best' that cannot be mathematically defined.

Music is a natural area to apply evolutionary interfaces. The composer Michel Redolfi used Mutator at a series of concerts (MANCAT festival in Nice, 1997). Others have tried similar experiments (Kurt Thywissen, private communication). However, selecting from images on a screen does not provide a natural interaction technique for musicians. The mind must switch between listening to and evaluating the sounds, and expressing the evaluation via a graphical user interface.

In this interactive experience the musician uses a portion of the keyboard for expressing judgements. The note is in three sections: applications of Mutator to music, the Mutator interface for musicians, and implementation details of the interface.

2 Mutating Music

Mutation can be used at different granularities for sound and music. At the finest granularity it controls the sound of each note; mutated parameters control details such as the attack, decay, vibrato and spectral content. At the next level Mutator controls a 'texture' of notes fired as a result of a single 'input' note; the notes may fire as a chord or spread as a motif. For both these levels, the source of input notes may be the musician at a keyboard, or a midi file.

At a wider granularity Mutator controls continuous algorithmically generated music (as generated by Koan Pro). Parameters include the density of notes, the rhythmic regularity and pattern, and the degree of harmonisation or discord. The musician does not typically provide any note input to this process.

Mutator is not so suitable for larger granularity

music control, such as complete pieces. The time taken to listen to each suggestion limits the number of judgements and thus the effect of evolution.

3 Musician Interface

The musician interface to Mutator eliminates the need to use the GUI. Basically the GUI provides two features: decision of the object to judge, and recording the judgement.

In the musician interface, Matator automatically makes the decision of which sound to play. Sounds must be heard and judged serially. Mutator adds sounds judged as good to the pool of potential parent sounds, and rejects ones judged as poor.

The judgement is made by the use of a keyboard. Where the musician is already providing note input via a music keyboard, Mutator reserves a region of this keyboard for judgements, typically, the bottom half an octave or so. The lowest note signifies 'worst', and the highest note in the region 'best'. Where the note input is being provided from a midi file, the computer keyboard may be more suitable for selection input. 0 (bad), 1 (ok), 2 (good) and 3 (excellent) in the numeric keypad are convenient.

Once the user has judged one sound, Mutator switches to another one. This may be a sound already in the pool, or a new sound generated from parents in the pool. As evolution occurs the quality of sounds in the pool improves. The user always makes judgement relative to other recently heard sounds. Thus a sound that is judged good when it is first introduced may well be judged bad at a later stage when the competition has improved.

The need for serial judgement is an inherent limitation to music mutation. The non-GUI interaction imposes additional limitations. The user cannot explicitly revisit a particular sound for comparison. Advanced Mutation features are lost. For example the user cannot breed for different desired properties in different windows, and then crossbreed the result. The GUI remains available for these advanced interactions.

4 Implementation

The implementation of the interface is fairly straightforward. The most interesting aspect is deciding the best size for the pool and the revisiting pattern for sounds in the pool.

Informal experiments (practical and theoretical) on the standard GUI version of Mutator indicate that twelve is a good population size, with the best four being carried over as parents for the next generation. Even though Mutator permits cross-breeding between more than two parents, we have found it best to limit each child to two parents chosen from the four.

The 'generation' concept is less clear with the serial interface. There is no point in making a complete generation of objects that cannot be immediately presented for judgement. It is better to generate objects on demand, taking advantage of all the latest judgements.

Mutator typically keeps a pool of 6 potential parents. Parents fall from the pool when they are judged poor in comparison with the rest of the pool. This makes space for new objects to be created, judged and potentially become new parents.

5 Conclusion

We have described a variation on the Mutator process that replaces its standard GUI interface with an interface that can be used 'blind'. This interface is suitable for the Mutation of musical sounds. The interface is limited, but permits a musician to use Mutation techniques without the distraction of switching between listening and looking.

References

Dawkins, R (1986) *The Blind Watchmaker*, Longmans Scientific and Technical

Sims, K (1991) "Artificial Evolution for Computer Graphics." *ACM Siggraph Conference Proceedings, Computer* Graphics, **25(4)** 319-328.

Todd, S and Latham, W (1990) "Mutator, a subjective human interface for evolution of computer sculptures", IBM UKSC Report 248.

Todd, S and Latham, W (1992) *Evolutionary Art and Computers*, Academic Press, London.

Part Seven

Tutorials

Human-Computer Interaction - INTERACT'99 (Volume II)
S. Brewster, A. Cawsey & G. Cockton (Editors)

Designing Movement in Interactive Multimedia: Making it Meaningful

Michelle Bacigalupi

Email: mbacigal@us.oracle.com

Abstract: This tutorial taught participants how to discuss, design, and analyze the creation of movement in multimedia. The material in this tutorial showed how, by examining what psychologists know about movement perception and by exploring the ways movement is used by visual artists, dancers and other non-verbal communicators, we can learn to develop a design vocabulary that aids in creating communicative and purposeful movement in interactive software. The scope of this tutorial included demonstrations and examples, a design vocabulary for identifying movement qualities and their communicative capabilities, and structured movement and prototyping exercises.

Keywords: interaction design, multimedia, formal movement qualities, expressive movement qualities, movement design vocabulary

1 Introduction

The world is full of movement! As human beings we use movement to help us interpret what is going on. In many of today's interfaces movement is largely arbitrary, often annoying, and provides little information. Psychologists demonstrated that we are wired physiologically to notice movement, particularly in our peripheral vision. Since we are visually drawn to movement, how can interaction designers think about it in a way that communicates effectively? This may in actuality involve using very subtle movements. How can we take advantage of the rich knowledge people possess about understanding movement, based on their interactions in the real world, to build interfaces that take these experiences into account? How can we add movement to enhance on-line cues? Interaction software designers have drawn heavily from graphic design, incorporating and adapting for the computer screen principles of color, layout, and typography to communicate more effectively. Yet interactive software is dynamic! Unfortunately, most of today's interfaces remain static, with either limited or irrelevant use of movement. In this tutorial we viewed and discussed whether the movement is used effectively and whether it was relevant to the information presented. We explored these ideas through developing a movement design vocabulary for interactive multimedia.

I demonstrated how interaction designers can draw from the studies of movement in graphic design, fine art, and psychology. Based on human perception, visual designers and artists have quantified forms with respect to line direction. For example, on the surface of the page or canvas a horizontal line implies stability whereas a diagonal line provides greater dynamic movement. Formalization of perspective in art added the ability to imply dynamic movement in 3-dimensional space within the context of static media.

From previous experiments with light and form that helped artists to develop ways to imply movement in static media to the kinetic sculptures of Calder, we explored how those tricks, relevant to interaction design, can be incorporated to imply movement. For example, many painters developed ways of communicating movement in both static and kinetic compositions. Formalists such as Klee and Kandinsky discussed how the shape or form of a static image effects its ability to communicate movement to the viewer. In Klee's Pedagogical Sketchbook he demonstrated how a line made of diagonals with sharp turns appears static. In comparison, if the same line is made round, a greater impression of fluid movement is communicated to the viewer. Later formalists such as Kepes and Moholy-Nage built on these concepts. They argued that communication increases when actual movement is initiated. Designers who have studied Gestalt psychology examined the role of past experience on the viewer's interpretation of images. We can learn from Amheim's experiments with visual illusions how the mind makes sense of visual images.

Dancers have also learned to take advantage of the intuitive understanding of movement to communicate ideas and emotions. Through observations of body rhythms and movement styles in everyday life, great choreographers such as Martha Graham captured and expanded on the human experience in their dances. Her work, through extremes in body tension, communicates body rhythms reflective of extreme emotional qualities. The innovative Broadway choreography of Jerome Robbins in "West Side Story" and of Anes de Mille in "Oklahoma," offers many excellent examples (albeit American) of every day activity translated into dance. These movements, extrapolated from the real world were discussed in the tutorial in the Effort/Shape terms of weight, time, space, and flow.

We also took a look at Sign language as a powerful and sophisticated form of communication. Similar to dance, it uses gestures reflective of the human experience in daily life. Further, it too depends on subtle tonalities that effect communication. For example, a conversation in sign language describing a sunset would have very different gestural qualities than one describing a fire burning down an apartment complex in the very early morning hours.

2 Movement Qualities

We defined basic qualities of movement as: rhythm, tempo, sequence, and direction. Just as notes on a musical scale, they form building blocks for analyzing movement. In music each composition has a range of possible qualities of expression: thus music can be played staccato (texture/style) or allegro (tempo), movement can also have qualities of eloquence and articulation. These expessive movement qualities, woven together with formal movement qualities, create a rich and complex fabric of communication through movement.

The key elements of expressive movement qualities were discussed in terms of empathy and kinesis. Kinesis illustrates how the movement is expressed and empathy the emotional or physical identification of the movement. Inherent expressive qualities are seen in rhythms that lend themselves to certain movement styles. This is apparent in nature: a humming bird moves with a quick rhythm and tempo often changing sequence and direction. By contrast a snail has a very slow rhythm and tempo and rarely changes sequence and direction. Each movement style has its purpose and intention but with very different movement qualities. Each movement is suited to the needs of each animal and their movement is adapted in support of their needs.

Throughout the tutorial we explored these movement concepts through a series of exercises Participants applied the movement design vocabulary to a prototyping project and incorporated the vocabulary to support the creation of movement in interactive software. Participants left with an understanding of the communicative nature of movement. After taking this tutorial they were able to identify various movement qualities and correlate communicative intention with these different qualities. Finally, they were be able to apply this design vocabulary to discuss, evaluate, and create meaningful movement in the development of interactive multimedia.

S. Brewster, A. Cawsey & G. Cockton (Editors)
Published by The British Computer Society © IFIP TC.13, 1999

Industry Standard Usability Tests

Nigel Bevan

Serco Usability Services, 4 Sandy Lane
Teddington, Middlesex, TW11 0DU, UK
Email: nbevan@usability.serco.com

Abstract: A Common Industry Format (CIF) for usability test reports is currently being agreed between major American software suppliers and purchasers. The objective is to raise the profile of usability in the procurement process, and to demonstrate the consequent benefits of acquiring products with increased usability. For the reports to be useful, they should contain reliable measures of usability. This requires a carefully designed evaluation procedure and use of appropriate metrics.

Keywords: usability test, usability evaluation, standards

1 Objectives

Usability will only be taken seriously when it is part of the acceptance criteria for a product, and this requires a means to specify usability goals and assess their achievement. In many organisations usability is ignored because there are no objective criteria for usability when developing and procuring products.

A Common Industry Format for usability test reports is currently being agreed between major American software suppliers and purchasers in an initiative co-ordinated by NIST (the US National Institute of Standards and Technology) (Blanchard, 1998).

In making purchase decisions, companies and organisations have traditionally had little indication of how usable a product would be, how productive its users will be, or how much training and support its users would need. The situation has made it difficult to compare products, to plan for support, or estimate the total cost of ownership.

The goals of the NIST initiative are to:

- Encourage software suppliers to work more closely with consumer organisations to understand the needs of the users.
- Develop a common usability reporting format for sharing usability data with consumer organisations.
- Conduct a pilot study to determine how well the usability reporting format works and to determine the value of using this information for software procurement.

The scheme is due to be published and start pilot testing in mid 1999.

2 Who Performs the Test

The usability test may be performed by the software supplier using its own usability group or by contracting with an independent testing facility or a consumer organisation. The consumer organisation interested in purchasing this software may accept the test results or may replicate the test.

In many cases, the supplier organisation will provide the results of the last usability test conducted in the course of software development to the consumer organisation. This allows organisations that have a usability testing program in place to participate without incurring the expense of additional usability testing.

3 Pilot Study

NIST is planning to co-ordinate a 30-month trial of the CIF. Pairs of supplier and consumer companies will enter into an agreement with NIST. An important component of the trial is to collect business data that will demonstrate the benefits of incorporating usability into procurement decision making. Consumer companies will supply NIST with internal data on overhead, productivity and user satisfaction, and record it in a common format in the NIST database.

4 Report Format

One of the issues being discussed is the extent to which the report format should require a particular style of test. Many consumer organisations would like reports to contain usability measures that would enable comparisons to be made between products. However, the primary objective of much usability testing is to identify problems rather than to produce measures. A test that is optimised to provide feedback into design may provide little information of any value to a purchaser. The most effective formative usability tests give rapid iterative feedback using three to five participants (Nielsen, 1993). These tests will frequently be exploratory, with the observer discussing the interaction with the participant and giving hints when necessary. Providing the results of such a test to a potential purchaser indicates that attempts have been made to improve the usability of the product, but does not demonstrate whether the product has adequate usability.

The purchaser needs to know how usable the product will be for particular types of users carrying out defined tasks in a specific environment. This is not just a matter of the ease of use of the interface – it is the extent to which the product can meet the needs of the user as a result of providing appropriate functionality, performance, reliability and ease of use (Bevan, 1997). This is the approach to usability taken in ISO 9241-11, and operationalised in the MUSiCmethods (Bevan and Macleod, 1994).

5 Usability and Quality in Use

To distinguish this approach to usability measurement from narrower concerns with ease of use, the broad objective of meeting user needs is also known as quality in use (Bevan, 1995). ISO/IEC 14598-1 takes this broad view, explaining that quality in use is the user's view of the quality of a system, and is measured in terms of the result of using the system, rather than properties of the system itself. Quality in use is the combined effect of the system quality characteristics for the end user. A product meets the requirements of a particular user if it enables the user to be effective, productive in use of time and resources, and satisfied, regardless of the specific attributes the product possesses.

6 Tutorial

The tutorial explained the potential benefits of the scheme to producers and purchasers, and how organisations outside the United States can become involved. The tutorial explained how MUSiC methods (Macleod et al 1997) can be used to provide test results which can be reported in the Common Industry Format. The tutorial also explained the wider benefits of specifying and measuring usability as a quality objective during product development.

References

Bevan N (1995) Measuring usability as quality of use. *Journal of Software Quality, 4, 115-130.*

Bevan N (1997) Quality and usability: a new framework. In: *Achieving software product quality*, van Veenendaal, E, and McMullan, J (eds) Tutein Nolthenius, Netherlands.

Bevan N and Azuma M (1997) Quality in use: Incorporating human factors into the software engineering lifecycle. In: *Proc. Third IEEE International Software Engineering Standards Symposium*, p169-179.

Bevan N and Macleod M (1994) Usability measurement in context. *Behaviour and Information Technology*, 13, 132-145.

Blanchard H (1998) The application of usability testing results as procurement criteria for software. *SIGCHI Bulletin, July 1998.*

ISO/IEC FCD 9126-1 (1998) Software product quality - Part 1: Quality model.

ISO 9241-11 (1998) Ergonomic requirements for office work with visual display terminals (VDT)s - Part 11 Guidance on usability.

ISO/IEC 14598-1 (1998) Evaluation of Software Products - Part 1 General guide.

Kirakowski J (1996) The software usability measurement inventory: background and usage. In: *P Jordan, B Thomas, & B Weerdmeester, Usability Evaluation in Industry.* Taylor & Frances, UK.

Macleod M, Bowden R, Bevan N and Curson I. (1997) The MUSiC Performance Measurement Method. Behaviour and Information Technology, 16.

Nielsen J (1993) Usability Engineering. Academic Press.

Human-Computer Interaction - INTERACT'99 (Volume II)
S. Brewster, A. Cawsey & G. Cockton (Editors)
Published by The British Computer Society © IFIP TC.13, 1999

Planning and Implementing User-Centred Design

Nigel Bevan

Serco Usability Services, 4 Sandy Lane
Teddington, Middlesex, TW11 0DU, UK
Email: nbevan@usability.serco.com

Abstract: The tutorial presented a structured approach to user centred design, based on the principles of the International Standard "Human centred design processes for interactive systems" (ISO 13407) and other related standards. A core set of practical methods which support the approach was described. These have been selected by the European Usability Support Centres on the basis of their applicability, maturity, availability, and cost-effectiveness. The tutorial gave an overview of each method, and described criteria which can be used for selecting appropriate methods. The benefits of demonstrating conformance to ISO 13407 were explained.

Keywords: User-centred design, usability evaluation, standards

1 Objectives

Many organisations now recognise the need for usability in interactive systems, and the benefits that usable systems deliver. But guidance about how to "do" usability tends to be technique-centred, concentrating on specific approaches for designing or evaluating systems. How can organisations at different levels of usability maturity, and with different criteria for usable systems, discover how to improve the usability of their systems?

ISO 13407 describes how a human-centred design process can be used to achieve usable systems. The standard provides a framework for applying human-centred de-sign and evaluation techniques, and is intended to supplement existing lifecycle models.

Different organisations are at different levels of usability maturity – from not recognising usability as an issue, to having processes in place which ensure the development of consistently usable systems. The principles of ISO 13407 can be integrated into their existing development process incrementally, to achieve an appropriate maturity level.

ISO 13407 specifies types of activity to be performed during the development of an interactive system, but does not demand nor recommend particular techniques or methods. The European Usability Support Centres (set up by the EU INUSE project) have agreed a set of core techniques to support the human-centred design process, selected on the basis of their applicability, maturity, availability, and cost-effectiveness. These are described in a handbook (Daly-Jones et al, 1997) which accompanied the tutorial.

2 User Centred Design Principles

The tutorial started by explaining the approach to usability and user centred design which is now embodied in a set of related international standards. Usability is defined in ISO 9241-11 as a high level quality objective: to achieve effectiveness, efficiency and satisfaction. This requires not only ease of use, but also appropriate functionality, reliability, computer performance, etc. It is thus synonymous with "quality in use", which is the user's view of software quality (Bevan, 1997, Bevan and Azuma, 1997). ISO software quality standards make quality in use the ultimate objective of systems design, thus providing the authority for giving usability a very strategic role in the development process. Achieving quality in use requires a user centred design process, and the use of appropriate usability evaluation techniques.

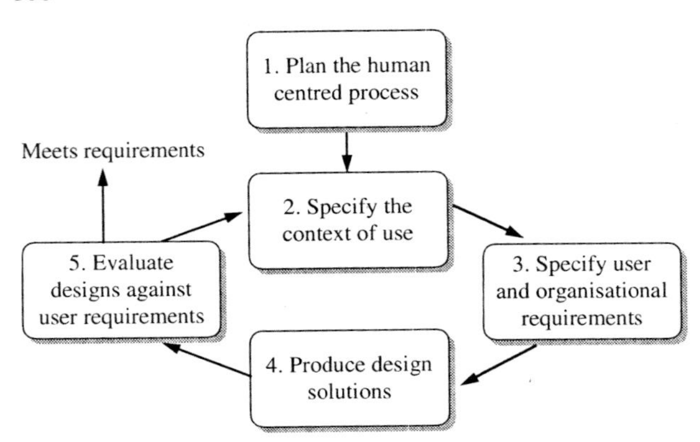

Figure 1: User centred design process.

The steps in the process are illustrated in Figure 1 (based on ISO 13407), and involve an iterative cycle of specifying the context in which the product will be used and the user and organisational requirements, and then producing design solutions which can be evaluated against these requirements. Early in design the requirements will be at a high level and the design solutions are likely to be mock ups. As design progresses higher fidelity prototypes will be evaluated against more detailed requirements.

3 User Centred Design Methods

The first step is to plan which methods are expected to be used at different stages of development. This will depend on the business case for usability, and will take account of the budget, timescales, resources, skills and other constraints. For each potential method, the handbook (Daly-Jones et al, 1997) provides information which includes when the method should be used, the type of results provided, the number of usability experts and users required, and the typical range of person days involved.

One essential prerequisite for user centred design is to define in detail the context of use of the product. The method recommended in this tutorial, Usability Context Analysis (Bevan and Macleod, 1994), is based on ISO 9241-11, and provides a structured approach to gathering and documenting information about the characteristics of the intended users, tasks and environments. The resulting specification of context of use can be used to inform design, and to specify valid and consistent evaluations.

The tutorial described the following other types of methods:

- Guidance and standards
- Early development methods
- Late development methods

3.1 Assuring Usability

How can a purchaser judge whether a product is usable? The supplier could state the results of a usability test, but it can be difficult for the purchaser to know whether the results are valid or relevant. A partial solution is to use a Common Industry Format usability test report (Bevan, 1999). Another approach is to provide evidence that a user centred design process was used when developing the product. The *ISO 13407 lite conformity scheme* (Earthy, 1998) can provide this assurance.

References

Bevan N (1997) Quality and usability: a new framework. In: *Achieving software product quality*, van Veenendaal, E, and McMullan, J (eds) Tutein Nolthenius, Netherlands.

Bevan N (1999) Industry standard usability tests. In: *Human-Computer Interaction – INTERACT '99 (Volume II)*. S. Brewster, A. Cawsey & G. Cockton (editors). British Computer Society

Bevan N and Azuma M (1997) Quality in use: Incorporating human factors into the software engineering lifecycle. In: *Proc. Third IEEE International Software Engineering Standards Symposium, p169-179.*

Bevan N and Macleod M (1994) Usability measurement in context. *Behaviour and Information Technology, 13, 132-145.*

Daly-Jones, O, Thomas, C, Bevan, N. (1997) Handbook of user centred design. National Physical Laboratory, Teddington, Middx, UK.

Earthy, J (1998) Usability Maturity Model: Attitude Scale. INUSE deliverable D5.1.4s - see INUSE (1997)

INUSE (1997) see http://www.npl.co.uk/inuse

ISO/IEC FDIS 9126-1 (1999) Software quality characteristics and metrics - Part 1: Quality characteristics and sub-characteristics.

ISO 9241-11 (1998) Ergonomic requirements for office work with visual display terminals (VDT)s - Part 11 Guidance on usability.

ISO 13407 (1999) Human centred design processes for interactive systems.

ISO/IEC 14598-1 (1998) Information Technology - Evaluation of Software Products - Part 1 General guide.

Human-Computer Interaction - INTERACT'99 (Volume II)
S. Brewster, A. Cawsey & G. Cockton (Editors)
Published by The British Computer Society © IFIP TC.13, 1999

Solution Engineering Techniques

Anthony Crawford

Process Improvement Institute
461, Lakeshore Road West, Oakville
Ontario, L6K 1G4
Canada
Email: tony@crawford-jad.com

1 Tutorial Overview

This tutorial demonstrates an approach to model business engineering that promotes user involvement in product solutions design and pre-implementation phases of systems development. The approach is presented in the context of recommendations and ISO standards for quality design, human factors and ergonomics for operating interfaces with technology.

2 Analysis with Design in Mind

Classic*JAD** is a workshop approach to ***Advance Business Concepts in plans that increase business performance from process redesign and appropriate applications of technology. Compared to traditional methods, the difference is a complete approach to analysis for business details in solutions design. In this approach, people focus vision and requirements as Process Improvement Expectations (**PIE**) and procedures and specifications in an intuitively clear, easy to use Process Improvement Model (**PIM**).

These unique methods overcome typical problems found in many methodologies. The approach promotes a practical operational view of business from the start and develops progressive solution guidelines for implementation. It encourages people to think of ***business engineering with design in mind*** for:

- Change assessment and resource management
- Action plans with guidance and support
- Business vision and goals analysis
- Organization and process redesign requirements
- Procedure specifications and information dialogues
- Software development and system customization
- Solution implementation and training materials

3 Systematic Approach

The idea of business engineering with design in mind has many advantages. You can use it for a wide range of plans including the application of change management and organization needs analysis through business process design and also systems development.

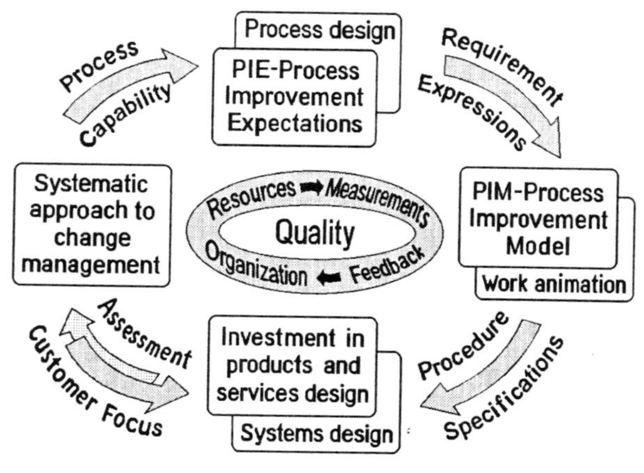

The approach provides several benefits:

- Focus on customer satisfaction and infrastructure design for quality products and services
- Analysis technique for management organization with defined roles and responsibilities
- Measurable objectives for increased business performance and software process improvement

- Systematic approach for change management and technology integration
- Progressive development using workshop techniques for appropriate analysis and design
- Solution acceptance through teamwork and participation in business process redesign

5 Teamwork

The basis of *Classic*JAD is to involve business representatives and information technologists in a collaborative effort to redesign business processes and define system solutions together. A good measure of success is a well-documented design with all the necessary details to facilitate a large or small change initiative.

6 Organization for Analysis

Business analysis during a workshop is supported by a unique structure designed to focus ideas in a pre-prepared discussion document. Participants review the scope of design and business objectives along with summary illustrations of current functions and process redesign scenarios including plausible screen designs for a computerized information dialogue.

Here, an experienced session leader presents background materials for all to see, while guiding the analysis for consensus and an acceptable solution.

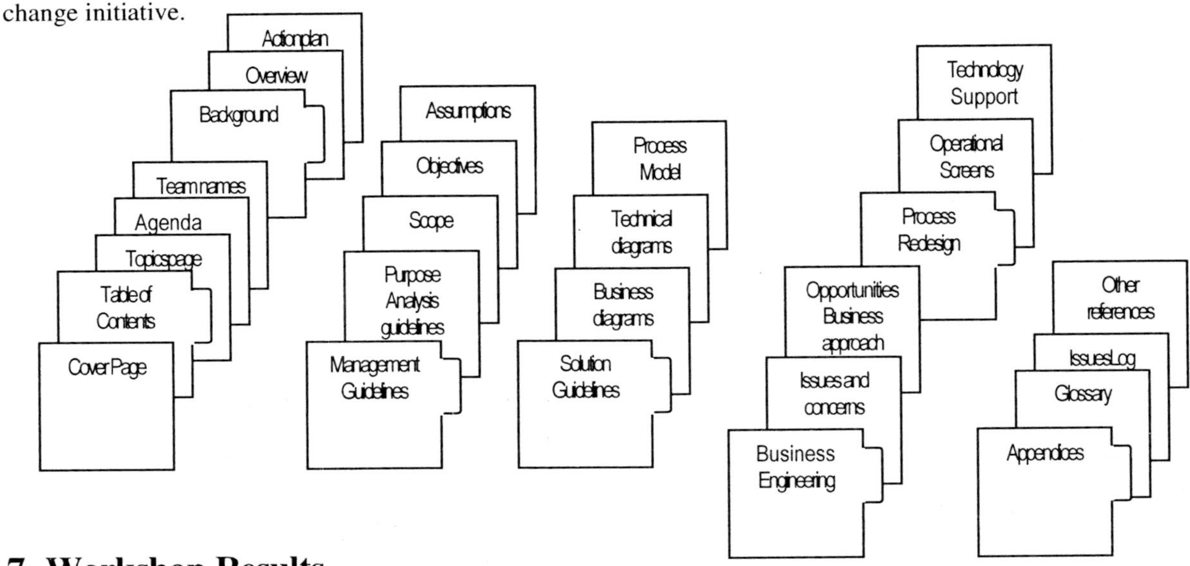

7 Workshop Results

Impartial facilitation and teamwork in a workshop setting is key to successful participation. Rather than merely automating current processes, good ideas and creative designs emerge from teamwork. The result is a well-documented solution using on-line documentation for immediate review and approval of design plans for implementation

With an emphasis on quality results and team productivity, a good choice in analysis technique and workshop support is increasingly important for good participation in thoughtful analysis for process redesign and systems development activities.

Participants are usually eager to talk about what they must do to achieve their business objectives. And they want to discuss problems and concerns while they design practical solutions. With the issues identified and documented, conversation continues to focus various ideas as they relate to opportunities for improvements in processes and systems design.

Reprinted with client permission from Solution Engineering Techniques
ISBN 0-9698952-8-3 Toronto University Press, Hushion House Canada

Human-Computer Interaction - INTERACT'99 (Volume II)
S. Brewster, A. Cawsey & G. Cockton (Editors)
Published by The British Computer Society © IFIP TC.13, 1999

Producing Usable Artefacts with Java 2.0

Fintan Culwin

South Bank University
Borough Road
London SE1 0AA
UK
Email: fintan@sbu.ac.uk

Abstract: The use of State Transition Diagrams (STD) to model the interaction between a user and an interface can be the starting point for a defined software construction process. This tutorial introduced STD notation and illustrated how it can be used, in conjunction with other notations, to derive a complete the design. The realisation of the design, using the Java Foundation Class (JFC) interface components, illustrated the applicability of these techniques.

Keywords: GUI, Three-Layer Model, Java, AWT, JFC, STD, Statechart

1 Introduction

The rapid proliferation of Java artefacts, most noticeably as interactive content on the World Wide Web, is leading to a 'hypercard effect'. That is the technology is being used without due regard to usability or software engineering considerations, leading to the production of seemingly sophisticated visual interfaces containing many usability faults and inadequate application functionality. One factor contributing to these problems was the small number of widgets supplied in the Abstract Windowing Toolkit (AWT) and their visual and functional paucity. The inclusion of the Java Foundation Classes (JFC) as a part of the Java 2.0 release obviates some of these problems.

2 Overview

The tutorial was divided into two major parts, the first of which was a detailed introduction to some fundamental mechanisms and notations. The most central notation was State Transition Diagrams (Culwin 1999), also known as statecharts (Horrocks 1999) to describe the interaction between a user and an interface. The STD was subsequently used to inform the design of class instance diagrams. The design of visual aspects of the interface was facilitated by the use of layout management diagrams. The processes underpinning the consequences of user actions, leading to closure, were illustrated by the use of object interaction diagrams.

The second part of the tutorial consolidated the material supplied in the introduction and commenced with a participatory exercise where attendees constructed STDs for a number of simple interfaces presented to them. The tutorial concluded with a tour of many, but not all, of the interface components supplied by the JFC.

3 The Stopwatch Artefact

Figure 1 contains the STD for the *Stopwatch* artefact whose construction process was illustrated in the first part of the tutorial. A STD contains states linked by transitions, shown as arrows, which have a three-part label. The first part of the label is the event which must occur for the transition to be considered, the second part is the precondition which must be true for the transition to be followed and the third part is the consequences of following the transition. (All of the preconditions in this simple example are empty which are taken as being true).

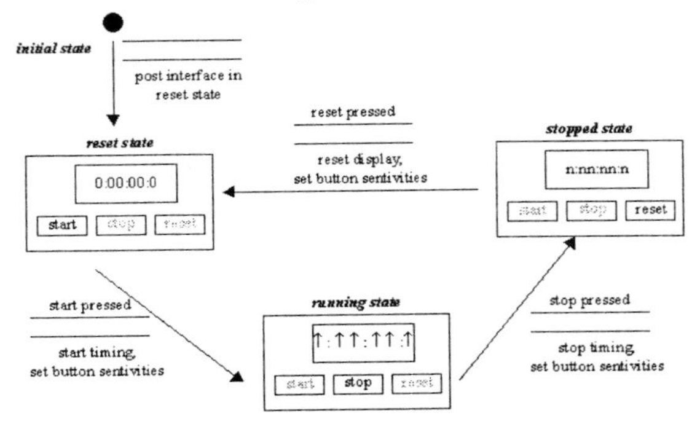

Figure 1. *Stopwatch* STD.

A three-later model divides an artefact that has a GUI into three distinct layers. The part that is visible to the user is contained within a *presentation layer* which contains no behavioural or application intelligence. The *application layer* contains the essential functionality of the artefact, implemented without regard to any particular interface or interface style. The *translation layer* inter-connects the other two layers and implements the behaviour expressed in the STD. In a simple Java artefact these layers are supplied as instances of particular classes and the relationships between them can be expressed on an object instance diagram. The object instance diagram for the *Stopwatch* artefact is given in Figure 2.

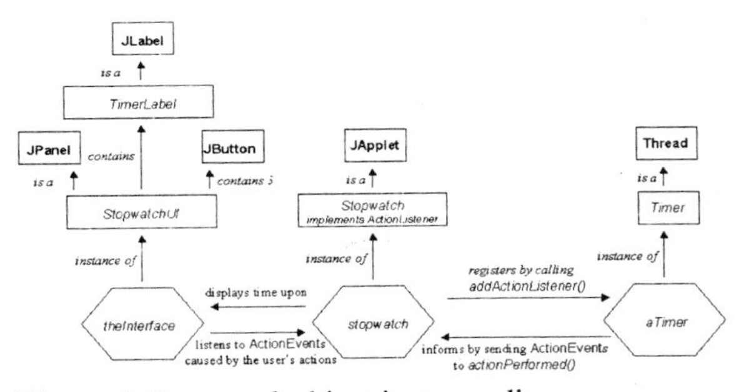

Figure 2 *Stopwatch* object instance diagram.

This diagram clearly illustrates the role of events in the behaviour of the artefact. The translation object, in the middle identified as *stopwatch*, is listening to the events dispatched from the three buttons contained within the presentation object, on the left identified as *theInterface*. The *stopwatch* is also listening to events dispatched from the application object, on the right identified as *aTimer*.

The *stopwatch* object implements the behaviour shown on the STD when it responds to the events originating from the presentation object. The receipt of an event causes the stopwatch object to move itself into a new state and send appropriate messages to the other two objects to effect the state change. The *stopwatch* object is also continually receiving events from the *aTimer* object which, when it is in the *running* state, causes it to send a message to *theInterface* to update the time it is displaying.

3 The JFC Components

The development of artefacts whose user interface is more complex than the *Stopwatch* example will require the use of other components. The JFC supplies a range of components including various types of buttons, text input areas, sliders, combo boxes, layout managers, tree and table views, modal and non-modal dialogs, menu bars and menu items of various types.

Within a half-day tutorial it was not possible to provide a comprehensive overview of all JFC components. Instead an in-depth look at the JLabel class was supplied, using an artefact which allowed the interactive exploration of other classes. For example, Figure 3 illustrates the *TabbedLabelDemo* artefact with the *CustomColor* interface active. This allowed the JSlider class to be introduced and showed how it dispatches events when the user interacts with it. This consolidated the concepts from the first part of the tutorial by illustrating their applicability to a different artefact, with the intention that they could be further extended to the classes which were not introduced.

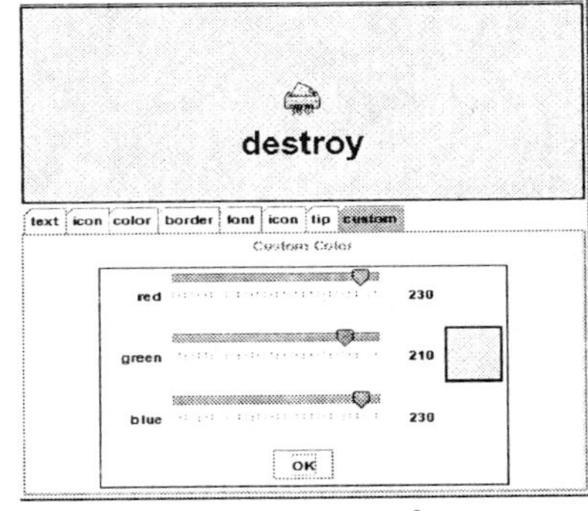

Figure 3 *TabbedLabelDemo* artefact.

References

Culwin, F. *A Java GUI Programmers' Primer*. Prentice Hall UK,.ISBN 0139088490.

Horrocks, I. (1998) *Constructing the User Interface with Statecharts*. Prentice Hall UK,.ISBN 0201342782.

Human-Computer Interaction - INTERACT'99 (Volume II)
S. Brewster, A. Cawsey & G. Cockton (Editors)
Published by The British Computer Society © IFIP TC.13, 1999

From Components to JavaBeans

Fintan Culwin

South Bank University
Borough Road
London SE1 0AA
UK
Email: fintan@sbu.ac.uk

Abstract: The Java Foundation Classes (JFC) supply a large number of user interface components, but cannot supply a suitable component for every possible requirement. The Object Oriented nature of Java facilitates the extension of the supplied components to produce specialised components, suitable for particular requirements. In order for these specialised components to be fully interoperable with the JFC components, specialised components from other developers and with bean-aware software development tools they should be designed and constructed with regard to the JavaBean component architecture specifications.

Keywords: Java, JavaBeans, GUI, Three-Layer Model, JFC, STD, Statechart

1 Introduction

The Object Orientated nature of the Java Programming Language, in particular inheritance, allows the components supplied by the Java Foundation Classes (JFC) to be (relatively) easily extended to supply specialised components suitable for particular requirements. In the first part of this tutorial two case studies of examples of this process were described.

A JavaBean is defined by the Java Bean specification (Sun 1999) as "a reusable software component that can be manipulated visually in a builder tool". The major advantage of developing a specialised component with regard to the JavaBean specification is so that it can inter-operate efficiently with other bean-compliant components, including all the JFC components.

The other major advantage is that the bean can be loaded into a bean-aware software development tool and manipulated as a constituent part of a user interface. In the second part of the tutorial the essential features of a bean were described and one of the examples from the first part of the tutorial was further developed so as to become fully bean compliant.

The usability of a bean within a software development tool can be enhanced by the provision of additional classes support it. Examples of BeanInfo and specialised property editor classes were given and the developer-oriented usability improvements that they provide was demonstrated.

2 Specialised Components

The first specialised components, whose design and implementation were presented, consisted of a set of *numericinput* components. The JTextField class, a single line text input area, could be used for the input of numeric values. However, there could be no guarantee that the user would always restrict their input to a numeric value, possibly within a required range.

Figure 1 illustrates the three *numericinput* components which were developed in the first part of the tutorial. At the top is an instance of the *NumericInputField* class, which extends the JTextField class and allows for the input of any floating point value. Below it are three instances of the *IntegerTextField* class that extends the *NumericInputField* class, restricting the user's input to integer values within a defined range. The final component is an instance of the *SpinBox* class, which is a composite component which contains an *IntegerTextField* and two *ArrowBoxes*.

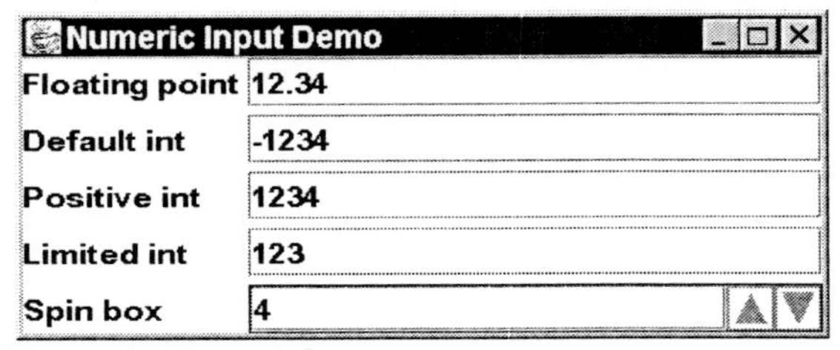

Figure 1: *NumericInput* components.

The development of the *numericinput* components required techniques for the internal handling of events originating from the keyboard to be processed. The second example, the *TimeInput* component shown in Figure 2, extended this knowledge to the processing of events that originate from the mouse.

Figure 2: The *TimeInput* component.

A user can use the *TimeInput* component to indicate a time of day by dragging the clock hands around the clock face and by selecting the morning or evening icon at the top. The current setting is confirmed by the feedback at the bottom of the component.

2 Javabeans

The defining characteristics of a JavaBean are:

introspection, allowing a bean's resources to be revealed.
event handling, using the source/ listener model.
properties which determine both appearance and behaviour.
customisation of the bean by setting the values of its properties.
persistence allowing the state of a bean to be serialised and stored.
internationalisation and *localisation* for use in different locales.

The specialised components were shown to be already partially bean compliant requiring little additional work to make them fully compliant.

The ease with which a developer can customise a bean within a development tool is facilitated if a BeanInfo class is supplied and specialised property editors are made available. Figure 3 shows the BeanBox property sheet configured in response to the *TimeInputBeanInfo* class and from which the *TimeInputValue* specialised editor has been posted to allow the developer to set the time shown on the bean.

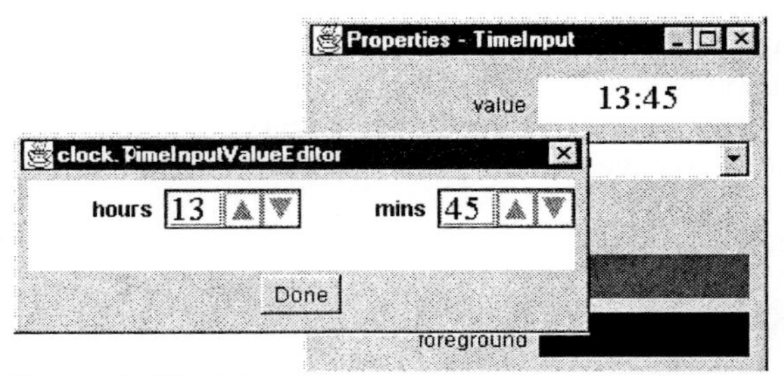

Figure 3: The *TimeInput* property sheet & editor.

The property editor is making use of two instances of the *SpinBox* class illustrating the effective (re)use of these components in a different setting. The BeanBox was also used to demonstrate persistence by saving a configured *TimeInput* instance to a file and subsequently deserialising it from the file into a example applet, shown in Figure 2.

The final defining property, I18n, L12n & C10n, of a bean was not easily demonstrated with either of the components used in the substantive part of the tutorial. Instead these mechanisms were illustrated by the automatic configuration of the *ColaMachine* simulation for use in different locales.

References

Sun Microsystems (1999). *JavaBeans API Specification version 1.01*, www.javasoft.com/beans/docs/beans.101.pdf

Human-Computer Interaction - INTERACT'99 (Volume II)
S. Brewster, A. Cawsey & G. Cockton (Editors)
Published by The British Computer Society © IFIP TC.13, 1999

Human-Centred Processes, Their Maturity and Their Improvement

Jonathan Earthy
Lloyd's Register
Email:
jonathan.earthy@lr.org

Brian Sherwood-Jones
BAeSEMA

Jenny Weston
Philips

Abstract: The software engineering community is gaining business benefit from identifying, assessing and improving its **processes**. This tutorial describes how HCI can do the same.

1 Introduction

A survey of European IT developers (Maguire and Graham, 1996) suggests that concern over user issues is widespread. 91% of respondents felt that user and organisational issues are important and 58% felt that they did not address these issues properly. An international study (Hefley, 1996) indicates that while 70% of organizations use a process for managing product quality, only 32% explicitly addressed usability as an integral part. Thus, 68% of the organizations either do not follow a process for managing quality or do not address usability as an integral part. Of the organizations surveyed, only 11% *always* integrate their process with their overall product creation process. Only 36% of the organizations surveyed follow a defined process that explicitly addresses usability/ease of use as an integral part of this process.

Even when usability is addressed it is rarely approached in the right way. Hakiel (1998) reports the software industry's current (misbelief) that improvements in practice are achieved by simply extending the repertoire of software engineering methods to include Human Computer Interaction (HCI) methods. As a usability design solution, this corresponds to a restricted view of usability; that it is concerned only with the ease of use of the specified function. Under this approach usability engineering is limited to accepting or identifying the user interactions associated with specified functions and providing user interfaces to support those interactions. The major problem with this approach is that a software product design is presumed to exist, and the problem for HCI is to make it usable. Human-centred design (HCD) methods can of course be applied under this approach, and could well result in a better solution than might be derived in the absence of such methods. But, in this context, HCD methods are only concerned with ensuring that the user interfaces to be provided are optimised from users' points of view. However, from a general Human Factors perspective this whole approach to usability design is inherently limited, and all usability solutions derived by this approach are likely to be sub-optimal.

Problems deriving from this restricted approach to usability are avoided by taking an extended view of usability which subsumes utility (utility being the functions to be provided to the user) and shifts the focus from the development of software to the development of systems. This is because the system functions provided to support user tasks contribute about 60% of the ease of use whereas the specific design of user interfaces to software contributes only 10% (IBM, 1992). Activities concerning the identification and specification of such functions from the end user's point of view should therefore be part of the overall design process. Adopting an extended view of usability implies a substantial, if not radical, change in the role of HCI/Usability engineering in the design of software-based products. Under this approach, specification of function cannot be considered to be simply a software engineering activity and must be based on considerations relating to disciplines quite different from those on which software engineering is based.

Under this broader view process improvement moves away from the current capability modelling approaches which focus on the developer's concerns with the software process and turns towards a focus on system lifecycle processes and the users' concerns about the product that they are to use. The question is how process improvement should take account of this broader view? One crucial factor is for the HF/HCI community to understand and employ the process approach. This tutorial is intended to explain the process and process improvement to that community with the goal of situating the necessary ownership of usability process with the HF/HCI community, not the systems/software community.

2 The Process Approach and Process Maturity

For a product to achieve a guaranteed level of usability its development process should be human-centred. In order to be effective, human-centred methods have to be integrated into the product development process. This integration has to take account of the current state of the developer's processes and the overall attitude to usability (or the maturity of the human-centredness) of the organisation. Philip Crosby's well-known Quality Management Process Maturity Grid (Crosby, 1978) can be applied to an organisation's attitude to product usability.

Stage	Typical Attitude
Ignorance	"We don't have problems with usability"
Uncertainty	"We don't know why we have problems with usability"
Awakening	"Do we always have to have these problems with usability?"
Enlightenment	"Through management commitment and improvement of human-centred processes we are identifying and resolving our problems"
Wisdom	"Usability defect prevention is a routine part of our operation"

These attitudes give goals for the level of maturity of the management and development processes in an organisation. In order to select which goals are appropriate for a particular business, and to plan how to reach these goals, an organisation needs an overview of the usability-related parts of its development processes. A human-centred (HC) maturity model provides such an overview. It describes all of the HC activities which have to be carried out in order to ensure that products are usable. Such a model also contains criteria for deciding how well human-centred management and project activities are being performed. Examples of the use of an HC maturity model are:

- a high level plan for setting up usability activities
- basis of workshops to identify and resolve barriers to effective exchange of usability information
- assessment of the capability of sub-contractors or service providers
- benchmarking of usability process in an organisation against its competitors.

There are three initiatives in Europe which have developed models for the HC aspects of system development:

1. at Philips (as part of the Humanware Process Improvement programme)
2. at BAeSEMA (the Total Systems Maturity Index)
3. at Lloyd's Register (as part of EC 2016, INUSE).

The tutorial is presented by the leaders of these three initiatives. They have unparalleled experience in the area of human-centred process modelling, assessment and improvement. In addition to their previous experience new findings from current work for IBM, DERA and SERCO will be available in time for the tutorial and will be described.

References

Crosby P. B. (1978) Quality is Free: The Art of Making Quality Certain, New York: McGraw-Hill.

Hakiel S. (1998) Human centred Processes, Panel session at HCI'98, Sheffield August 1998

Hefley W. (1996) Results from the ACM interactions survey, Personal communication

IBM Corporation (1992) Object-Oriented Interface Design: IBM Common User Access (TM) Guidelines (Carmel, Que Corporation) p16.

INUSE (1998a) Usability Maturity Model: Processes, Lloyd's Register, project IE2016 INUSE Deliverable D5.1.4p. http://info.lboro.ac.uk/research/husat/inuse

INUSE (1998b) Usability Maturity Model: Human-Centredness Scale, Lloyd's Register, project IE2016 INUSE Deliverable D5.1.4s. http://info.lboro.ac.uk/research/husat/inuse

Maguire M. and Graham R. (1996) Results of Market Survey, INUSE deliverable D7.1.2, HUSAT Research Institute, The Elms, Elms Grove, Loughborough, Leics. LE11 1RG, UK.

Human-Computer Interaction - INTERACT'99 (Volume II)
S. Brewster, A. Cawsey & G. Cockton (Editors)
Published by The British Computer Society © IFIP TC.13, 1999

Computing Outside the Box

Chris Esposito

Advanced User Environments Group
Boeing, Phantom Works Research Division
PO Box 3707, Mail Code 7L-48
Seattle, Washington
USA
Email: Christopher.esposito@boeing.com

Abstract: Several U.S. information technology consulting groups have recently projected that in less than 5 years desktop PCs will constitute a minority of computing devices in general. The remaining majority will be in our phones, held in our hands, stuffed in our pockets, or worn somewhere on our bodies. Instead of mice and keyboards, these new devices use speech, pens and hand gestures. Small, lightweight displays will be more popular, some flat, some folding like paper, some hanging in front of one or both eyes. The early versions of these devices are being used in environments that have never seen computers before. The design of these devices, their applications, and the user interface designs for these applications are often very different from that of their desktop counterparts. This tutorial described these new devices, discussed some of these new design challenges, and presented some recent case studies where they have been successfully met.

Keywords: Handheld, wearable, pervasive, speech, pen, small displays, head mounted display

1 Tutorial Description

The tutorial had five major sections. The first section described the new environments, new tasks, and new users that are involved with these new devices. Some of the new environments described were aircraft assembly lines, an African jungle, and a desert military campaign. Some of these new applications included wire bundle assembly, tank inspection, navigation in city streets for the visually impaired, and aircraft troubleshooting and maintenance. Evaluating system components such as input and display devices for survivability and suitability for these environments and applications turns out to be a bit more complicated than choosing between the various mice and keyboards currently on the market.

The second section described many of the new software tools and hardware devices. The software tools include Sun Microsystems' Jini and Personal Java, Microsoft Windows CE, and 3Coms' PalmOS. The hardware subsection was a bit of a show-and-tell format with new devices such as wearable computers, palm-sized computers, head-mounted displays, and microcameras. Examples of most of these devices were passed around for the attendees to examine and try out.

The third section discussed how physical characteristics of the environments, devices, and users created new issues for evaluating system design, system component selection (e.g., input devices) and some aspects of user interface design.

The fourth section discussed how the design and implementation of the software and user interface portions of these new systems differs from that of more conventional desktop applications. This included issues like:

- Designing for low resolution (VGA & below) and grayscale screens
- Techniques for viewing large graphics on small displays

- Matching input device characteristics with application task requirements
- A more active and automatic approach to managing the application user interface
- Pen/handwriting interface design guidelines
- Speech interface design guidelines

The fifth and final section was a collection of brief case studies of successful applications for these new systems. These included several applications from Boeing, collaborative troubleshooting using wireless networks and head-mounted cameras, and inspection and battle management applications from the US military that used handheld devices.

Human-Computer Interaction - INTERACT'99 (Volume II)
S. Brewster, A. Cawsey & G. Cockton (Editors)
Published by The British Computer Society © IFIP TC.13, 1999

Programming Collaborative Applications for the Web

Andreas Girgensohn

FX Palo Alto Laboratory
Palo Alto, CA 94304
USA
Email: andreasg@pal.xerox.com

Alison Lee

IBM TJ Watson Research Center
Hawthorne, NY 10532
USA
Email: alisonl@us.ibm.com

Abstract: The World Wide Web is often viewed as the latest and most user friendly way of providing information over the Internet (i.e., server of documents). It is not customarily viewed as a platform for developing and deploying applications. In this tutorial, we introduced, demonstrated, and discussed how Web technologies like CGI scripts, Javascript, and Java can be used in combination with Web browsers to design, create, distribute and execute collaborative applications. We discussed constraints with the Web approach as well as recent extensions that support application development.

Keywords: Collaborative applications, interactive applications, forms, HTML, MIME, CGI, HTTP, URL, Java, JavaScript, WebL, web server, web browsers, cookies, proxy servers, software development, chat, desktop video conference, voting application, group calendar, multi-user games.

1 Introduction

Building collaborative applications is a challenging task that requires balancing social, user interface, and technical concerns. The Web provides building blocks (e.g., servlets, Javascript, Java, proxy servers) that lower the technical hurdles and allows researchers, designers and developers to focus on exploring and understanding the social and HCI concerns. Using concrete examples, we demonstrated how these building blocks are used to develop applications consisting of components such as awareness, shared objects, and conversational tools. We provided insights into and understanding of the Web building blocks and their use for rapid prototyping.

The tutorial was broken into a morning and afternoon session, each consisting of a formal presentation and an exercise. The presentation introduced Web tools for developing the use, interaction, server-side functionality, and client-side functionality of collaborative applications.

We sketched how these tools can be used to build fragments of a number of small collaborative applications. For instance, we demonstrated how a proxy server can integrate information about the users looking at a document by modifying the document before it is presented to the user. The example applications included a group calendar, an annotations viewer, a video conference tool, an issues voting tool, an awareness tool, meeting notes editor, a turn-taking word game, a chat tool, and an auction tool.

As well, the applications provided a basis for discussing how to address issues related to interactivity, customization, data and tool integration, control, synchronization, firewall support, scalability, user identification/authentication, and security. Where appropriate, we discussed tradeoffs in using one particular building block over another. Some of these discussions focussed on different considerations and tradeoffs in implementing variants of the auction and chat services.

In the exercise portions of the tutorial, attendees gathered in small groups to work on a specially constructed collaborative application (i.e., Web-based asynchronous auction). The morning exercise involved designing the user interface for auctions (e.g., auction listing, auction login, bid on auction). The afternoon exercise involved modifying the auction servlet code to display the number and names of people at an auction.

The tutorial concluded with a Q&A session, a discussion of the limitations of the Web approach and the enhancements being made to building blocks.

Human-Computer Interaction - INTERACT'99 (Volume II)
S. Brewster, A. Cawsey & G. Cockton (Editors)
Published by The British Computer Society © IFIP TC.13, 1999

Cognitive Factors in Design: Basic Phenomena in Human Memory and Problem Solving

Thomas T. Hewett

Department of Psychology, Sociology, and Anthropology
Drexel University, Philadelphia, PA 19104
USA
Email: hewett@drexel.edu

Abstract: This tutorial provides a "hands-on" (actually, "minds-on") exploration of several basic processes and phenomena of human memory, and problem solving. The emphasis is on developing both intuitive and formal knowledge useful in making educated design judgements when design guidelines fail, conflict, or are nonexistent. Demonstrations emphasize phenomena with which any theory of memory or problem solving must deal. In addition, the tutorial suggests general implications of these phenomena for designing interactive systems.

Keywords: memory, problem solving, design, cognitive factors

1 Introduction and Caveat

The emphasis in this tutorial is on demonstrations and exercises which highlight some of the remarkable things human beings do in interacting with, in learning about, and in making sense out of the world around them. These things often seem to be quite ordinary simply because we do them regularly, often without deliberation. Nonetheless, some of them are quite complex and not well understood. Many of the demonstrations replicate phenomena studied under controlled laboratory conditions and some are drawn directly from research studies.

2 Memory

In one model of memory, short-term memory (STM) is described (Solso, 1994) as having a limited storage capacity (seven plus or minus two chunks) for a relatively brief duration (estimates range from 12 to 30 seconds without rehearsal). Information can be maintained in STM for longer periods of time with maintenance rehearsal (MR). Elaborative rehearsal (ER) appears to be the most effective set of processes for the transfer of information into long-term storage.

LTM has a large capacity for storage of information for long periods of time. Several types of information are represented in LTM, including such things as facts and events, motor and perceptual skills, knowledge of physical laws and systems of mathematics, a spatial model of the world around us, attitudes and beliefs about oneself and others, etc. This information is more or less well organized in a variety of ways and varies in its accessibility as a function of several factors. The factors determining accessibility of the information in LTM include the conditions which existed at the time the information was stored, the recency of its last use, its degree of inter-relationship with other knowledge, its degree of uniqueness relative to other information, etc. Most discussions of failure to recall from LTM focus on explanations such as interference, the absence of or inappropriateness of retrieval cues, or some type of organic dysfunction such as brain damage.

An alternative model memory holds there is no need to postulate a STM. Rather, there is a working memory which is part of the larger memory system and not a separate memory. Different degrees of persistence of information in memory are thought to be a function of the elaborateness or the depth to which information has been processed. The greater the degree of processing, the longer the retention period. In this model, chunks are organizational units in LTM and the capacity limitation is on how much information can be actively scanned or held in working memory at any given time.

While the bulk of the evidence supports the model which includes working memory (Anderson, 1994), there are basic phenomena with which any theory of memory must deal. For example, regardless of whether one thinks of the capacity limitation as the result of a limited capacity memory or as a result of a limit on the amount of information which can be activated and maintained in an active state any given time, it is clear there is a capacity limitation. Similarly, regardless of whether one thinks that memory rehearsal processes have different degrees of depth and elaboration or that there are two different kinds of rehearsal processes, each associated with a different memory store, it is clear that elaborative rehearsal is more effective than maintenance rehearsal in insuring information will be accessible in memory for a long period of time.

3 Problem Solving

A major turning point in the literature on problem solving occurred with the work of Newell and Simon (1972). In their view, a problem can be analyzed by means of a "problem space" representing various states of knowledge of the problem solver, a series of transformations between states, and a set of operators which produce those transformations. A problem exists when we have a gap between an initial state and a goal state. The means of solving the problem involves applying the appropriate set of operators required to complete a series of state transformations that will eliminate the gap. These transformations must be accomplished without violating any of the conditions on the operators.

As a result of repeated experience with problems, solvers build up an organized body of knowledge or information about the properties of a particular type of problem and the operations or steps required to solve it. This organized body of information is usually referred to as a problem solving schema (e.g., Norman, 1982). Humans develop a wide variety of familiar problem schemas (Newell & Simon, 1972), and the typical individual has built up a wide stock of such schemas which come into play in solving problems problems with which one has prior experience. Some schemas are so familiar they are activated almost automatically and without much thought.

Typically, the effect of problem solving schemas is to help provide reasonably efficient methods of solving frequently encountered kinds of problems. Sometimes, however, a schema can interfere with the problem solving process. Since it influences the problem solver's early analysis of the problem and determines which schema, or schemas, will be brought to bear in solving a particular problem, the way in which that problem is represented can make a vital difference in how easily the problem can be solved. When a problem is not solved as easily as expected. it is often quite fruitful to look to the adequacy of the representation of the problem, and to give thought to changing that representation.

4 Implications for Design

In considering the nature of human memory it is clear designers need to take account of the limited number of "chunks" of information with which a user can actively cope at any given time. While the size of those chunks can be affected by the development of additional new knowledge structures, that growth of knowledge requires the user be actively engaged in elaborating and assimilating knowledge. In addition demands upon human learning and memory can be reduced by providing appropriate mnemonic cues in the interface and the flow of interaction.

In considering human problem solving it is clear designers need to take account of user's established problem solving strategies developed from having solved problems encountered frequently in the past. While established strategies can be used to facilitate usage they can also create process blockages which may only be solved by changing the way the problems of interaction are presented to the user.

References

Anderson, J. R. (1994) *Cognitive Psychology and Its Implications.* 4th ed. W. H. Freeman, New York, NY.

Hayes, J. R. (1981) *The Complete Problem Solver.* The Franklin Institute Press, Philadelphia, PA.

Newell, A. & Simon, H. A. (1972) *Human Problem Solving.* Prentice-Hall, Englewood Cliffs, NJ.

Norman, D. A. (1982) *Learning and Memory.* New York: W. H. Freeman, New York, NY.

Solso R. L. (1994) *Cognitive Psychology.* 4th ed. Allyn and Bacon, Needham Heights, MA.

Human-Computer Interaction - INTERACT'99 (Volume II)
S. Brewster, A. Cawsey & G. Cockton (Editors)
Published by The British Computer Society © IFIP TC.13, 1999

Contextual Inquiry: Gathering and Using Customer Data

Karen Holtzblatt

InContext Enterprises, Inc.
249 Ayer Rd., Suite 301
Harvard, MA 01451
USA
Email: karen@incent.com

Hugh Beyer

InContext Enterprises, Inc.
249 Ayer Rd., Suite 301
Harvard, MA 01451
USA
Email: beyer@incent.com

Abstract: This tutorial presents some of the principal techniques of Contextual Design, a leading approach to customer-centred design. Taught by the originators of the process, the tutorial is a practical introduction to the use of field research in designing computer systems that support and extend people's work. Participants learn about and practice the Contextual Inquiry approach to interviewing and analysis, simple work modelling, consolidation, and how to set up a customer-centred project. The instructors draw examples from their experience working with product companies and Information Technology organisations to develop requirements, define products and strategies, and design information systems.

Keywords: analysis methods, design techniques, customer-centred design, ethnography, usability engineering, methodology, team design, domain analysis, work modelling, software engineering, task analysis, user models, user studies, work analysis

1 Content

Contextual Design is a state-of-the-art approach to designing products directly from an understanding of how the customer works. Great product ideas come from a marriage of the detailed understanding of a customer need with the in-depth understanding of technology. The best product designs happen when the product's designers are involved in collecting and interpreting customer data. Contextual Design gives designers the tools to do just that.

In this tutorial, we cover some key techniques from Contextual Design:

1.1 Contextual Inquiry

Contextual Inquiry is a technique for interviewing and observing users in their own workplace as they work. The technique is designed to be effective given the time constraints and work situations of engineering teams. The technique drives initial design concepts by forming an accurate understanding of how people work. This is the basis for effective design action. We cover the key principles of Contextual Inquiry, discuss the structure of an interview, and practice two kinds of contextual interviews.

1.2 Work Modelling

Understanding work is hard: there is no discipline of understanding how people work, the concepts, distinctions, and issues of work practice are not general knowledge, and we have no language for describing work practice. Without a language, it is hard to communicate work practice to others. To remedy this deficiency, we have developed *work models*, drawings that incorporate important distinctions about work. These models show the roles people play in the organisation and how they communicate; the social and emotional context in which work happens; the sequence of actions which accomplish work; the details of the physical site and work place in which work happens; and the artefacts which support work and capture work results.

In this section of the tutorial, we introduce work models as a way of representing contextual data. We describe key kinds of work models for understanding customer tasks.

1.3 Interpretation Session

Team interpretation sessions enable a cross-functional team to bring their unique perspectives to the data. They share design, marketing, and business implications, raise and capture issues, draw work models, and develop a shared view of all customers and their needs. Interpretation sessions offer an effective way to handle the overwhelming amount of data qualitative methods provide.

In this section of the tutorial, we describe and practice running an interpretation session using the data collected during the interview exercise. We capture key insights from the data and draw sequence, physical, and artefact work models to represent the work practice.

1.4 Characterising a Market

Products and systems are built for sale to a market or use by a department; they are not built for individual users. But we gather data from individual users—how do we represent what these users tell us about all users? Without a well-defined way to generalise from specific users, we appear to be designing from anecdotal evidence. *Work model consolidation* is such a well-defined process, resulting in a small set (5-7) of work models which characterise the work structure and basic work strategies across all customers. These models can be shown to account or fail to account for the work practice of any individual user.

In this part of the tutorial we describe and practice two key techniques for characterising a market. First, the *affinity diagram*, which brings together issues across all customers to reveal the scope and nature of the problem. Second, *work model consolidation*, which brings together individual work models to show common patterns, structure, and intents across all customers.

In this section of the tutorial, we practice building affinity diagrams, and walk through the process of work model consolidation, discussing how to derive design insight from the consolidated model.

1.5 Running the Project

The best techniques in the world cannot help you if you cannot manage the project to deliver a result. We discuss the unique problems raised by introducing customer-centred processes into traditional organisations. We discuss key leverage points where new approaches can be successful, and suggest how to manage the process for success given each different project situation.

2 Conclusion

A clearly defined, customer-centred design process guiding a team from initial data gathering to system design is possible today. In this tutorial we lead participants through key transitions in that process: gathering detailed, valid customer data; making customer work practice concrete; generalising to a market or department; and seeing the implications for the system design. We show how the material in this tutorial links to the later design process which formalises and elaborates the initial design.

References

Beyer, H. and Holtzblatt, K. (1997). *Contextual Design: Defining Customer-Centered Systems,* Morgan Kaufmann Publishers Inc., San Francisco.

Greenbaum, J. and Kyng, M. (Eds.), (1991). *Design at Work*, Hillsdale, NJ: Lawrence Earlbaum Pub..

Norman, D. A. and Draper, S. W. (Eds.), (1986). *User Centered System Design.* New Jersey: Lawrence Earlbaum Associates.

Suchman, L., (Ed.) (1995). 'Representations of Work' (special issue), *Communications of the ACM*, September, **38** (9).

Suchman, L., (1989). *Plans and Situated Actions*, Cambridge University Press, Cambridge.

Holtzblatt, K. (ed.) (1999). "Special Section on Contextual Design" in *interactions* Jan/Feb **1**(1).

Winograd, T., (1996). *Bringing Design to Software*, ACM Press, NY, NY.

Wixon, D. and Ramey, J. (Eds.) (1996). *Field Methods Case Book for Product Design*, John Wiley & Sons, Inc., NY, NY.

Human-Computer Interaction - INTERACT'99 (Volume II)
S. Brewster, A. Cawsey & G. Cockton (Editors)
Published by The British Computer Society © IFIP TC.13, 1999

Designing Speech-driven User Interfaces

Tony Rose

Canon Research Centre
Surrey Research Park
Guildford, Surrey GU2 5YJ
UK
Email: tgr@cre.canon.co.uk

Elisa del Galdo

Cambridge Technology Partners
Eton House, 18-24 Paradise Road
Richmond, Surrey TW9 1SE
UK
Email: egaldo@ctp.com

Abstract: This half-day tutorial provided participants with an understanding of the fundamental concepts in speech recognition, and how best to use this technology in the design of user interfaces. A number of guidelines and case studies were presented and discussed. The tutorial finished with a group exercise that allowed participants to apply the design guidelines to an actual device.

Keywords: User interface design, speech recognition, guidelines, input methods

1 Introduction

This tutorial provided an overview of speech recognition technology and investigated the important user interface design issues for speech-driven applications. Each design issue was discussed in the context of how it affects usability or user satisfaction, and was accompanied by the corresponding specific guidelines. This introductory-level tutorial also provided an opportunity to apply the knowledge gained, via a practical exercise.

2 Speech Recognition Technology

The purpose of the opening section was to provide a brief technological overview of the process of speech recognition, in order to familiarise the interface designer with the technical characteristics of this novel input medium. Speech recognition technology encompasses a wide range of academic disciplines, and a comprehensive treatment of the subject is evidently beyond the scope of a short tutorial. The reader is thus provided with suitable references should further detail be required (e.g. Rabiner and Juang, 1993). Indeed, it is possible for good design to take place even in the absence of such knowledge, simply by treating the recogniser as a "black box". However, some awareness of the recognition process is inevitably required to fully appreciate the limitations of the technology and to anticipate the impact that future developments will have on the use of speech within interface design (Schmandt, 1994). The following topics were covered by this section:

- Why speech recognition is a difficult problem
- How speech recognisers work
- Different types of recogniser
- Examples of small and large vocabulary systems
- Future directions

The practicalities of these topics were further illustrated by live demonstrations using a PC-based speech recogniser.

Speech recognition has made considerable progress in recent years, and systems that were once confined to the research laboratory are now becoming commercially available. The utility of speech interaction is spreading rapidly: from dictation programs on PCs, through speech driven PDAs to interactive voice response telephony services. Furthermore, performance is continually improving: many PC dictation products now claim a word accuracy of 95% or more, and smaller vocabulary command and control systems can return an accuracy of 99% or more, for speaker-dependent, non-noisy conditions.

3 Advantages of Spoken Interaction

Many situations were identified in which spoken input to machines is highly effective. These situations typically include cases when the user's hands or eyes are busy, or when the user is physically disabled (Lindsay-Carter, 1995). In addition, recent technological developments have led to the proliferation of small (yet powerful) portable devices such as PDAs, and advances in speech technology have made the use of speech input a viable option. The disadvantage of the more traditional input methods is that they do not always allow effective and efficient access to the complete functionality of the application. Interaction with such devices requires input methods that are fast, accurate, robust and compact.

Speech can provide users with an input method that is more powerful and potentially less complicated. By taking full advantage of spoken interaction, and not just mimicking the work patterns of non-speech interfaces, speech recognition can transform the way users interact with machines. An understanding of the design issues, benefits and limitations of speech technology can therefore facilitate more effective user interface design.

4 Design Issues and Guidelines

There is sometimes a misconception that the accuracy of the speech recogniser alone determines the usability of a speech-driven application. Clearly, accuracy is a key factor, but other issues can be equally important in the overall system design. Research has demonstrated that well-conceived, simple interface design strategies can have a significant impact on the management of spoken input (Oviatt, 1996). However, such user-centred approaches often remain under-exploited, and the interface design issues for many systems are frequently inadequately investigated.

The tutorial discussed these issues and focused on the relevant design guidelines and case studies. The guidelines were based on the results of recent research combined with an examination of the relevant HCI guidelines and heuristic evaluation of existing speech-driven applications. The case studies were supported by demonstrations of actual devices to illustrate the application of specific guidelines. Example design issues included:

- The benefits of spoken interaction vs. other methods;
- The way in which interface design is affected by user context and speaker dependency;
- Designing for different input speech types, such as discrete, continuous, or keyword;
- How to manage the acquisition of speech training data;
- Improving interaction by the use of feedback, prompts and error resolution;
- How to design a vocabulary for maximum usability.

5 Practical Exercise

The guidelines were followed by a practical design exercise in which attendees, in small groups, were given the opportunity to put into practice the material presented in the first half of the tutorial. Each group was provided with a (non-speech) device and asked to redesign the user interface to incorporate speech input. Attendees were not expected to produce a complete user interface design, but to evaluate the advantages, limitations and potential of speech input for their chosen device. Attendees then illustrated their conclusions using scenarios and example interactions.

References

Lindsay-Carter, E. (1995) "*Placing the user at the centre of design: contextual research in speech recognition*" http://kcox.cityu.edu.hk/ct1995/carter. Advanced Technologies Group, Novell Corporation, Orem, UT, USA.

Oviatt, S. (1996) "*User-Centered Modeling for Spoken Language and Multimodal Interfaces*" http://www.cse.ogi.edu/~1chen/SharonPaper/Ieee/Ieee.html. Center for Human-Computer Communication, Oregon Graduate Institute of Science & Technology.

Rabiner, L. and Juang, B. (1993) "*Fundamentals of Speech Recognition*". Prentice Hall, NJ.

Schmandt, C. (1994) "*Voice Communication with Computers*". Von Nostrand Reinhhold, New York.

Designing Multimedia Presentations

Alistair Sutcliffe and Stephanie Wilson

Centre for HCI Design, School of Informatics
City University
Northampton Square
London EC1V 0HB
UK
Email: a.g.sutcliffe, s.m.wilson@city.ac.uk

Abstract: This tutorial presents a comprehensive method for multimedia presentation design which addresses problems such as how best to organise the design process, how to select appropriate media in order to deliver content that is comprehensible to the user and how to script for effective user navigation and control. The approach is based on extensive research and practical experience in industrial multimedia design.

Keywords: Multimedia, design guidelines, scripting, dialogue design, media selection

1 Overview

This tutorial presents a comprehensive design method for multimedia presentations which is based on extensive research at City University (Sutcliffe and Faraday 1994, Faraday and Sutcliffe 1997) as well as practical experience in industrial multimedia design (Faraday and Sutcliffe 1998). The method addresses key problems in presentation design including how best to organise the design process, how to select appropriate media in order to deliver content that is comprehensible to the user, how to ensure the user perceives and comprehends important information in the presentation and how to script for effective user navigation and control. Participants will gain knowledge of and practice in the method and will also be introduced to the forthcoming multimedia user interface design standard (ISO 1998) which is edited by Prof. Sutcliffe.

2 Content

The tutorial covers the entire design process for multimedia presentations, from initial task analysis and requirements, through media selection and scripting to final dialogue design and navigation control. A variety teaching formats are used throughout, including lectures, question and answer sessions, demonstrations of multimedia products on video and CD ROM, and practical hands-on exercises. The content is structured into four sections as outlined below.

2.1 Psychological Background and Principles

The first section introduces the design process in outline and provides a summary of the relevant psychological knowledge for multimedia design. Key features of human perceptual and cognitive processing of visual and audio media are outlined, as well as the limitations of human information processing for each medium. Topics to be covered include working and long term memories, issues of selective attention, learning and comprehension. For example, multimedia designers can influence what users look at by controlling attention with display techniques such as use of movement, highlighting and salient icons. The limitations and properties of different media will be explained in relation to the psychology of perception and comprehension, for instance, the differences between static and dynamic media (e.g. users only extract very high level or 'gist' information from moving images). The section will conclude with a set of multimedia design principles based on human psychology.

2.2 Media Selection and Combination

The second section first gives detail on requirements specification and creation of a task model incorporating a specification of information requirements. This is based on the assumption that the presentation content should be specified in logical terms before media are selected. Only when the 'amodal' specification of content has been produced should media selection and design proceed. This is followed by definitions of media and advice on selecting appropriate media for the information requirements. Mapping rules and heuristics are described for media selection and combination. Task and user characteristics influence media choice; for instance, verbal media are more appropriate to language based and logical reasoning tasks; whereas visual media are suitable for spatial tasks involving moving, positioning and orienting objects.

2.3 Scripting, Integration and Attention

In the third section, the first cut script is elaborated to deal with topic focus and integration. Design techniques are described for directing the users viewing/reading sequence to ensure that important information is perceived and the message thread can be followed effectively across different components in a multimedia application.

Issues concerning user attention to both time varying and static media are explored. First, attention directing techniques are proposed for each medium e.g. text, speech, still image, moving image, and then techniques to link media segments together are described. The need for focus shifts between information components are identified and a set of techniques are described for establishing contact points between media. A contact point is where the message in one medium continues in another, hence a bridge has to be built. The techniques direct the user's attention by overt directions to look or attend to another medium or by indirect reference to contents being presented. The use of presentation bar charts to plan the sequence and duration of media delivery is explained.

3 Dialogue and Tutorial Multimedia

The final section covers dialogue and navigation design for interactive multimedia and ends with a brief review of high level design concepts for tutorial multimedia. Dialogue design includes selecting devices for communication from the wide variety that are now available such as speech input/output, gesture, hand writing input and virtual reality devices. Heuristics to guide this choice of communication modality are described. Dialogue design in multimedia elaborates presentation scripts to add features for user navigation through a set of media resources and for access to system functions. Guidelines and design features to support user navigation are covered, ranging from design of hypermedia navigation structures, to visit lists, bookmarks, search mechanisms, overview maps, etc.

Time precludes an extensive coverage of tutorial multimedia design, however, some time is devoted to this topic as it is a major application area and designers often request coverage of design for learning and training systems. The features of modern tutorial multimedia are reviewed and the implications of learning theory for direct engagement and guided discovery learning are discussed along with their design implications. High level scripts and architectures for tutorial media are described and cross referenced to media selection and combination covered earlier.

References

Faraday P.M. and Sutcliffe A.G. (1996) An Empirical Study of Attending and Comprehending Multimedia Presentations. *ACM Multimedia 96,* Boston USA, 265-277.

Faraday, P.M. and Sutcliffe, A.G. (1997) Designing Effective Multimedia Presentations, *In Human Factors in Computing Systems, Proceedings of CHI 97*, ACM Press , 272-279.

Faraday, P.M. and Sutcliffe, A.G, (1998), Providing Advice for Multimedia Designers, In *Human Factors in Computing Systems CHI 98,* Los Angeles USA, ACM Press , 124-131.

ISO (1998) ISO 14915 *Multimedia User Interface Design Software Ergonomic Requirements* – Part 1: Introduction and Framework, and Part 3: Media Combination and Selection.

Sutcliffe, A.G and Faraday, P.M. (1994) Designing Presentation in Multimedia Interfaces, In *Human Factors in Computing Systems, CHI '94*, Boston, USA, ACM Press, 92-98.

Part Eight

Workshops

Human-Computer Interaction - INTERACT'99 (Volume II)
S. Brewster, A. Cawsey & G. Cockton (Editors)
Published by The British Computer Society © IFIP TC.13, 1999

Second Workshop on Human-Computer Interaction with Mobile Devices

Stephen Brewster and Mark Dunlop

Department of Computing Science
University of Glasgow
Glasgow, G12 8QQ, UK
Email: {stephen, mark}@dcs.gla.ac.uk
Web: http://www.dcs.gla.ac.uk/mobile99/

Keywords: mobile devices, PDAs, mobile telephones, usability

The last 3-4 years have seen the development and marketing of a vast array of mobile computing devices. These systems herald what we believe to be a new era of 'ubiquitous' computing. The utility of these devices is reduced by the problems of accessing information resources through tiny displays. This can be especially problematic where that information is 'perishable'; where its value is only relevant to particular locations and times. The utility of mobile devices is further reduced by the problems of manipulating miniaturised versions of `standard' keyboards and pointing devices. Users are also forced to perform numerous, delicate operations by selecting very small icons.

This workshop provides a forum for academics and practitioners to discuss the challenges and potential solutions for effective interaction with mobile systems and builds on the success of the First Workshop on Human Computer Interaction with Mobile Devices held in Glasgow in May 1998. The workshop is intended to cover not only PDAs but also voice terminals, smart phones and laptops.

Papers were invited on the following topics:

- visualisation techniques for large data sets on small displays;
- speech input for portable devices;
- evaluations of mobile devices being used in remote/hazardous locations;
- safety issues in the operation of mobile devices;
- case studies of the existing tasks performed by mobile users;
- requirements engineering for location dependent (and location independent) computing;
- interfaces that support the integration of mobile devices and telecommunications;
- ergonomics of hand-held devices;
- authoring Web pages for hand-held devices;
- novel screen-based user interfaces for hand held devices;
- screen quality and the success of hand held devices;
- sound in mobile computing devices.

The proceedings of this workshop will be formally published in the journal *Personal Technologies* after the conference.

Human-Computer Interaction - INTERACT'99 (Volume II)
S. Brewster, A. Cawsey & G. Cockton (Editors)
Published by The British Computer Society © IFIP TC.13, 1999

HCI — Theory or Practice in Education

Margaret Cox[1], Lars Oestreicher[2], Clark Quinn[3], Matthias Rauterberg[4] and Markus Stoltze[5]

[1]King's College, Strand
London WC2R 2LS
England,UK
Email: mj.cox@kcl.ac.uk

[2]Dept. of Information Science
Uppsala University
P.O. Box 513
751 20 Uppsala
Sweden
Email: larsoe@csd.uu.se

[3]School of Computer Science and Engineering
The University of New South Wales
Sydney 2052, Australia
Email: cnquinn@cse.unsw.edu.au

[4]IPO
Technical University of Eindhoven (TUE)
Den Dolech 2,
5612 AZ Eindhoven,
The Netherlands
Email: rauterberg@ipo.tue.nl

[5]IBM Zurich Research Laboratory
Säumerstrasse 4
CH-8803 Rüschlikon
Switzerland
Email: mrs@zurich.ibm.com

Keywords: education, teaching, HCI, practice, theory, multimedia

The workshop aims at identifying how education programs in Human-Computer Interaction (HCI) can benefit from modern teaching techniques and how collaboration between industry and academia can be improved for a better understanding of the mutual educational needs. Some immediate issues are:

(1) Can we use multimedia technology to implement networks of teaching excellence?
(2) What kind of support do we need for teaching both at undergraduate and postgraduate level?
(3) Which is the role for HCI within e.g. software engineering, psychology and sociology?
(4) What is a PhD in HCI, i.e. what criteria should we impose in a multi-disciplinary subject?

Education in HCI is a task that incorporates many different aspects on the area. Students are to be taught how to apply their knowledge in many different knowledge fields, as well as involve themselves in the traditional software design processes, rapidly producing good interfaces for the software. The clash between practical, easily accessible knowledge, and the theoretical fundaments of the topic areas needs to be addressed in education. This has to be done in a way that is fruitful to both academic institutions and the practitioners in the field.

The role of an HCI expert will in many cases be to know when and why HCI problems may or will occur, and make sure that proper preparations will be made before the problem occurs. Thus, HCI education has to be shaped to produce this kind of experts —as a complement to the HCI practitioners.

Furthermore, HCI, by its title as well as its very nature is an interdisciplinary activity. Involving humans indicates contributions from fields including psychology, sociology, and anthropology. The computer side indicates contributions from at least computer science, software engineering, and artificial intelligence, though it can extend to electrical engineering and industrial design. The interaction side starts involving communication fields including graphic design, writing, ergonomics, and sound in its various incarnations.

This interdisciplinarity requires an integrative approach, and argues for a project-based learning environment. Ideally, students from different disciplines will converge on courses in this area, to be grouped in teams to solve problems. Also ideally, the problems can arise from real industrial needs that can situate and motivate the learning. It is important to scaffold the tasks with rapid prototyping tools, allowing learners to iterate designs quickly.

Interdisciplinarity is an increasing benefit to the learner and the employer, and facilitating these links provides a better framework for learning. In this way, we may arrive at professionals who in their work combine a good theoretical understanding with minute practical skill.

Human-Computer Interaction - INTERACT'99 (Volume II)
S. Brewster, A. Cawsey & G. Cockton (Editors)
Published by The British Computer Society © IFIP TC.13, 1999

Usability Pattern Language: Creating a community

Richard N. Griffiths
Lyn Pemberton

University of Brighton
Faculty of Information Technology
Brighton, BN2 4GJ
UK
Email: r.n.griffiths@brighton.ac.uk
Email: lp22@brighton.ac.uk

Jan O. Borchers

University of Linz
Telecooperation Group
Department of Computer Science
Altenberger Str. 69, 4040 Linz
Austria
Email: jan@tk.uni-linz.ac.at

Keywords: usability, interaction, interface, pattern, pattern language, design

1 The Workshop Topic

The idea of patterns and pattern language originally developed by the architect Christopher Alexander and colleagues in the 1960's (Alexander, 1977), has been widely applied in the area of object-oriented software design. On the face of it, Alexander's original use of pattern language for the planning of towns and design of architecture has a more immediate applicability to user interface design. Researchers and designers in HCI are faced with the similar challenge of creating interfaces, systems and settings for systems which have that "quality without a name", which in our community we acknowledge via terms such as "user friendliness," "affordance," "intuitive," "transparent" and so on. Also there are very direct analogies between the architectural and HCI domains: we constantly appeal to spatial notions in HCI design whether we are discussing screen layout, information visualisation, web navigation or interaction in virtual reality environments. Alexander's ideas have recently begun to be explored for application to the practice of HCI design, most notably in the Design Patterns Workshop at CHI'97, (Erickson, 1997) and usability pattern languages have started to appear. For a substantial example, see Jenny Tidwell's Web site, (Tidwell, 1998).

2 The Aims of the Workshop

This workshop is intended to develop the idea of using pattern languages for recording and disseminating good practice in usability design, and to build a community of HCI design pattern practitioners. It will address the following issues with the aim of initiating a continuous process of pattern development and review: How best to find, document, maintain and disseminate pattern languages; How to use them to bridge interdisciplinary gaps; How to apply patterns; How to evaluate patterns; How to evaluate the application of patterns; Case studies and examples.

References

Alexander, C., Ishikawa, S. & Silverstein, M. (1977) "A Pattern Language: Towns, Buildings, Construction." Oxford University Press.

Erickson, T. (1997). "Report on Design Patterns Workshop CHI '97." Available at: http://www.pliant.org/personal/Tom_Erickson/.

Tidwell, J. (1998). "Common Ground: A Pattern Language for Human-Computer Interface Design." Available at: http://www.mit.edu/~jtidwell/common_ground.html.

Human-Computer Interaction - INTERACT'99 (Volume II)
S. Brewster, A. Cawsey & G. Cockton (Editors)
Published by The British Computer Society © IFIP TC.13, 1999

How to Make User Centred Design Usable

Jan Gulliksen
Department of HCI,
University of Uppsala,
Uppsala
Jan.Gulliksen@hci.uu.se

Ann Lantz
CID
Royal Institute of
Technology, Stockholm,
alz@nada.kth.se

Inger Boivie
Enator AB
Stockholm
inger.boivie@enator.se

Web: http://www.nada.kth.se/cid/interact99/workshop/index.html

This workshop on user-centred design in practice is a follow-up to the workshop "User-Centred Design in Practice - Problems and Possibilities", held at the Participatory Design Conference (PDC '98). The PDC workshop touched on a great number of issues within the field of user-centred design but left little time to explore any of the subjects in depth. For more information, see the PDC workshop web site http://www.nada.kth.se/cid/pdc98/workshop/ Matters that were discussed were among others:

- User-centred design (UCD) versus participatory design (PD) - what are the intentions?
- Work without users - what do you do when your users are not available?
- The role of the UCD facilitator
- Should users participate in the actual user interface design, and in such case how?
- Organisational aspects and power structures
- Attitudes about UCD and users

This workshop will continue the discussion about UCD in practice and bring up a few issues for in-depth discussions. For the purpose of this workshop we would like to define UCD in accordance with ISO/DIS 13407 (Human Centred Design Process for Interactive Systems) which specifies the following four principles for UCD: 1. an appropriate allocation of function between user and system, 2. active involvement of users, 3. iterations of design solutions and 4. multidisciplinary design teams.

This workshop will discuss UCD from a slightly different viewpoint - that of the system developer and the designer. Few people would refute the necessity of user involvement in systems development, but in reality, user participation and usability activities are often reduced or removed from the itinerary when the project is pressed for time as the deadline is coming close. Moreover, in traditional systems development, there are few methods for user interface design, and the user interface designer is often a software engineer. User participation is concentrated to the early phases of modelling and analysis, whereas the actual interface design is done with a minimum amount of communication with the users, in as little time as possible. Usability activities are scheduled late in the project, if included at all. Where does UCD come into the picture?

This workshop focus on certain issues regarding how to make UCD help the interface designers in their work and help them meet their deadlines, i.e. how to make the UCD process usable for its users. Such issues include, for instance:

- *Organisational aspects - how do we create a in the project?*
- *Roles - how does UCD change the role and work of the designer?*
- *Tools - do prototypes and mock-ups help in creating a shared understanding of the context?*

The workshop is intended for practitioners and researchers with practical experiences within the field of UCD as well as system developers and designers with an interest for the field. It will provide a possibility to discuss these matters and exchange experiences.

Workshop on the Organisational Aspects of Human Error and Systems Failure

Chris Johnson

Department of Computing Science
University of Glasgow
Glasgow, G12 8QQ
Scotland
Email: johnson@dcs.gla.ac.uk

Keywords: human error, safety, organisational failure, management

Human error has long been seen as a contributory factor in the causation and exacerbation of accidents. In the past, this has resulted in an emphasis upon the individual human factors that lead to error: high workload; fatigue; poor situation awareness etc. However, there is an increasing realisation that accidents can only be prevented by also looking at the organisational factors that place individuals in situations where they are likely to make errors. This workshop will provide a common forum for academics and practitioners to review techniques that can be used to identify and avoid these error-inducing contexts.

Our intention is to focus on techniques that can be easily integrated into existing systems engineering practices. We will discuss the impact of new technology in safety-critical organisations. This includes workplace studies, ethnography and more focussed forms of human reliability analysis. We will also consider the managerial problems associated with maintaining a safety "culture" with existing equipment and legacy systems. This includes the way in which risk analysis must inform and be informed by wider organisational objectives. We are also interested in the legislative frameworks that govern the design and operation of safety-critical systems.

The following list includes some of the higher level questions that will be addressed:

- is it possible to predict the effect that organisational change will have on the safety of an application either in terms of human 'error' or systems 'failure'?

- do previous failures provide a useful means of assessing the impact that organisational factors have upon the safety of future systems?

- is it possible to extend incident reporting systems from the narrow confines of operator error and component failures to provide effective warnings about wider managerial and regulatory issues?

Human-Computer Interaction - INTERACT'99 (Volume II)
S. Brewster, A. Cawsey & G. Cockton (Editors)
Published by The British Computer Society © IFIP TC.13, 1999

Methodology for Design: CUI, GUI or Web

Joseph Kramer

IBM Research
30 Saw Mill River Road
Hawthorne, NY 10532, USA
Email: kramerjo@us.ibm.com

Eugenie Bertus

IBM
11401 Burnet
Austin, TX 78758, USA
Email: ebertus@us.ibm.com

Abstract: There are a number of distinct styles that could be used when designing software user interfaces. In the late '80s, character based (CUI) interfaces were discarded in favour of the more appealing graphical user interfaces (GUI). The current trend in interface design is moving toward web browser interfaces and beyond. Unfortunately, the decision of interface style often is dictated, by the fad of the day, which may be a detriment to the intended users. Each interface style has advantageous and disadvantages. The goals of this workshop are to document the advantages and disadvantages of each style, and include recommendations for proper usage for each style.

Keywords: CUI, GUI, Web, Browser Interface, Design

1 Workshop Description

In the workshop, the characteristics of the different styles that can be used when designing software user interfaces will be explored. The hypothesis is that each interface style can be advantageous to the user if used in the appropriate context. This assertion assumes that interfaces loose favour due to popular trends, and not to the inadequacies in meeting users needs.

The outcome of this workshop will be a job-aid (decision tree) to help guide decision makers to choose the appropriate interface style. The job-aid will include advantages and disadvantages of each style, recommendations for proper usage for each style, and what questions a designer should ask to help guide them into making the appropriate decisions. The workshop participants will decide on an appropriate method of making the product of the workshop accessible to a wider audience.

2 Agenda

Participants will begin, by describing the characteristics for each interface style. Participants will split into style specific groups and generate lists of characteristics which they feel identify their particular interface style. Inclusion of concrete examples will be strongly encouraged. The entire workshop will then re-congregate to formulate a commonly agreed upon list for each style identified.

Next, the style specific groups will list the advantages and disadvantages of each interface style. Again, participants will be encouraged to draw upon their experiences and give concrete examples from projects they have participated in. A commonly agreed upon list of advantages and disadvantages will be formulated and discussed for each style identified.

The participants will then formulate the methods and questions necessary to determine what design is optimal for a proposed interface. This will enable the construction of a decision tree to be used as a job-aid.

3 Benefits

Participants in this workshop will gain a greater appreciation and understanding of the different choices available for design. In turn, aiding their teams in understanding the ramifications of interface style choices.

Making Designers Aware of Existing Guidelines for Accessibility

Monique Noirhomme-Fraiture, Julio Gonzalez-Abascal and Colette Nicolle

University of Namur
Institut d'Informatique
21, rue Grandgagnage
B-5000 Namur, Belgium
Email: mno@info.fundp.ac.be

University of the Basque Country
Laboratory of HCI for Special Needs, Spain
Email: julio@si.ehu.es

HUSAT Research Institute,
Loughborough, UK
Email:
c.a.nicolle@lboro.ac.uk

Keywords: People with disabilities, Accessibility, Guidelines, Regulations, Web Design.

The access of people with disabilities to the New Technologies of Information and Communication (NTIC) is crucial on many grounds. Indeed, the society is evolving in a direction where these technologies are part of everyday life and a two-speed society is not acceptable. At the same time, such technologies offer a substantial help in the process of improving the way of live of people with disabilities.

In order to make NTIC accessible by people with disabilities, it is absolutely necessary to raise the awareness of the designers and developers. This workshop will focus on the ways to achieve it. For the moment, there exist relevant guidelines dedicated to software and hardware designers. But, do the designers read them? Often, these guidelines represent large documents readable by disability specialists. Is this the best way to proceed? What do the designers think about regulations (e.g. the Americans with Disabilities Act in the U.S., the Disability Discrimination Act in the U.K., and the European Commissions 1996 White Paper - Equal Opportunities and Non-Discrimination for people with disabilities)? How can designers ensure that they know how to implement these regulations? What do designers think about guidelines accessible on the Web and about the use of awareness campaigns? On the assumption that guidelines are known by the designers, how do they use them and what are their habits? These are as much questions to be discussed by the participants of the workshop.

The workshop is intended for anybody concerned about the design of interfaces also accessible by people with disabilities: the ergonomists and the interface specialists but also all the designers and the developers interested in sharing their practice and their views. This in fact ought to include them, given legislation that now exists which could (and should) have far-reaching implications for the future.

The topics exposed and discussed are:

- Are the designers and developers aware of existing sets of guidelines for the design of accessible interfaces and do they use them?
- Is there best means to make them aware of guidelines?
- What is their practice using guidelines?
- What are the possibilities to present the guidelines and is there a best way to do it?
- What do the designers think about regulations?

The workshop is organised on behalf of IFIP WG 13.3 "Human-Computer Interaction and Disability".

Human-Computer Interaction - INTERACT'99 (Volume II)
S. Brewster, A. Cawsey & G. Cockton (Editors)
Published by The British Computer Society © IFIP TC.13, 1999

Representational Support for User-Developer Communication in Systems Development

Eamonn O'Neill, Hilary Johnson, Peter Johnson and Pat Healey

Department of Computer Science
Queen Mary and Westfield College
University of London
London E1 4NS
Email: {eamonn, hilaryj, pete, ph}@dcs.qmw.ac.uk

Keywords: Representations, communication, user, participation, systems development.

1 Introduction

User-developer communication in systems development relies upon diverse representations. In addition to supporting communication about the subjects of the systems development activities, the representations must (often simultaneously) support communication amongst the participants about the development activities themselves. In fulfilling these roles, multiple representations are often used in combination and in series, demanding frequent transformations between representations.

Surveys, case studies and anecdotes all provide illustrations of successes and, too often, failures of the use of different forms of representation in supporting user-developer communication.

2 Objectives and Issues

This workshop brings together researchers and practitioners with interests in processes of communication between users and developers in software systems development and in representations used to support this communication.

The workshop runs for one day, tackling a set of related questions:

What features of user-developer communication can or should be supported by such representations?

What properties of a representation contribute to making it an effective communicative aid?

Which forms of representation exhibit these properties and in which contexts?

How are representations transformed in the course of use for communication?

What relations are there between effective support for communication within user-developer co-operation and for communication outside those collaborative activities, e.g. in communicating the results of their work to system implementors or others who may not have participated in the creation of the representations?

The workshop contributes to both research and practice. The workshop discussions identify gaps in our current understanding of the communicative role of representations in systems development and lay the groundwork for a research agenda to explore these and other issues which arise through the discussions. The workshop conclusions also lead to recommendations for the selection and use of a range of representational forms to support user-developer communication in systems development practice. This in turn may lead to proposals for technologies to support communication through representations.

Human-Computer Interaction - INTERACT'99 (Volume II)
S. Brewster, A. Cawsey & G. Cockton (Editors)
Published by The British Computer Society © IFIP TC.13, 1999

Is Cognitive Engineering the Way Forward for HCI?

Adam Stork, John Long and Tony Lambie

Ergonomics and HCI Unit
University College London
26 Bedford Way
London WC1H 0AP
Email: a.stork@ucl.ac.uk

Keywords Cognitive Engineering, Human-Computer Interaction

1 Workshop Topic

Cognitive Engineering (CE) has been proposed as being the way forward for Human-Computer Interaction (HCI). This workshop is intended to debate the proper meaning and value of CE to HCI in the long- and medium-terms.

The idea of CE has been around for some time in various forms and under various guises. HCI has also developed in various ways, during this period. Over the last ten years or so, CE and HCI have made contact of different sorts. For example, the notion of domain' from CE is finding some (belated) favour in HCI. More concern with human-computer interactions is now the case in CE. Research initiatives and conferences often accommodate both CE and HCI. We feel this CE/HCI contact points up the need for a workshop on the proper meaning and value of CE to HCI in the long- and medium-terms.

2 Workshop Plan

The workshop is a one-day workshop. Position papers on the workshop topic are contributed by participants, and are circulated to all participants before the workshop. The plan comprises:

- Workshop Introduction
- Cognitive Engineering for the Long-Term: Summary of the Position Papers
- Cognitive Engineering for the Long-Term: Discussion
- Cognitive Engineering for the Medium-Term: Summary of the Position Papers
- Cognitive Engineering for the Medium-Term: Discussion
- Workshop Dissemination
- Future Workshops
- Conclusion

3 Workshop Emphasis

Discussion, and the dissemination of that discussion, are the primary aims of the workshop. All participants are encouraged to take part.

It is expected that dissemination is to be by an informal poster and web report that summarises the content and outcome of the workshop for Interact '99. The organisers will prepare a more fulsome report for publication, after circulation and agreement amongst the participants after the workshop. A decision over publication of the position papers, or extended position papers, is to be taken during the workshop.

A discussion is to be initiated on potential CE topics for future workshops.

Part Nine

Professional Practice and Experience

Human Factors and the Design of an Enhanced GUI to Support Post-Production Tasks

Clare Borras and Richard Foster

Sony Broadcast & Professional Europe
R&D Advanced Technology
Jays Close, Viables
Basingstoke
UK
Email: {cb, rdf}@adv.sonybpe.com

Abstract: This paper describes a Graphic User Interface, (GUI), for use within the post-production industry. Post-production software tools are designed on a 'needs led' basis lacking structured Human Factors (HF) input. Window based systems proliferate the industry, inserting an additional computing layer to post-production tasks. Extant User Interface (UI) design reveals non-optimal allocation of perceptual modality to information representation. The graph, a central component when designing special effects, fails to utilise the whole visual field, and quickly becomes complex causing navigation problems. Based on Psychological, HF and Broadcast specific literature, EditWorld presents a GUI that exploits human experience of living in a 3D world and operating 3D objects through a design that incorporates a 3D work-space, direct manipulation objects, and multimedia multimodal (M^4) technology for information representation. An enhanced graph design is presented that utilises the whole visual field and provides a more rational means of presenting complex data structures in 3D environments.

Keywords: post-production, direct manipulation objects, M^4 technology, 3D, GUI, enhanced graph

1 Scope and Purpose

EditWorld is a research project concerned with the design of a post-production special effects tool to more effectively and efficiently support Human-Computer-Interaction (HCI). Such tools are used to perform detailed special effects edits on image contents across a sequence of clips, lasting in the region of a few seconds to a few minutes. The industry refers to such tasks as 'short-form' editing.

EditWorld is the first step in the design of an innovative and intuitive special effects tool that encourages and supports Users in the creative and exploratory tasks that characterise short-form editing.

The overall design goal for EditWorld is to increase the communication bandwidth within the human computer interaction by improving the quality and quantity of information flow. The design solution accommodates the capabilities and limitations of human cognition by incorporating the following technologies:

- Graphic representations of direct manipulation objects in a 3D workspace. A design solution that draws on human experience of living in a 3D world and operating 3D objects, combined with graphic representations of direct manipulation objects within human computer interaction has added attraction. The design of direct manipulation objects incorporate 'ecological' visual cues that optimise human cognition due to the 'naturalness' of perceived objects.

- Applying M^4 technology to information representation through a design that exploits human multi-sensory channels, enhancing the interactive nature of the human computer interaction by enabling Users to more effectively and efficiently manipulate information.
- Enhanced graph metaphor is a graph designed to work in harmony with the whole visual field and the ability to focus on detail and simultaneously maintain an overview. As the User moves towards an object of interest, the object becomes increasingly magnified. Other objects are presented in decreasing size and detail relative to increasing distance from the object of interest. An overview map will link the detailed and summary view through a coding methodology yet to be decided.

To this end, the paper goes some way to defining the design problem, characterises short-form edit tasks and presents an initial design solution. The colour correct tool, which modifies colour values, is used to demonstrate a graphic representation of a direct manipulation object, the effective application of M4 technology to information representation within an enhanced graph and a 3D workspace.

2 The Design Problem

The scope of the general problem for HCI is summarised as "humans and computers interacting to perform work effectively", (Long and Dowell 1989). From this, a specific design problem for EditWorld can be summarised as 'humans and computers interacting to perform efficient and effective short-form edits within a system that encourages creativity and exploration'.

Analyses of the interaction process with extant post-production systems reveal the design issues HCI must address. More specifically, the post-production systems currently available alienate Users from the creative task by implementing a multi-media window based UI inserting a computerised layer into the work process. This layer requires additional learning and navigation skills, and causes Users to indirectly perform edit tasks. The mismatch of information representation to domain task in extant systems result in a variety of interaction problems.

The graph component is the established industry metaphor to structure and organise special effect tasks. However, graphs quickly become complex and densely populated causing navigation problems. Also, to perform detailed tasks on image contents, work has to be transferred to another component, requiring the User to integrate information between system components, incurring further cognitive costs.

3 Domain Task Model

With information derived from editors and industry experts, involvement on post-production courses, and examination of domain specific literature, short-form edit tasks can be characterised as being creative and exploratory visual processes performed on images and image structures. Typically, attention and time are dedicated to a sub-section of an image with intermittent overviews of the entire image to ensure an adequate idea of how detailed tasks relate to the overall project. Users add, delete and modifying graphical aspects of image components within a clip or over a sequence of clip frames.

Due to high financial costs incurred using the specialist skills of editors and post-production equipment, the finished product must result in a high quality productive work output.

From this, it can be seen that this area of research is directly linked to the utility, perceived utility, financial benefits and production output gained from using one system over another. Therefore, obvious benefits are made where the information bandwidth within the human computer interaction is expanded.

4 The Design Solution

In short, the intention is to remove obstacles to creativity and exploration through the combinatory effect of implementing the technologies detailed above. More specifically, Users will be able to preview the outcome of a special effect on an image without having to perform the actual task. Tasks are to be reversible in that Users can 'walk out' of, rather than undo task sequences. Special effects will be manipulated on the actual image, or image sequence. As effect attributes change, the changes are visible in the appearance of the image and the special effect direct manipulation object. The design of direct manipulation objects and the background workspace will be recognisable and reflect functionality.

EditWorld looks to human to human communication and the natural employment of perceptual modality to information representation where the use of multi-media to present information and the employment of multiple perceptual modalities to handle incoming information is 'naturalised', resulting in minimal cognitive costs. As the component technologies of spatial and temporal information representation have limitations a synergy of technologies is used to increase the information bandwidth.

The enhanced graph is intended to more effectively present complex information structures by using 'ecological' cues to, for example denote areas of intense detail and make use of the whole visual field by presenting information at an appropriate level of detail whilst mapping a detailed view to the overview.

4.1 A Graphical Representation of a Direct Manipulation Object

Using graphic representations of direct manipulation objects is well suited to creative spatial tasks. Users become more closely involved with the creative and exploratory aspects of such tasks.

Well designed graphic representations of direct manipulation objects adhere to many HF principles. Principles of 'virtuality', whereby realistic representations of reality can be effectively manipulated, and 'transparency', whereby skills can be directly applied to tasks, are detailed in Shneiderman (1998). Problem-solving and learning skills are enhanced when problems and solutions have a suitable visible representation as memory is better equipped to retain physical spatial graphic representations. Finally, knowledge learnt in a physical visual-spatial format can be more effectively applied to other related problems.

Using direct manipulation objects during interaction leads to more efficient interaction due to the following attributes:

- Combined location of data display with data entry
- Immediate feedback reduces logical errors

A design solution that incorporates direct manipulation objects should reflect the way people manipulate objects in the real world. Card et al (1999) suggest designs include the following aspects:

- Continuous representation of objects and actions of interest (maintains visual momentum)
- Objects be manipulated by physical actions or directional keys
- Operations are visible, rapid and reversible
- Direct manipulation objects be designed as recognisable objects and reflect real world actions

Also, where these principles are adhered to the following benefits will be evident in a system such as EditWorld:

- Immediate feedback allows Users to monitor actions in relation to goals. Where actions are counter-productive Users can easily change direction through inverse actions
- Rapid manipulation of objects of interest
- Data display and entry is in the same location
- Physical and visual representations are easier to manipulate and retain in memory
- More effective navigation through complex scenarios
- Anxiety is minimised as the system is comprehensible and actions are easily reversed
- Intermittent Users retain operational concepts

From this, a graphic representation of a direct manipulation tool for colour correction is presented.

Figure 1 demonstrates an image overlaid with a colour tool reflecting. 1: Shows a colour sampler represented by a small rectangle. 2: Represents direct manipulation tools unique to colour correction functionality to, for example, change the colour space, view user defined colours etc. 3: Represents the Red, Green, Blue, (R, G, B) colour space with three nodes, the arms of which can be dragged out or pushed in to change a colour value. The R, G, B colour nodes are accompanied by a numerical information which can also be directly edited. 4: Represents a boundary function to define the area to be modified.

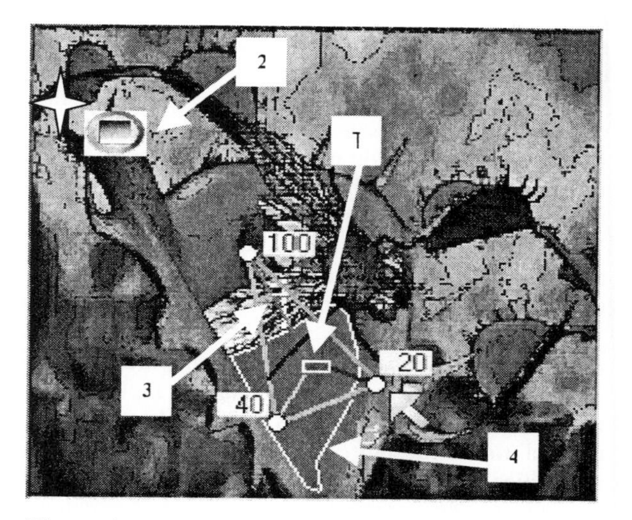

Figure 1.

Once the colour tool has been overlaid on the image, the colour sampler becomes active and visible. This causes the colour nodes and associated numeric values to reflect the current colour values within the colour sampler. During colour correction the sampler maintains the original colour until a preferred colour is accepted, providing a way of comparing old and new colours. Alternatively, the User may need to see how modifications affect the whole image to make adequate creative judgements.

A means of defining the sampler and boundary to the colour correction task has yet to be designed. It may be that a default shape can be directly edited, to change its shape and size, or the User may access a library of shapes. Ultimately, the means to manipulate boundary and sampler components will need to be consistently represented.

The colour nodes can be moved to increase or decrease individual colour values or the associated numerical values can be edited. When colour nodes are manipulated the associated numerical values change in harmony and visa versa. It is expected that user trials may find the design will need to incorporate more traditional ways of defining colour, (possibly similar to that used in graphics packages).

4.2 M⁴ Technology

Firstly, M^4 technology is an abbreviation of the terms 'multimodal' and 'multimedia'. Dix, Finlay, Abowd and Beale (1993) supply the following distinction between these terms. A multimodal system refers to the exploitation of the human multi-sensory channels to increase the communication bandwidth between the human and computer. By utilising more than one sense, or mode, of communication, the interactive nature of the system is enhanced. A multimodal system may use a number of different media to communicate additional or, redundant information.

By comparison a multimedia system refers to the objects used to present information to the User. Multimedia may exploit multi-sensory channels or an intra-sensory channel by presenting more than one type of, for example, visual information. Finally, 'layering' refers to instances when a modality, such as language, uses more than one media type, even though they use the same modality, and, when a single medium uses many modalities, for example a piece of paper may use language and graphics.

The human facility to exploit multiple input/output media in the real world needs to be understood and applied to UI design. A description of sensory modalities and cognitive processing is outlined with a view to the optimal allocation of perceptual modality to domain task processing code. Subsequently, this will have an impact on the efficiency of tasks performed and contribute to the effectiveness of work by presenting information in an appropriate format for particular tasks.

Firstly, resource modality refers to the channels by which stimuli are perceived, or the mental operations carried out, to then perform responses. Processing code refers to the form of information representation in human memory. Spatial code presents information in an analogue spatial form like graphical images. Verbal or phonetic code represents information in linguistic form as words or sounds.

Each sensory modality has varying capabilities and limitations affecting the quality and quantity of information flow, and that of subsequent information flow. To enhance information processing 'stimuli-response compatibility' (SRC) should be optimised, for example, verbal stimuli are best attended to by a spoken response (see Wickens 1992). The effective implementation of SRC on the GUI is an area that EditWorld can distinguish itself from competitor products.

In the instance of dual task performance within limited space that demands separate resource modalities, such as audio-visual, rather than a common resource, such as audio-audio, will result in the following:

- Cognitive time-sharing is more efficient.
- Current task difficulty is less likely to have implications on subsequent tasks.

In short, cross modal time-sharing is more efficient than intra-modal, unless competing intra-modal resources are far enough apart. Competing intra-modal resources too close together cause confusion, for example two auditory messages competing to be heard mask each other.

From this, when considering the application of M^4 technology to GUI design to enhance performance in special effects tasks whilst incorporating direct manipulation devices. It is necessary to consider how direct manipulation devices will be used in relation to the image or sequence of images.

Special effects tasks are performed on image contents, a sub section of image contents, on a single image frame, or over a series of image frames. The special effect will modify, add or remove aspects of the image within a x-y, or x-y-z space. When experimenting with a colour correct tool, the User starts by identifying the colour to be changed, then judgements are made as to how much the colour is going to change. The User may have a vague pre-defined requirement expressed in subjective terms, such as produce a 'moody' feel, or change the insects' wings to look more metallic and so on: The domain expertise of editors is such that Users will either go directly to a colour or explore alternative options on a try it and see basis.

Again referring to Figure 1, it can be seen that the current design solution accommodates the above User requirements. The colour corrector can be positioned on the actual image, so the component is closely related to the object of interest. The colour to be changed is identified and its values presented by the colour sampler, a change in the colour node arms and their associated values reflects the colour in the colour sampler. The User is then able to define a boundary area to which the colour modification will apply. The User stretches out the colour node arms, making creative judgements as the colour changes within the bounded area. Alternatively, the User can input numeric values in the numeric section above the colour node arms, or access a more traditional way or selecting colour through one of the direct manipulation tools dedicated to colour correct tool.

4.3 Enhanced Graph Metaphor

Space is a critical aspect when performing any post-production tasks. Special effect tools and aspects of an image need to be located and navigated through an information space. An enhanced graph design needs to more adequately represent spatial distance and make use of the capabilities and limitations of the eye.

Our ability to perceive and understand spatial relationships is anchored in an analogue understanding of the world whereby larger spatial differences are more important than smaller ones. An example of this is the way a graph or meter is read in analogue form, for example, estimations are made in terms of 'about half full'. Meanings attached to differences within spatial representations are significant to the reader. In comparison, the meaning attached to a digital meter exhibiting two numerical values (e.g. 344444 and 677777 to signify comparable differences in capacity) is limited, as the numerical information has to be converted into a more suitable format when representing spatial information.

Visual tasks are spread across the whole visual field, using both foveal and peripheral vision. Foveal vision enables focused and detailed attention within a small (2°) area. Peripheral vision, although unable to attend to detail, may be exploited to perceive changes in, for example, speed and direction, and supplies summary information, effective for tracking and monitoring tasks. Peripheral and foveal vision are simultaneously employed supplying two different types of information that can be used together.

The usefulness of peripheral vision is lost where display information is restricted to using foveal vision through a layout that requires attention to be directed at a number of different objects. Such a layout requires each object to be attended to separately and then integrated to obtain summary information.

Solutions to the integration of summary and detailed information in a display to effectively exploit the whole visual field are as follows:

- Incorporate a magnifier, so that areas of interest can be examined in detail, with external information in decreasing detail providing a summary view.
- Provide a link between the detailed and summary views
- Rationalise the UI by designing an 'ecological' display to exploit natural visual cues to perceive information about objects to signify information concerning the depth or age of tasks

Figure 2 demonstrates the first two issues mentioned above. 1: Shows a magnified view in the 3D workspace, with a colour correct tool overlaying an image clip. 2: Shows an overview of the project. The magnified view is highlighted in the overview to orientate the user and integrate the two views. 3: Demonstrates the decreasing detail of information representation of objects positioned away from the object of interest.

Figure 3 (represented as 3: on Figure 2) shows a way of rationalising the graph components by allowing tasks to be layered on top of each other. 1: Signifies instances of a history of tasks a depth metaphor is applied to the 'pile of objects'. 2: Demonstrates a task layer and its associated attributes being re-visited by 'pulling it out' of the task pile.

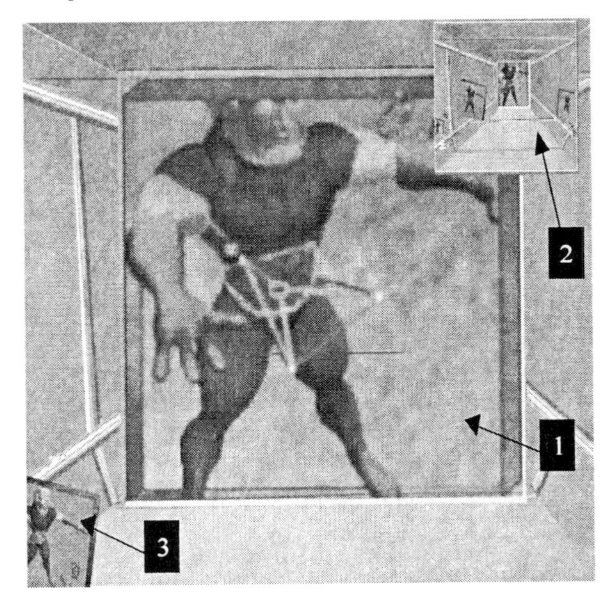

Figure 2.

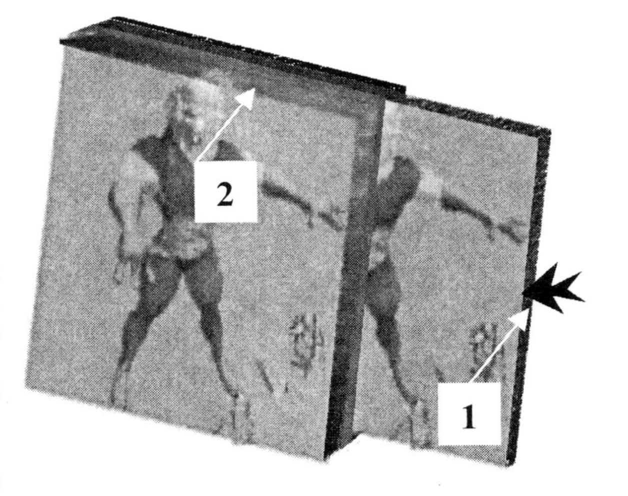

Figure 3.

5 Conclusion

The above outlines a sub-section of the initial stage of a research project centred around the design of an innovative task-based GUI to more adequately support special effect tasks. The combinatory effect of the above design concepts within the design solution seeks to enhance the human computer interaction process. The research contributes to understanding and finding ways to removing task obstacles, providing a means to enable Users to better concentrate on domain tasks and harness the additional 'magical' qualities that technology can bring to special effects and short-form editing.

The extent to which the design more effectively and efficiently represents the domain, domain tasks and adequately accommodates the capabilities and limitations of human cognition will be revealed through extensive testing and iterative design amendments planned for future stages.

References

Card, S., K., Mackinlay, J., D., and Shneiderman, B. (1999) *Readings in Information Visualisation – Using Vision to Think,* Morgan Kaufmann Publishers Inc.

Dix, A., Finlay, J., Abowd, G., and Beale, R. (1993) *Human-Computer-Interaction,* Prentice Hall International (UK) Limited.

Eakins, J. P., and Graham, M. E. (1999) *Content-Based Image Retrieval – A Report to the JISC Technology Applications Programme (final draft for comment),* Northumbria Image Data Research Institute.

Garber, S. R. and Grunes, M. B. (1992) The Art of Search: A Study of Art Directors, *Proc. of CHI 1992.*

Long, J. B., and Dowell, J. (1989) Conceptions of the Discipline of HCI: Craft, Applied Science and Engineering. In Sutcliffe, A. and Maculay, L. eds., *Proceedings of the Fifth Conference of the BCS HCI SIG,* Cambridge University Press.

Norman, D. A. (1998) *The Invisible Computer,* The MIT Press.

Ohanian, T. A. (1993) *Digital Non-linear Editing: New Approaches to Editing Film and Video,* Butterworth-Heinemann.

Posner, M. I. ed. (1993) *Foundations of Cognitive Science,* The MIT Press.

Sarkar, M. and Brown, M, H. (1992) *Graphical Fisheye Views of Graphs,* CHI 1992.

Shneiderman, B. (1998) *Designing the User Interface – Strategies for Effective Human-Computer-Interaction (third edition),* Addison-Wesley.

Wickens, C. D. (1992) *Engineering Psychology and Human Performance (second edition),* Harper Collins.

Human-Computer Interaction - INTERACT'99 (Volume II)
S. Brewster, A. Cawsey & G. Cockton (Editors)
Published by The British Computer Society © IFIP TC.13, 1999

More Than Meets the Eye! Usability and Iris Verification at the ATM Interface

Lynne Coventry

NCR Financial Solutions Group Ltd
St Davids Drive, Dalgety Bay
Fife
Scotland
Email:
lynne.coventry@scotland.ncr.com

Graham I. Johnson

NCR Knowledge Lab
206 Marylebone Road
London
UK
Email:
graham.johnson@scotland.ncr.com

Abstract: This paper describes some of the consumer-driven usability research conducted by NCR Self-Service Solutions in the development of an understanding of usability and user acceptance of leading-edge biometrics verification techniques. We discuss the background and present a case study, which focuses upon the usability phases and issues, associated with iris verification technology at the ATM user interface. The paper concludes with a review of some of the major research issues encountered, and an outline of future work in the area.

Keywords: biometrics technology, iris verification, ATMs, usability techniques, consumer research.

1 Introduction

Until recently, (e.g. Baber et al, 1998) there has been relatively little interest in public technology, such as the Automated Teller Machine (ATM), the ubiquitous cash machine, from the field of usability and human-computer interaction (HCI). There have been ATM-related studies, for instance, in relation to older adults (see e.g. Adams & Thieben, 1991), of the mental models held by users (e.g. Payne, 1991), of novel self-service user interfaces (e.g. Johnson, 1996), and of overall ATM usability (e.g. Hatta & Iljama 1991; Johnson & Westwater, 1996). However, these are few in comparison with the multitude of studies, essentially of similar technology, to be found in the workplace. This is clearly despite the growing numbers and importance of this technology in our lives, a technology which is evolving quickly in terms of complexity, convergence, and the variety of potential applications of such devices (see www.ncr.com).

Biometrics technology at the ATM, and specifically speech-driven end-points have been investigated (Baber et al., 1997; Hone et al, 1998) revealing the importance of convenience, speed and familiarity of the ATM interface, and underlining the diversity of the ATM user population. Other behaviourally-based biometrics techniques have also received attention from a user's perspective (e.g. Deane, 1995a and 1995b), albeit in an occupational setting and application.

This paper describes our recent user-centred research in understanding attitudes towards, and behaviour with, biometrics verification at the ATM interface. Following a brief introduction to biometrics technology, we present the case study noting usability methods adopted, findings, and briefly conclude with an outline of future research.

2 Biometrics Technology

Traditionally, access to secure areas or sensitive information has been controlled by possession of a particular artefact, such as a card or key and/or knowledge of a specific piece of information such as a Personal Identification Number (PIN) or password

(Feustel & Velius, 1989). Today, many people have PINs and passwords for a multitude of devices from the car radio and mobile phone, to the computer and their bank information. Herein lies a major difficulty involving the trade-off between usability and security. Methods for increasing the security of this information such as regularly changing PINs and passwords, and ensuring all are different, makes them more difficult to remember and, therefore, error- prone. Of course, these traditional methods rely upon the assumption that the artifact (such as key or card) will be in the possession of the rightful owner and that the information to activate it will be kept secret. Unfortunately, neither of these assumptions can be wholly relied upon.

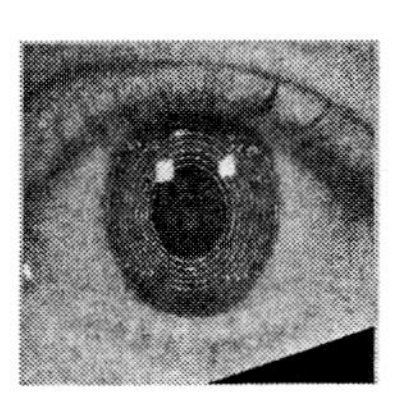

Figure 1: Iris image showing template.

Gong et al (1992) note that if people are permitted to choose their own passwords they tend to select ones which are easily guessed. People tend to choose ones that are related to their everyday life (Adams & Chang, 1993). They choose ones, which are easy to remember, and, typically, easily predicted, or they change all PINs to be the same. Also, people are often lax about the security of this information and may deliberately share the information, say with a spouse or family member, or write the PIN down and even keep it with the card itself. Other approaches, such as biometrics verification, are being investigated with a view to their general introduction, either in combination with or as a replacement of card and PIN solutions.

The term biometrics refers to any and all of a variety of identification techniques, which are based on some physical, or behavioural characteristics of the individual, contrasted with those of the population. Unique digital identifiers are created from the measurement of the characteristic.

Physiological and anthropometric biometrics techniques include those based on the verification of: fingerprint, hand and/or finger geometry, Eye (retina or iris), face, wrist (vein), and so forth. Behavioural techniques include those based on voice, signature, typing behaviour, and pointing.

All biometrics approaches follow a similar operation: a digital template is created during an enrolment process, then the template is stored in a database. On attempted verification, the relevant template is extracted and compared with the data input, say in the form of a fingerprint, or an acquired iris image, for positive identification. Biometrics techniques tend to be differentiated in terms of their technical accuracy, measured by False Reject Rates (FRR), and False Accept Rates (FAR), together with template size, and the speed of enrolment and recognition or verification.

Clarke (1994) presents the desirable characteristics of a human identifier, an ideal biometrics measure. It seems that not all these objectives can be fully achieved by any current method. These ideal characteristics are - universal, unique and exclusive, permanent through life, indispensable, digitally storable, precise, easy to record, efficient to record, and acceptable to contemporary social standards.

2.1 Iris Verification

Figure 2: Showing final self service prototype.

With iris verification, as developed by Sensar Inc. (www.sensar.com) for application at ATMs, a wide-angle camera finds the head of the person to be identified. A zoom lens then targets in on the user's iris and takes a digital photo. A template of concentric lines is laid on the iris image (see Figure 1) and 266 specific points are recorded and the information converted into a digital template. This can then be compared with others and for verification and identification purposes.

The general interest in iris verification applied to public technology is centred upon its accuracy or reliability, which is much greater than say fingerprints, and the fact that the biometric itself can be acquired without the individual having to come into physical contact with the end-point. The next section of this paper reviews our work in the pursuit of an understanding of financial consumers with regard to biometrics in general, and iris verification in particular.

3 Case Study

At NCR Self-Service Solutions, investigations into the use of biometrics to verify and/or identify bank customers have been undertaken over a number of years. These investigations have used a variety of methods with the aim of gradually acquiring a sound understanding of the issues from the consumers' perspective. This section outlines some of the research undertaken, addressing iris verification at the ATM user interface. We describe focus groups, dynamic anthropometry study, laboratory-based usability evaluations, and an extensive field trial with customers.

3.1 Focus Groups

Over the last few years, a number of focus groups have been held, frequently in association with different financial institutions and in different locations around the world.

The aim of the focus groups was to gauge the consumer attitudes towards biometrics technology in general, and on occasion a particular biometric, such as iris verification, has been the primary interest. A focus group involves a pre-selected group of consumers, and a moderated discussion, following a set guide of topics with the purpose of eliciting commonly held views, their range, and underlying attitudes.

There are many issues which influence consumers and their perceptions of public technology. It is important to separate general attitudes from actual behaviour. What consumers think and what they really do does not necessarily follow an obvious relationship. This is particularly true when dealing with the diversity of the general public, and with technology, services or concepts that have rarely been encountered before.

The focus groups have shown that there is a general lack of public understanding of how a biometric, or even a PIN works. This is often expressed in terms of a level of suspicion or distrust. In general, people believe facial recognition could work, as they believe that is the way humans identify each other, and that fingerprint technology must work, after all, they are used as evidence in law enforcement. Summarising the major findings of the series of focus groups: :

(a) There is little perceived need for the addition of biometrics. Years of experience with PIN have led consumers to believe that it is sufficiently secure. Consumers rarely report forgetting their PIN, unless prompted. They do report the potential for others to acquire their PIN, but they also can misuse this by giving their cards and PINs to friends and family on occasions.

(b) Consumers have difficulty believing that such 'futuristic' technology can work well. In the case of iris verification technology, consumers assume there are difficulties with the process of image capture and even the uniqueness of the iris. They also worry that the technique could fail to recognise them leaving them unable to access their money at a critical time.

(c) There is a general concern about the potential for the misuse of personal, biometrics data collected, which is seen as violating their privacy and civil liberties. This issue is reviewed extensively by Woodward (1997).

(d) Consumers also express some concerns about potential health risks associated with the technology. Misunderstandings of iris verification can lead the consumer to believe the technology involved may lead to eye damage.

The initial focus groups with iris verification highlighted several general, negative attitudes from potential users. However, we know that attitudes can be changed provided that the consumer has a successful experience with the technology. It may be that fears could be alleviated by a careful marketing campaign, or through utilising the enrolment process as an educational opportunity, or simply through exposure to, and experience with, the technology.

Later focus groups specifically addressed key acceptance issues. Participants were asked how they would convince others to use the system. They were also asked to comment on a first draft of a marketing leaflet. Comments made within these groups suggested that the marketing information should stress how simple the process is, and use the analogy of a photograph. Also, the perceived value to the consumer, of speed and convenience, was raised.

3.2 Eye Tracking and User Envelopes

Alongside understanding consumer attitudes, it is also necessary to understand the physical characteristics of potential users that will impact the design of a self-service technology. One design must attempt to fit all consumers. The iris image must be acquired in a non-obtrusive manner. This means that the user can not be expected to be standing with the eye in a predefined position. Thus, the ATM-iris unit must cope with a naturally wide range of consumers' eye positions in front of the ATM.

In contrast to the qualitative nature of focus groups, an in-depth investigation of the dynamic anthropometry of consumers and their eye positions when using ATMs was carried out (see Hide et al., 1999). The aim of this study was to produce three-dimensional co-ordinates of consumers' eye positions at three key stages, during an everyday ATM transaction. Those points were card entry, PIN entry and general screen use. A series of LED markers in combination wit CODA (gait) motion analysis system were used to determine these 3-D co-ordinates. A sample of over 100 participants from the ages of 13 to 79 years took part in the study, including some wheelchair-bound users. The measurements were taken on two different ATM machines, upon which the angle of the screen was varied.

The eye positions recorded demonstrated that for non-wheel chair users, the majority of eye positions fall within a relatively small envelope, of 300mm across the face of the interface, 300mm vertical and 400mm away from the front of the machine.

This study has provided real dimensions upon which to base the requirements for the ATM-iris unit, so that it is able to easily locate user's iris, where that user is drawn from the general population, without requiring any self-positioning when using the ATM.

3.3 Functional Prototype Evaluation

One of the first iris verification technologies, with the potential to be utilised within a self-service environment was developed by Sensar Inc. An early prototype of this technology underwent usability and feasibility testing. This trial was carried out with approximately 300 participants.

As a first test of the prototype the evaluation was mainly focused on the actual performance of the technology, specifically, its accuracy and reliability. The technology was not fully integrated into a self-service environment, and required that the participants remember what to do. This caused some problems with mistiming and misdirected gaze. Participants also noted that the system was slower than expectation, and 31% reported experiencing problems using the system as they kept looking at the associated computer screen, rather than the verification unit. This meant that iris images were not easily captured. Perhaps, not surprisingly, iris verification was not favoured, by the majority of participants.

This work with the early, functional prototype revealed that at that stage of maturity of the technology was not generally acceptable to the general public, and that further iterations were required to improve speed and enhance the system's ability to acquire a quality iris image.

3.4 Experimental, Laboratory Evaluation

The iris verification unit underwent several changes and was incorporated into a self-service ATM with appropriate graphical lead-through for users. During the prototype development it was crucial to, firstly, ensure that usability was maximised and, secondly, to ensure that the acceptance of the technology would be influenced by actual usage of the system.

Recruited from our own organisation, 42 people who were not involved with the biometrics self-service projects, were asked to take part in the lab-based usability trial. The height of participants varied form 4 ft 10 in to 6 ft 2 in. The majority of participants were young (under 40) males (69%), of whom 14 % wore contact lenses, and 17% wore spectacles.

To understand the general acceptance issues, qualitative data were captured via questionnaires at three points in the study: Firstly, before participants had any experience with the system, then after they had taken part in the enrolment procedure and lastly after they had used the prototype iris-ATM system. Usage of the system by individual participants averaged 6 times during a three-day period.

The results showed that, even with internal, largely technically-aware staff, before enrolling over a third had concerns about using the system as it might be implemented in their own bank. These concerns were in the areas of reliability, health issues and misuse of data. Around a third, at pre-trial stage, also said their concerns were so great that they would not feel very confident using the system.

After enrolment with the iris verification system, 26% said that enrolment had caused a positive change in their opinion of the system. Further, *after* use of the system to carry out normal transactions such as withdrawing cash, 31% quoted a positive change in attitude. Only a small number still had some concerns, and these were primarily about potential misuse of personal data. Following, full use of the prototype system, 96% of the participants said they would now be confident in using the system in future.

From the usability perspective, performance data were collected by using the system to log the 'verify time' and videotaping the prototype usage. The verification time (i.e. how long it takes for a user to be 'recognised' by the system) achieved by users varied greatly from a min of 2.2 seconds to a max of 33.5 seconds. Only 2 users could not achieve at least one verification time of less than 4 seconds, which compares very favourably with PIN entry. The mean verification time was 4.6 seconds.

In further reviewing the behavioural evidence, the videotape records, many of the usability issues were attributable to the user being distracted and looking away when the verification process started. However, the issue of misdirected gaze was still not fully resolved. This was due to the distance between the screen on the machine and this prototype unit. Occasionally, the user would look down at the screen to see what was happening and would then not have the iris in view of the system for verification. Two immediate recommendations were made for the prototype development, either increase the visibility of the cueing on the prototype unit (similar to a photo-booth's red light flashing) and or incorporate an audio cue to signal that the 'picture' has been taken. Ultimately, it would be preferably if the user did not have to look away from the screen when the iris image was being captured.

The in-house work has ensured that the potential usability issues with the system were understood, and could be acted on. It also provided concrete evidence that the experience with the system was sufficient to positively influence participants' attitude. However, this in-house evaluation did not fully answer the fundamental question of whether consumer attitudes would be translated into actual behaviour in the field: Would people use the system in real life, with their own money?

3.5 Field Trial

After the in-house, laboratory-based work, it was important to investigate whether or not the system would be usable and acceptable in a real environment with consumers using the system to access their own money. A 6-month field trial was established with a major UK financial institution.

The trial was located in Swindon, the site chosen as there was a small branch accessible to both the general public and a large population of the institution's staff, who were also customers. A refined prototype IRIS ATM replaced the existing ATM, and the three teller (counter) stations were equipped with iris verification units, to replace traditional signature methods.

A basic marketing campaign was developed to inform customers of the trial and invite then to 'convert' to iris verification in place of PIN. No incentives were provided. During the trial over 1,000 people enrolled in the system of which 39% of these were general public.

Two types of data were collected. Attitudinal data were collected via telephone surveys carried out by an independent market research bureau. Performance data were collected via system logging of the performance details for each and every transaction.

A total of 411 participants were interviewed during two waves of market research. The first wave occurred just after enrolment, and the second wave took place three months later. This market research showed that 70% of enrolees used the system at least once. 44% of those interviewed after enrolment said they were comfortable using the system, after extended usage, the second wave of interviews revealed that this had increased to 94% of users.

Of the 72% of people who continued to use the system until the end of the 6 month trial. Over 90% of the interviewees were satisfied with the iris verification and would elect iris over PIN or signature. These consumers regarded the system as more secure, more reliable and faster. Of those who did not continue to use the system, the main reason given was that they had not been at the branch. Following use of the system, no one expressed any major negative attitude towards the concept.

4 Issues and Future Work

It is clear from our experiences with the on-going development of the iris verification prototypes, that there exists a gulf between those general pre-usage attitudes, and subjective opinion following iris-ATM use. Our ability to predict consumer acceptance of new technologies and services, requires that we acknowledge some of the inherent limitations of focus groups. Whether these are developed with scenarios, or involve grounded discussion, our experiences demonstrate clearly that there is no substitute for 'hands-on' experience with functional prototypes that adhere to the contextual attributes of the task. The earlier we engage consumers with prototypes of the intended system, the better.

Some of the main issues emerging from our research with the iris verification technology are specific to this type of non-contact approach (e.g. 'natural' user positioning), whilst others relate to more general concerns (e.g. potential use of personal data). Future development of the iris technology for ATMs will take full account of the range of consumer issues highlighted. The development of this biometrics approach for ATM consumers, whether via an iris or an alternative, will now be well informed as a result of these studies.

It should be noted that our progress with definition and resolution of some of the usability aspects of the proposed system has been the result of a pluralist approach as far as methods are concerned. The value of qualitative techniques in identifying potential barriers, and the use of sophisticated technology is determining user positions and envelopes, shows that a deliberately wide variety of usability methods need to be incorporated in the pursuit of ease-of-use.

Future research needs to understand better the nature of trust as it relates both to the technology *per se*, and the service provider (in this case the financial institution) as we look beyond the public end-point as a channel via which to carry out transactions which are biometrics-authenticated.

5 Conclusions

This paper has provided an overview of the user-centred work focussed upon the provision of biometrics verification at the ATM user interface. Having adopted a variety of qualitative and quantitative methods, with laboratory- and field-based studies, our research has revealed a number of non-trivial issues with the introduction of this type of technology to the general public. Moreover, as a result of our interventions we have made progress in significantly improving, from users' perspective, the implementation of this leading-edge technology.

Finally, our understanding of user issues with respect to public technology, and specifically the ubiquitous ATM, is enhanced, as is our understanding of the relevance and application of usability techniques at different stages of the design and development lifecycle.

6 Acknowledgements

We would like to thank our design, development and usability colleagues of NCR Financial Solutions Ltd., for their support and encouragement of this work.

References

Adams, A. S. and Thieben, K. A. (1991) Automatic teller machines and the older population, *Applied Ergonomics*, **22** (2), 85-90.

Adams, D. A. and Chang, S. Y. (1993) An investigation of keypad interface security, *Information & Management,* **24**, 53-59.

Baber, C., Johnson, G. I. and Cleaver, D. (1997) Factors affecting users' choice of words in speech-based interaction with public technology, *International Journal of Speech Technology*, **2** (1), 45-60.

Baber, C., Stanton, N. and Johnson, G. I. (1998) From public computing to ubiquitous computing: implications for ergonomics, *Ergonomics*, **41** (7), 921-926.

Clarke, R. (1994) Human Identification in Information Systems: Management Challenges and Public Policy Issues, *Information technology and People*, **74**, 6-37.

Davies, S. (1992) *Big brother: Australia's growing web of surveillance*, Simon and Shuster.

Deane, F. P., Henderson, R. D., Mahar, D. P. and A. J. Saliba (1995a) Theoretical examination of the effects of anxiety and electronic performance monitoring on biometric security systems, *Interacting with Computers*, **7**, 395-411.

Deane, F. P., Barelle, K., Henderson, R. D., and Mahar, D. P. (1995b) Employee acceptance of computerised biometrics security systems, *Computers and Security*, **14**, 225-231.

Feustal, T. C. and Velius, G. A. (1989) Speaker identity verification over telephone lines: where we are and where we are going, *Proceedings of the 1989 International Carahan conference on security technology,* (3-5 Oct), 181-182.

Gong, L., Lomas, M. A., Needham, R. M. and Saltzer, J. H. (1993) Protecting poorly chosen secrets from guessing attacks, *IEEE Journal on Selected Areas in Communications*, **11**(5), 648-656.

Hatta, K. and Iljama, Y. (1991) Ergonomic study of automatic teller machine operability, *International Journal of Human-Computer Interaction*, **3**(3), 295-309.

Hide, S., Haslegrave, C. M., Hopkinson, N., Robertson, D. and Johnson, G. I. (1999) Tracking eye positions during the use of an Automatic Teller Machine (ATM), *Proceedings of CAES '99*, Barcelona, Spain.

Hone, K. S., Graham, R., Maguire, M. C., Baber, C, and Johnson, G. I. (1998) Speech technology for automatic teller machines: an investigation of user attitude and performance, *Ergonomics*, **41**(7), 962-981.

Johnson, Graham I. (1996) Exploring novel banking user interfaces: Usability Challenges in design and evaluation, *IEE Colloquium: 'Interfaces - The Leading Edge', (Group C5, Human-Computer Interaction),* Institute of Electrical Engineers, Digest 96/126, Abertay University, Dundee.

Johnson, G. I. and Westwater, M. G. (1996) Usability and Self-service information technology: Cognitive Engineering in Product Design and Evaluation, *AT&T Technical Journal*, January/February, 64-73.

Mahar, D., Henderson, R., Laverty, W. and Napier, R. (1998) "The effects of password length and reference profile size on the performance of multivariate text-dependent typist verification system." *Interacting with Computers*, **10**, 375-383.

Payne, S. J. (1991) A descriptive study of mental models, *Behaviour and Information Technology*, **10** (1), 3-21.

Woodward, J. D. (1997) Biometrics: Privacy's Foe or Privacy's Friend? *Proceedings of IEEE*, **85**(9), 1480-1492.

Human-Computer Interaction - INTERACT'99 (Volume II)
S. Brewster, A. Cawsey & G. Cockton (Editors)
Published by The British Computer Society © IFIP TC.13, 1999

Turbo-Prototyping: Ultra Rapid User Centred Web Development

Gautam Ghosh

Objectware AS
Slemdalsvn. 37
N-0319 Oslo
Norway
Email: gautam.ghosh@objectware.no

Abstract: Turbo-prototyping is a fast and reasonable method for specifying and designing small web-applications, intranets and extranets. Its objectives are to enhance user participation in the design process and to actually produce a deliverable (a prototype) within a limited time.

Keywords: Professional practice and experience, web design, usability, user involvement, prototyping, methods, participative design experience.

1 Satisfying the Client's Needs

1.1 The Business Perspective

Organisations and enterprises aim at providing their services efficiently and effectively. Though these services have economical, technological and organisational constraints, the client often takes the view that IT systems will inadvertently add value to and reduce costs of their services. They are however often rather unclear and evasive when challenged about their aims and goals of their business processes.

One of the answers these days is the web. What the question is can often be rather uncertain. It is often left up to the web-project to clarify what the goals are, how they can be implemented and what benefits the client can expect to reap. Not long ago every second web project seemed to be initiated simply because the organisation or enterprise felt the need to "be on the web". To avoid being classified as old-fashioned, your organisation's presence on the Internet was crucial.

1.2 The Project's Perspective

The speed with which web projects have to be completed has set many an organisation under considerable pressure. The clients and their users often have very fuzzy notions of what they actually want to achieve, but expect web developers to come up with something tangible within extremely short time-spans.

Seen from the perspective of the software consulting business, the trend in the market has shifted slightly from being focussed on purely Internet based projects to Intranet and extranet services. These projects have some similarities to Internet projects:

- they are based on the same underlying technology
- they still suffer from a lack of clear goals
- they are initiated or controlled by the client's IT department
- clients expect to have something up and running quickly.

The difference between yesterdays internet projects and the intra-/extranet projects of today is the fact that the new projects are applications offering functionality to support the user's tasks, not just information and marketing as many of the internet sites do.

So we're back to developing applications, and though some of the parameters have changed, these projects entail several aspects of traditional software development, e.g. involving users, system security, interfacing with underlying systems, structured methods, documentation, etc. Unlike the Internet projects, the intra-/extranet projects don't require the attention and new approach of marketing gurus, art directors and copywriters. Quite the contrary, these projects are all about providing appropriate functionality, high usability and modern technology, thereby resembling traditional system development projects which require the efforts of system developers, usability experts, designers and least but not least the users.

1.3 The Challenge

The challenges many of today's web project faces are:

- Assisting the clients in clarifying and defining their goals
- Involving the users in the process
- Designing for the possibilities and limitations of the web
- Meeting client expectations within the project constraints
- Being able to deliver something quickly

When an organisation or enterprise engages a consulting company like ours, it generally has an idea of what it wants to do and often has a requirement specification ready. It is our experience, however, that these specifications seldom reflect which goals it expect target groups to achieve using its new system.

Most organisations claim that their projects always focus on their users first. But in reality most of these claims are a modification of the truth, since the project teams spend literally all their time developing features and specifications without once mentioning, let alone spending time with, the user.

Quite a few of the web-projects that we encounter, be they for the internet, intranet or extranet, have limited budgets and seem to be proof-of-concept projects. This basically means that the clients want to investigate certain ideas before committing themselves to a concept. The limited budget aspect obviously limits the scope of the project and is a paradox since the projects are often of an exploratory nature.

In our experience, successful projects don't go through long processes to refine and perfect ideas. They focus on keeping the development cycle short by doing frequent, fast iterations.

2 Our Approach

Turbo-prototyping is very similar to a turbo-charged engine. Ideas, constraints, possibilities and clarifications from the prototyping process are fed back into the process immediately, giving the decision-making process an extra boost thereby speeding it up.

Turbo-prototyping is based on well-known and well-tried techniques, and is therefore nothing new in itself. It is however a very fast and reasonable method for specifying and designing small web-applications, intranets and extranets. One objective is to enhance user participation in the design process and collaboration between designers and users. Another objective is to actually produce a deliverable (a prototype) within a limited time.

The Turbo-prototyping method comprises of the following steps, each taking 1-2 working days:

- Planning and preparing for the process
- a JAD workshop for vision, goals and requirements-specification
- a JAD workshop for designing a prototype
- Documenting the process and results

2.1 Planning the Process

The facilitator (see role description in The Participants below) plans the entire process and scopes the outcome in alliance with the project manager and client's representative(s). Facilities are reserved and the appropriate people are invited to the JAD workshops. Necessary equipment is reserved for use.

2.2 JAD Workshop for Vision, Goals and Requirements-Specification

The first JAD session reviews and refines the vision, goals and requirements developing them into tasks, functions and scenarios.

- Gather together the participants (see The participants below) under the direction of an experienced facilitator.
- Give the participants an orientation about the purpose and format of the session.
- Identify and decompose the vision and the goals into the operations needed to achieve them.

- Identify requirements and known constraints (security, speed, usability, etc.)
- Identify intended users, their tasks and contextual factors.
- Decompose and exemplify tasks into task scenarios.
- Document the process using a visual tool (see ObjectWallware below) during the entire workshop.

2.3 JAD Workshop for Designing a Prototype

Based on requirements, task descriptions and scenarios developed in the first JAD workshop, the second workshop aims at designing a prototype which can be evaluated and endorsed by the participants.

- Prepare rough sketches for a prototype before the session. These do not need to be detailed, but serve as a starting point for the design process.
- Run through the task scenarios one-by-one designing an interface for each task.
- Start out with your own design-suggestion for each web page using ObjectWeb (see ObjectWeb below) on the whiteboard.
- Modify each web page making sure that all the participants agree to the contents and navigation scheme for each page.
- Note navigational details in the margins outside the ObjectWeb page.
- Document each completed page by photographing it with the digital camera. Transfer the photographs to the computer.
- The web-developer imports each photograph into a web-tool like Microsoft FrontPage® and inserts fields and other input fields, makes depictions of buttons and other navigational mechanisms in the photograph active hot-spots, linking them to other pages. This work can be done within an hour or so, thereby enabling the remaining participants to go out for lunch.
- The entire team evaluates the prototype by displaying it on a wall using a projector connected to the computer. The users are encouraged to go through task scenarios. Problems and deficiencies in the prototype are noted so that they can be integrated into the design documentation (changes are not made to the prototype at this stage)
- Problems, deficiencies and changes that have been noted during the prototype evaluation, are listed, grouped and prioritised by the workshop participants. The prioritised list serves as a basis for actions to be taken on the prototype after the session.

2.4 Documenting the Process and Results

Though Turbo-prototyping takes many short cuts past traditional documents and deliverables, it is still important to document the results of the workshops to give the project members and others insight into issues that have been covered and decisions taken as a part of the process. Our approach to this is

- taking pictures of the ObjectWallware diagrams that we develop in the workshops, and transcribing the results in a written document at a later stage.
- including the developed prototypes as live documentation.
- describing the navigational model that is developed during the process.
- taking pictures of the participants and including these in all documentation to make their participation visible. This often leads to a feeling of ownership of the result amongst the participants.

3 The Process Components

Successful Turbo-prototyping depends on the following:

- JAD workshops
- The participants
- ObjectWallware
- ObjectWeb toolkit
- A digital camera
- A computer + wall-projector

3.1 JAD Workshops

JAD Workshops are set up in which 6-20 individuals make decisions through the consensus building leadership of a trained, unbiased facilitator who is not a stakeholder in the future system. Users and information systems professionals are drawn together to design a system jointly in a facilitated group session. A session produces formal outputs such as entity-relationship models, which can be input directly into the system specification.

It is important that a JAD session explores ideas within a predefined scope and that the participants of the session are in a position to make decisions about the outcome of the process. This means that all the participants must be enabled to make decisions on behalf of the stakeholders that they represent. (J. Stapleton, 1997).

The success of the workshop relies on the presence of a facilitator chairing the meeting. The main role of this person is to ensure that the group stay focused upon the design problem and ensuring that every member of the group is given the opportunity to stand up and present his or her own ideas. Another role is to summarise all the ideas after the session for presentation to a design team meeting.

The outcome of such a participatory design session is a series of ideas for screens, layouts, navigation structure, that are evaluated by the design team to assess their technical feasibility and usability. They thus serve as a draft of design specifications. This approach results in immense savings compared to traditional approval processes, which often entail design documents being sent back and forth between decision-makers for their approval. A 20% to 60% increase in productivity over traditional design methods is claimed.

3.2 The Participants

Turbo-prototyping is about making decisions about:

- the scope and requirements
- which alternatives to choose
- functionality, navigation and content of a system
- look-and-feel
- who is to do what and when

Before any decisions can be made a fair amount of investigation and exploration of ideas is required, both of which involve the participation of the right people. A typical Turbo-prototyping workshop will involve:

- The client's representative: can take decisions that involve the cost and scope of the project (optional)
- Domain experts: know the details of what is to be achieved in tasks supported by the system
- End users: actually carry out tasks in the (business) domain
- Project manager: Is ultimately responsible for the project reaching its goals and can act as a corrective in the process.
- Graphical web designer: can visualise ideas and suggest solutions based on experience from other projects
- Web programmer: can put together web-prototypes on the fly, as well as participating in the process with knowledge about the possibilities and constraints of the web.
- Facilitator: designs and runs the entire process including the JAD workshops.

3.3 ObjectWallware

Many organisations use paper-based techniques to create models of processes, systems, data-flows and the like. We have developed our own version of this concept that comprises

- Stiff paper or cardboard in 5 different shapes and 6 colours
- Blue-tack to fasten the paper to a wall
- Wide-tip pens in various colours

We use ObjectWallware in the following manner:

- Each idea in the session is noted using large letters and hung up under an appropriate heading (goals, users, benefits, requirements, etc.) on a wall that is visible to all the participants.
- At regular intervals, the ideas are sorted and grouped, structuring them as much as possible.
- The end-result is documented using a digital camera and is later transcribed into a document.

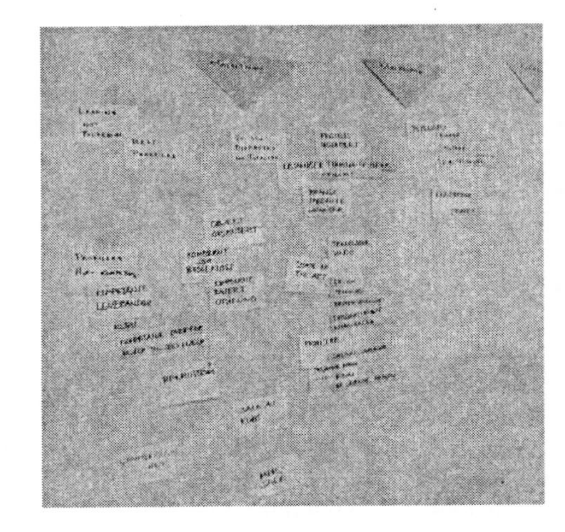

Figure 1: ObjectWallware.

Using the wall as a workspace ensures all ideas of being brought forth, and can hinder unnecessary repetitions. By assigning one portion of the work-space as a "parking-lot", ideas that fall outside of the scope of the process can be effectively parked there, thus demonstrating that the idea has been handled.

3.4 ObjectWeb

We have been building lo-fidelity prototypes based on ideas of M.Rettig (1994) and others for a long time. New developments and changing expectations from project participants have however led us to improve on some of the techniques, resulting in our ObjectWeb toolkit.

The ObjectWeb toolkit is a set of magnetic components that are used on a whiteboard. The user-interface components (for web interfaces) are printed onto a magnetic metal sheet. Our toolkit presently contains

- Browser elements (separate items for all 4 sides, including the standard menus, buttons, etc.)
- 50 buttons with predefined texts (OK, Cancel, Print, Save, etc)
- 20 labels with predefined texts (Name, Address, Password, etc.)
- Blank buttons
- Blank listboxes
- Input fields in 3 different sizes
- Graphical elements and common button icons
- Sets of check-boxes and radio-buttons
- Lines, separators.

The components are to scale (1,5 mm : 1 pixel) and can be used to represent a 800x600 pixel screen on a 120cmx90cm whiteboard (most whiteboards are larger – thus letting us use superfluous area on the board for comments about navigation and links). By visualising screen components at a realistic size we avoid mismatches between our design and the actual product.

We always let a web-designer set up an initial interpretation of a screen using ObjectWeb on the whiteboard, before involving the remaining workshop participants in the design process. Ideas that cannot be represented by ObjectWeb components (e.g. graphics) are drawn onto the whiteboard using standard markers. It is important to permit and encourage the team-members to participate in the design process by letting them move things around if they want to, since this often leads to the revelation of details that might have been otherwise overlooked.

Once the group approves a web page, it is photographed using the digital camera and the picture is transferred to the computer.

3.5 The Digital Camera

The digital camera – we use an Olympus C900 camera – is central in the Turbo-prototyping process. It is utilised to document the result of the process using ObjectWallware and is indispensable in the prototype design process when we use ObjectWeb. The camera must have high resolution and preferably zoom functionality.

3.6 The PC and Projector

The computer is used as a database for pictures taken by the digital camera. It is also used to create a prototype by importing the pictures into a tool like Microsoft FrontPage ®. This prototype is later displayed for evaluation via a projector, while a user runs through task scenarios.

3.7 Case study: Extranet Service for Telecom Company

One of Norway's telecom companies engaged us to design and construct an extranet service. The company sells Internet subscriptions through a chain of high street retailers of electronic goods and wished to offer the shops on-line registration of subscriptions.

Using Turbo-prototyping as our method, we put together a team composed of marketing representatives from the telecom company, end-users from the high street retailers, web designers and developers, the project manager and a facilitator. The team carried out the process and produced a prototype that was evaluated by the team. The evaluation revealed that

- the sequencing of actions (choosing the type internet subscription before entering customer data) was cumbersome and could lead to incorrect registrations.
- the prototype didn't handle the issue of printing a contract a second time (printer-jams are a problem).
- the prototype didn't address the issue of registering several subscriptions for a single customer (relating to SMEs).
- the terminology was too "computerish".
- issues related to logging on and off were inadequately addressed.

The prototype, process documentation and evaluation results were used in the next phase of the project (which contained both more prototyping and usability evaluations)

4 Lessons Learned

The Turbo-prototyping sessions so far have taught us a few new things as well as reinforced some of our earlier beliefs, so we have been able to draw some conclusions about the process and its outcome:

- The process encourages and enables high-level decision-making.
- The method is best suited for small projects or for pilot-projects for larger systems.
- Only minimal resources and materials are required to convey product feel.
- Usability problems can be detected very early in the process.
- Prototypes are quick to build and refine, and thus support iterative design and evaluation.
- We are not left second-guessing what the users do or expect the system to do.
- Communication and collaboration between designers and users is established early in the project.
- The process promotes co-operation, understanding and teamwork among the various user groups and IT experts.
- An experienced facilitator must be used to ensure results within a short time-span.
- Group sessions needs skilful running to ensure the team that they are productive and reach a consensus. Strong personalities in the team can side-track the process preventing the team from covering all the major issues
- The process requires the participation of persons with programming or model building skills to produce the prototypes.
- It is not always possible to get hold of representative users.
- It is often difficult knowing when to stop – prototyping can be fun.
- Workshops tie up stakeholders often for several days at a time.

5 Conclusion

Though Turbo-prototyping in its present form is quite new for us, we have practised almost all of the techniques and methods mentioned in this article in different contexts earlier. We have succeeded in using this method to elicit information, get decisions and produce results in short pilot projects as well as small self-contained projects. Turbo-prototyping is yet another rapid prototyping method, but has an advantage over some of the other methods due to its speed and the results it can produce.

References

Stapleton, J. (1998) *DSDM – Dynamic systems development method – The method in practice,* Addison Wesley Longman Limited, Harlow, England

Rettig, M. (1994) Prototyping for tiny fingers, *Communications of the ACM*, April, **37**(4).

Human-Computer Interaction - INTERACT'99 (Volume II)
S. Brewster, A. Cawsey & G. Cockton (Editors)
Published by The British Computer Society © IFIP TC.13, 1999

Usability Designers Improve the User-Centred Design Process

Bengt Göransson[a,c] and Torsten Sandbäck[b]

[a]Redina Informatik AB, Smedsgränd 95A, SE-753 20 Uppsala, Sweden
Email: Bengt.Goransson@redina.se
[b]Orbil, Kungsängsgatan 17-19, SE-753 22 Uppsala, Sweden
Email: Torsten.Sandback@orbil.com
[c]Department of Human-Computer Interaction, Uppsala University, Lägerhyddvägen 18, SE-752 37 Uppsala, Sweden

Abstract: This paper introduces the idea of having a usability designer role in development team following a user centred approach. There are difficulties in incorporating the user-centred activities into an existing development process, as a user-centred life cycle among other things requires new ways of searching for solutions. Often there is a need for more direct communication and co-operation between users and developers. Somebody has to strengthen this communication as well as to keep the usability method on track. This role is responsible for the usability in all phases of development. In our opinion there exists a need for a person with ability to, for example, specify usability goals; conduct user and task analyses; make the user interface design and lead the design team.

Keywords: user centred design, usability designer, development process

1 Introduction

How can we keep focus on the users, the users' tasks and the usability aspects during a systems life cycle? Processes such as the ISO/FDIS 13407 – "Human-centred design processes for interactive systems" [ISO/FDIS 13407, 1998] are necessary concepts, but does not really give us much support in terms of how to develop usable systems. We need to find,— and define,— practical methods and work procedures to actually be able to incorporate a user-centred view along with active user involvement, multi-disciplinary design etc. into the iterative development process. Among other things, we think that this calls for a new, multi-disciplinary, role in development projects – usability designer. The main purpose of this role is to bridge the gaps between the user-centred activities, but also between the development organisation and the user organisation. This role is responsible for keeping the development process user-centred.

The draft international standard ISO 13407 – "Human- centred design processes for interactive systems" defines a conceptual model that can be used by software companies as an add-on to more traditional system development life cycle processes. ISO 13407 refines models such the classical waterfall model. The four main principles of this conceptual model are:

- An appropriate allocation of function between user and system,
- the active involvement of users,
- the iteration of design solutions,
- the use of multi-disciplinary design teams.

These principles aim to put the users, the users' tasks and the usability of the forthcoming system in focus. To achieve this the ISO 13407 concept introduces four activities that have to be carried out in a project in order to certify that the development is human-centred:

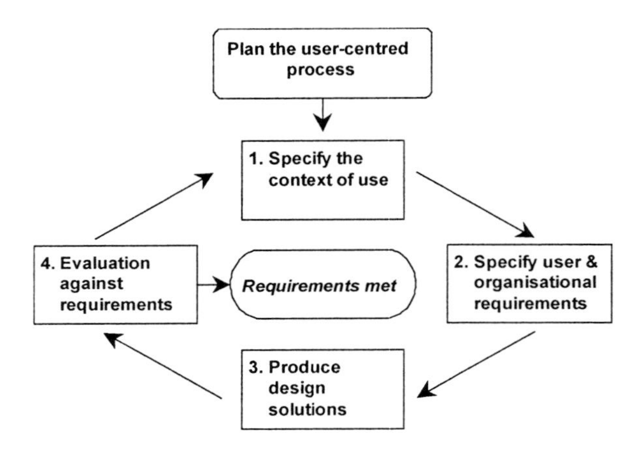

Figure 1: Activities in ISO 13407.

1. Specify the context of use: – the characteristics of the users, tasks and the organisational and physical environment.
2. Specify user and organisational requirements: – functional and other requirements.
3. Design: – create artefacts and evaluate against design objectives.
4. Evaluation: – against user and organisational requirements.

The iteration ends when step 4 is executed with a satisfactory result.

There are difficulties Development organizations still have great problems in incorporating the user-centred (we prefer to use the phrase user instead of human) activities into an existing development process. There are many reasons for this. However, to a great extent they can be related to the fact that an iterative and user-centred life cycle requires new ways to search for solutions, new methods, new project roles, other ways of planning and allocating resources for a project etc. Furthermore, the relationship between the user organisation and the developer organisation has to change. There is a need for more direct communication and co-operation between these groups. We consider this to be mainly a This is mainly a question of moving the development process closer to the users. A user-centred approach, as ISO 13407, can be seen as a shift in development paradigm for an organisation rather than just a new way of developing systems.

2 Case Studies

2.1 Methods

As action practitioners developers we have been involved in several projects trying to assimilate use a user-centred model. We have tried to introduce this model to customers and developers in our own organisation and to practice the role of a usability designer into an existing waterfall model. This process has shaped some theories about how to conduct the iterative user-centred design process successfully. Right now, we are in the phase of forming and testing (verifying) these theories deductively.

2.2 Case One—Government Agency

2.2.1 Background

This project was a contract development job at a Swedish government agency (the client). The client doesn't develop any information systems in-house, but they have a development process they assume the contract developers to follow. This process is a " straightforward waterfall model:; pre-study, requirements specification, system design, construction, test and deployment. Our mission was to make the system design for an administrative office system.

2.2.2 Project accomplishment

We assembled a project team: one domain expert, one system architect and one usability designer. Even though the client didn't specifically ask for a user centred approach, we did set up the project as user centred as possible within the client's framework. This mainly as a result of the usability designer's earlier experiences with failing waterfall processes etc. We didn't manage to get full time end user involvement, but we did convince the client to let us have access to the users a certain amount of hours per week. We did engaged three users (out of a total of about 40) that corresponded to the user population and user profiles. This project set up was totally new for the client. They were not used to have this kind of active user involvement *after* the requirements specification phase. We did also introduce the concept of prototyping as a way of visualising the future system. What we tried to accomplish was a user centred and iterative, prototyping driven system design. This in a framework of a "frozen requirement" specification and a final deadline for the system design, with a construction (or implementation) phase to follow. So we did set some goals; user and task orientation instead of function orientation; prototype instead of written formal documentation; active user involvement instead of passive. These were the three main goals that we tried to accomplish. This in contrast to other development projects already in the construction phase at the client's site.

We started with a user analysis followed by a work task analysis. This was a little bit frustrating for the users since they had been through a lot of conceptual modelling seminars etc. to write the requirements specification. Not admitting it at the start of the project, they now told us that the modelling seminars were very hard to understand and actually didn't give them very much in envisaging the future system. Given the requirements specification, user analysis and the work task analysis we started to sketch on a paper prototype later transferred to an executable prototype. From this point and on we didn't hear a positive word about the earlier modelling seminars, and as soon as we started to work on the prototype the users said—we should have done this much earlier. The prototype was continuously refined through an iterative process: design sessions, implementation and evaluation until Then the design was evaluated and refined and so on, until the prototype covered pretty much the whole requirements specification.

2.2.3 Discussion

In our project we actually tried to practised the concept of user centred design. It became clear that the process needed a role that had the power to lead the team, including the users, through the design process.

The result from of our the system design (yet to be implemented) was quite a success among the users and made an impact on the client. They realised that active user involvement and prototyping resulted in a much more user centred, task oriented and accepted system design. The impact of the usability designer was large. Instead of focusing on functionality, as expressed in the requirement specification, the usability designer managed to move the focus to the user's tasks. This was not an easy thing to do, since the users were not familiar to work so closely with the developers and they thought that the requirement specification documents contained enough information for the team to design a well suited system. We didn't fully accomplish in our mission to let the prototype replace the written documentation. We sort of made it half way in that sense that the prototype considered to be a part of the system design accompanied by paper documentation explaining the look and behaviour of the prototype.

2.2.4 Discussion

Earlier system designs in other projects at the client's site had not had the impact of a usability designer. Those project teams were made of one domain expert and a couple of developers. The only user involvement they had were a passive "question-answer dialogue". When comparing development approaches they realised the benefits of having a person in charge of the design process and the usability. The usability designer led the team, including the users, through the design process. He (it was a male) also made almost all of the screen design.

In this project we actually practised the concept of user centred design. It became clear that the process needed a role who had the power to lead the as it was so easy to drift away from the user centred path.

Benefit from the user centred methodology or the usability designer?

We did also talk to the developers in the projects already designed and under construction. They expressed their positive...

We do not have any numeric results, but we have...

We did only try to be user centred in one phase of the whole development cycle... Is that enough?

2.3 Case Two—Natur och Kultur Publisher

2.3.1 Background

The project was conducted at Natur och Kultur (the client), which is a Swedish publisher (the client). As a complement to publish literature, Natur och Kultur the client has an extending course business. The course department needed help to make a system which handles participators, booking, statistics etc..

2.3.2 Project Accomplishment

This was a small project, involving one designer and two programmers. We could use our own development process. From the start it was decided that we should have a user centred approach, iterate and make prototypes. We made a pre-study including three prototypes evaluated and refined, followed by implementation. When the system was deployed and used for one month, yet an evaluation was conducted.

The designer made the analysis in the pre-study and the paper prototypes as well. As it was a rather small project, the designer led the development team and was responsible for the contact with the users as well as the client customer. During the pre-study the users, needs of the users and information were studied. This resulted in a requirement specification document describing their needs and a paper prototype visualising the a user interface. The paper prototype was the collecting unit of information to all project members and users. It showed the static layout of the interface. We discussed the information visualised in the prototypes, not the requirements specification itself as the visualisation was more concrete.

The programmers used the third paper prototype as the basis for building the system as no formal requirement specification was written. When new requirements arose during the implementation phase they were designed and implemented, the programmers didn't have enough knowledge about the users and the domain so the user interface first was put together in the software tool, then redesigned by the designer to fit with the ideas and design criteria emanating from the prototypes. . In this case the designer brought the experience from the earlier and new analyses. The designer had come to know the user roles, how they think, their domain specific language well and could therefore make solutions suggestions that was accepted almost directly by the users.

2.3.3 Discussion

This approach of working—user centred, iterative and prototype driven—was new to the two programmers and to the customer. The designer acted as an information carrier within the project, explaining why the system should work in a certain way. Sometimes the programmers made a solution with wrongly taken assumptions of the usage of the information and interaction design, so the designer had to reviewed the user interface and to make made adjustments. This sometimes became a "review relationship" where they wanted the designer to acknowledge the solution.

This may sound negative; the designer steered the programmers, but it did actually work was a help as the designer had the whole picture; from analyse, implementation and to evaluation.

Having one person understanding the background of the requirements and bringing that directly to the programmers, This actually meant that it was possible to keep focus on delivering a usable and by the users and the customer accepted system. to speed up the work and still keep high quality. One might claim that one should be able to be read the background in some written documentation, but the time that would have been spent on detailed description on every aspect and unspoken issue from the users could now been invested in actually making the design. It was more fruitful for us to discuss the solution, instead of having to spread all information to everyone. One can look upon it as delivering right piece of information when asked upon.

3 Discussion

In contrast to traditional processes, the activities mentioned above in (figure 1) have to be tightly coupled. One activity can not be performed by developers in isolation and then handed over to the next group of programmers. The transition over the gaps has to be smooth and easy. In every transition informally gained knowledge and unspoken information is lost – information that never will be revealed in formal documentation. No matter how precise the documentation is; the recipient will always have his own interpretation. To minimise the risk of misinterpretation we recommend that a category of people continuously participate in the different activities. As these persons take part in activities where developers and users try to communicate, it is equally important that these persons understands both the users and the developers, since we know that users and developers almost never speak the "same language".

We have experienced the problems mentioned above; the gap between activities; the gap between users and developers, when moving from a traditional process to a user- centred process. In search for solutions we have among others studied Norman's [Norman, 1986] prescriptions for design principles, for example: the urge of taking interface seriously and do user-centred system design. But we did not find a solution, there were still pieces missing. Who in the development team pay attention to the various aspects that leads to a usable system well suited for the user's work tasks and to the business' objectives? We do see a need for multi-disciplinary teams, but also a need for a multinter-disciplinary usability designer.

We are aware that our case studies were quite small projects, and that the role of the usability designer certainly will be different in larger and more complex projects. For instance there will be a demand for more written documentation, formal reviews etc.

3.1 Definition of Usability Designer

The usability designer is responsible for keeping the development process user-centred and focusing on usability aspects. It is very important crucial that the usability designer actually takes an active part in the e design and development process, and just not becomes another project manager. We emphasise the importance of one person participating in all the user-centred activities, in order not to lose valuable information in the transitions between the activities.

Define usability goals, design criterion, conduct task analyse, make the design—or in large project; lead the design team, participate in the evaluation.

The usability designer works close to the user organisation and participates in different analyses applying to usability. The result from these analyses is then transferred into the design activities by the usability designer usability designer then transfers the result from these analyses into the design activities. The continuation is maintained as he/she participates in designing the prototypes. By taking part in the succeeding evaluation activities, the iterative design cycle is closed.

Examples of tasks this role may lead: specify usability goals; specify design criterion; conduct user and task analyses; elicit the user needs and requirements; make the user interface design—or in large project; lead the design team; participate in the evaluation.

The usability designer has to be a human-computer interaction specialist capable of performing the above mentioned tasks. The interdisciplinary characteristics are absolutely necessary for this role. These are all preliminary research results that we will continue to work on in future projects.

4 Conclusion

One has to make an effort to successfully adopt a user centred approach. We argue for having an official role that keeps the projects' focus on the users. To improve the development process, it is important vital to have an explicit role that has an overall view and responsibility of the usability aspects. We see a need for a dewlap in software development.

References

International Organisation for Standardisation (1998) *ISO/FDIS 13407 Human Centred Design Process for Interactive Systems*, Draft International Standard.

Norman D. A. (1986) Cognitive Engineering, In *User Centered System Design*, Norman D. A. and Draper S. eds., Lawrence Erlbaum Ass. Inc., Hillsdale, New Jersey.

Stapleton J. (1997) *DSDM—Dynamic Systems Development Method*, Addison Wesley Longman Limited, Essex England.

Human-Computer Interaction - INTERACT'99 (Volume II)
S. Brewster, A. Cawsey & G. Cockton (Editors)
Published by The British Computer Society © IFIP TC.13, 1999

Measuring the Usability of WWW Sites: Lessons Learned in a Commercial Development Environment

Karen Gunn

Ericsson Australia
5/207 Bouverie St
Carlton, Victoria 3053
Australia
Email: Karengunn@usa.net

Abstract: Usability metrics have the potential to provide designers of World Wide Web sites with valuable information about the impact of design changes and the relative usability of one site compared with another. This paper presents what has been learned from a study where usability metrics were collected for a functional WWW site. The study shoed that using efficiency and effectiveness as measure of WWW site usability has a number of limitations when used in the context of a user-centred WWW design process. It is proposed that a single approach to measuring WWW usability is flawed, both conceptually and in application. A more useful approach might involve the development of a taxonomy of usability evaluation techniques customised to a particular family of sites.

Keywords: metrics, WWW, usability evaluation, ISO 9241-11, measurement, efficiency, effectiveness

1 Introduction

In a commercial World Wide Web (WWW) development environment the need arises from time to time to justify the benefit of a user-centred design approach, to compare the usability of one site against another or to demonstrate improved levels of usability across design iterations. One possible solution to issues like this is to use metrics to measure WWW site usability.

This paper describes an attempt to apply performance metrics to a functional WWW site, the Australian Yellow Pages® site. As a key revenue earner for Pacific Access and a widely used and popular product in its paper form, the Yellow Pages on the WWW has always been viewed by the company as the number one priority site for usability activities. The paper describes some of the issues, benefits and problems associated with measuring WWW site usability.

The International Organization for Standardization International Standard 9241-11 defines usability as the extent to which a product can be used by specified users to achieve specified goals with effectiveness, efficiency and satisfaction in a specified context of use (ISO, 1998). An International Standard was chosen as this appeared to be a 'best practice' approach and one that would resonate with senior management.

2 Objective

Our objective was to investigate how well the measurement of efficiency and effectiveness might be applied to a functional WWW site within the context of a user-centred design process in a commercial WWW development environment. We were interested in the performance measures only,

® Registered trade mark of Telstra Corporation Limited.

namely efficiency and effectiveness. According to ISO 9241-11, effectiveness describes how correctly and completely goals are achieved. This may be expressed as a percentage. Efficiency relates effectiveness to the effort (time) required to achieve that goal.

As usability professionals, we were interested in proving the value of our contribution to the WWW design process. The use of metrics appeared to be a means of providing such proof, but it was not a method we had used on many previous occasions.

3 The Study

We took the measures of efficiency and effectiveness as part of a formal usability evaluation, conducted at the Pacific Access Usability Laboratory in Melbourne, Australia. During the evaluation ten subjects were asked to complete six tasks where they were required to find particular pieces of information from the Australian Yellow Pages site.

We used a range of methods to evaluate the process of measuring usability based on efficiency and effectiveness. We compared the metrics-based usability study to a previous study we had conducted two months earlier, where the objective was only to give design feedback and where no measures of performance had been collected. In addition to our own observations, feedback from the developers was a key input.

We were interested in assessing the following aspects of the metrics-based approach:

- Resource requirements
- Compatibility with a user-centred design approach
- Reliability
- Validity
- Appropriateness of using performance metrics for WWW sites

4 Results

4.1 Resource Requirements

Measuring usability with a subject-based approach brings with it a significant cost in terms of the time required for planning the evaluation, recruiting subjects, conducting the tests and presenting the results. Collecting performance data did not significantly increase the time required for these activities, compared to the study which focussed on design feedback.

Staff did, however, need to be trained in how to collect and analyse the performance measures. This does represent an additional overhead. We found that an investment of eight person weeks would be required for all the activities associated with establishing measurement protocols, setting up the study, collecting, analysing and presenting the usability data. With practice in collecting this type of data, the time required might be reduced.

Measuring task time and completion rates was greatly assisted by having an established usability laboratory, the ability to record multiple camera angles and equipment that allowed us to play back multiple videotaped images concurrently. This type of equipment represents a significant investment to any commercial development group.

4.2 Compatibility with our User-Centred Design Approach

Pacific Access is committed to applying user-centred principles to its WWW design activities as usability is seen as critical to product success. Empirical measurement is one of the three main components of a user-centred design process as defined by Gould and Lewis (1985), the other two being an early focus on users and iterative design.

Taking measures of efficiency and effectiveness in task completion is an empirical approach. Furthermore, it strongly supports iteration in the sense that the measures become meaningful only when compared. An efficiency score of 60% in itself says very little about a WWW site. Compared to a score of 40% for a previous iteration, however, it begins to have meaning.

In the metrics-focused study, the subjects worked alone and were only asked to comment on the tasks after they had completed them all. This resulted in two problems - subjects could not recall what strategies they had used; and the opportunity was lost to gain insight into the subject's behaviour while they were undertaking the task. Both aspects resulted in a loss of richness of data to assist with diagnostic analysis of problems. In the feedback-focused evaluation, by contrast, both concurrent thinking aloud and post-task debriefs were used, yielding rich diagnostic data. Smith, Smith and Kupstas (1993) hold that concurrent think-aloud protocols offer a source of rich and finely nuanced data which are unattainable by other means. That proposition is supported by our professional experience.

We found the post-task debrief was very valuable for diagnostic feedback. If no debrief had taken place, opportunities would have existed to misinterpret observed behaviour. For example, one subject swore while undertaking one of the tasks. It would be easy to assume that that subject was having difficulty with the task he was working on at the time but the post-task debrief showed that he actually swore because he realised he had used an incorrect strategy for the *previous* task.

The developers told us that the most useful part of any usability evaluation is the description of usability problems and the presentation of proposed design solutions by the usability team. At Pacific Access, a video highlights tape is often used as a communications device to illustrate usability problems. We did not prepare a video highlights tape in the metrics-focused evaluation. One developer felt that this reduced the value of the usability feedback as he preferred to learn from observation rather than from statistical quantification. Performance metrics do not give any clear indication about how to improve the interface, whereas a highlights tape at least makes it clear where redesign efforts need to be directed.

4.3 Reliability

We found a large amount of variation in the efficiency scores for each task, something which worried us and the developers. This variation is shown in the standard deviations for task efficiency measures, which ranged from a minimum of 24% for one task to a maximum of 36% for another. This degree of variation would make it extremely difficult to attribute any changes in the task efficiency scores in a subsequent design iteration to anything but chance.

Tasks are always open to some degree of interpretation by the subject, despite the attempts made in the pilot evaluations to make the tasks read as clearly and unambiguously as possible. This can apply to any experiment where the subjects are asked to complete tasks that they have not developed themselves. It is, however, a consideration that should be borne in mind when considering the reliability of any task-based usability evaluation that relies on users.

In addition to this, the developers were concerned about what they perceived to be too small a sample (ten people) used in the metrics-focused study. The study which focused on design feedback had a similar sample size, but this had not been a concern to the developers. The higher level of concern can probably be attributed to the greater emphasis on measurement and comparison in the metrics-focused study.

4.4 Validity

In order to confidently report the results of a metrics-based study, the usability professional must feel confident that the measures do reflect what they claim to measure and that the findings are representative of 'real world' behaviour.

Smith (1996) points out a number of problems with using time to complete a task as a measure of efficiency. The user's experience level, confidence and natural tempo may all impact on the time taken to complete a task. We found through the post-session debrief that subjects approached the tasks with notably different styles. One subject reported having double-checked many of his answers, with a corresponding increase in task-completion time.

One of the developers voiced a concern about the validity of the results from any usability evaluation conducted in a usability laboratory, saying that data collected in this type of environment is intrinsically flawed because a laboratory setting is unnatural.

The other developer had a different concern, also related to the perceived artificiality of the laboratory setting. This developer felt that in the usability laboratory subjects have an expectation that there is an answer to the task they have been asked to complete and that they therefore persevere longer than they might otherwise do. In previous Australian Yellow Pages WWW site evaluations where a concurrent thinking-aloud protocol was used, subjects occasionally voiced a preference for completing the task by dialing an operator-assisted service or consulting a printed directory. Our experience therefore suggests that this concern may be justified.

4.5 Appropriateness for WWW Sites

Continued use of a metrics-based approach could only be justified in a commercial development environment if the approach was felt to assist the task at hand, namely building highly usable WWW sites.

Measures of efficiency are time-based, and the usefulness of relying strongly on time based-measures can be questioned in the case of the WWW where download times are highly variable.

Efficiency is a particularly difficult area in the context of the WWW because the nature of many sites is that they are designed to encourage browsing, an activity where the concept of efficiency must be viewed differently. Efficiency usually implies a goal directed activity with a 'known' outcome whereas browsing implies an exploratory type of behaviour where the outcome may not be known. The properties of hypertext make browsing as valid a means of using the WWW as searching is. Browsing defies the thinking implicit in a number of the definitions of usability where there is an implication of goal-directed behaviour. This is an area dealt with by a number of authors including Smith (1996) who uses 'lostness' as a metric for hypertext usability.

The usability issues relating to browser capabilities, modem speeds and related WWW technological issues are not addressed in any direct way by taking measures of effectiveness and efficiency.

5 Lessons Learned

As a result of this study, we have concluded that efficiency and effectiveness alone do not provide a comprehensive solution to measuring WWW usability and that this approach alone does not adequately support the WWW design process.

Usability metrics based on the ISO 9241-11 definition assume some kind of task-based user behaviour. The study described here used highly goal directed tasks, namely retrieving business listings from a database. It can not be assumed that all WWW sites will have task-focused objectives with such predictable outcomes. This limits the applicability of using efficiency and effectiveness as measures of the usability of WWW sites.

The range of purposes that WWW sites are created for means that a single methodology for measuring usability would be extremely difficult to develop. For example, in content-rich sites a short visit might be an undesirable usability objective.

Usability measurement of the type described in this case study is better suited to summative evaluation than to formative evaluation, due to its emphasis on counting and measuring. The measures of usability do not have meaning unless used for the purpose of comparison to other measures or to predefined usability goals.

It is reasonable to question whether any one methodology for measuring usability can meet the objectives of measuring usability and providing diagnostic feedback to a development team, without some degree of compromise in the quality of the data provided.

Concentrating on measurement and diagnosis at the same time is a challenge because each implies a different data collection approach. Collecting data about task completion in an environment which mimics the context of use impacts on the ability of the usability professional to gain diagnostic data about what the user is actually thinking and their reasons for following a particular course of action, as is observed by Lausen (1997.)

A metric which would allow businesses to compare the usability of different WWW sites could be very helpful in certain circumstances, for example, in evaluating alternative suppliers of WWW systems such as electronic commerce payment systems or for measuring the usability impacts of different WWW site version releases. However, to allow reliable comparison a sufficiently large sample of users would be required to ensure that any differences noted were not simply the result of random fluctuation. The results of this case study indicate that a sample size of ten subjects is not adequate for this purpose.

Furthermore, to allow for comparison across tests and systems the evaluations would need to be conducted with a high degree of control over influencing variables. In particular, the environment of use, tasks and skill level of test subjects would need to be controlled for within the study design.

An ideal WWW usability metric would be easy to apply by either usability professionals or developers themselves and would have a low resource overhead in terms of training and physical resources. This is an extremely difficult goal to achieve.

While we did not observe any differences in the response time achieved in different evaluation sessions, collecting task completion time data is potentially hazardous for Internet applications where system response times are impacted on by the amount of traffic on the WWW at any given time. This is noted by Vora (1998) who describes a usability study conducted at US West, where no time-based data was collected, but where considerable variability was noted in response times depending on the time of day when the usability sessions were conducted.

It may be appropriate to consider surrogates for time-based measures, that correlate with, but are independent of system response times. In the case study described here, an appropriate alternative measure would be to count the number of times the search button was clicked to submit a new search query.

The findings from this usability study indicate that attempting to provide both a quantification of the usability of a system and a set of diagnostic tools to support the user-centred design process is very ambitious. There is a tension between the two goals of objective quantification of usability and provision of design feedback during the development process. These two goals may not be contemporaneously solvable, because each goal requires a different approach with respect to sample size, type of data collected and method of analysis.

For the purposes of measurement of WWW usability, use of a highly standardised data collection approach applied in a controlled environment is worthy of consideration. This might involve little or no experimenter interaction with the subject. In resource terms, a remote testing approach might facilitate the collection of data from relatively large sample sizes so as to provide measures where differences could confidently be thought of as reflecting differences in the usability of the systems under investigation rather than simply being random fluctuations.

Many elements of WWW usability that relate to technical considerations are very resource intensive to check using subject-based evaluation methods. It is more effective to do this using an expert-based approach. There is no need to 'waste' valuable users in verifying that, for example, alternative text is available to users who chose to view the WWW site with images turned off on their browser.

A high degree of variability in the context of use is likely when developing or assessing WWW applications. The environment of use is possibly subject to greater variation in the WWW than with other applications because of the significant variations in end-user technology. There can be significant variation in terms of browser capabilities (both due to manufacturer and the installed version of the browser), modem speeds and hardware configuration. Where the end user's computer configuration and browser type can not be ascertained, it points to the need for a low-technology alternative to be provided by the developer in order to accommodate those users with low-level computer systems, slow modems and outdated browser software.

Technical and media items can and should be checked for usability impacts prior to any end-user testing. Actions that fall into this category include browser testing, checking page download times with different modem speeds, and verification that the pages appear consistently and as the designer intended across the platforms and browser versions used by the site's audience.

The optimal use of resources for performing formative usability evaluations of WWW sites is to combine technical testing and expert-based evaluation against guidelines with user-based evaluation methods. User-based evaluation methods might measure behaviour and/or attitudes.

It appears unlikely that use of any single measurement or evaluation methodology could work across all stages of the development process nor across all types of WWW sites. The development of a set of usability evaluation tools to address the multiplicity of WWW sites and objectives is not a task which can be accomplished quickly or easily, but it is a worthwhile endeavour.

6 What We Need

While this case study has contributed to the knowledge and approaches which might be taken to measuring the usability of WWW sites, a number of issues require further investigation.

The results of this investigation indicate that future work in the area of measuring WWW usability as part of a user-centred design approach would benefit from a formal classification of WWW sites, based on the site owner's purpose and the resultant usability objectives for the site.

Approaches to evaluating and measuring WWW usability must acknowledge the wide range of objectives that can exist for a site. These can include browsing behaviours and entertainment as well as the highly task-focused behaviours measured in the study described here. A solution might be provided by developing a taxonomy of WWW sites to classify them by their purpose and usability objectives. Having classified the sites, the taxonomy could then be extended to include guidelines and measures of usability, validated for each family of sites. This is not a trivial task, though some work has already been undertaken in this area.

Shneiderman (1997) and Nielsen (1997) have both proposed different usability metrics for different types of WWW sites, and this work provides an excellent starting point.

Any approach taken to measuring the usability of WWW sites for the purposes of comparison would, however, be limited by the difficulty associated with the impact of potentially confounding variables such as differences in task selection, the characteristics of the sample and the environment of use.

As the range of applications widens, to which WWW technology is used, and the medium incorporates greater levels of complexity, both at the user-interface and in the systems design, user-based design and evaluation approaches will become more critical to product success.

While the concept of a 'universal' usability measurement method based on ISO standards is very appealing, in order to serve the requirements of the developer and the human factors professional, a more finely tailored tool is required. Such a tool can only be developed on a foundation of understanding the unique characteristics of the WWW as a medium, technology and functional device.

The usability community must meet the challenge of a more sophisticated WWW environment by developing and disseminating a range of evaluation tools, based on user involvement and reflecting the variety of site purposes. Until bandwidth and server capacity cease to fluctuate, time-based measures of site performance must be abandoned in favour of measures that are reliable and consistent. The development of such evaluation tools will facilitate validation of WWW design guidelines, thereby providing an environment where expert-based and user-based evaluation methods can be combined to maximise the use of development and evaluation resources.

The development of a set of user-based WWW evaluation tools provides a rich opportunity for developers and human factors professionals.

References

Gould, J. D. and Lewis, C. (1985) Designing for usability: key principles and what designers think, *Communications of the ACM*, **28**(3), 300-301.

International Organization for Standardization (1998) ISO 9241 - 11, *Ergonomic requirements for office work with visual display terminals (VDT's) - Part 11: Guidance on Usability.*

Lauesen, S. (1997) Usability engineering in industrial practice, *Proceedings of Interact '97, IFIP TC13 International Conference on Human-Computer Interaction,* Howard, S., Hammond, S, J. and Lindgaard, G. eds, 15 – 22.

Nielsen, J. (1997) *Alertbox*, Measuring the Usability of Reading on the Web, available online 11 February, 1998, at http://www.useit.com/alertbox/readingmetrics.html

Shneiderman, B. (1997) Designing information-abundant web sites: issues & recommendations, *International Journal of Human-Computer Studies*, **47**, 5-29

Smith, P. A. (1996) Towards a practical measure of hypertext usability, *Interacting with Computers*, **8**(4), 365-381.

Smith, J. B., Smith, D. K. and Kupstas, (1993) Automated Protocol Analysis, *Human Computer Interaction*, **8**, 101-145.

Vora, P. (1998) Human factors methodology for designing web sites, *Human Factors and Web Development*, Forsythe, C., Grose, E., and Ratner, J. eds, Lawrence Erlbaum Associates Inc, New Jersey.

Human-Computer Interaction - INTERACT'99 (Volume II)
S. Brewster, A. Cawsey & G. Cockton (Editors)
Published by The British Computer Society © IFIP TC.13, 1999

Using Quantitative Usability Goals in the Design of a User Interface for a Cellular Phone

Timo Jokela and Jani Pirkola

Nokia Mobile Phones
P.O. Box 50
FIN-90570 Oulu
Finland
Email: {timo.jokela, jani.pirkola}@nokia.com

Abstract: We experimented the use of quantitative usability goals in our project where we designed a user interface concept for a mobile phone. A special challenge was that the usability evaluation had to be done at an early milestone of the project – at a stage where no working prototypes were available - so that the set of keys and type of display could be decided early. We used two usability attributes (average efficiency, overall usability). We defined the usability goals in relation with a reference product based on these two attributes, and measured the level of usability of our design in the end of the project through expert evaluation and keystroke level analysis. The experience was mainly positive. The use of quantitative usability goals gave a clear direction to the work in the project, and evaluation of our design was relatively easy and fast. The evaluation results indicate that we well met the targets. The main open question is the validity of the evaluation results. Even if we feel that we did achieve good usability in our design, we can be sure of that only after the design is evaluated with true usability tests with working products.

Keywords: usability, case study, measurements, efficiency

1 Introduction

Small size is characteristic to the user interface of cellular phones. Small size means tough restrictions on the design of the user interface. The display is small, and the means for input is limited. Another characteristics of cellular phones are that they are mechanical devices. While phones are manufactured in very big quantities, there are very high requirements for the quality of mechanical design.

In order to give time for industrial and mechanical design, one has to make a decision about two elementary components of user interface - the set of keys and the type of display - very early in the development life cycle. Especially the early decision about the keys makes a difference in the development process compared with desktop software systems. A design issue that comes typically in the detailed design phase in the development of the user interface is something that needs to be decided very early in the development of cellular phones.

The need for this kind of early decision making sets special requirements for the user interface development process. The decision about the set of keys and type of display should be made at an early milestone of the development project when there are no working prototypes, nor software available. In a typical case, we do not even have time to build mock-up simulations that run on a computer. Thus, the challenge is that we need to make a decision about fundamental characteristics of the user interface concept at a phase of development where no extensive usability tests can be made in a traditional way.

It is generally regarded as a good quality and project management practice to have quantitative goals for product characteristics (e.g. Wesner,

1994). Clear goals give a project a clear direction. It is also recommended to use quantitative goals for usability. For example, the evolving standard (ISO 13407, 1999) states that one should specify 'clear statement of human-centred design goals and provide measurable benchmarks in the requirements phase'.

Traditionally usability has not been among the quantitative goals in the product development programs at Nokia Mobile Phones. Either it has not been regarded relevant to define usability goals, or it has been experienced too difficult to do that. In a previous user interface development project, the usability goals were defined qualitatively. The experience, however, was negative: the evaluation of the design was found very problematic. Qualitative goal setting meant that the evaluation was practically done based on subjective opinions.

Consequently, this time there was a clear demand from the management board of the project for quantitative usability evaluation to help decision making. "There needs to be quantitative quality goals for the project, to give the project the right direction and to make the objective evaluation of the quality of the concept feasible".

In this paper, we describe how we used quantitative usability goals as a part of this kind of development process. We discuss how we defined quantitative usability goals for the milestone where the decision about the set of keys and display had to be made; how we defined the usability attributes and goals based on these attributes, how the measuring was done and what were the lessons learnt.

2 Defining the Usability Attributes

2.1 Requirements for the Usability Attributes

As the first step, we needed to define what are the relevant usability attributes, how to define unambiguously the usability goals. We had to select a set of appropriate attributes, from the many potential ones. For example, Nielsen proposes (Nielsen, 1993) five main usability attributes: learnability, efficiency, errors, remembering, and satisfaction.

The main restriction was that the goals should be of high level enough. This was a requirement from the management board of the project. Typically, there are five quantitative goals set to a project. While the usability goals are not only the ones in a project, the number of usability goals was limited to be less than four.

In addition, there were a number of different factors that we had to take into account when selecting the attributes:

- A big number of different end user tasks is characteristic to cellular phones. For illustration, one can identify many tasks related to the basic phone functions:
    - calling by entering digits manually
    - calling to a person from phone book
    - using quick dialling to call
    - inserting a new entry into phone book
    - editing name of number in the phone book
    - answering a call
    - answering to a waiting call
    - swapping between two calls.

  In addition, when we take into account all the other applications that are typical to an advanced cellular phone - e.g. voice messaging, text messaging, different settings (ringing tone, volume) and modes of operation, call transfer and forwarding functions, calendar, the new data applications - the number of tasks is very high. The high number of tasks means that measuring usability cannot be based on a limited set of tasks only; it would not give valid data about the total usability of the phone.

- Another characteristic of cellular phones is that they are products that are used frequently, many times a day. This means that efficiency - every day use - is a critical usability attribute. This aspect should be taken into account when selecting the attributes.

- The usability attributes should be such that they can be practically measured early in the life cycle. We should be able the have usability measured in a situation where we do not have a functioning prototype of the product. The attributes should be defined so that measuring at this stage is feasible.

- The goals should be relevant for the business case. They should direct the design of the UI to the right way to support business. This means that special attention should be paid on applications that are critical business wise.

2.2 Selection of Attributes

In the selection of attributes, our first decision was to set the attributes in relation with a reference product. This made the goals setting easier and the measuring itself became more practical as it was not necessary to have any previous benchmark data.

After a number of brainstorming sessions and discussions with the management, we then came up with the following set of attributes:

1. Average Efficiency

Efficiency is a usability attribute that is relevant to the use of a phone in the daily life. Our strategy to set the goal for efficiency was as follows:

- Identification of a representative set of time critical user tasks. Such tasks are for example those that users would perform frequently in their daily life.
- Comparing the efficiency of the new and the reference user interface in relation with each of these tasks.
- Using the *average efficiency* increase as the quantitative usability attribute.

We planned to measure efficiency using a simple version of keystroke level analysis method (Card, 1983).

2. Overall Usability

This attribute describes the overall design of the user interface: how users learn to use the phone quickly; whether the design metaphors and paradigms are of good quality and use of keys is logical; the style remains consistent through the different applications and users do not make errors (and if they do, they can recover from them) etc.

There was a practical reason for selecting this attribute: the way we planned to do the evaluation.

Three usability experts (expert teams) would do expert evaluation independently, and give quantitative scoring based on their total view using a subjective scale 1 … 7. The new UI concept as well as the reference concept would be evaluated in the same scale.

With these two different attributes, we hoped to get a balanced picture of the total usability. Different attributes and different evaluators would bring credibility to the evaluation results, especially if their conclusions were in line with each other.

At the stage of goal setting, we had only preliminary ideas how to do measuring. The exact way of how to carry out measuring was done later.

3 Setting Usability Goals

In goal setting, we identified two categories of applications (sets of functions that are in the phone). The *focus* applications were those where a clear improvement of usability was seen strategically important for the business; the *baseline* applications were those where usability is important but where a more modest increase of usability was acceptable.

As a result, we identified four usability attributes to be measured: efficiency and overall usability for the two different categories of applications, focus and baseline applications.

Setting of quantitative goals to these attributes was more guessing than science. The goals were set together with the management on the basis what we thought is realistic. It was anyway the first time when this kind of goal setting was done. We naturally set tougher usability goals for the focus applications than for the baseline applications.

As a result we had the following kind of table for the goals:

Applications	Increase to Overall Usability (scale 1 .. 7)	Increase to Average Efficiency
Focus	+ 2 points	+30 %
Baseline	+1 points	+10 %

Table 1: Improvement goals in contrast with a reference product. (NOTE. The figures are for illustration purposes only.).

The goals were to be measured against a reference product, which – again – was agreed together with the management.

4 Performing the Evaluation

After the goal setting, we carried out several iterations of designs. We produced different concepts, and made qualitative usability evaluations - mainly through paper prototyping. We were able to experiment different designs with the many different applications that would run on a cellular phone.

We finally selected one of the several user interface concepts that we had experimented as a candidate for evaluation at the milestone. At this point, we did not have any quantitative data about the quality of the concept; the selection was based on the experience and vision we had gained through the number of different alternatives we had explored.

We prepared a set of different scenarios of about how the user interface would behave in different situations and with different applications, and documented those in PowerPoint slides. We did not even aim for thorough specification and documentation of the user interface in the short period of time we had. However, we 'knew' in our minds the details of our design: how our design would work in the different applications and situations.

The evaluation had to be carried out with these limitations. We had only limited documentation, but the knowledge that the team had was much broader. Our strategy was to use the team members as 'prototypes' for the evaluators. The way of doing that was presentations, answering to questions etc.

4.1 Measuring Efficiency

To keep the calculations practical, we decided to measure the efficiency using the following procedure:

1. Define a representative set of efficiency critical tasks

2. For each task:
- If our concept is more efficient, the score is 1
- If equal, then the score is 0
- If worse, the score is -1.

3. The total efficiency:
(sum of scores/number of tasks) * 100%

Following that procedure, we identified a representative set of efficiency critical tasks for both of the two categories. This was done together with representatives of product marketing and application specialists. The main criteria for the selection of the efficiency critical tasks were:

- tasks that are done frequently
- tasks that need to be done quickly.

As a result, we ended up with sets of tasks for both categories, each containing 20 ... 30 tasks.

Using the procedure described above, measuring of efficiency per task was rather straightforward: it was easy to determine which one of the two user interfaces provided a more efficient way of accomplishing a task. No detailed level keystroke level analysis calculation was required. The total effort to do the measuring was a couple of days.

A usability expert (not belonging to the project) did comparison together with the key designers of the project. If not documented, the members of our design team explained how a specific task would be done with our design. - There existed detailed knowledge about the functionality of the reference concept.

4.2 Measuring Overall Usability

We organised presentation sessions where our user interface and the reference concept were presented to the evaluators. We briefed the evaluators about our business case: what are the drivers, what is the goal user segment, what are the key applications. While we did not have a running prototype, we presented the behaviour through slides and by answering questions that the evaluators asked.

We asked the evaluators to score the quality of the usability of both concepts in a subjective scale:

1: poor: would not recommend to anybody
.
.
7 excellent: would recommend to a colleague

The scoring was asked separately for the focus applications and baseline applications.

In addition, we asked the evaluators to give qualitative comments. While one reason was to get feedback to further improve our design, a very essential reason was to gain confidence to the validity of the evaluation. If the comments were in line with each other, it would give confirmation to the validity of the results.

5 Results

Even if the drivers and goals of the project were well known by the project team, it was a bit of excitement to the team to wait for the results. The results, when they came out, indicated clearly that we had been successful: there was improvement in all of the areas.

The efficiency measures were very clear: we got an exact score on how much better our design was compared with the reference. The evaluators produced also a table that shows all the tasks that were gone through, and the score of each task.

The measures about the overall usability were very much in line with each other - even if the evaluators did the work independently, without any mutual communication. An interesting thing was that they used different usability evaluation methods: two teams used heuristic evaluation (Nielsen 1994) while one team used SUS (Brooke 1995).

In addition, the qualitative feedback from the evaluators was very similar. This makes us believe that the results of the 'overall usability' are rather valid.

6 Discussion

This was our first time to use quantitative measures in the design of user interface style of a cellular phone. In that sense, it was experimental.

We can find both positive and potentially problematic aspects in our approach. A very positive aspect simply was that it 'it could be done'. We did specify quantitative usability goals, we measured our design against these goals, and we got the results.

We also found it very useful to have quantitative usability goals 'project wise'. Compared with some earlier user interface concept projects, we now had clear and shared view on the user interface concept what we are aiming at.

Our approach was practical. The efficiency evaluation took just a couple of days. Expert evaluation required more effort, but still it was done in less than one week.

The biggest potential problem is the validity of the usability results. If we look at the results, they indicate that our design was a success. We reached our goals. The problem, however, is that evaluation was done on one had at rather abstract level, on another hand with numeric calculations. There is a clear risk that these evaluations do not tell the whole truth. To do the reliable usability evaluation, one naturally needs to do the evaluation using real products and real users, which is a future issue.

Anyway, we think that we did capture some essential usability in our measures. We covered quite a large spectrum of user tasks in two simple measures. At this stage, we 'feel' that we really gained good results in usability.

Another positive thing was that quantitative measures are a very good means of communication to the management (who are not usability professionals). For example, explaining the results of efficiency evaluation by saying that 'n % of user tasks are quicker to do with our design than with the reference product' made sense. When telling the names and positions of the usability experts were gave credibility to the results of expert evaluation.

Naturally, there is a lot of space for improvements. A more sound means should be established for defining the efficiency critical user tasks. In this project, the tasks were identified in a brainstorming session. In the future, those should be based more on true data received from user studies. In expert evaluations, we organised presentation sessions to introduce the concepts. The main feedback from the experts was that it had been easier if we had given some preliminary documentation to them a couple of days earlier.

Afterwards, we have also been thinking of some other attributes that could have been used instead of (or in addition to) efficiency and overall usability. One such attribute could have been *the number of major usability problems* and the goal – naturally – to decrease the number of these major usability problems.

This attribute might have been more laborious to measure. There also might have been some contradictory opinions: what is a major usability problem and what is not. However, communication with this kind of attribute could probably be even more tangible to the management than was with the attribute we used. By claiming that we have been able to overcome such and such a number of major usability problems with this new design compared with the old user interface should make clear sense to anybody.

References

Brooke, J. SUS – A quick and dirty usability scale. (1995). In: *Usability Evaluation in Industry*, Pat Jordan (ed.), Taylor&Francis,

Card, S. K., Moran, T.P., and Newell, A. (1983) The Psychology of Human-Computer Interaction. Hillsdale, NJ:

ISO 13407: Human centred design processes for interactive systems. 1999.

Nielsen, J. (1993). Usability Engineering. AP Professional.

Nielsen, J., Mack, R. (1994). Usability Inspection Methods John Wiley & Sons, New York.

Wesner J., Hiatt J., Trimble D. (1994). Winning with Quality. Applying Quality Principles in Product Development. Addison Wesley. Reading, Massachusetts.

Human-Computer Interaction - INTERACT'99 (Volume II)
S. Brewster, A. Cawsey & G. Cockton (Editors)
Published by The British Computer Society © IFIP TC.13, 1999

Microwave Bank: Consumers in Context

Paula Lynch and Alexandra Trabak

NCR Knowledge Lab
206 Marylebone Road
London
UK
Email: {paula.lynch, alexandra.trabak}@unitedkingdom.ncr.com

Abstract: The NCR Knowledge Lab aims to drive the creation of future e-commerce by involving potential consumers, as early as practically possible, in the design lifecycle. This paper will focus on how we involved consumers in the design and development of an innovative concept - the NCR Microwave Bank. The Microwave Bank case study is an example of involving people in design from the very early stages - during concept creation itself. The paper will discuss the aims of and rationale for the development of the Microwave concept, and the method we employed to understand consumer issues associated with online access in the kitchen environment using a familiar domestic appliance. Key methodological lessons derived from this research will also be reported throughout the paper.

Keywords: concept design, user involvement, e-commerce, Relationship Technologies

1 Background

The Knowledge Lab was launched by NCR to research and understand the future of financial services, its technologies, and its consumers. The research is supported by NCR and a consortium of over twenty world leading financial institutions. Its overall aim is to create Relationship Technologies which are technologies that are there when we need them, are easy to communicate with, are sensitive to our needs, know and understand who we are and what we want, and are technologies that we trust.

Relationship Technologies will evolve in reaction to consumers' need for easier-to-use online home devices. The latest figures from Odyssey show that, after two decades, only 45% of US homes have a PC, and that although prices keep falling relatively few PCs are being sold to new households (Interactive Home, 1998). The PC one-size-fits-all approach to computing does not seem to satisfy the requirements of most consumers who perceive home-PC as either too costly, too complex or having no utility. International Data Corporation (IDC) predicts that the sale of easier to use, Internet enabled appliances will nearly match that of PCs in 2002 and thereafter greatly exceed them (The Economist, 1998). These devices will better meet the needs of households by creating useful context sensitive services within easily usable interfaces. NCR's Microwave Bank is one such "information appliance".

The objectives of this paper are:

- to describe how the NCR Knowledge Lab involved potential consumers in the design of the Microwave Bank concept;
- to discuss some of the consumers issues associated with online access in the kitchen environment using a familiar domestic appliance;
- to highlight some of the methodological issues we faced when involving potential users in the early concept design.

The following section describes the main aims of and rationale for the development of the Microwave concept before moving on to discuss the Microwave Bank consumer studies.

2 Microwave Bank - What Is It?

A working prototype has been developed by the Knowledge Lab to demonstrate the potential for future Relationship Technologies to be situated within the shell of existing domestic technologies.

Figure 1: Microwave Bank prototype.

The idea for the Microwave Bank grew out of our research into developing new ways of providing electronic services, such as banking and shopping, to the home in order to broaden the consumer base beyond current PC users and to deliver via appropriate channels. The microwave was chosen as the design focus for a number of reasons, including the familiarity of this household appliance (NCR, 1998).

There are other research laboratories that are focusing on developing kitchen-centric intelligent products and services, such as MIT and ICL (ICL, 1999). The idea of embedding intelligence in to the kitchen environment is gaining much attention. However, to date, there are no commercially available Internet enabled devices designed specifically for the kitchen. The kitchen is a place in the home characterised by domestic activities, where people want *to 'get things done'*, rather than a place for relaxation, and is therefore a popular room for managing household tasks, such as bill paying and writing shopping lists. It was these contextual elements of the kitchen that led us to identify it as a promising location for non-PC based home banking and shopping, rather than the living room. The Microwave concept offers users a set of services that are sensitive to user needs in the kitchen, such as automatic food ordering, recipe information, bill payment and money transfer.

3 Consumer Trials of the Concept

The following section describes the methods we employed to understand potential users' acceptance of the concept and to understand consumer issues associated with online access in the kitchen environment through a familiar domestic appliance. Two consumer studies have been conducted on the Microwave concept.

3.1 Study One: Early Consumer Feedback

A preliminary study was completed with 36 individuals in order to gather initial feedback for the development of the prototype. The study used the following techniques: a photography task followed by participation in a discussion group. All participants had some experience of using a computer and half had a home PC. Having some experience of computers and the Internet was considered important for the preliminary study since it meant that individuals could assess the rationale behind the innovative concept, based on their own experiences of using existing technologies.

During the preliminary study, participants were given disposable cameras and were instructed to take specific pictures (e.g. location of their microwave, where they normally carry out financial tasks, etc.). We found that the photographs were excellent for gaining a better understanding of why, during the discussion group, people said what they did. For example, some people said that they did not have any *chairs* in their kitchen, which meant they were less likely to want to use the microwave concept for financial services. Using the photographs we were able to reveal that for these individuals their current mode of financial management required a table and/or a chair. These individuals therefore found it difficult to see beyond their current time consuming, paper-based practice to a time when they could use alternative digital transactional processes, like those that were demonstrated by the Microwave concept.

Participants returned the cameras during the discussion group session that followed. Six qualitative discussion groups were conducted in three locations in the UK (Surrey, Manchester and London). Each session began with a discussion about participants' attitudes towards computers and their current financial practices, such as experience of telephone banking, before the Microwave concept was introduced. At the time of this study, there was no prototype so we used a short video to show the developing Microwave and the services that it could potentially offer, for example, using a bar code scanner to compile an electronic shopping list.

3.2 Study Two: Consumer Acceptance of the Concept

In the second study 39 individuals took part in six qualitative group sessions in London. Each session contained individuals who had little or no Internet experience and had no home PC. The sessions differed from the preliminary study in that there was no photography task, individuals completed a financial usage scenario, and that the video stimuli was replaced with a demonstration of the actual Microwave prototype. The session began with a discussion about participants' attitudes and experience of using computers, and included reasons for not having a home computer and their likelihood of getting one in the near future. In order to understand how participants currently carry out financial tasks available on the Microwave Bank, participants were asked to develop a financial usage scenario describing a recent experience using any of the following options: Checking a balance, getting a statement, paying bills, setting up either a loan, an overdraft or a direct debit, transferring money.

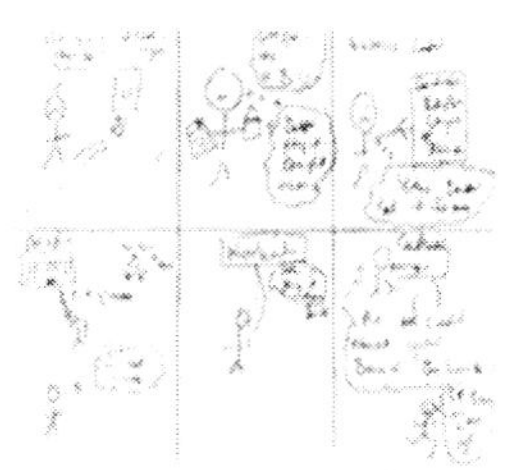

Figure 2: An example of a financial usage scenario.

Participants were asked to think about what they did, how it happened, the environment that they were in, the presence of other people, and how they were feeling. Participants were given approximately five minutes to create their usage scenario. The aim of this task was to help contextualise the users' own practices, and to exemplify an everyday situation (Chin, 1997). Each individual was asked to read out their story to the group. The facilitator probed for both positive and negative points about the experience, and for solutions that could counteract the negative aspects. These comments were written up on a flip chart.

During the next part of the session the facilitator demonstrated the prototype to the group. Initial reactions were captured during the discussions, and then each of the potential services were demonstrated and discussed, for example: check bank balance, find a recipe, etc. The order of presentation of these services was randomised between each group session to prevent an order effect influencing the findings. Once all services had been discussed, the group compared their earlier comments, about factors that affect current usage of financial channels, with the possibility of completing the same financial task using the concept.

The session ended with a short questionnaire that covered household responsibilities for shopping and banking, ownership and aspirations for home technology, current usage of financial channels (e.g. ATM, Internet, branch), and a *usefulness* rating for each service demonstrated on the Microwave.

In both studies one researcher facilitated each group, whilst another observed and took notes (behind a two-way mirror). In addition, each group was videotaped for analysis. Each session lasted an hour and a half, and each participant received £25 for participating.

3.3 Analysis

The following qualitative analysis was conducted:
Photographic data

The photographs were developed digitally and clustered into categories such as the location of microwaves. An artefact audit was carried out to gain visual insight into the position and relationship of artefacts in each picture, and then the photos were re-analysed to show the similarities and differences between participants.

Discussion group data

The sessions were transcribed and then analysed using content analysis. This involved grouping the raw data into subjects, for example attitudes to using the microwave for banking, and further breaking the data into sub-groups of naturally occurring themes, for example control, privacy, trust and environment of use, etc.

4 People's Thoughts about the Concept

It is the intention of this section to focus on one of the key consumer issues associated with the Microwave concept - locating an intelligent device in the kitchen environment.

This research demonstrated that the drivers for the adoption of kitchen-based intelligent appliances include the relevance of the environment of use and the social dynamics and current practices within the household.

4.1 Relevance of the Kitchen Environment to Current Practices

By embedding Internet technology within the physical shell of a contemporary microwave oven a number of our participants found it difficult to understand the link between a cooking device and services not related to cooking (e.g. banking). However, this lack of synergy was less of a problem for people who associated the kitchen environment with specific household tasks, e.g. paying bills.

Kitchen related services were popular, (e.g. recipe finders, online grocery shopping, and a notice board facility). This can be explained by the fact that these services are sensitive to current practices within the kitchen environment. For example, participants were enthusiastic about using the innovation for on-line shopping, and just under a half of participants expressed an interest in using the Microwave as a future home channel for grocery shopping. Unsurprisingly, they perceived a synergy between shopping, the recipe finder and the kitchen environment. Another context sensitive service was the electronic notice board and most participants agreed that it would be a useful service on the microwave to aid intra-family communication. The kitchen is a communication crossroads where individuals currently use paper based signals to communicate with other household members, e.g. calendars and notes that are magnetised on to the fridge (Fleuriot, 1998). The Microwave concept offered individuals an electronic alternative to aid intra-family communications.

The photographic task highlights the fact that current financial management behaviour involves sitting down, possibly for an extended period of time. Therefore, participants with more spacious kitchens, and those with a kitchen table, were more likely to conduct their financial activities in this environment. Those participants who currently perform their financial tasks outside the kitchen perceived the environment in which the Microwave concept is located as a potential barrier to for any banking transactions. This was not a surprising result since they evaluated the concept relative to their current practices (predominantly paper-based) of managing their household tasks.

4.2 Social Dynamics of the Kitchen

Another important factor raised by almost all participants in this research as a driver in the adoption and use of such an appliance was the feeling of comfort in carrying out financial activities. This again reflects current practices related to financial tasks within the home that do not allow consumers to envisage standing in the kitchen for prolonged period of time using any appliance. Various rooms within the home tend to be associated with different levels of comfort. In our study, rooms predominantly associated with feelings of comfort were the lounge and the bedroom. Comfortable environments such as the living room often mean environments for relaxation. The television is a context sensitive appliance, but it is sensitive to the context of the social dynamics of the living room, which is predominantly group (family) relaxation. This is an entirely different context to the kitchen and the social dynamics of the kitchen, which is predominantly about activity and task (cooking, shopping) performing as opposed to relaxation.

" Transfer it to different locations depending on what you are using it for, recipes & shopping in the kitchen, banking in the bedroom or lounge" (Female, aged 25-35 yrs old)

Finally, whilst just over a third said that they would like to use the Intelligent Microwave in the future for their banking others were concerned over privacy in relation to the environment of use. They perceived the kitchen as an open and public space, and felt a need for their privacy within the household to be maintained. A mobile unit was perceived as an attractive proposition for these individuals who wanted to have the option to access sensitive financial information as well as more time consuming services in private, in comfort and wherever the need arises.

5 Methodological Issues

Knowing the needs, attitudes and requirements of potential end users is key to the successful design of any developing product. Factors that will ultimately affect the adoption and use of an innovation are obviously better identified early on in development, as the costs associated with making design changes increase exponentially throughout the design lifecycle. During ideas generation and concept design user requirements should be captured and endorsed in design specification for an embryonic design. However, there are a number of obvious methodological issues associated with asking people what they want, need and desire in a future design of a product, particularly if the product under development is innovative. Rogers defined an 'innovation' in the following terms:

'An idea, practice, or object that is perceived as new by an individual...which presents an individual...with a new alternative...with new meaning of solving problems.' (Rogers, 1983)

One known limitation of involving people in the design of future technologies is that when faced with an unfamiliar technology, individuals can have difficulties in relating it to the context of use in their future lives (Dixon et al, 1997; Ireland & Johnson, 1995). Consumer research techniques such as focus groups, questionnaires, and interviews have significant shortcomings when used to provide insight into individuals future behaviours (Anderson, et al, 1999). It is unrealistic to expect research participants to be able to predict their future behaviour. Hence one of the aims of research within the Knowledge Lab is to develop new tools and techniques that will better support the design team in understanding the user group of a developing product. Hence, we employed a combination of methodologies and research approaches in order to get a rich picture of how people behave. The combination of different methodologies also allowed us to maximise the strengths of individual methods whilst overcoming their individual weaknesses. Lessons learnt relate to the following issues: Understanding the concept, the context of environment of use and finally current financial practices.

- Understanding the concept

A challenge that we had to overcome was the nature of the concept being a familiar device that was offering novel applications. Using demonstration techniques, the video and the prototype, helped in facilitating participants understanding of the concept. Findings from this study, however, highlighted that the stimulus video material used to introduce the concept was insufficient and too abstract for many participants to fully understand the potential for the idea and that it was important to give participants the opportunity to 'see and touch' the prototype.

- Context of the environment

The aim of the photographic task was to gain contextual information about the environment of use of home technologies, and to gain insight into the location where people carry out specific household tasks. Photographs are effective in gathering information that would have been impossible to collect using existing consumer research techniques such as discussion groups. People would have found it difficult to remember and recount verbally the level of detail that was captured in the pictures. '...Photographs are there to remind us of what we forget' (Berger, 1992).

Figure 3: Participant's photo showing location in the home where they pay bills.

One of the advantages of this technique is that it is a simple, quick and familiar task to ask participants to complete, although it may be perceived by some people as intrusive. In our study, the technique proved to be extremely successful since everybody returned the cameras. This success may be attributed to the fact that participants were allowed control over what information they gave out. Another advantage of using this technique, from the researchers perspective, is that disposable cameras are relatively cheap, although the cost of digitising the material needs to be taken into account. Ideally, you would want to talk to participants about the content of their photographs, something that we did not do due to time constraints. It is worth mentioning that photography has been used before as a technique to collect "inspirational data" to stimulate designers imaginations rather than define a set of problems (Gaver, Dunne, Pacenti, 1999). Within our analysis, however, we tried to conduct an artefact audit to quantify where participants carry out various household activities and where they locate certain technologies within the home. In doing so, care needs to be taken during analysis of photographs in order not to over state what researchers subjectively perceive in them. Since photography misses out on the wider context of use and only captures a static point in time.

- Context of current practices

Financial usage scenarios were used during discussion groups to capture contextual information related to people's financial activities. This technique was used as a tool to raise participants' awareness of current financial practices and enable a richer discussion to take place. This was achieved by giving participants time to individually think about how they achieved a certain task before the discussion took place. The outcome in our case was that as a result of usage scenarios, individuals were better able to critique and relate to the concept. One of the advantages of this technique is that it allows expression of feelings such as mood through text and drawings. Although it is a quick data capture technique that can be entertaining for participants at the same time, it relies heavily on people's ability to recall their past behaviour. However, it could be argued that participants may recount what they consider distinctive issues for the particular task. In our study, we found that it does not appeal to all participants and that those with limited artistic skills felt embarrassed and a little intimidated by this task. For these individuals text-only usage scenarios were completed. Overall, we found this technique to be extremely effective at instigating discussion around current financial experience and practices.

6 Conclusions

The microwave concept has been designed to demonstrate the potential of Relationship Technologies for bringing electronic services into the home through intelligent consumer electronic appliances.

This paper has highlighted some of the methodological issues we faced when potential users were involved in the early concept design of this innovation, and thus has raised the need for better tools and techniques for involving potential end-users in concept creation. Secondly, the paper described the key consumer issues associated with locating an intelligent device in the kitchen environment. Our findings suggest that the Microwave was perceived as particularly useful for households who viewed their kitchen as the hub of family life. However, the idea of having simple access to online services was a key benefit for nearly all of our consumers.

The key strength of the concept is that it offers *context sensitive* information through a usable interface. The key lesson learnt from an opportunity perspective is that this concept demonstrates the likely *future* for next generation home-centred computers. Ultimately, the Microwave fits the model of the emerging networked society, where computing and networks are embedded – and invisible – within the fabric of everyday things.

References

Anderson, B, McWilliam, A., Lacohee, H, Clucas, E. and Gershuny, J., *Family Life in the Digital Home – domestic telecommunications at the end of the 20th century*, BT Technology Journal, Vol 17, No 1, January 1999-04-29

Berger, J., 1992, *Keeping a Rendezvous, How Fast Does It Go?*, <http://www.hi.is/hakona/photo/nonframe/b3.htm>

Chin, G., Rosson, B., & Carroll, J., 1997, *Participatory Analysis: Shared Development of Requirements from Scenarios*, CHI 97 conference proceedings, (22-27 March), 162-169.

Dixon, P., Vaske, B., & Neervoort, P., 1997, *User Involvement in Concept Creation,* Proceedings of DIS97, Amsterdam, (August), 97-99.

Fleuriot, C., Meech, J., & Thomas, P., 1998, *Diaries as Family Communication Tools,* Student Poster CHI 98 Conference Proceedings, (18-23 April), 361-362.

Gaver, B., Dunne, T., & Pacenti, E., 1999 *Cultural Probes*, Interactions (January+February) VI.1, 21-29

ICL Press Release, 1999, The Fridge that Goes Shopping for You, (10 February), http://www.icl.com/news/pressfeb99/10feb99c.htm

Interactive Home, 1998, *The Emerging International Internet*, (1 February).

Ireland, C, & Johnson, B, 1995, *Exploring the Future in the Present*, Design Management Journal, 6(2), 55-64.

NCR Press Release, 1998, Do my shopping, Pay my bills, Cook my dinner, (10 September), http://www3.ncr.com/press_release/pr091098b.html

Rogers, Everett M., 1993, *Diffusion of Innovations* (Third Edition). The Free Press: New York

The Economist, 1998, *The Future of Computing: After the PC.* (12 September), 79-81.

Human-Computer Interaction - INTERACT'99 (Volume II)
S. Brewster, A. Cawsey & G. Cockton (Editors)
Published by The British Computer Society © IFIP TC.13, 1999

Supporting Collaboration in Multimedia Design

Marianne Graves Petersen and Kim Halskov Madsen

interMedia, Aarhus University
Åbogade 34, DK 8200 Århus N, Denmark
Email: mgraves@daimi.au.dk, halskov@imv.au.dk

Abstract: Using the development project of the integrated television and PC concept of Bang & Olufsen, as the setting for experimenting with different ways of organising design sessions, this paper addresses the issue of how collaboration between designers is mediated by design materials and use of physical space. Based on an analysis of two design meetings, which represent rather different strategies for applying design materials and physical space, we provide recommendations on how these means can support collaboration in a multi-disciplinary team of designers. The main recommendations include to use a diverse set of flexible design materials for supporting communication and exploration of design ideas among the designers. Further, we provide examples of how the way people are physically organised may influence their engagement in discussions and modifications of design proposals.

Keywords: the design process, collaboration, materials, physical space, TV and PC integration

1 Introduction

The emergence of multimedia technology poses new challenges for designers of interactive systems. The competencies needed in the design process can no longer be covered by designers with a uniform background. Thus we see software engineers working together with for instance anthropologists, psychologists and communications design people when designing multimedia products. In the BIDI project (Brugbarhedsarbejde I Dansk Industri, Eng. Usability work in Danish industry), we work with developing methods and settings that allow for these very different perspectives to be integrated in the development process. This involves experimenting with new forms of participation as well as identifying tools that support collaboration and synthesis amongst different disciplines. Starting from an analysis of two specific design sessions of quite different nature, this paper describes how collaboration between designers is mediated by design materials, and how the dynamic of a design sessions also depends on the use of physical space in which the setting is situated.

The specific development project, which provided the setting for experimenting with design practice, was the development process of Bang & Olufsen's *PC-TV living room*. Bang & Olufsen is a major Danish hi-fi manufacturer and one of the commercial partners in the BIDI project. The vision of *PC-TV living room* is to provide users of a traditional television with access to PC functionality and applications when seated in the sofa in the living room. Bang & Olufsen have already developed the counterpart product of *PC-TV living room*, the *PC-TV office*, which allows users to watch television or listen to radio or CDs, from the computer. The products exploit the BeoLink® concept of Bang & Olufsen which allows audio and video devices to share services, such that for instance a person from one room can select and listen to a track from a CD loaded in the CD player placed in another room. The technology is multimedia in the sense that it is the integration of a mass media and the computer as a media, rather than in the sense of combination of picture, sound and text.

As the platform for our analysis we apply the work of D. Schön (1983, 1988 & 1992). Through his exploration of how reflection and action are intimately connected in the world of practitioners, Schön provides a valuable perspective on design practice. His notion of design as a reflective conversation with materials supports our analysis of the role of materials in the design process. We have found it productive for the purpose of our analysis to expand his theoretical framework concerning the number of people involved, the materials available, and his notion of seeing and moving. In addition we have added a concern for the role of physical space.

2 The Set-Up of the Two Design Sessions

The empirical basis for our analysis consists of the first design meeting in the *PC-TV living room* project and a workshop conducted as part of the project three weeks later. In the following, we will term the two sessions the 'meeting' and the 'workshop', respectively. The total number of people involved in the two sessions was 14; 10 of them participated in the meeting and 12 of them in the workshop. Participating in the meeting were five people from the usability group, three from the multimedia department, one from the communications department, and one person from our research group. Participating in the workshop were four people from the usability group, two from the multimedia department, one from the communications department, two from the other industrial partners of BIDI, and three people from our research group, whose main responsibility was to organise the event. The people involved represented expertise from a broad range of domains, including software engineering, psychology, anthropology, aesthetics design, communication, and multimedia.

2.1 The meeting

At this first design meeting, the first prototype of the *PC-TV living room* was presented by the multimedia department, for the usability group to comment on it. The goal of the meeting was to start a process where people with different competencies would comment on the technological initiative in the form of a prototype and hereby provide recommendations for how the prototype should be modified to form an improved version. The only design representation available at the session was a prototype of the PC-TV living room, which was set up with access to two different kinds of web sites - a local newspaper and a European art museum. In addition a page with favourite links and a button panel had been designed. The meeting started off by a demonstration of the prototype by the manager of the multimedia department, followed by a discussion between multimedia developers and usability people on a wide variety of issues concerning the design of the PC-TV living room. The meeting took place in a room equipped as a three-piece suite, where the people from the usability group were comfortably seated in sofas while discussing the prototype.

Figure 1: The meeting.

2.2 The workshop

The goal of the workshop was to further develop the design concept of the PC-TV living room. The workshop took place in a room equipped with products and prototypes of relevance to the PC- TV living room. Moreover, video was shown from a previously conducted workshop with users concerning the design of the PC-TV living room. The workshop started out with the participants split in two multidisciplinary teams who in turn visited different stands which presented products and prototypes related to the PC-TV living room and a video which presented highlights and key-issues from the workshop with users. At the stands, design dilemmas and statements from users were presented on posters on the wall, and the participants were asked to comment on these and summarise their discussions on post-it notes. Based on the discussions held in this first round, two specific design issues were chosen which the two groups should then work on. Each team was asked to produce their design solution in a tangible form, for instance as a paper prototype. The idea was that after approximately half an hour, the two groups presented each their design proposal for the other team, and then swapped design topics. For the second round a team could either start from scratch or start out from what the other team had produced.

Whereas people had been standing while discussing posters and prototypes, during the last part of this session they were seated around a table. At their disposition were various design materials including pens, paper in various sizes, Scotch tape, Post Its, etc. In addition, screen dumps from the current prototype of PC-TV living room were available.

Figure 2: The workshop.

3 Analysing Design as a Reflective Conversation with Design Materials

In order to analyse the strengths and weaknesses of the two design sessions, we apply the framework of Schön (1983, 1988 & 1992), who sees design as a reflective conversations with design materials. According to Schön, design is a kind of experimentation that consists in reflective 'conversation' with materials. The interaction with materials is a conversation between the designer and the materials in a metaphorical sense. For instance when "working in some visual medium (...) the designer sees what is 'there' in some representation (...), draws in relation to it, sees what has been drawn, thereby informing further designing" (Schön 1992 p. 135). Keeping with the metaphor, the materials talk back to the designer, which guides further moves and the process becomes one where the designer sees, moves while taking account of previously unanticipated result of his moves, and sees again (Schön 1983 p. 158). The design representations are virtual worlds, which may facilitate experimentation at low risk and cost by eliminating or inhibiting constraints of the built world (Ibid. pp. 157-8). "But the virtual world of drawing can function reliably as a context for experiments only insofar as the results can be transferred to the built world" (Ibid. p. 159).

Although we base our analysis on the work of Schön, we have found it necessary to expand his framework as regards the number of designers, the range of design materials and finally we have sought to clarify his terms of seeing and moving, such that an analysis of a specific design session is enabled.

The prototypical design case reported by Schön involves *one* designer. One of the widely used examples in his work is about a student of architecture who makes and reflects on a series of sketches of building layout (Schön 1983 p. 76-104). Though the design situation also includes a master designer he does not include the interaction between the student and the master designer as subject for his analysis. Our case involves several people and in our analysis we have found it important to incorporate a concern for the collaboration between them. In Schön's general discussions of design he puts great emphasis on the role of design materials, for instance by discussing how the designer works selectively in different media or materials experimenting with different aspects of his design. Having originally been concerned with the design practice of architects, he has quite naturally primarily been concerned with material like paper, wood, and cardboard. However, in our case, a number of different kinds of material are being used in addition to various kinds of pens and paper: Software prototypes of for instance the *PC-TV living room*, hardware prototypes of for instance a remote control with tracker ball, prints of screen images, pictures of products, posters, and Post Its.

The terms seeing and moving are by Schön used in a fairly loose way and we have found it productive to use them in a little bit more accurate way. We use the term moving in two different ways: 1A) in the sense that somebody *says* something, which moves the design ahead 2A) in the sense that a design representation in some material is being *modified.* Similarly we distinguish between two kinds seeing: 1B) in the sense of *visual apprehension* of for instance a design sketch or listening to what some one else says, and 2B) in the sense of *actively* experiencing how it would be, for instance, to apply a certain interaction principle by trying out a prototype. That is, we make the following distinctions:

A) Moving:
1. Verbal expression
2. Material modification

B) Seeing:
1. Visual apprehension
2. Actively experiencing

Visual apprehension and actively experiencing is not a dichotomy but rather the two end points of a continuum as illustrated by the following list of ways of *seeing* a remote control:

1. looking at a picture of a remote control
2. looking at a remote control
3. holding the remote control in the hand
4. holding the remote control in the hand and imagining how it would be to use it, for instance by pushing the buttons
5. using the remote control to control a TV set or a prototype of a TV set

4 Two Forms of Collaboration In Design

The two sessions were quite different with respect to the way collaboration was supported.

4.1 Brainstorm at the meeting

The nature of the meeting was most of all a brainstorm of problems to be considered in the future work on designing the PC living room product. Numerous issues were touched upon, inspired by the prototype presented at the session, ranging from aspects of functionality to aesthetic concerns regarding the graphical appearance of the PC-TV living room. However, most of these issues were left standing alone and were not elaborated on by the rest of the participants. This loose coherence among moves taken at the meeting was partly due to the limited and inflexible materials available at the session. The hardware and software used for implementing the prototype did not support the creation of alternative design solutions – not to mention on the spot experiments.

In terms of moving, the session represented only verbal moves, that is the list of topics raised during the session were not documented in any way, except for some sporadic notes produced by the head of the multimedia department in his private notebook. Again no materials were available for documenting the reflections and observation, thus many of the rich and valuable comments produced at the meeting was in jeopardy of being lost in relation to future work. Though we in general would argue in favour of having strong coherence between statements and contributions from different participants, a session like the meeting where a number of issues are raised, is important as well - in particular in the early phase of a design process. What seems to be needed are better ways for materialising the moves while at the same time maintaining the dynamics of raising a number of issues within a short time frame. Elements of Future Workshops, (Jungk & Müllert 1987) could be an important source of inspiration here. A Future Workshop is a way of organising a meeting where the goal is to handle a complex problematic situation but has also been applied in design, see for instance (Kensing & Madsen 1991). Parts of a Future Workshop is conducted according to a set of rules which include formulating and writing short statements on posters on the wall. The speaking time is restricted to 30 seconds to make it easier for all participants to raise their voice. Another principle at this particular part of the process is that there is no need for rational arguments for points raised.

As regards seeing, the prototype was at the meeting experienced in the sense of literal visual apprehension and only on rare occasions did anybody actively experience the prototype by using the remote control. The main exception being the manager of the multimedia department who gave the introduction to the prototype. The fact that the participants of the session were seated as a fairly large group in front of the TV may to some extend account for the lack of interest in trying out the prototype. In retrospect, minor changes to the set-up of the meeting could have supported more active ways of seeing than what actually took place. By having ten people sharing one prototype to a large extend prevented active exploration from taking place. Either more prototypes or some short sessions with minor groups exploring the prototype could have provided a better background for the discussions taking place in this session. Further an awareness of the importance of active exploration could have been reflected in the agenda such that participants were encouraged or asked to actively try out the prototype.

4.2 The co-operative workshop

Compared to the set up of the meeting, the setting of the workshop turned out to support more collaboration between the designers in a form where the contributions of the participants complemented each other rather than being isolated, undocumented statements. However, given the experiences from the workshop, we see room for improvements of this type of design work too. As an example of the collaborative nature of the workshop consider how one group explored ways of using the remote control for navigating among the hot spots on an internet page viewed on a TV-set in the living room. In this case, the designers started out from the idea of using the arrow keys on the remote control to direct the position of a cursor on the screen. The initial idea was investigated in series of seeing and moving which involved the use of both the remote control at hand, some screen dumps from the present prototype, pens and paper. The screen dumps facilitated in a very productive manner on the spot experimentation as people were able point to the screendump and not least to add modifications to the screen dump using various materials including post its and pens. Further, separate notes were produced on paper for later reference.

Thus the collaborative nature seen at the workshop can be attributed to several aspects of the organisation of the event. By asking the participants to solve a specific design task, and by providing them with flexible materials such as screen dumps on paper, pens and post-its, the designers were to a larger extent able to relate to each others comments thus supporting coherence among seeing and moving. Further, the participants used the materials for expressing their ideas in a tangible way, which in conjunction with the fact that the participants were seated in a small group around a table, made the implications of the design proposal easier to explain and build upon among the participants.

Figure 3: Materials at the workshop.

In the workshop, the materials like screen dumps, to a large extent supported seeing in the terms of active exploration when used to play through scenarios of future use. But this setting also turned out to be problematic in other respects. First of all, it was a problem that the design solutions were only tried out actively in one specific case, i.e. on one specific web-page and that the setting did not support an awareness of the limitations of the material. For instance, what would be a good navigation form on a page with few links positioned vertically on one side of the page, may not be a useful navigation form in a case with many links evenly distributed all over the web-page. Obviously, more example materials in terms of print out of web pages would help overcome this limitation. Further, seeing representations in the form of paper prototypes, as was the case in the workshop, raises the issue of whether the experiences from seeing a design representation is in accordance with seeing a corresponding real life implementation of the representation. Obviously this is not the case with respect to the aesthetic experience of a design presented on a piece of paper, which is of great importance in the case of Bang & Olufsen products. Thus although paper based materials are useful due to the flexibility and modifiability they offer, they are limited with respect to especially their realism regarding aesthetics.

At the workshop, we used the physical space as one of the means of setting up a productive workshop, but this is still an area with room for improvements. One of our experiences was that material from the posters on the walls presenting design dilemmas and users' statements was only used a little during the later design discussions, which might be due to the fact that the session took place in a rather large room. Karat and Bennett (1991) suggest to use a room large enough for two to eight people and small enough so that all walls are nearby. Another general guideline pointed out by Karat and Bennett (1991) is to use each of the walls in the room for separate design issues similar to that we had a stand in three of the four corners. Several designers and researchers, for instance Beyer & Holtzblatt, K. (1998), have pointed out the value of having a design room available throughout the design process as a way of keeping design ideas and reflection accessible for everybody involved throughout the process.

In terms of the different ways of seeing, the meeting and the workshop represent each their ends of the spectrum ranging from pure visual apprehension to actively experiencing. At the meeting, in which one prototype was mainly demonstrated for the designers by the head of the multimedia department and only few of the meeting participants actually tried out the prototype themselves. At the other extreme, we have the workshop in which the paper screen dumps were actively used to play through future scenarios of use and where the participants in turn took the existing remote control in their hand and played through a use-session using the remote as a dummy remote control. This served to provide each designer with an impression of how the design would come into play in future use situations and thus provided the designers with a basis for the next moves. Given the positive experiences from the workshop in terms of iterations and coherence of discussions, we argue that it is crucial that the designers actively try out design representations at design meetings. This is very much in line with the Scandinavian design tradition, (Greenbaum & Kyng 1993), where it is argued design proposals in the form of mock ups or prototypes support the collaboration between designers and users. However, given the insights gained in this study we argue that such techniques are also useful in a setting where multiple designers with different backgrounds need to collaborate.

5 Guidelines

We summarise our experiences from analysing the two forms of design practice in the following set of guidelines.

Supporting collaboration in multimedia design work

- make available a diverse set of materials to support communication and reflection among the participants;
- flexible materials can support cohesion among seeing and moving;
- the layout of the room may be used as a means of creating dynamic and interactive sessions;
- asking the participants to solve a specific design task within a certain time limit may stimulate productivity;

- use the agenda to balance out brain storming and elaboration of design ideas.

Support active hands on experience
- adjust the number of participants to the number of prototypes available;
- put active exploration on the agenda of the design session;
- make sure that people are seated in a way which encourage trying out prototypes;
- use design scenarios to stimulate trying out prototypes in an active way;
- consider how to pay respect to the aesthetic qualities;

Support experimentation
- provide flexible materials like screen dumps, post its and pens, to support the creation of alternative design solutions;
- use example data, like screen dumps, to facilitate on the spot experimentation;
- be aware of the limitations of the example material

Ideas for possible design materials
- pens
- paper
- cardboard
- post-it notes
- screen dumps
- posters
- mock-ups
- prototypes
- video
- previously developed products

Acknowledgements

The research project *Usability in Danish Industry* is sponsored by The Danish National Center for IT Research through grant no: 23. In addition, this research have been supported by The Danish Research Councils grant no 9600869 (*The Staging of Virtual 3D Spaces*). We would like to thank Bang and Olufsen for their active participation in both seeing and moving. We would like to thank Susanne Bødker for her comments on an earlier version of this article.

References

Beyer, H. & Holtzblatt, K. (1998): Contextual Design, Defining Customer-Centered Systems. San Francisco: Morgan Kaufmann Publishers.

Greenbaum, J. and Kyng, M. (1991): Design at Work: Cooperative Design of Computer Systems. Lawrence Erlbaum Associates.

Jungk, R. & Müllert, N. (1987): Future workshops: How to create a desirable future. London, UK: Institute of Social Invention.

Karat, J. and Bennett, J. L. (1991): Working within the Design Process: Supporting Effective and Efficient Design. In Designing Interaction: Psychology at the Human-Computer Interface. Carroll, J. M. (ed).

Kensing, F. & Madsen, K.H.: Generating Visions: Future Workshops and Metaphors, in Greenbaum, J. & Kyng, M.: Design at Work, Lawrence Earlbaum 1991 (155-168).

Schön, D. (1983): The Reflective Practitioner. New York: Basic Books.

Schön, D. (1988): Designing: Rules, types and worlds. Design studies, vol. 9 no 3 July 1988.

Schön, D. (1992): Kinds of seeing and their role in design. Design studies, vol. 13 no 2 April 1992.

Human-Computer Interaction - INTERACT'99 (Volume II)
S. Brewster, A. Cawsey & G. Cockton (Editors)
Published by The British Computer Society © IFIP TC.13, 1999

Scenario-Based System Validation by Users

Barbara Schmidt-Belz, Dietmar Fleischhauer and Oliver Märker

GMD--German National Research Center for Information Technology
Schloss Birlinghoven
D-53754 Sankt Augustin
Germany
Email: Barbara.Schmidt-Belz@gmd.de

Abstract: We report on using experimental games to validate innovative systems applications. Within a user oriented systems development, we have found this a very useful method to validate a new system as soon as a prototype is available. At two different stages of the system development we were able set up experimental games for three groups of prospective users (10 - 16 persons each group) and we got a rich feedback about ergonomic and usability issues of the system and its application in a certain domain. The participating users found this method very useful. First, it serves as a tutorial, second, it allows them a close-to-reality experience, and third, it is a sound basis for validation and further implementation planning.

Keywords: Scenario-based usability validation, user-oriented software design process, innovative systems and applications, experimental games, validation experiments

1 Introduction

An important stage in a user oriented system development process usually is the delivery of a prototype to the users. The idea is to let users try this out, then use their feedback for some improvements of the system before its final delivery and implementation it in the real working environment. The ideal basis of the usability validation would be a "field test", that is, users perform their everyday work supported by the prototype.

With innovative systems, we often encounter problems when we ask users to perform this real-world validation:

- The system may affect not only isolated workplaces but a whole group or department.
- Efficient use of the system may require some changes in the workflow.
- The domain may have high standards of reliability (as in public administration or factory management).
- The users may still lack the appropriate technical equipment.
- Employees under high work pressure are reluctant to commit to additional efforts.

In such cases the test of a prototype would be expensive (both money and time), risky and hard to recover from in case of a failure.

We therefore developed a procedure that allows users to validate the system in a realistic working context, but without the risks of a real-life application. We set up an experiment with a realistic scenario and ask a group of users to perform tasks using the prototype. Within a workshop of one, two, or three days (depending on the scenario and the tasks to perform) they get tutoring and experience, and we can apply different methods to get user feedback during this time. We have profited from watching the users work with the system, their questions about how to use it, we have used questionnaires, and we have had group discussion or focus group sessions. Users have profited from the workshops by being trained (free of their every-day pressure) gaining personal, close-to-reality experience about the benefits or problems of the system, they had another chance to influence the final development, and after the session they felt well prepared to plan and decide upon the implementation of the system in their organisation.

2 Our Experiences

We have developed and used this approach within a user oriented development of a system called ZENO. ZENO is an Internet-based groupware including discussion forums and other services. It is based on the World Wide Web, its main concepts are shared virtual workspaces for groups with access control, and a discussion forum according to an argumentation framework called Issue Based Information System (IBIS), see Gordon and Karacapilidis (1997). The system is generic and can be applied in different domains. We have user partners who want to use ZENO in urban planning including public participation. Other partners want to use ZENO for co-operation in technical development projects, like software development or production process reengineering.

At two different stages of the development process we have used scenario-based validation experiments.

A first prototype of the ZENO system was validated in April 1997. We set up a scenario of use and invited two groups of potential users to a workshop, where they used the system according to this scenario and gave us feedback. The scenario was not very specific (i.e. not specifically taken from the domain of Urban planning and Citizen Participation) but oriented at the (more generic) clusters of systems support (e.g. to use a shared virtual workspace, to organise a shared workspace, to use a discussion forum). One group of 16 employees of the City of Bonn had a two-day workshop, another group of 11 geography students had a three-day workshop.

The second prototype of ZENO was validated in December 1998. This time, we have set up a rather specific scenario and made it an experimental game: ZENO was used to mediate a conflict between the (fictive) city of "Knopfheim" and several interest groups of Knopfheim citizens. The story was, that a large area of a former button factory near the old centre of Knopfheim should be developed. The City together with an investor preferred a huge shopping centre, while the Knopfheim merchants and some citizen interest groups had quite different goals and ideas.

This game had only two half-day sessions, including validation. We had one group of 12 people from different professions take part in this game.

3 The Results of our Validation Experiments

A discussion of results should consider the three aspects:

- performance of the experiment,
- validation feedback, and
- learning success of the users.
-

In all cases, the experiments could be performed quite successfully. Users were at ease, they performed the tasks as suggested, and engaged in their roles in the game quite seriously.

From the first validation, the main result was a rich feedback about ergonomic issues. We got less feedback about advantages or disadvantages of the system. Users were vague and ambivalent in their assessment of the benefits of the system. We found two possible reasons for this: First, the first prototype had an insufficient user interface, so this was the dominant user concern. And second, the experimental game was not very specific, so it gave basis for only a rather speculative assessment of the impact of the system for each user's job.

From the second validation we again got some feedback about ergonomic issues, but mostly on missing functionality (which is not a bad sign). And we got a lot of feedback about usability for the scenario in question. The reasons for this are, first, that the second prototype was much improved compared to the first one, and second, that an experimental game allows a very concrete experience of applying the system and thus is a better basis to assess usefulness.

The goal of training users within this validation process was quite obviously successful. For other groups of users we have also given pure training courses of one-day duration (5-7 hours, depending on previous user competence). They were set up similar to the first type of scenario based validation (see above), but they lacked the group discussion about the use of the system. The training participants decided at the end of the courses, that they now needed to meet again (at their organisation) to discuss details about how to use ZENO in their special domain.

4 Difficulties we Encountered

Of course, the first difficulty was to find appropriate scenarios for the validation experiments, and to choose the validation methods. We discuss this in detail in the next section.

One problem in our cases was, that the low time budget of users forced us to squeeze a discussion via the ZENO discussion forum into one afternoon, which is not a realistic setting for an asynchronous interaction.

Another difficulty has been to separate ergonomic from usability issues (handling of system - usefulness of its application). Of course handling and usefulness of a system have mutual influence on one another. But we had to make sure that both aspects were validated in their own right. A similar effort had to be made in order to distinguish different dimensions of ergonomics (handling, functionality, response time etc.), and dimensions of usefulness (benefits, problems, costs, added values etc). It is more easy when the moderator of the focus group or group discussion has a clear understanding of usability; otherwise you have to apply techniques like clustering when you analyse the feedback.

During the discussion of the ergonomic issues, some users tend to make very concrete suggestions how to improve the system (like "I need this stop button big and red in the top left corner" or "I prefer the look and feel of Windows 95"). You must not suppress their ideas, but make sure you always ask for the reason, and what is the problem with the current version. Otherwise you get a list of concrete requirements, which are hard to ignore, but sometimes rather worthless because the items are incompatible, contradictory and not state of the art. It is the job of users to validate the current prototype, but it is the job of the development team to design an improved system.

At the first time we roughly underestimated the time we needed to analyse the validation results. The questionnaires we used were easy to summarise, but compared to the group discussions, they gave us a rather meagre feedback. During all sessions, the stages of the experiments as well as the group and focus group discussions, we had several people taking notes. We also succeeded in a good moderation of all discussion sessions. We refrained from tape recording the sessions, which in our opinion was a wise decision considering the effort of preparing transcription and other well known problems. All the same, it took us many days to come up with a final report that could be used by the development team.

5 How to Design Validation Experiments

Validation Experiments can be very different, taking into account the system to be validated and the kind of results you need. Some important parameters of such experiments shall be discussed here.

Above all, it is important not to focus on the functions of your system but on its use and the context of its use. The scenario may be more or less specific for the application domain. Games usually need more specific scenarios. Simple experiments (and training courses as well) can be based on more generic scenarios (e.g. such as derived from use cases). We found that games give users a more vivid experience, which is a good basis for identifying benefits and problems of the system application. But you may need several different games to cover your domain. Less specific scenarios are quite sufficient to get feedback on ergonomic issues. It is easier to cover the scope of your system by less specific scenarios (like use cases, see for instance Schneider and Winters (1998). But they tend to be abstract and users need a lot more imagination in matching the laboratory experience with their real working life.

You can set up experiments with single users or with user groups. If the system supports isolated working places, you can set up scenarios and experiments for one user being supported by the new system, and perform this experiment with a certain number of single users. If the system aims at supporting user interaction, like supporting co-operation or workflow management, the experiment has to involve user groups and their co-operation. In both cases it may be sensible to have a group of users discuss the system, not only interviews of single users (see below).

One constraint of validation experiments will be time. While real-life tasks often need several days or weeks to be accomplished, you probably are lucky if you find users willing to spend one or two days with your experiment. So you need to select short, but still meaningful parts of the real world tasks, and combine them in your scenario. They can be linked together by a story, which helps to remember the real world context. Another consideration concerning time is whether the system is to support synchronous or asynchronous communication, or if the tasks have to be performed in a certain workflow. You have to find an appropriate way to schedule your experiments.

When choosing the setting, the incentives, and preparing a data background for an experimental game, do it with a profound knowledge of the domain and a true love for detail. Any unrealistic detail may distract users and add to a general irritation. For instance, most users cannot distinguish between the functionality of a system and the data contents. In the end, you have trouble in distinguishing feedback concerning the usability of the system from irritations caused by details of the experimental game. (Of course you can pep up your game with some funny details, but don't overdo it.)

The experiment has to be accompanied and completed by methods of collecting and analysing the user feedback. There is a great choice of methods available, see for instance ELPUB (1995). We have chosen a combination of methods with a clear bias in favour of qualitative methods.

Quantitative methods, like questionnaires to measure usability, are necessary when you have to demonstrate or prove the quality of your system. For a valid result you will need a certain number of users. We used the "Software usability measurement inventory SUMI" for this purpose, see SUMI (1996), which is generally applicable to assess the usability of software systems. There are others available.

When you design your own questionnaire, as most projects do, you can ask more specific questions and get a more concrete feedback about your system. But you need several users to test and adjust the questionnaire itself, and you then need a good number of users if you want to achieve statistically significant results.

When you need feedback to improve your system (not to prove something), we found qualitative methods more useful: to watch users, to interview them and to arrange group discussions. You do not need a lot of users, sometimes 3-5 users will do, and you can achieve very specific, detailed and useful feedback about the quality of your system. Among other techniques, Focus Groups are applicable, see Caplan (1990) or Greenbaum (1993).

Here, we cannot go into details of appropriate qualitative methods for observation, interviewing or discussion groups, see ELPUB (1995) or MEGATAQ (1997) for a qualified survey of suitable methods and references.

6 Role of Validation Experiments

A simple, "cascading" model of a user oriented systems development process begins with acquiring users requirements, specifying the system, realising the software, testing it and finally implementing it at the users site. Usually there are additional efforts to facilitate user participation, like

- using mock-ups to help users find their requirements,
- iterative realisation with intermediate steps of validation and redesign of the system, or
- giving users a prototype to try out, before the new system becomes finished and organisationally implemented.

Why should we need experimental games within such a user oriented approach? Users probably have been involved from the beginning of the project, in defining user requirements, specifying use cases and so on.

When the new system is innovative or its application in a domain is innovative, the user guided design is not as straight forward as developers often assume. For an innovative system application, system engineers and users co-operate in the construction of a new reality, often struggle for a common understanding of this new reality. Under these circumstances, the first prototype is the users first real chance to get a feeling for the innovation and what it would mean for their own work. Often the system engineers are shocked when at this (rather late) stage users reconsider their requirements and reassess the concept of the system.

So a prototype is necessary for usability validation of innovative system applications. Why not deliver the prototype, let users play with it and ask for feedback by means of a questionnaire? In this case, the user organisation has to cope with the innovation all by them selves. If they perform an inappropriate test, the basis for users assessment is insufficient. Often the response quote to the questionnaire is rather low. The feedback that can be achieved by a questionnaire is rough and superficial, compared to the possibilities of interviews or group discussions.

On the other hand, scenario based validation experiments are time-consuming and therefore rather expensive. Another difficulty may be that you need both domain and system knowledge to design the experiments, and a good moderator to perform them. So, whenever the application domain can afford real-life experiments or when plenty of experiences from similar applications are available, experimental games are not necessary and probably too expensive.

7 Summary and Outlook

Within a user-oriented development of innovative systems, we found it necessary to bridge the gap between delivery of a prototype and its real application. In our experience, a scenario based usability validation by performing experimental games with users as soon as a prototype of the system is available, has proved very useful both for users and developers.

We also suggest that this kind of validation experiments might be very useful in the process of deciding upon which standard software to buy and how exactly to reorganise business in order to make the best use of the new system.

In the near future, we shall develop a variation of the above described validation experiments: ZENO shall be offered to be used in a real public participation process. However, we expect that for the time being, most citizens stick to the traditional means of participation such as writing letters or talking to the urban planners in their offices. By simulating the real process by a synchronous or a retrospective application of ZENO ("as if they had used ZENO"), we hope, in spite of this problem, to get valuable experience for the urban planers, and to demonstrate the use of the system to the public. We also hope, that what was a simulation at the beginning, might prove as an ice-breaker, and result in a real use of the system.

8 Acknowledgements

We wish to thank our colleagues Tom Gordon, Eckehard Gross, and Lothar Oppor who have designed and implemented the ZENO system taking user orientation very seriously, and who are making great efforts to realise user requirements. And last but not least, we thank our user partners at the City of Bonn, especially Ulrich Ziegenhagen and Martin Seelbach, who have supported the experimental games with their great domain knowledge and enthusiasm.

References

Caplan, S. (1990). "Using focus group methodology for ergonomic design". *Ergonomics* **33**(5), 527-533.

ELPUB (1995). "Handbook for practical usability engineering in IE projects", Report ELPUB 105 10107. 1995

Gordon, T. F. and Karacapilidis, N. I. (1997). "The Zeno Argumentation Framework". *Proceedings of the International Conference on Artificial Intelligence and Law -- ICAIL-97*, ACM, Melbourne, 1997.

Greenbaum, T. L. (1993). "The Handbook for Focus Group Research". New York, Oxford, Singapore, Sydney, 1993.

Inbar, M. and Stoll, C. S. (1972). "Simulation and Gaming in Social Science". New York, 1972: Free Press.

MEGATAQ (1997). "Evaluating User Aspects of Telematic Applications; A model and Inventory of Techniques. EU project MEGATAQ TE 2007.

Schmidt-Belz, B. and Gordon, T.F. and Voß, H. (1998). "Urban Planning with GeoMed - First User Experiences" *Proceedings of the 4th* European Digital Cities Conference: Changing Patterns of Urban Life, 135-138.

Schneider, G. and Winters, J. P. (1998). "Applying Use Cases. A practical guide". Reading, Massachusets.

SUMI (1996). "Software usability measurement inventory". Human Factors Research Group, University of Cork, Ireland. 1996.

Weidenhaupt, K. and Pohl, K. and Jarke, M. and Haumer, P. (1998). "Scenarios in System Development: Current Practice." *IEEE Software* March/April 1998, 34-45.

Human-Computer Interaction - INTERACT'99 (Volume II)
S. Brewster, A. Cawsey & G. Cockton (Editors)
Published by The British Computer Society © IFIP TC.13, 1999

Experiences (Painful and Good) Developing HCI Standards

Tom Stewart

System Concepts
2 Savoy Court, Strand
London, WC2R 0EZ
UK
Email: tom@system-concepts.com

Abstract: The purpose of this paper is to explain why the author believes that the sixteen years he has spent developing International Standards concerned with the ergonomics of human system interaction have not been wasted. He describes some of the issues involved in standardisation and explains the thinking behind ISO 9241 Ergonomic requirements for office work with visual display terminals (VDTs) and a new standard ISO 13407:1999 Human centred design processes for interactive systems.

Keywords: user interface standards, ergonomics, HCI

1 Background

In the late 1970s, there was growing concern about the ergonomics of visual display terminals (also called visual display units). The prime concern at that time concerned the possibility that prolonged use (especially of displays with poor image quality) might cause deterioration in users eyesight.

When a new work item to address this concern was proposed, the Information Technology committee decided that this was a suitable topic for the recently formed ergonomics committee ISO/TC 159. The work item was allocated to the sub-committee ISO/TC 159/SC4 Signals and Controls and an inaugral meeting was held at BSI in Manchester in 1983. The meeting was well attended with delegates from many countries and a few key decisions were made.

At that time, there was a proliferation of office based systems and we decided to focus on office tasks (word processing, spreadsheet etc) rather than try to include Computer Aided Design or process control applications. We also decided that we would need a multi-part standard to cover the wide range of ergonomics issues which we believed needed to be addressed in order to improve the ergonomics of display screen work. Six initial parts were identified and working groups established (see Table 1) . At the end of that first meeting, one of participants was heard to complain that we had been meeting for three days and still had not standardised anything. Little did any of us realise that it would be nearly seven years before the first parts of ISO 9241 were published and that it would take us to the end of the century to publish all seventeen parts.

2 The Structure of ISO 9241

The structure of the standard was decided at a time when there were clear distinctions between hardware and software and monochrome Cathode Ray Tube (CRT) displays were the norm. The first six parts were therefore primarily concerned with hardware (which, in our naivete we thought would be easier and less contentious to standardise). However, even within this hardware domain, we recognised the importance of job and task design in ensuring that users could work safely, comfortably and efficiently – so part 2 was inserted before the more technical hardware oriented parts.

Later, software parts (10 to 17) were added, reflecting the different styles of user system interaction which were available at the time and additional hardware parts were added to deal with reflections (7), colour displays (8) and non-keyboard input devices eg mouse (9). The structure therefore reflected the practicalities and history of standard making and unfortunately is not very user-centred (one of the key principles of ergonomics).

Table 1: Shows the status of all seventeen parts in May 1999.

ISO 9241 Ergonomic requirements for office work with visual display terminals (VDTs)	**Status May 1999**
Part 1: General introduction	IS
Part 2: Guidance on task requirements	IS
Part 3: Visual display requirements	IS
Part 4: Keyboard requirements	IS
Part 5: Workstation layout and postural requirements	IS
Part 6: Guidance on the work environment	FDIS
Part 7: Requirements for displays with reflections	IS
Part 8: Requirements for displayed colours	IS
Part 9: Requirements for non-keyboard input devices	FDIS
Part 10: Dialogue principles	IS
Part 11: Guidance on usability	IS
Part 12: Presentation of information	IS
Part 13: User guidance	IS
Part 14: Menu dialogues	IS
Part 15: Command dialogues	IS
Part 16: Direct manipulation dialogues	FDIS
Part 17: Form filling dialogues	IS

3 How to Use ISO 9241

ISO 9241 was developed to be used in a number of different human-computer interaction (HCI) design activities, including:

- Analysing and defining system requirements
- Designing user-system dialogues and interface navigation
- Designing or selecting displays
- Designing or selecting keyboards and other input devices
- Designing workplaces for display screen users
- Supporting and training users
- Designing jobs and tasks

In the following sections, I describe how various parts of ISO 9241 support these activities.

3.1 Analysing and Defining System Requirements

Engineering usability into products requires a commitment to usability requirements as well as functionality requirements. However, setting usability objectives in these requirements only make sense if there is an agreed way of specifying usability. *ISO 9241-11:1998 Guidance on usability* was developed to provide an internationally agreed framework for such a statement of usability.

It provides guidance on usability specification which includes descriptions of the context of use, the evaluation procedures to be carried out and the criterion measures to be satisfied when the usability of the system is to be evaluated. There are various situations in which usability may be evaluated, for example in product development, in procurement or in product certification. The common framework presented in this part should be useful in all of these situations.

3.2 Designing User-System Dialogues and Interface Navigation

ISO 9241 10:1996 Dialogue principles presents high level ergonomic principles which apply to the design of dialogues between humans and information systems. These include suitability for the task, controllability and error tolerance amongst others. The principles are supported by a number of scenarios which indicate the relative priorities and importance of the different principles in practical applications.

ISO 9241-14 :1997 Menu dialogues provides recommendations on menu structure, navigation, option selection and execution, and menu presentation (by various techniques including windowing, panels, buttons, fields, etc.).

ISO 9241-15:1998 Command dialogues provides recommendations on command language structure and syntax, command representations, input and output considerations, feedback and help.

ISO FDIS 9241-16 :1998 Direct manipulation dialogues provides recommendations on the manipulation of objects, and the design of metaphors, objects and attributes. It covers those aspects of "Graphical User Interfaces" which are directly manipulated, and not covered by other parts of ISO 9241.

ISO 9241-17:1998 Form-filling dialogues provides recommendations on form structure and output considerations, input considerations, and form navigation.

3.3 Designing or Selecting Displays

Display hardware specification and design for office VDTs is covered in *ISO 9241-3:1992 Display requirements*. This part deals with the design of screen hardware for visual display terminals. In addition to design specifications, this part also contains a proposed user performance test as an alternative route to conformance.

ISO 9241-7:1998 Requirements for displays with reflections deals with the ergonomic requirements, for and details of, methods of measurement of reflections from the surface of display screens, including those with surface treatments.

ISO 9241-8:1997 Requirements for displayed colours deals with the ergonomic requirements for multi-colour displays which supplement the monochrome requirements in Part 3. Displays for control rooms are dealt with separately in ISO 11064 (this is still under development).

Software aspects of display design are covered in *ISO 9241-12:1998 Presentation of information.* This part deals with the specific ergonomics issues involved in representing and presenting information in visual form. It includes guidance on ways of representing complex information, screen layout and design as well as the use of windows.

There is already a substantial body of material available in guidelines and recommendations and this part represents a distillation of the most useful and relevant ones.

3.4 Designing or Selecting Keyboards and Other Input Devices

Keyboard specification and design (in terms of the operation of the keys and its ergonomic qualities) is covered in *ISO 9241-4:1998 Keyboard requirements.* This deals with alphanumeric keyboard design. In addition to design specifications, this part also contains a proposed user performance test as an alternative route to conformance. It deals with the ergonomic aspects of the keyboard, not the layout which is specified in *ISO 9995 Keyboard layouts for text office systems.*

Non-keyboard input devices are becoming increasingly popular and *ISO FDIS 9241-9: 1998 Requirements for non-keyboard input devices* deals with the ergonomic requirements for pointing devices including the mouse, tracker ball etc. which can be used in conjunction with a visual display terminal.

3.5 Designing Workplaces for Display Screen Users

Office workplaces incorporating VDTs are covered in some detail in *ISO 9241-5:1998 Workstation layout and postural requirements.* This part deals with the ergonomic requirements for a visual display terminal workstation which will allow the user to adopt a comfortable and efficient posture. Workplaces in control rooms are dealt with separately in *ISO DIS 11064-3:1998 Control Room Layout.* Environmental considerations (visual, acoustic and thermal) are covered in *ISO 9241-6:1998 Guidance on the work environment.*

3.6 Supporting and Training Users

In assessing the usability of a product in practice, real users take account of the documentation, manuals and training received as well as the specific characteristics of the product itself. *ISO 9241-13:1998 User guidance* covers some of these aspects and provides recommendations for the design and evaluation of user guidance attributes of software user interfaces including Prompts, Feedback, Status, On-line Help and Error Management.

3.7 Designing Jobs and Tasks

In developing ISO 9241, there was a clear recognition that many of the problems often attributed to poor equipment or workplace design may in fact stem from poor job design. Thus *ISO 9241-2:1992 Guidance on task requirements* provides guidance on the design of display screen tasks based on nearly half a century of research and organisational practice in socio-technical systems.

4 Painful Experiences

Although ergonomics standards are generally concerned with such mundane topics as keyboard design or menu structures, they nonetheless generate considerable emotion amongst standards makers. Sometimes this is because the resulting standard could have a major impact on product sales or legal liabilities. Other times the reason for the passion is less clear. Nonetheless, the strong feelings have resulted in the following painful experiences in the process of standardisation, especially for me as committee chairman. These have included:

4.1 Undue Influence

Large multinational companies can try to exert undue influence by dominating national committees. Although draft standards are usually publicly available from national standards bodies, they are not widely publicised. This means that it is relatively easy for well informed large companies to provide sufficient experts at the national level to ensure that they can virtually dictate the final vote and comments from a country.

4.2 Horse Trading

End user's requirements can be compromised as part of 'horse trading' between conflicting viewpoints. In the interests of reaching agreement, delegates may resort to making political trade-offs largely independent of the technical merits of the issue.

4.3 Uncritical Support

National pride can lead to uncritical support for a particular approach or methodology. In theory, participants in Working Group meetings are experts nominated by member bodies in the different countries. They are not there to represent a national viewpoint but are supposed to act as individuals. However, as one disillusioned expert explained to me 'sometimes the loudest noise at a Working Group meeting is the grinding of axes'

4.3 Unusable Standards

It is not just the process which can be painful. The standards themselves can leave much to be desired in terms of brevity, clarity and usability as a result of:

- **stilted language and boring formats.** The unfriendliness of the language is illustrated by the fact that although the organisation is known by the acronym ISO, its full English title is the International Organisation for Standardisation. The language and style are governed by a set of Directives and these encourage a wordy and impersonal style.

- **problems with translation and the use of 'Near English'.** There are three official languages in ISO - English, French and Russian. In practice, much of the work is conducted in English, often by non-native speakers. As someone who only speaks English, I have the utmost respect for those who can work in more than one language. However, the result of this is that the English used in standards is often not quite correct - it is 'near English'. The words are usually correct but the combination often makes the exact meaning unclear. These problems are exacerbated when the text is translated.

- **confusions between requirements and recommendations.** In ISO standards, there are usually some parts which specify what has to be done to conform to the standard. These are indicated by the use of the word 'shall'. However, in ergonomics standards, we often want to make recommendations as well. These are indicated by the use of the word 'should'. Such subtleties are often lost on readers of standards, especially those in different countries. For example, in the Nordic countries, they follow recommendations (shoulds) as well as requirements (shalls), so the distinction is diminished. In the USA, they tend to ignore the 'shoulds' and only act on the 'shalls'.

5 Good Experiences

I would not spend my time (largely unfunded) developing standards if I did not believe that they are largely a force for good. Major strengths in the process are that it is:

5.1 Based on Consensus

Manufacturers (and ergonomists) make wildly different claims about what represents good ergonomics. This is a major weakness for our customers who may conclude that all claims are equally valid and there is no sound basis for any of it. Standards force a consensus and therefore have real authority in the minds of our customers. Achieving consensus requires compromises, but then so does life.

5.2 International

Although there are national and regional differences in populations, the world is becoming a single market with the major suppliers taking a global perspective.

Variations in national standards and requirements not only increase costs and complexity, they also tend to compromise individual choice. Making standards international is one way of ensuring that they have impact and can help improve the ergonomics quality of products for everyone.

6 Technology Push

One of the problems we experienced during the development of ISO 9241, was that the technology was developing faster than we could reach agreement on the standards.

So we started work on a process standard *ISO 13407 Human-centred design processes for interactive systems* which aims to provide guidance for project managers to help them follow a human-centred design process. By undertaking the activities and following the principles described in the standard, managers can be confident that the resulting systems will be usable and work well for their users.

The standard describes four principles of human-centred design:

- active involvement of users (or those who speak for them)
- appropriate allocation of function (making sure human skill is used properly)
- iteration of design solutions (allowing time for iteration in project planning)
- multi-disciplinary design (but beware over large design teams)

and four key human-centred design activities:

- understand and specify the context of use (make it explicit - avoid assuming it is obvious)
- specify user and organisational requirements (note there will be a variety of different viewpoints and individual perspectives)
- produce design solutions (note plural, multiple designs encourage creativity)
- evaluate designs against requirements (involves real user testing not just convincing demonstrations)

In order to claim conformance, the standard requires that the procedures used, the information collected and the use made of results are specified (a checklist is provided as an annex to help). We have developed this approach to conformance in a number of parts of ISO 9241 since so many ergonomics recommendations are context specific. Thus there is often only one 'shall' in these standards which generally prescribes what kind of evidence is required to convince another party that the relevant recommendations in the standard have been identified and followed.

There has already been considerable international interest in ISO 13407 and we believe there will be increasing demands from large customers for evidence that their system suppliers follow this kind of process.

7 And Finally...

I believe that we have produced a number of useful standards over the past few years. These are not only useful in providing technical information in their own right but serve to ensure that ergonomics issues are firmly placed on management agendas. Many organisations feel obliged to take standards seriously and therefore even if they were not predisposed towards ergonomics initially, the existence of International Standards ensures that they are given due consideration. As consultants, we know that basing our recommendations on agreed standards gives them far greater authority than citing relevant research.

Human-Computer Interaction - INTERACT'99 (Volume II)
S. Brewster, A. Cawsey & G. Cockton (Editors)
Published by The British Computer Society © IFIP TC.13, 1999

No Pain, No Gain - Applying User-Centered Design in Product Concept Development

Tiina Hynninen, Tea Liukkonen-Olmiala and Timo Kinnunen

Nokia Mobile Phones
P.O. Box 50
FIN-90571 OULU
Finland
Email: {tiina.m.hynninen, tea.liukkonen-olmiala, timo.v.kinnunen}@nokia.com

Abstract: A third generation mobile phone concepting project was carried out at Nokia Mobile Phones. The concepting project had two goals. Its first goal was to create a third generation mobile communication device concept for teenagers. The resulting concept is not presented here for propriety reasons. The second goal of the project was to explore different methods in obtaining knowledge of the end-user. The methods were tested in a multi-disciplinary team, which consisted of representatives from different fields: concept design, graphical design, industrial design, qualitative research, etc. The findings of the project are presented in the discussion concerning the applied methods and evaluation of the teamwork. From these experiences it can be concluded that various specialists recognize the importance of the end-user study, but the practice itself is not easy. Studying human behavior may not give direct answers to the design process, but it certainly increases the understanding of the end-user.

Keywords: user-centered design, product conception, end-user needs.

1 Introduction

This product concepting project at Nokia Mobile Phones (NMP), Finland, was started in October 1998. Its goal was to create a 3rd generation mobile communication device concept and the demonstrator focused on teenage users. Third Generation (3G) mobile phones are smart phones and communicators, which are able to transmit and receive a combination of digital information including speech, pictures, video, and various kinds of information content.

The project was started in October/98 and completed by the end of March/99. The design team consisted of two representatives from user interface (UI) concept design and usability; one graphical designer, one representative from a field of usability and qualitative research, one representative from information studies, one software and simulation designer, and two students of industrial design from the University of Lapland in Finland. Apart from the students of industrial design from the University of Lapland, all team members are employees at NMP.

Another goal of the project was to explore different methods in obtaining knowledge of the end-user in a multidisciplinary design team. An on going, internal sociological research related to the topic provided data background for the team.

2 User Needs As Design Drive

Design drives for the concept were a result of the brainstorming in the design team. The sociological study served as one of the main sources for the brainstorming. The team raised eleven user needs to function as design drives for the project. Having investigated into needs of the target user group, technological possibilities were explored for 3G concept.

2.1 User Needs Inquiry Process

To validate the user needs introduced from the sociological study for our purposes, teenager interviews were arranged. A total of 13 Finnish teenagers were interviewed for the purpose in seven interview sessions. The interviews were made in pairs, so that a pair of team members interviewed a pair of teenagers at a time. The interviews were made in pairs to optimize free association from teenagers, through which as much feedback as possible could be obtained. A new structure of interviews was experimented, because the design team felt that it might be difficult for teenagers to imagine a product with new features that do not yet exist. The interviews thus consisted of fictitious use case scenarios, in which an imagined end user describes different situations, where s/he has used the future product. The use case scenarios were written stories without pictures. The teenagers read the scenarios, and commented ideas introduced in them. They were also asked to compare the fictitious stories to their own everyday lives and experiences, so that the predefined user needs could be checked against their responses. In the end of the interviews, the interviewees were asked to rate the scenarios from their own point of view. On the one hand, they rated the most interesting / most applicable scenario and on the other hand, the least interesting one.

As a result of these ratings, the most desired functionalities for the concept could be listed. On the top of the most desired functionalities was a general category of pictures. According to the teenagers, pictures enable expression of feelings a lot better than traditional means in mobile devices. Another important functionality for teenagers is overall communication with friends – anytime and anywhere. Requirements were also set for the UI of the concept, individuality as the strongest one. This may be a counter reaction to advertisers; teenagers form a target group for many mass production purposes today. As a result of that, many teenagers have begun to regard individuality as one of the leading ideologies.

Next the most desired functionalities were explored with a Contextual Inquiry study (Holtzblatt & Beyer, 1998). The design team used an applied version of Contextual Inquiry emphasizing artefacts, which, in this case, are teenagers' current tools and devices for carrying out their tasks. The team selected uses of email/SMS, calendar/diary, phone/phonebook, and photo album/home videos as the foci for the Contextual Inquiry.

Seven interview sessions were arranged, and at this phase the teenagers who were most advanced in mobile device use were selected for interviews. The idea was to approach the end user in the place, where one finds it comfortable and natural to send messages, write calendar entries, etc. In the interview session, the selected artefacts were walked through with the user, and good cases that could be used as examples or taken into further analysis were copied (calendar pages, email-messages, etc.). Interviews were analyzed and interpreted further in sub-teams by drawing artefact models of collected artefacts and documenting findings as notes.

According to the method of Contextual Inquiry, in order to find common practices among teenagers, individual artefact models of interviews were consolidated into a single model which represents common usage patterns and intents for using the artefact. Interview notes were used to build a bottom up affinity diagram that reveals the themes and common issues among teenagers using their current artefacts.

2.2 Concept Design Process

At the first phase, Contextual Design (Holtzblatt & Beyer, 1998) was selected as a working method. Validated use case scenario results, consolidated artefact models and affinity diagrams were used to trigger design ideas. The design team created three different visions of the new concept in brainstorming sessions. Visions were then designed into more detailed storyboards, in which it was defined step by step how the user uses the concept to perform his or her task. In addition to storyboarding phase, to define one system structure for the concept, the team created a User Environment Design (UED), which could also be called a software floorplan. Finally, paper prototype mock-up was created for walking through the designs from the storyboards and UED with end-users. In this study, walkthrough can be understood as a method in which the user performs one's tasks and codesigns the concept together with the interviewer. The team selected one form factor model as the basis for the paper prototype mock-up.

In the first mock-up walkthrough, three users from the target segment were interviewed about the concept in their own environment. Thus the sessions were arranged at school cafeterias and homes. A couple of designers from the team participated the interviews as well, and one worked with a prototype (as a human computer) and others took notes. In the session, the users performed their current communication tasks with their current devices (SMS, phone calls, email, etc.). Once completed the tasks, users repeated each task with the new concept. They were also encouraged to employ new ideas and possibilities provided by the concept. If the concept did not work according to the user needs, it was developed and co-designed with the user during the walkthrough session. Also, areas that did not work at all were documented as issues to be developed in further design.

Issues found from the mock-up walkthroughs were analyzed in the team. The team made changes and developments in the concept according to the issues with the help of storyboarding method. Having done the changes in design, the system UED was updated, and a paper mock-up version for the second walkthrough was created.

The second mock-up walkthrough session was arranged according to same principles that guided the first mock-up sessions. The second case indicated that some of the changes from the earlier concept were correct, but there was still room for improvement left. In the issue analysis of the second mock-up walkthrough, the team learned that many focus areas of the concept were in a fairly good shape, some additional functions were needed in each focus area.

3 Benefits

Benefits of user-centered design procedures are countless. First of all, they provide a good basis for user interface concept design, because it keeps the user as the main focus in the design process. The data collection procedures do not question designers' insights; on the contrary, the user data increase designers' knowledge.

Design process in the multi-professional group is useful for all of its participants. In the group, all the important information is shared easily, and representatives of various professions bring different viewpoints into the design process.

Contextual design as a qualitative method does not bring anything new into qualitative data collection or research in general. However, it introduces strict formalism to field methods in user-centered design process. By following the principles of contextual design, designers and researchers are constantly aware of the stages in design process, i.e. they always know what they are doing, and what they are supposed to do next. As qualitative research sometimes leads the researcher into endless supplies of data, the frames and structure that contextual design follows help in organizing and making use of the data.

Similarly with many other qualitative studies, our user-centered design process was spiral in nature. Its first phase was acquiring knowledge of existing practices. This was done with the methods described earlier in this paper. After analyzing and organizing the user data, which is the second phase, the design team starts with the actual design work that is based on the user data. If the team realizes it does not have enough data that would guide the team in design process, it returns to the users to obtain more data, and redesigns the work model. The mock-ups and prototypes are checked with users as well. The spiral nature assures that the direction the team has chosen in its design is correct, and it also improves the designers' insights. In the spiral process, each phase brings more data about the user and the usability of the product, which should increase the designer's or the team's confidence concerning the product.

As mentioned earlier, different qualitative methods were applied in the multi-disciplinary group. Since all these specialists approach design issues from different perspectives, there were no simple solutions to problems rising from the design issues. All the team members had strong opinions that they did not hesitate to express. This meant that all the arguments had to be grounded on real facts or data, of which the conclusions were drawn. This all was done together in the group sessions, in which all the team members participated. However, in the evaluative workshop after the project, this was seen as one of the greatest benefits of the multi-disciplinary team.

4 Challenges

Although the team regarded the user centered design as a powerful and useful way to start design, there were many issues that the team had to overcome during the process. These issues are probably very typical within qualitative studies and group design. The team came to notice that the problems that people attempt to overcome with new methods and techniques do not disappear anywhere. The basic problems appear in different forms and are perhaps dealt with in a more structured and sophisticated way. This is, in fact, the point in new approaches: the same problems are still faced, but the greatest difference is in the way they are handled.

4.1 Interviews

Since the number of the sample is small in qualitative studies, the selection of the interviewees becomes a crucial issue in practising user-centered design. Therefore the study sample should be as diverse as possible. In this kind of concepting project these requirements can be hard to fill, because there are confidentiality issues involved.

Multidisciplinary team, i.e. people with different backgrounds, skills, and ideas create a productive atmosphere. This means that group members are good at different things, but a new question emerges: should all team members be good interviewers as well? In some cases it was discussed whether certain interviews were done in a proper way. Consequently, the team had to ask itself what is the value of the data, if it is not gathered in an acceptable manner. On the other hand, it cannot be expected that people with varied skills would all make a good interviewer. After all, it is quite natural that people are eager to sell their own ideas to the user. However, a somewhat worse consequence may be the fact that the interviewers are sometimes not critical or objective about how the user responses and what he or she may even take back from the given opinions. On the other hand from the team work point of view, too much criticism on certain interview data can violate the team spirit and complicate later work. Should the team use data that they do not consider as valid in order to work smoothly together, i.e., is team spirit more important that the 100% valid data?

4.2 Interpretation

One benefit in user centered design is that designers' feelings or opinions do not lead the discussion, but the user data, which should help in decision process. However, it is not a black and white issue. It is also a matter of data interpretation, which may take many forms since no exact guidelines can be drawn from data. When it comes to human behavior, there are no countable, scientific causalities that could be objectively discovered and generalized to concern everybody. This caused some disagreements within the team; for example, what does some given piece of information really mean, and how details should be interpreted, etc.

After the interviews, the team members are usually loaded with a huge pile of unstructured data. Abundance of details and the interpretation of details, i.e. conclusion drawing, are a challenge. First interpretations are made in the field through observations - further interpretations are made in the storytelling part of the process. Some people may have difficulties with the credibility of the method, because they may come from disciplines, where the facts are presented according to, for example, positivist tradition. For them the unacceptable part is that there is no statistical evidence for interpretations.

After having gathered and analyzed the data the design can be started. Details and cases of the data are summarized on posters on the walls. The question still remains: how much of those data can be seen in the design? How can one be sure that the gathered data are really used in design? Sometimes a designer may just invent something, but s/he cannot really explain where the invention comes from. Does the brain really synthesize all the material in the course of the contextual design process, as it is claimed (Holtzblatt & Beyer 1998)?

4.3 Design for the Future

Imagining that a team is designing for the far future raises another problem; how can one expect that users are able to comment on solutions that are far from today's? This is a problem, because current models of some phenomenom are so far from what they will be in the future with new technologies supporting it.

In some cases the team was uncertain what the correct reference products would be for this product. Is it correct to refer to current phones, if the team questions whether this product is like a personal digital assistant (PDA) with a phone, or a conventional mobile phone. Furthermore, this leads to a question: what features should be provided at the cost of some other features in this procuct? Knowing now that the teenagers use their phones in a certain way today, raises a question whether we should support the same strategies in the new product or is the product perhaps a whole new concept of which the teenagers create a totally new culture?

4.4 Do the Designers Know Better Than the Users?

Some disagreements concerned the question of extent, i.e. how much the data, that is not always unambigous, should really drive the design? Opinions of the team members were divided in this question. Some team members were more willing to question users' comments than others. It is generally approved that the user data should drive the design but the question is more about the extent. Users might sometimes suggest ideas or features that designers cannot think a good purpose for. They might make suggestions just to say something. Also, when responding to new products with new features, the user may at first say something as his or her opinion, which will be taken back once the user has understood the whole idea of the product. Thus it may not always be wise to follow all the feedback the user gives in an orthodox manner, because the context of the interview may lead the user to say something that he or she would not really mean, if one knew the functionality of the product more thoroughly. Sometimes the users implicated this by saying something like "Now I get the idea why it was not possible to do this like that in the first place..." . On the other hand, this kind of thought can also be interpreted as forcing the user to think of something and perform in a desired manner.

4.5 Organizational Challenges - Who is Willing to do the 'Hard Work'

Since the user-centered methods require a lot of resources, different people in the organization may have difficulties in committing to data gathering and analysis that take a long time. One really has to believe in the benefits that can be obtained from the data gathering, in order to put a lot of effort and commitment on the work. How can people be made committed in something, if the results can be seen only after weeks of hard work? And even this being the case, one can ask whether this could have been achieved without any user data at all. Moreover, what would the result be like if the team had done the field research without any deeper data analysis? Would the insight obtained from the interviews been enough for the design?

In addition to the challenges presented above, user-centered design requires certain attitude from its practitioners. They must be humble, prepared to do unconventional things, and finally, some creative craziness is definitely a benefit. All this flavored with the huge amount of work can be a big challenge, when introducing these approaches into an organisation.

5 Possible Solutions

Based on the experiences obtained from this study, some solutions to challenges could be applied in other studies. For example, less experienced interviewers in the team could pair with an experienced, qualified interviewer on the field. Although this inevitably means that the team gets fewer users to the study, however, the data is deeper and richer, because there are four eyes and ears observing the same focus. On the other hand, letting only more experienced interviewers do the field research may give quality data, but reduce the sharing experience with other team members.

To support data interpretation, videotaping and recording might provide the opportunity for re-analysis, but this means extra work. Also carrying a video camera in a mobile test case may be impossible. Bringing the users to laboratories would allow more observers to see what is happening, but it also may reduce the important information that emerges from the real context interview.

Studying the user needs for the future product is always problematic to some extent, but in this case the users were let to imagine the future with the help of written scenarios. We intentionally left out the pictures from the stories to allow room for imagination. Another effort to reduce the problematic nature of this kind of study was to select innovative and advanced users to the interviews, although the sample would not represent the entire target segment. No design method itself can make a good design; which means that there is always room for designers' innovation and experience to make design better. A design team may want to bring new solutions and change to the user culture; thus it is their responsibility to build up the optimal design solution for the case. However, it is important to see the difference between current use and the new design in order to avoid too high steps when introducing the new product.

To reduce organizational resistance to cross-functional design work, there needs to be a certain amount of generalism in practitioners' attitudes. Of course some special process areas may be divided between field researchers and designers, but this may hinder the information sharing. A fundamental change may be needed in education, so that design schools and universities would train people to be both cross-functional team workers and end-user practitioners. Then the organizations would definitely be ready for user-centered approach.

6 Future

How to proceed from this? The first thing to do, would be to organize user studies and testing in other target cultures. The design team has so far concentrated on Finnish teenagers, but as to other cultures, the user data is missing. On the other hand, it could be argued that human behaviour and user needs are basically the same in other target cultures, which could be called advanced in technology to some extent. However, this has not been studied, which means that cross-cultural generalizations cannot be drawn.

Design of UI elements and user interaction have not been completed in this project. Some of the issues may already have been taken care of during the design process, because usability specialists naturally approach design issues from the usability point of view. However, no conscious effort has been made for this issue.

The design team had a 'lessons learned' discussion' after the design project, in which they analyzed the course of the project. One of the main ideas of that discussion was clear: multidisciplinary team work is suitable for design work, but the team could be even more multidisciplinary, so that also the areas oriented to harder technology would be participating in the process. Everybody in the team agreed that they know a lot more about the end-user now, than they did before.

References

Holtzblatt, K. & Beyer, H. 1998. *Contextual Design.* San Francisco, Morgan Kauffman Publishers.

Part Ten

Panels

Human-Computer Interaction - INTERACT'99 (Volume II)
S. Brewster, A. Cawsey & G. Cockton (Editors)
Published by The British Computer Society © IFIP TC.13, 1999

Story and the Design of Participatory Media

Ivor Benjamin (Panellist)
City University, London, ivorb@cix.co.uk
Kim Binsted (Panellist)
Sony Computer Science Lab, Tokyo, kimb@csl.sony.co.jp
Lydia Plowman (Moderator)
Scottish Council for Research in Education, Lydia.Plowman@scre.ac.uk
Sharon Springel (Panellist)
University of Cambridge, s.springel@ccsr.cam.ac.uk
John C Thomas (Panellist)
IBM, New York, jcthomas@us.ibm.com

Abstract: Stories and the act of telling stories are deeply embedded in our culture. We will consider how this affects the ways in which we engage with computer-based media and participation in stories. This panel will examine ways in which designers and HCI specialists can think about and develop participatory media models and consider the extent to which participation is a useful way of conceptualising the relationship between people and computers and the level of engagement to which designers may aspire.

Keywords: story, participatory and interactive media, narrative, authorship, design

1 Overview of Panel Topic

One of the oldest forms of human communication is telling stories. This can be a highly participatory event involving rich interplay between storyteller and audience - of one or many - who will inevitably offer their own numerous tangents and interruptions. But apart from day-to-day gossip and anecdotes most people in the West now experience story only as finished product, whether television, books, theatre or films. Notions of sequence, connectedness, linearity and predetermined content are implicit in a western European concept of a well-formed story and shape our expectations.

Active participation in the creation of meaning in a computer-based product implies displacement of the author because the narrative thread and the unity imposed by an author is not necessarily present. Stories in media such as film, television and books traditionally deny their construction. There may be an illusion of authorlessness, of the narrative unfolding by itself, even though the audience is being led by the author. Barthes describes this as texts being 'tyrannically centred on the author'.

The wide availability of 'authoring' tools and the Internet itself has meant that there is a shift to a model of co-construction of experiences formed out of the interplay between producers and consumers. In these circumstances the journey, let alone the outcome, is no longer fully determined prior to the event. Some conventions help shape and guide these experiences, without resorting to dictatorial control over them. The archetypes of the journey, the evolving story line and the processes of cause, effect and consequences are useful models because we all understand how these patterns work and the importance of both process and outcome.

Our goal is to provide a forum in which designers, practitioners and researchers can discuss theory and practice relating to story and participatory media. We have used the term 'participatory' in preference to 'interactive' for two reasons: to emphasise a richer level of engagement than 'interactive' usually implies and to acknowledge the centrality of the user's creativity.

2 Summary of Panellists' Positions

2.1 Ivor Benjamin

Whenever and wherever people pretend to be someone else, they rehearse the world as drama, just as children play. As adults, we have developed a long and noble tradition of "paying the players to play the play", an economy of scale that leads from theatre to film and television, and a lessening of involvement for audience in their drama. Computer games and virtual environments hand back some of that involvement and interaction to the participants, but the rules of engagement have changed. A theatre director for fifteen years, and a systems analyst for five, I am interested in the boundary between the live theatre as dramatic interaction and human interaction in virtual worlds as drama. What are fit subjects for this kind of interaction? What are the structures for a new drama, without beginning, middle or end? And what place is there for writer, director and designer in this new drama?
http://www.soi.city.ac.uk/homes/ivor/research.html

2.2 Kim Binsted

When authors create stories in non-interactive media, they use their understanding of normal human behaviour to predict and manipulate the audience's response at each point in the narrative. When creating for interactive media, we rarely have this luxury, unless we overconstrain the interaction. The audience can move along any number of paths towards the story's conclusion, so how can we design the narrative landscape so that all possible paths have desired shape(s), such as the traditional story-arc? One possibility, which we are currently exploring, is to use emotionally-relevant psychophysiological feedback to inform the interactive narrative system about the audience's current affective state. This, in combination with information about earlier events in the interaction, could allow the system to time crises so that they build to an exciting climax and satisfying resolution.
http://www.csl.sony.co.jp/person/kimb/

2.3 Lydia Plowman

Stories and storying are not simply aesthetic issues because narrative and cognition are so intertwined. The generation of narrative is an active process of meaning-making, a process through which we create a structure for interpreting and understanding connections and links between people, texts and events. We are skilled at imposing order in this way, but this is not necessarily an efficient use of cognitive resources when seeking story in interactive texts. Our research on interactive learning environments recognises the importance of structure but emphasises that narrative cannot be studied in isolation from the dynamic processes of interaction and communication.
http://meno.open.ac.uk/meno/

2.4 Sharon Springel

Previous forms of mass market entertainment have been largely locked into a linear, one-to-many, pre-scripted format. Initial forms of interactive content have often been guilty of copying this pattern through the re-packaging of conventional forms of media, the point and click navigational mechanism amounting to little more than electronic page turning. Research programmes now investigating the tempting possibilities suggested by the combination of computers, RAM, drama and the individual tend to focus on the user to system relationship, rather than the user to user relationship. Our approach is built upon drawing together technologies to enable explorations of shared virtual spaces, combining them with practical models for the design of creative participatory experiences which are collaboratively created through the co-operative interplay between the scenario designers and the end users themselves.
http://www.ccsr.cam.ac.uk/index.html

2.5 John C. Thomas

There are many ways to support well-structured information that has been captured in a computer. Yet, we know that in real communities of practice, much of the most important knowledge creation and sharing is done through semi-structured forms such as stories. We are engaged in a project to understand better the relationship among social, cognitive, organizational and technological issues in the creation and sharing of stories for business purposes. The second goal is to work with a user community in a business context to help create a storybase and an associated set of tools to support the creation and capture of stories, as well as the organization, search, and utilization. Ultimately, we believe the power of the computer may help unlock previously hidden patterns of solving problems in ill-defined domains through mining a large enough storybase.
http://www.truthtable.com/

'Artificial Morality': Representations of Trust in Interactive Systems

Elisabeth Davenport[1], Harold Thimbleby[2], Steve Marsh[3] and Mark Dibben[4]

[1]Napier University, Email: e.davenport@napier.ac.uk, Moderator
[2]Middlesex University, Email: h.thimbleby@mdx.ac.uk, Panellist
[3]National Research Council of Canada, Email: s.marsh@iit.nrc.ca, Panellist
[4]University of Aberdeen, Email: m.dibben@abdn.ac.uk, Panellist

Abstract: Trust in the 'wired world' is a hot topic. A recent CHI 99 panel addressed the issue in terms of 'social capital', or 'the extent to which we trust and work for a common good'. In this panel, the focus is representation and design: what are the components of trust, and how may they be engineered into congenial interactive systems? These must support a number of relationships: humans trusting humans in contexts where they do not see each other; humans trusting systems; humans trusting agents who operate within systems; and agents trusting other agents. The view from e-commerce has emphasised contractual trust, and focused on technological issues like security and authentication. Representations of trust, trustingness and trustworthiness which take a more socially-oriented approach, can enrich the design of systems for computer mediated transactions in a number of contexts.

Keywords: Non-contractual trust, representation, engineering, situations, agents, interactive systems

1 Overview of Panel Topic

How may the components of trust be represented and engineered into trustworthy computer-based interactions? Working systems designed by by members of the panel have taken studies of trust in the non-electronic world as a starting point, specifically studies of trust in 'temporary organisations'; relevant work is reported in the edited research monograph by Kramer and Tyler (1996). Marsh (1996), drawing on such work, has analysed the components of trust and developed formalisms on which agents may base their interactions with humans and other other agents; Dibbin, has operationalised Marsh's work in the context of partnerships in investor banking (1997). Marsh and Dibbin state that in cases of 'temporary organisation', situational trust (Lewicki and Bunker, 1996) must be addressed. Members of the panel will be asked to anatomise the concept of trust, and indicate how, in their experience, it may be captured and represented in human computer interactions. The evaluation of trust in interactive systems will also be discussed.

2 Panel Format

The moderator will explain why the panel has been convened, and each panelist will be asked to speak for up to ten minutes on their experience of anatomising and representing the components of trust, and to comment on the achievements and limitations of the systems which they have engineered. In the second part of the session, the audience will be invited to relate experiences and make observations, and the moderator will conclude with a session position statement.

3 Panellist Statements

Harold Thimbleby is Professor of Computing Research, Middlesex University. He is a member of IFIP 9.2.2. (Computers and Ethics), and his concerns with trust in user interfaces have resulted in papers on cryptography, artificial life, and on Trojan and computer viruses -- for example, "Concepts of cooperation in artificial life', written with. Pullinger and Witten and 'A framework for modelling Trojans and Computer Virus Infection', written with Anderson and Cairns.

Steve Marsh thinks interacting with each other is hard enough, and asks 'What of agents?' Jaron Lanier, amongst others, thinks agents are going to result in a general 'dumbing down' of users (Lanier, 1997) as we make ourselves behave in such a way that we feel that the agents are in some way intelligent. If this state of affairs is to be prevented, there has to be a way of ensuring that the users feel empowerment rather than submissiveness and meek acceptance of whatever the agent decides to throw at us, be it information or attitude. Maes (1996) identified this problem as one of control - we have to be able to trust the agent to do for us what we want, and to feel that at any time we can regain control of it actions. How can we achieve this? One way is to embed social knowledge in the interface agent so as to enable it to facilitate trust between the user and itself. With a 'knowledge' of trust, ethics, morals and so on, it is possible to imagine the agent reasoning about how to behave in order to present the user with a coherent but comfortable experience in their interactions. (Marsh, 1995) Though agents are here to, it is important that we not forget that the ultimate users of these systems are humans, with all that implies. Presenting humans with more and more social, trustworthy interfaces, can be no bad thing in this respect.

Mark Dibben is a research associate with a leading Scottish management consultancy applying models of trust and cooperation with a number of major Scottish companies. His book 'Exploring Interpersonal Trust in the Entrepreneurial Venture' which develops the AI work of Steve Marsh is due out in the Autumn. He has identified three problematics in 'atomising' trust for AI conceptualisation: 1) conceptualising and operationalising the nature and extent of an interaction or situation in which trust operates; 2) conceiving of a means by which to accurately represent the process of trust development in and between agents in and across situations; 3) attempting the measurement of a quality in development given an 'atomistic' or elemental approach to the subject that (probably) relies on quantity as its primary measuring mechanism.

References

Dibbin, M. R., Harrison, R.T. and Mason, C. The role of trust in the informal investor's investment decision: an exploratory analysis. *Entrepreneurship Theory and Practice*. Special Issue on Informal Venture Capital, 1997.

Friedman, B. and Thomas, J.C. Trust me, I'm accountable: trust and accountability online. Extended panel abstract. *CHI 99 Extended Abstracts*, New York: ACM, 1999, 79 - 80.

Kramer, R.K. and T.R. Tyler (eds.) *Trust in organizations*. London: Sage, 1996

Lanier, J., Agents of alienation, http://www.well.com /user/jaron/agentalien.html, 1997

Lewicki, R.J. and Bunker, B.B. Developing and maintaining trust in working relationships. In R.K. Kramer and T.R. Tyler (eds.) *Trust in organizations*. London: Sage, 1996, 114 - 139.

Maes, P. Agents that reduce work and information overload, *Communications of the ACM*, Vol. 37, No. 7, July 1994, pp31 - 40.

Marsh, S. Trust in distributed artificial intelligence. In Castelfranchi and Werner, *Artificial Social Systems*, Springer LNAI, 330, 1996, 95 - 112.

Thimbleby, H., Witten,I. H. and Pullinger D.J. "Concepts of cooperation in artificial life', *IEEE Transactions in Systems, Man & Cybernetics*, 25 (7), pp. 1166 - 1171, 1995

Thimbleby, H., Anderson, S.O. and Cairns, P. A framework for modelling Trojans and Computer Virus Infection, *Computer Journal*, 41 (7), pp444 - 458, 1999.

Human-Computer Interaction - INTERACT'99 (Volume II)
S. Brewster, A. Cawsey & G. Cockton (Editors)
Published by The British Computer Society © IFIP TC.13, 1999

Gender and Human-Computer Interaction

D. Ramanee Peiris[1], Alison Crerar[2], Peter Gregor[1], Britta Schinzel[3] and indigo V[1]

[1]Department of Applied Computing,
University of Dundee, Dundee, DD1 4HN, UK
Email: {rpeiris, pgregor, indigo}@computing.dundee.ac.uk

[2]School of Computing, Napier University, Craiglockhart Campus,
219 Colinton Road, Edinburgh, EH14 1DJ, UK
Email: a.crerar@dcs.napier.ac.uk

[3]Institut für Informatik und Gesellschaft, Friedrichstr. 50,
D-79098 Freiburg, Germany
Email: schinzel@modell.iig.uni-freiburg.de

Abstract: HCI and gender cannot be separated - men and women **are** different, in the way they process information, the way they work, the way they design and the way they communicate with others. This panel will explore several of the issues in this area - from the need to encourage more women into Computing and User-Centred Design, to new interfaces for software, web pages and our "desktop".

Keywords: Interface design, gender, women into computing, user-centred design

1 Panel Overview

Women and men are different - physiologically and psychologically - in the way we approach tasks, in the mental models we create and use, and in the way we process information. Research presented at Human-Computer Interaction (HCI) conferences and in the HCI literature has considered user differences due to age, culture and a range of special needs, but few have considered gender.

It can be argued that gender differences when using technology set us poles apart, and therefore women and men need different user interfaces. Or, it can be argued that there is a continuum with extreme masculinity and extreme femininity at each end. In either case, it has been assumed that one interface is suitable for all.

Similarly, men and women may design radically different interfaces from each other - whether due to their own gender differences or due to the different way in which they work with the users involved.

From the panelists statements below, it can be seen that gender plays an important part in HCI. This includes user-centred design, where female characteristics may allow the designer to elicit what the user actually wants. Whereas, in the actual design process - men and women may design differently; male and female users may need different interfaces.

2 Panel Format

The chair (Ramanee Peiris) will introduce the panel session, and ask each of the panellists to present their position in under 10 minutes. Each panellist may be asked one or two questions, and after all the panellists have presented, the chair will lead a discussion on the main issues raised.

3 Position Statements

3.1 Alison Crerar

The number of women taking up computing course is falling. Female students seem to seek out courses and professions which allow them to "work with people". Clearly, user-centred design is all about people.

There is a widespread public misconception about what careers in IT involve. The range of job opportunities is not appreciated and the fundamental point that Computing is about helping people to communicate has been missed.

There is a huge challenge to be faced in rectifying this situation if women are to be encouraged to play their full part in the emerging information society.

3.2 Peter Gregor

Computer interface design has historically been a man's world - why else would terms such as "kill" and "abort" have been used to instruct a computer to stop doing something.

The move to graphical user interfaces (GUI) brought us variations of so-called intuitive WIMP (Windows, Icons, Menus and Pointers) interfaces. If the GUI had been designed for non-command orientated users, including women, something else might have been the result. In particular, designers could have considered the way in which different people organise their work. For example, our needs might be different at different times of the day.

3.3 Britta Schinzel

In general, women play fewer computer games than men; women are less likely to "mess about" with computers than men; and women are more afraid of "breaking" computers than men.

However, computer experience is gained by "playing", that is, trial and error, rather than reading books. Much modern software is highly complex, and trial and error seems the best approach to learning. Software interfaces need to be developed to help users explore packages without fear of irreversibly changing something.

3.4 indigo V

The World Wide Web provides plentiful examples of interface design. Interfaces which have been created by amateurs and professionals for a variety of purposes. The nature of the web is such that page design is not constrained by the same screen widgets as conventional software development.

A study of personal web sites may allow us to classify what makes a "male" or a "female" design, and thus a "male" or a "female" user interface. It is hoped that this will lead to guidelines for web developers, who may currently not be considering the gender differences of their users when designing.

4 Conclusion

There are many issues in the area of gender and the computer interface; from who the designers are to who their users are. A fresh look at interface design from a female perspective may lead to better interfaces for us all, or interfaces which can better adapt to us as individuals.

The contributors to this panel wish to ensure that the user-centred designers of the future have a greater understanding of gender issues.

Human-Computer Interaction - INTERACT'99 (Volume II)
S. Brewster, A. Cawsey & G. Cockton (Editors)
Published by The British Computer Society © IFIP TC.13, 1999

Interfaces with an Attitude

Govert de Vries and Paula Lynch

NCR Knowledge Lab
206 Marylebone Road
London
United Kingdom
Email: govert.devries@unitedkingdom.ncr.com

Abstract: In this panel, a number of professionals working in academia and industry will discuss the opportunities that 'user interfaces with an attitude' offer to enhance the quality of interaction with products and services. Perspectives are mostly pragmatic. The panelists discuss issues that they are facing in developing 'user interfaces with an attitude' and will present their thoughts and ideas about how these issues might be addressed and what the future will bring us.

Keywords: personality, user interfaces, attitude, interaction

1 Introduction

Most of today's user interfaces are rigid in the sense that they do not reflect or respond to their users' preferences, goals, moods, wishes, tastes, etc. Many studies have shown that the quality of user interfaces can play a big influence on: product usage, the overall perception of the service that the product delivers and ultimately on the brand that provides the service (Tractinsky, 1997). Also, some companies have shown that by investing in the quality of their products' user interfaces, they can develop a competitive edge (e.g. Palm Pilot, Apple computer).

Reeves and Nass (1998) have found that people respond socially and naturally to media (and thus also to computers) even though they believe it is not reasonable to do so, and even though they don't think that these responses characterise themselves. People automatically use social rules from real life to guide interactions with computers.

2 Panel Format

The panel is organised in three rounds. It will begin with a brief overview by the moderator, followed by a 10 minute statement by each panelists in which their view on 'products with attitude' will be outlined. Each panelist will also discuss a particularly good and a particularly bad example of a product or service that can be or has been personalised. The third round will be driven by audience questions and panelists discussion. In this round, the following issues will be addressed:

- How do we design products with attitude?
- What sort of personalities and interaction style can we incorporate in products or services without making the interaction substantially elaborate, lengthy and thus less efficient?
- How do we ensure that people interact with an interface that expresses the personality that is appropriate for them?
- What sort of products and services are most suitable to be 'enhanced' with an attitude?
- A product, for example and ATM, may have an attitude, express opinions, be angry with you, make fun of you, be patient, understanding, etc. How can it be expressive but also maintain trustworthy?

3 Position Statements

Anthony Creed, Sony USA
Customers are becoming less interested in the technologies underlying their products and more interested in the services that those products provide (e.g. "music", "photos", "chopped onions"). At the same time, there is increasing interest in the secondary value of products, e.g. product as lifestyle statement; product as ornament. Thus the interface has a pivotal role in customer perception: it defines the nature of a customer's access to the services a product provides, and influences or even dictates a product's design. My position is that a product's design attracts a potential customer, but it's the interface that 'clinches the deal'. If an interface has no 'personality' or no 'attitude', this sale is less likely to be made.

Kay Hofmeester, Dutch Design Institute
People attach emotions to every product or object. For example, products are seen as trustworthy, happy, professional, sturdy, or sensual. Designers try to enhance these emotions attached to products by a process that is hard to communicate or make explicit. The designer and the design commissioner do not have a common language or process to determine which emotions to enhance in the design, or how to do this. If this process is made more explicit, products can be designed more purposefully based on emotions, and thus become better products for their users.

Marco Susani, Domus Academy, Italy
Through the presentation of the results of the Presence project by Domus Academy Research Center, the theme of "Emotional Communication" will be introduced. Using existing state of the art (or conventional) technologies together with new interfaces, the project aims to investigate new communication languages that mix real-time communication with collaborative "family" environments. The project deals particularly with handheld mobile technologies combined with agent systems and smart databases. From the interface point of view - major part of our contribution - we experimented the use of "cosmographies", on-screen-graphic structures to organise and represent the persons with which we communicate. These structures are used as a space for navigation, and also as a representation of the persons. We could take these interfaces as "Interfaces with attitude" in the sense that they have some self-configuring features, and also because they represent the communication "attitude" of people.

Michael Waller, NCR Knowledge Lab
The success of creating excellent information services that are tailored to individuals in a mass information market place all hinges on the individual's ability to access the information he or she requires and enjoy the process of the interaction. In order to gain a better, more tailored service to our individual needs, we need objects to begin to learn what we want from them, personality in object could be seen as a step towards objects taking particular attitudes towards us to gain our best response and attention. Our experiences as children are full of characterisation of the things both fictional and real. This I believe helps us to define the world around us. My interest is in how could this be applied to every day objects.

Peter Verbeek, Philips Design
When people interact with exciting new products, they develop a relationship with them: they learn to appreciate the positive aspects and learn to live with the negative aspects. As with other types of relationships, the element of excitement wears off over time. However useful, certain values or functions of products may become implicit. There is an opportunity in (re)-designing the interaction with familiar products to specifically address the excitement factor without jeopardising the usability of it's implicit functionality. The added value of the product would then be in it's 'character'.

References

Picard, R. W. (1997). *Affective Computing*, M.I.T., Camebridge, MA

Reeves, B. and Nass, C. (1996) *The Media Equation: How people Treat Computers, Televisions, and New Media Like Real People and Places*. Stanford, CA: CLSI

Tractinsky, N. (1997) Aesthetics and Apparent Usability: Empirically Assessing Cultural and Methodological Issues. *CHI 1997*: 115-1220

S. Brewster, A. Cawsey & G. Cockton (Editors)
Published by The British Computer Society © IFIP TC.13, 1999

From Analysis to Design: Do Different Analytical Methods Make a Difference?

Catherine G. Wolf*(organizer), Christine Halverson, Victor Kaptelinin, Andrew Shepherd (panellists) and John Karat (discussant)

*IBM T. J. Watson Research Center
Hawthorne, NY 10532 USA
Email: cwolf@us.ibm.com

Abstract: This panel asks the question: Do different analytical methods for capturing and representing information about current and potential work practices impact the resulting system design? Panellists representing the perspectives of Distributed Cognition, Activity Theory, and Task Analysis will apply their approach to some work practice data and then propose a design to address some aspect of the data. Each panellist will rationalize the design in terms of the analytical approach.

Keywords: design rationale, analytical methods, requirements capture

1 Panelists

Christine Halverson, IBM T. J. Watson Research Center, Hawthorne, NY, USA
Victor Kaptelinin, Department of Informatics, Umeå University, Umeå, SWEDEN
Andrew Shepherd, Department of Human Sciences, Loughborough University, Loughborough, UK
John Karat, IBM T. J. Watson Research Center, Hawthorne, NY, USA (discussant)

2 Overview of Panel

At Interact, CHI, CSCW and other conferences there are papers and tutorials extolling the virtues of a particular analytical method for capturing and/or representing information useful for system design. The process of going from analysis to design remains something of a black art. This panel asks the question: Do different analytical methods for capturing and representing information about current and potential work practices impact the resulting system design?

This panel asks several experts in different analytical approaches to apply their approach to some work practice data and then propose a design to address a problem in the data. Each panel participant will rationalize the design in terms of the analytical approach. The panelists will do this exercise in advance of the panel and share results.

3 Statements

3.1 Distributed Cognition (Christine Halverson)

Distributed cognition (DCog) is particularly useful for understanding complex socio-technical systems. This theory, developed by Hutchins and colleagues at UCSD in the 1980s and 90s, has roots in cognitive science and anthropology. A key premise is that cognition and its residua surround us. Taking advantage of the observable nature of cognitive phenomena on a system scale, DCog focuses on the distributed nature of these phenomena across individuals, artifacts and internal and external representations, and on the interactions between the distributed structures. DCog's theoretical language describes the phenomena in terms of 'representational states' and 'media', where the role of artifacts, individuals, and social phenomena are treated on an equal footing exposing details about the interaction between them.

An analysis begins by understanding the function of the system and then examines different identifying cognitive properties at each level. These properties are explained by reference to processes that transform representational states inside the system. Using different units of analysis, based on functional and temporal constraints, provides flexibility. One result of the analysis is the description of a range of cognitive systems, whereby some subsume others.

DCog provides a methodology for examining the interactions between people and artifacts that is not possible with more traditional cognitive task analyses. It highlights the complex interdependencies between people and artifacts in their collaborative activities, which in turn can lead to a better understanding of why seemingly trivial breakdowns can have significant and sometimes drastic consequences. This information is critical for the design of new technology placed in a complex socio-technical system.

3.2 Activity Theory (Victor Kaptelinin)

Activity theory is a broad conceptual framework for describing the structure, development, and context of human activity, with a special emphasis on social phenomena and mutual transformations of internal and external processes. This approach has its origins in Russian psychology of the '20s and is currently being applied to a variety of problems.

According to activity theory, computers are artifacts that mediate purposeful human interaction with the world. Therefore, understanding of how to design, evaluate, implement, or customize a technology can be achieved through understanding the human activities supported by the technology and how the technology is integrated into these activities.

To make the application of activity theory more practical, Kaptelinin and Nardi (1997) developed an analytical tool based on this approach, the Activity Checklist. It is intended to elucidate the most important contextual factors of human-computer interaction.

The Checklist lays out a kind of "contextual design space" by representing the key areas of context specified by activity theory. The structure of the Checklist reflects the basic principles of activity theory. The principle of tool mediation has been applied throughout the Checklist and systematically combined with the other principles. It results in four sections corresponding to four main perspectives on the use of the "target technology" to be evaluated or designed: (a) means and ends, (b) social and physical aspects of the environment, (c) learning, cognition and articulation, and (c) development. The Activity Checklist appears to be most useful at early phases of system design and for evaluating existing systems.

3.3 Task Analysis (Andrew Shepherd)

Task analysis is the act of discovering how people carry out their work in terms of information and tools available to them, taking account of the context in which they are operating, and with a view to generating design hypotheses or hypotheses to account for performance inadequacies. This broad view has focused upon a number of narrower perspectives, including modelling goal hierarchies, representing information flows and representing cognition.

Hierarchical Task Analysis (HTA) is a method that considers tasks in terms of a hierarchy of goals and sub-goals, together with plans that govern the conditions when sub-goals are carried out. In some quarters this is represented as a model of behavior, but this is difficult to sustain and so cognitive methods have been sought. HTA is best considered as a general framework for task analysis, enabling the analyst to work systematically through various aspects of the task until suitable task data have been recorded. In this way the analyst's attention is directed towards different aspects of the task in terms of criticality. As different issues are encountered, the analyst adopts and adapts different methods, from investigating physical attributes to eliciting and representing cognition and social interaction. A project is guided by the nature of the task, the requirements of a client, and the costs of both methods of enquiry and hypotheses proffered. The full effectiveness of the task analysis is dependent upon the skills and expertise that the analyst brings to the process.

Part Eleven

Laboratory Overviews

Human-Computer Interaction - INTERACT'99 (Volume II)
S. Brewster, A. Cawsey & G. Cockton (Editors)
Published by The British Computer Society © IFIP TC.13, 1999

E.S.R.C. Cognitive Engineering Programme

Anne H. Anderson*, Rose Luckin, Andrew Monk, Jean McKendree and Tom Ormerod

University of Glasgow, University of Sussex, University of York, University of Edinburgh & University of Lancaster

*Director E.S.R.C. Cognitive Engineering Programme
Department of Psychology, University of Glasgow, Glasgow G12 8QB
Email: anne@mcg.gla.ac.uk

Abstract: Developing effective user-friendly IT systems is the goal of HCI. A UK research programme in Cognitive Engineering aims to help in the design of such future systems by bringing people as individuals and groups into the heart of research on design problems. By studying how people interact with each other and with existing IT systems, in the lab and in the work place, the research teams aim to produce design guidelines for improved future systems. The programme brings together over forty researchers from several different academic disciplines, working closely with end users and liasing with research users such as commercial developers.

Keywords: Design, user-centred, research on user

1 Introduction

Information and communication technologies are increasingly affecting many aspects of work, education and domestic life. These technological developments have not always fulfilled their potential because our understanding of how such technologies should be designed to maximise their benefits to users has been inadequate. To address these problems, in 1995 the UK Economic and Social Research Council funded a £2.4 million research programme in Cognitive Engineering. The main objective of the Cognitive Engineering Programme (CEP) is to bring people, as individuals and as groups, into the heart of research on design problems.

Cognitive engineering models the design problems associated with interactive cognitive systems involving people, computers and organisations. Interactions occur among groups of people, and between people and computers, and the larger cognitive system includes the software systems implemented on people's computers. Understanding these complex interactions and how they might be improved is the scientific and applied goal of the programme. The CEP thus focuses on key design and HCI problems in information storage and retrieval, communication, and education and training.

CEP research addresses a wide range of domains of application including telemedicine, computer assisted learning and computer supported co-operative work. The programme is fortunate in tackling a large number of questions which are both scientifically challenging and of obvious importance to research users, from the general public to more specialised audiences in industry and government. A strength of the CEP is the way in which these diverse communities of 'research users' are involved in the research process by the academic researchers.

Despite the breadth of domains of application, common themes run through the research programme: understanding more about users, their behaviour, context and real needs for IT support.

The CEP is a distributed community of researchers each working on their own project in their own university, but meeting for programme events such as workshops about every six months. The fifteen funded projects across the UK draw on researchers from a spectrum of disciplinary backgrounds:

psychologists, cognitive scientists, educationalists, sociologists, computer scientists. The projects use a wide variety of scientific methods: computational modelling, software prototyping, laboratory studies, and detailed observations of users in the workplace.

2 Examples of CEP Projects

Project 4: Laurillard, Plowman, Stratfold & Taylor, explore the design of educational multimedia and how children learn from such resources. From studies in schools, they found that narrative structure of materials is very important and that children often lack the multimedia literacy skills to benefit from much existing multimedia which is often poorly designed. Following from these studies, they produced and tested, in real school curriculum settings, versions of an educational CD-ROM and verified that learners' behaviour is affected by narrative structure. A theory of narrative guidance and construction has been developed to inform design and classroom use of educational multimedia.

Project 6: Mayes & Lee, have explored new forms of educational IT, investigating if on-line dialogues between tutor and learner, or between learners, can be captured and made available to other learners, and if such 'vicarious learning' is valuable. They captured and indexed dialogues in two university courses and are exploring how this might be extended to school work. They have shown that learning benefits accrue to those with access to vicarious learning. They are working with the BT Tomorrow's Customers Project and have influenced BT's thinking on new forms of educational IT.

Project 7: Monk, has been studying multimedia communications technology in supporting access to remote expertise. Three field studies of telemedicine were observed where local practitioners were guided by a remote expert through a medical procedure. Patients valued this expert link, and identified several important design features for the technology. Lab studies derived from these observations, have shown differences in what is recalled from different video configurations. Methods for guiding designers to identify key aspects of communications technologies for supporting remote collaborations were developed.

Project 8: Ormerod, Ball & Mariani, has been observing studying IT in the workplace. They investigated how designers in major companies re-use previous materials in innovative ways. Studies of design re-use are being used to develop an IT indexing system to support such processes. They have found ways to combine techniques from ethnography and cognitive psychology, to capture their observations of designers' behaviour in the design of the computer support system. This system (DESPERADO) aims to make these processes more efficient. They are testing and refining the prototype.

3 Publications and Results

Since 1995 CEP researchers have been active in disseminating their findings both to research users and to other researchers. The programme has produced over 250 publications, with over 100 scientific journal articles, over 90 refereed conference proceedings and over 30 book chapters.

A variety of events have also been held specifically for research users in education, public services and industry. These range from large-scale events to smaller more specialised workshops. Other forms of output include methodologies, and software prototypes from authoring and information retrieval systems to educational CD-ROMs.

4 Future Plans

The programme to date has significantly advanced our understanding of how users interact with IT and how interactive systems should be designed to maximise their effectiveness. We soon hope to launch a substantial follow-on programme in this area, under the UK government LINK scheme which fosters collaborations between academic researchers and UK companies. Substantial funding for this has been provisionally agreed by the UK Economic and Social Research Council (£2 million) and the UK Engineering and Physical Sciences Research Council (£2 million) and negotiations are in progress with the UK Department of Trade and Industry for funding (£3 million) to support companies' participation.

Further information on the CEP and its funded projects is available at:

http://www.cogeng.gla.ac.uk/.

Human-Computer Interaction - INTERACT'99 (Volume II)
S. Brewster, A. Cawsey & G. Cockton (Editors)
Published by The British Computer Society © IFIP TC.13, 1999

Designing the Human Experience at Nortel Networks

Mike Atyeo, Judith Ramsay and Judith Rattle

Design Interpretive
Nortel Networks
Ottawa, Canada and
Harlow, UK
Email: {atyeo, jramsay, jrattle}@nortelnetworks.com

Abstract: At Design Interpretive within Nortel Networks, we develop predictive product concepts and prototypes that reflect the needs and values of customers in exploiting emerging communications technology. The group's role is to drive technological research and development from an understanding of human behaviour. We aim to maintain Nortel Networks' leading market position as a supplier of communications infrastructure and services.

Keywords: Nortel Networks, Design Interpretive, telecommunications, Human factors, usability, rapid prototyping, interaction design, product design, value qualification, network management, healthcare

1 Role in Nortel Networks

Employing more than 75,000 people world-wide, Nortel Networks is a leading global supplier of telephony and IP-based data, wireline, and wireless networking solutions. In Design Interpretive, we help Nortel Networks to understand and design the human experience of communications, and to drive research and development of technology, maintaining Nortel Networks' market position.

We do this by producing predictive product concepts and prototypes that reflect customer needs and values and, at the same time, exploit emerging technological capabilities. We are as concerned with the *affective* qualities of human experience such as emotional engagement, as with traditional human factors concerns with productivity, etc (Campbell 1996). During the design process, we assess the user values and needs, and qualify our concepts against them (see, e.g. Tyson 1995).

We work as partners with Nortel Networks' lines of business and with industry affiliates, in which both partners invest effort and funding, focusing on the following areas:

- Building and deploying the network
- Managing the network
- Exploiting the network for business success
- Exploiting the network for Personal use

2 People, Teams, Facilities

There are 85 Design Interpretive people working in Ottawa, Canada, and 15 in Harlow, UK. We work in teams of about 3-6 people, with each multi-disciplinary team led by a Design Manager. Each team will include User Needs researchers, Interaction Designers, Industrial Designers and Mechanical Designers as appropriate, plus specific technical skills provided by our partners.

Our designers and researchers have varied backgrounds, including animation, architectural acoustics, linguistics, museum exhibit design, psychometrics, evolutionary biology, marketing, statistics, and fine arts. Our in-house facilities include a demonstration centre for customer visits and web-based presentations; a model shop for short production runs; a focus group room and fully equipped usability laboratories.

3 Our Design Approach

3.1 Generating Predictive Concepts

For each design project, we choose a focus which is rich in human needs and behaviour - for example remote medical consultation, or the planning and installation of a new enterprise network. We articulate key human issues, using primary and secondary research, then iterate through a series of design concepts, validating our hypotheses at each stage with various stakeholder groups.

We don't expect users to accurately predict their behaviour in a novel future situation. We try to build a small piece of the future and observe their reactions to it. Our prototypes are often *situational sketches* rather than product prototypes. For this reason, we find scenarios, video vignettes, role-playing and 'Improv', to be suitable and cost-effective techniques for exploring complex, situated human issues.

3.2 Value Qualification

We carry out much qualitative and quantitative research with customers and users, to de-risk investment decisions through immediate, unbiased customer feedback. Most of our research is carried out in the field, targeted at representatives of important Nortel Networks markets. For example, recent research has taken us to Asia, and Latin America. We have also started to use remote web-based research techniques with Beta-site customers.

4 Example Projects

Recent projects have included speech and multi-modal user interfaces, wearable devices, Call Centre evolution, remote collaboration, visualisation of complex networks, and eCommerce applications.

4.1 Behavioural Design of Network Management GUIs.

We apply our knowledge of cognitive issues of perception, monitoring, attention, and task structure to the design of Network Management Graphical User Interfaces (GUIs). We have developed a consistent graphic vocabulary, with redundant perceptual coding, to the representation of elements and links, and of alarm states (Talbott 1997). This graphic vocabulary helps build consistency across Nortel Networks products, has influenced international standards and has been adopted in third-party commercial products and toolkits.

4.2 Delivering Healthcare

In a recent project, we worked with the Ottawa Heart Institute to investigate remote diagnostic consultations, and ways in which future technology might be better able to support the human needs of this situation.

We investigated issues of trust, power, focus of attention, and presence, through interviews and observation, and using role-playing and videos. We mocked up a workstation and designed a gesture-based graphical user interface to support the social and cognitive behaviour of face-to-face interaction and enhance the interpersonal relationship between doctor and patient. The main value for Nortel Networks accrued from a greater understanding of the human needs that, in turn, gave requirements of future technology. Our model helped us define quality of service and billing architectures, for example.

4.3 GSM World Congress '99, Cannes

We worked with Nortel Networks' Wireless line of business to show how current and future wireless technologies such as GPRS (General Packet Radio Service) and UMTS (Universal Mobile Telecommunications System) can be exploited to achieve user goals. We used the results of user research to develop scenarios and demonstrations showing three subject areas: information, entertainment and corporate, including wireless Internet access. These web-based demonstrations were used as live working prototypes to give our customers an understanding of the capabilities of future wireless networks.

References

Campbell, A. (1996) A Fitting Approach to Interactive Service Design: The Importance of Emotional Needs *Design Management Journal*, Vol. 7, No. 4, Fall 1996

Talbott, D. (1997) "Coming to Our Senses: Multi-modal User Interfaces" *Design Management Journal*, Vol. 8, No. 3, Summer 1997

Tyson, J. (1995) "User-Centered Innovation." *Telesis* (100), 151-163.

Human-Computer Interaction - INTERACT'99 (Volume II)
S. Brewster, A. Cawsey & G. Cockton (Editors)
Published by The British Computer Society © IFIP TC.13, 1999

Applied Computing at the University of Dundee

Peter Gregor and Alan F. Newell

Department of Applied Computing
University of Dundee, Dundee, Scotland DD1 4HN
Email: pgregor@computing.dundee.ac.uk

Abstract: Dundee's Department of Applied Computing contains one of the largest and most influential academic groups in the world researching into communication systems for disabled people. It also has strong international and national reputations in other aspects of human computer interaction research and was awarded a top grade 5a in the 1996 RAE. It offers undergraduate and postgraduate Degrees in Applied Computing, in unique programmes where the learning of HCI and usability engineering techniques is integral throughout.

Keywords: disability, communication aids, HCI, usability, AAC, multimodal, telecoms, teaching, learning.

1 Core Research Skills

The Department, which has fifteen academic staff, has an engineering bias and brings together a unique blend of disciplines including computer scientists and engineers, psychologists, a therapist, a special education teacher, and staff who have benefited from interdisciplinary careers. Recently the Department has been strengthened by academic staff appointments in Digital Signal Processing with a particular interest in hearing and vision research, Linguistics and AI, the latter with a particular interest in Argumentation. The core research skills it can bring to bear on projects are:

- HCI and Usability Engineering
- AI techniques, Computational Linguistics and Conversation Modelling
- Special Education, Rehabilitation and Therapy
- Telecommunications for disabled people
- Software Engineering
- Signal Processing and Electronics
- Medical related issues
- Graph theory & combinatorial complexity

2 Research Foci

The Department is committed to the principles of usability engineering with a focus on developing academic and practical insights, and producing software that can be commercialised. Research is funded from a wide portfolio of funding agencies: Applied Computing has licensed many software products to commercial companies in the USA and Europe, and collaborates with commercial, academic and service organisations world-wide. The major foci of its research are:

- Human centred applications including elderly and disabled
- Telecommunications & remote learning
- Computer based interviewing & knowledge elicitation
- Health Informatics
- Space Systems

HCI and usability engineering is a major part of the first four of these foci. Detailed research in these areas is as follows:

2.1 Multimodal and Ordinary and Extra-Ordinary HCI

The group developed and concept within the HCI community that extra-ordinary (disabled) people operating in ordinary environments, pose similar problems to able-bodied (ordinary) people operating in extra-ordinary (high work load, environmentally unfriendly) situations. They have shown how simultaneous multimodal input, combined with user monitoring and plan recognition, can enhance the reliability of human-system interaction for pilots, air traffic controllers and people with disabilities. A recent project in collaboration with Daewoo is using systems which have been developed initially for disabled people, to explore novel means of controlling non-critical functions in automobiles.

2.2 Telecoms and Remote Learning

This group is investigating how data communication networks can improve the quality of life for disabled and elderly people. They have developed special services for interpersonal communication and demonstrated the advantages of novel graphical forms of communication as an enhancement to live video. This activity has been supported by research in multimedia services and HCI, and is linked with more recent research into the use of video and other support services for disabled and non-disabled students. Most of the research is collaborative, usually with European partners.

2.3 Interactive Communication Systems for Disabled People

This group is an international leader in the development of communication systems for disabled non-speaking people to help them to interact more effectively with others. Research projects have investigated several aspects of conversational modelling to aid in this task including word frequency, openings and closings, giving feedback, topic selections and movement, storytelling, and expressing emotions. Commercial products include: Predictability, a word prediction system; TALK, a system aiding social conversation; ScripTalker, a communication system based on scripts, and Talk:About, a storytelling aid. Related research projects include: Blissword, a predictive retrieval system for Blissymbolics; SeeWord, a word processing aid for dyslexics; HAMLET, a system for the investigation of emotion in synthetic speech; and Unicorn, a communication system making use of the internet.

2.4 Research into Technological Support for Ageing

Demography shows that there will be an increasing numbers of elderly people, some of whom will be disabled, but all of whom will have different performance characteristics than the traditional "user" of computer systems. These important changes are reflected in the Foresight exercise including a thematic panel considering how the ageing of the population should effect technological priorities. Within the Department, more emphasis is being placed on the HCI and other needs of elderly people. For example, the communication problems of people with Aphasia and the use of predictive and signal processing techniques are being investigated to assist with the maintenance and support of elderly people within the community.

2.5 Computer Based Interviewing and Knowledge Elicitation

Models of the structures of human interviews have been used to develop general purpose software to conduct computer based and computer facilitated interviews. A commercial product based on this work (ChatterBox), has been evaluated in use within schools. Further research is focused on more flexible models of computer interviewing and on the potential of computer based interviewing techniques to assist in a variety of settings from engagement with psychosis sufferers to employment pre-interviewing and software engineering requirements gathering. This research is leading to new insights concerning human computer interaction.

3 Applied Computing Degrees

To ensure close links between teaching and research, and to produce marketable graduates, in 1996 the Department ceased offering degrees in Computer Science and focussed on offering undergraduate and MSc (Conversion) Degrees in Applied Computing. The Department believed that this change responded to the needs of industry in the future, where more effort would need to be put into requirements gathering, usability and HCI than had been the case in the past. The degrees emphasise HCI and usability from day one, and the subjects underpin the whole programme. The new approach has proved popular with students and feedback from employers has confirmed that we are producing highly sought after graduates with a very marketable skill set.

For further information see:

http://www.computing.dundee.ac.uk/research/publication.asp

Human-Computer Interaction - INTERACT'99 (Volume II)
S. Brewster, A. Cawsey & G. Cockton (Editors)
Published by The British Computer Society © IFIP TC.13, 1999

Laboratory Overview: Human Communication Research Centre, University of Edinburgh

HCRC

HCRC, University of Edinburgh
2, Buccleuch Place
Edinburgh EH8 9LW
Scotland, UK
Email: hcrcinfo@cogsci.ed.ac.uk

Abstract: The Human Communication Research Centre (HCRC) has existed for ten years as an Interdisciplinary Research Centre set up by the UK Economic and Social Research Council (ESRC). Located at the Universities of Edinburgh and Glasgow, its mission is to apply the techniques and understandings of Cognitive Science to the field of human communication. Its research spans many areas in Psychology, Linguistics and Artificial Intelligence, with applications in HCI, language engineering, education, speech technology, etc.

Keywords: communication, cognition, language, HCI, education, Edinburgh, Glasgow

1 Introduction

The Human Communication Research Centre (HCRC) is an Interdisciplinary Research Centre at the Universities of Edinburgh and Glasgow, funded by the Economic and Social Research Council.

Established for an initial five-year period in 1989, its success was rewarded with a further grant for a second 5 years. The Centre has more than trebled its core grant by attracting other external funding, with an annual turnover now on the order of £2m.

HCRC is based on a core of senior staff contributed by the departments of Psychology at Edinburgh, Glasgow and also Durham, with the Division of Informatics and department of Theoretical and Applied Linguistics at Edinburgh. HCRC has become a major centre for postgraduate study and actively pursues training and research links with outside users in both the public and private sectors.

2 Research Activities

Within HCRC there are three Research Working Groups, specialising in Dialogue, Mechanisms of Language Processing, and Graphics & Language. In addition the Language Technology Group (LTG) and the Multimedia Communications Group (MCG) coordinate applied projects. All of the groups are available to help outside organisations and companies

2.1 Towards Computer Conversation

An important premise of the Dialogue Group's research is that natural dialogue can be effectively approached using existing technical tools which have so far tended to be limited to relatively artificial situations. Theoretical insights developed here will help us both to understand how human communication works, and to work towards computer systems that can engage in realistic conversation. Much of this research is relevant to the applied work of the MCG.

2.2 Language Processing

How language is processed is the central question being addressed by the Mechanisms of Language Processing (MLaP) Group. This topic is critical to the study of language use, and also in the development of language technology. The issues encompass all levels of processing, from sounds to meaning. A recent focus is on integration of rule-based and statistical methods of processing. Improved documentation design is also at the heart of the Group's concern with how presentation affects the processing and understanding of discourse. The mechanisms of production and comprehension are examined by integrating approaches from psychology and formal theory with the application of computational methods.

2.3 Graphical Communication Systems

The Graphics & Language Group uses formal and computational methods to study graphical communication and its setting in linguistic contexts. The relationships between graphics and language, and their uses in information transfer and reasoning, are immediately relevant to the effective use of multimedia computing systems. Applications are pursued especially in education, with implications for the development of "core skills" in representation, thinking and reasoning.

3 Interfacing with Industry

While HCRC's basic research is organised by Working Group, our interface with industry cross-cuts these groups. An overarching theme is improving the effectiveness of communication. All of HCRC's research has implications for the effectiveness of communication whether within companies and institutions or between company and customer. HCRC research addresses influences on communication over a broad range, all the way from the predictability of messages in context; through the differing expertise of participants; from familiarity with information technology to individual differences in cognitive styles among communicators.

The Language Technology Group brings together the projects in HCRC which are most directly applied to the development of computer systems. These span natural language interfaces, document generation, text analysis and intelligent editorial assistance. LTG developments embody the rapid application of basic research, and at the same time provide data from real-world applications to feed back into fundamental investigation.

The Multimedia Communications Group works most characteristically in the evaluation of multimedia communication systems, where HCRC research on dialogue and, for example, speech intelligibility is highly relevant to determining the applicability of technology.

4 Facilities

HCRC is comprehensively provided with facilities for research and development work, including fully networked computing resources. The Centre is able to collaborate with activities in all areas of IT, including multimedia and intelligent interfaces., experimental and evaluation work, etc.

5 Expertise

HCRC involves approximately 60 academic and related staff, offering an extremely wide range of expertise in human communication. The development and exploitation of Language Technology is a speciality, for which the LTG manager may be contacted direct.

HCRC can be visited on the World Wide Web at:

http://www.hcrc.ed.ac.uk/

Human-Computer Interaction - INTERACT'99 (Volume II)
S. Brewster, A. Cawsey & G. Cockton (Editors)
Published by The British Computer Society © IFIP TC.13, 1999

NCR Knowledge Lab

P. Lynch, S. J. Emmott and G. Johnson

NCR Knowledge Lab
206 Marylebone Road
London
UK
Email: knowledge.lab@unitedkingdom.ncr.com

Abstract: The Knowledge Lab is situated in the heart of the NCR's Financial Solutions Group headquarters, in London. The overall objective of the Lab is to explore, predict and create future technologies and services that will enable and build strong, lasting relationships between financial service providers and their consumers. We call these *Relationship Technologies*. This paper aims to briefly tell the story of why, what, how and who we are.

Keywords: Knowledge Lab, Relationship Technologies, financial services, consumer research

1 Why?

The financial services industry is rapidly changing as a result of consumer and market forces. The principles companies have relied upon to guide key market decisions are becoming less reliable as many markets form and transform in unexpected ways. For example, the adoption of the Internet and mobile telephony could not have been easily predicted by 'technology trends' alone. The relationship between consumers and providers is increasingly becoming more digital and remote. The Knowledge Lab was set up by NCR's Financial Solutions Group, in London (see figure one), to explore, predict and create technologies that will help support future consumer and provider relationships.

2 What?

At the Knowledge Lab, we believe that the solution to these market changes lies in evolving today's information technologies into appropriate *Relationship Technologies*; technologies that are there when we need them, are easy to communicate with, are sensitive to our needs, know and understand who we are and what we want, and are technologies that we trust. These are technologies that will define and shape the future of e-commerce.

Figure 1: The NCR Knowledge Lab, London.

Our chief research objectives are:

- To better understand, from a consumer's perspective, the context in which relationship technologies will emerge in the future network economy.

- To understand the inter-relationships between consumers, technology, information and e-commerce in the future.
- To identify, create, evaluate and exploit the emerging technologies that will form the platforms for relationship technologies for the financial services industry.

3 Who?

A consortium model lies behind the Knowledge Lab. We have over twenty leading financial organisations from around the world (including banks in Canada, UK, Australia, and US) who support, guide and have privileged access to our research program and its findings.

The research team has been built up over the last two years and comprises a talented group from a variety of disciplines. The teams include artists, mathematicians, designers, human factors, computer scientists, philosophers, economists and applied psychologists. In addition, we have many university alliances supporting the Lab's research program.

4 How and What?

Four teams, who work together on many projects, undertake the program of research. The teams are:

4.1 User Experience

The convergence of computing, networks and everyday things is key to the development of the future of computing. We focus not just on future technologies but also on the future of fashion, style, design and architecture. By doing so we extend the notion of Human Computer Interaction (HCI) beyond simply the Graphical User Interface (GUI) and into the inter-relationships between physical interaction, aesthetics and context sensitivity of interaction, function and form - *Relationship Technologies*. We are creating a new generation of consumer-centric computing that people will want to use for both inter-personal and commercial relationships. An example is the Lab's Microwave Bank concept that allows users to easily access a core set of online services via an intelligent microwave oven.

4.2 Emerging Technologies

The two key directions in the near future of technology seem to be divergent: communication protocols and computing devices. Communication protocols are becoming standardised, more universal, and becoming a key part of everything virtual and actual. Computing devices themselves are becoming more specialised, more particular and more tailored to individual needs.

Understanding, using and exploiting the potential of these emerging technologies is a key area of our research. Current projects include wearable technologies, and developing novel web-based applications.

4.3 Consumer Research

Understanding the inter-relationships between people, technology, lifestyle and consumerism is critical to creating Relationship Technologies. These inter-relationships tell us about how different types of people adopt and use technologies, and how this behaviour is influenced by factors such as service, brand, and style.

Typical market research approaches such as questionnaires and focus groups often have significant shortcomings for understanding consumers in this respect. Our aim is to evolve current methods for studying consumers and more importantly develop alternative tools and techniques.

4.4 Computational Modelling

Retailers and banks will increasingly be awash in an ocean of customer data. This information is potentially valuable to identify and retain profitable customers, but it is extremely difficult to know *how* to use the information effectively to increase profit.

In the Computational Modelling team we are developing the next generation of predictive models using Bayesian approaches because of its ability to quantify uncertainty and its flexibility in incorporating expert business knowledge. A major project is trying to model consumers' lifetime value.

5 Conclusion

In the NCR Knowledge Lab we are conducting research into the next generation of computing - Relationship Technologies. The diverse array of skills within the Lab and its consortium of leading financial institutions make our research. We are a young and rapidly growing research Lab that has already gained considerable world-wide recognition for pushing the boundaries of established research.

For more details see:

http://www.knowledgelab.com

Human-Computer Interaction - INTERACT'99 (Volume II)
S. Brewster, A. Cawsey & G. Cockton (Editors)
Published by The British Computer Society © IFIP TC.13, 1999

Many Irons in the Fire: A Strategic Usability Programme in Lucent Technologies Network Management

Rod Moyse

Lucent Technologies GSM R&D
The Quadrant, Westlea, Swindon SN5 7DJ UK
Email: rmoyse@lucent.com

Abstract: We describe a usability improvement programme for a Lucent Technologies network management product. Java technology is used with established HCI approaches to overcome architectural and resource problems. Solutions include a browser for complex object structures, a rule-based network consistency checker, and multi-layered topological views to visualise network connectivity.

Keywords: Usability; HCI; wireless networks; Java; digital maps; consistency checking; rule-based system

1 Introduction

Our task was to improve the usability of a Lucent Technologies network management system. This paper outlines some approaches we used to overcome problems arising from the product architecture and resource limits. The system manages the distributed software in the network elements of wireless telephone networks, and runs on UNIX servers. The product has served a narrow and highly technical sector of the mobile communications market where usability has not been seen as a priority and so was not emphasised in development. As the market has matured and competition has intensified, the rules have changed. Usability is now seen as a major element of product quality, particularly where service providers wish to reduce costs by using less technically sophisticated personnel for routine system operation. The size and complexity of the application, the need to integrate a new UI with the application core, and the dependence on base station development present us with a serious challenge.

Lucent Technologies is a US$30 billion global company with 128 years of experience. The company, with its headquarters in Murray Hill, NJ. USA, designs, builds and delivers a wide range of public and private networks, communications systems, data networking systems, business telephone systems and microelectronic components. Bell Laboratories is the research and development arm of the company (http://www.lucent.com).

2 Methods & Solutions

We faced a major issue in the number of windows being generated to display the Detail, Modify and Create modes for the thousands of objects in the system, such as radio terminals, channels, etc. Configuration or investigative work produced a large number of open windows that placed a major strain on operators' cognitive resources and interfered with their ability to focus on the current task. In order to give a detailed account of this and other problems we carried out at wide range of usability exercises. These included co-operative evaluations, observational studies, a questionnaire survey, extended interviews, analysis of customer-written 'fault' descriptions, and collation of documents from internal and external sources. We then identified "urgent" issues and gave a rationale for their selection, relevant scenarios, a statement of recommended solutions, and some prototype designs. The outcome was a new Object Manager browser which integrated dozens of windows into a single tool while giving the user strong navigational support based on the domain's object model. This greatly reduced the cognitive load imposed upon them. This integrated tool required a new GUI architecture, and our overriding goal in designing this was the complete abstraction of the GUI from the underlying application core. The cost of achieving this and all the new screens in C++ would have been prohibitive. Use of Java and Sun's Swing components gave a great increase in productivity and adequate run-time performance. It was also easy to move prototypes between platforms to show them widely and carry out co-operative evaluation exercises at various sites. In turn, this helped us to exploit a Rapid Application Development approach that directly involved customers.

These evaluation exercises were part of a sustained programme of lobbying and education intended to raise the profile of usability issues and to gain management support for the necessary solutions. Customer site visits were a highly significant step here. Clear and graphic evidence of customer requirements is hard to ignore. The Java implementations gained significant support as they allowed a more flexible and timely response to our customers' demands.

The scale of the proposed development meant that even with the productivity benefits of Java we had to reduce the work required if the project was to go ahead. The prototyping team sought a technical response to this issue: they produced a very neat Java Bean-based wizard where the developer/ designer graphically configures the components, data connections, and layouts that they desire. The Java layout manager then renders these onto the available panel and the configuration is saved. The necessary GUI screens are provided without a line of code being touched, and there are also run-time benefits.

A different problem concerned the consistency checking of wireless networks. Specific relationships must be maintained between parameters both within and across cells otherwise calls may be dropped or there may even be complete service failures. Errors may be easily introduced as frequency plans are adjusted or networks are expanded. The difficulty is at the level of flexibility: different service providers want to perform different checks and may frequently want to change or edit the checks that they perform. This makes it very difficult to have the checks compiled into a given product release. Anyone writing 'personalised' checks in e.g. SQL would need to be an expert in the structure of the database as well as in SQL. It is precisely this that we wish to avoid, as we require a flexible mechanism where checks can be edited or created by non-experts. We achieved this by encoding the checks in a small forward-chaining rule-based system. The logic is not complex but the ability to edit the text definition of the rules and to then execute them without re-compilation gives us the flexibility we require. The input data is pre-processed to allow a simple rule syntax. Also, swapping over the rule packets allows us to use the same tool to check data from widely differing systems. When resources allow, we intend to build a graphical rule editor. The output of the system is a report of the inconsistencies detected.

A quite different view of the network is provided by the 'Toplogical' or map-based view. This superimposes layers of vector graphics over digital mapping data. When thinking of their network 'in the large' or troubleshooting,, operators naturally use a geographical model. The usability challenge here is to provide a highly responsive tool that can display large quantities of data without undue clutter, and which will allow the user to zoom and pan rapidly without getting lost. Strong navigational support is essential. We used third-party Java software which allows multiple co-ordinated 'views' to be displayed in a single pane, so that a large zoomed-in 'detailed' display is co-ordinated with a smaller navigator pane which always shows the full mapping area. This combination of flexibility and navigation support has proved very popular. Layers for urban areas, roads, and major geographical features can be switched on and off, and the network connectivity can be displayed directly. Crucially we can display the 'virtual' links or 'handover' relationships that are of fundamental interest to the operators and which are not normally visible.

Some interesting HCI issues arise in this work. When do we switch to show streets rather than geographical features? If different types of cells are co-located, how are we to represent these without clutter or interference? Should we give them different layers, or should we displace them slightly on a single layer using a 'star' representation linked to the central point? A similar issue arises in relation to zooming: what representation should you use to prevent closely-located objects overlapping when you zoom out? Our work on these continues.

For further details see:

http://www.lucent.com

The Centre for HCI Design - City University

Alistair Sutcliffe, Director

Centre for HCI Design, School of Informatics,
City University, Northampton Square,
London EC1V 0HB, UK.
Email: a.g.sutcliffe@city.ac.uk

Abstract: The Centre for HCI Design at City University is a leading centre of excellence for research in cognitive engineering, requirements engineering and advanced interfaces including multimedia and virtual environments. This overview summarises the key areas of research within the Centre, highlighting our commitment to bringing theoretical perspectives to bear on the process and products of software development.

Keywords: Human-Computer Interaction, Requirements Engineering, Cognitive Engineering, Multimedia

1 Introduction

The Centre for HCI Design was formed in January 1991 as a focus of research excellence for human computer interaction design within City University. The Centre concentrates on HCI-in-the-large, i.e. user-centred design of complete applications rather than HCI-in-the-small for detailed design of interactive artefacts. The main aim of the Centre is to develop models, methods and tools to bring cognitive engineering research to bear on the process and products of software development. Within this strategic remit, the Centre conducts a spectrum of research ranging from cognitive science to design methodology and development of novel interface designs. The Centre has strong links with industry and commercial uptake of academic research is a key objective. The Centre is organised into three sub-groups according to funded projects and strategic interests.

Cognitive Engineering

The cognitive engineering group conducts basic research on theoretical models and methods for decision making and assessment in complex, safety-related domains. The EPSRC Project *DATUM* researched methods for risk assessment and safety design of human operation and human computer interaction in complex control systems. Another theme is investigation of designers' knowledge and practice in safety critical applications to understand how designers' reasoning may be supported. Human risk related judgement is being investigated in the MAFF sponsored *CROM (Cognitive Route Model)* project by theoretical and experimental studies to create a cognitive model which predicts human risk-related judgement for food choice according to personal profiles, type of risk, etc. Cognitive models of Information Retrieval (IR) are being researched in the ESRC project *Modelling Information Seeking Strategies and Resources*. In this work we have developed a theory that predicts users' information searching behaviour, their support requirements in an IR interface design, and help configuration/adaptation of IR services to individual users' changing needs.

Multimedia and Advanced Interfaces

The multimedia and advanced interfaces group researches theoretical models, methods and novel software architectures motivated by design issues in multimedia interfaces, 3D visualisation for information browsing and virtual reality applications. Experimental studies with complex 3D visualisations have given insight into the process of user interaction with complex visual interfaces leading to a design method that was applied to novel 3D interfaces for information browsing. In multimedia, experimental studies of human attention by eyetracking have led to new guidelines for multimedia design which have been incorporated into a method and are supported by a design tool. In virtual reality, a theory of interaction has been developed which has been operationalised as design principles and a walkthrough evaluation method. These research themes are continuing to be developed in the EU *Multimedia Broker* project which is developing retrieval, access and presentation services for multimedia applications over the Internet.

Requirements and Systems Engineering
The requirements engineering group investigates process for requirements acquisition, scenario based modelling and theories of generic knowledge which are applied in tools for software reuse and validation in requirements engineering. Generic models of domain knowledge have been developed to support specification reuse and requirements validation. The generic models have been validated by empirical studies with software designers, and a prototype toolset has demonstrated the utility of these models in requirements critiquing, validation and knowledge reuse. Methods for requirements analysis have been created which integrate scenario based analysis with walkthrough approaches and design rationales. The research continues in the EU long term research project *CREWS*. In business process design, we are researching methods for process redesign and IT requirements definition in the EPSRC *CORK* project.

2 Research Activity

The distinctive feature of the Centre is the application of cognitive theory to the design process. For example analogical memory theory was applied to matching domain for requirements engineering; while theories of attention and human information processing have been applied to design of multimedia interfaces and IR systems. The Centre is one of the few institutions with researchers in both software engineering and human computer interaction giving it a unique capability for synthesising multi-disciplinary research contributions to advance basic science and the design process in systems engineering. Finally the Centre has a strong commitment to application of ideas in realistic industrial contexts, as shown by our collaboration with several industrial partners. While the main themes of the Centre will continue in the future, we will concentrate research on design of complex socio technical systems- total systems engineering, and investigate both creative and formal approaches to design of interactive systems.
The Centre has 5 members of academic staff, 3 research fellows, and 7 research students. Research interests of staff are: Professor Alistair Sutcliffe, (Centre Director) cognitive modelling, design methodology for multimedia and virtual reality systems, visual human computer communication, information retrieval, human factors in safety critical systems, usability evaluation, requirements engineering, software reuse, structured development methods and business process design; Dr Neil Maiden, (senior lecturer) requirements engineering, requirements acquisition methods, procurement methods and software reuse; Dr Helen Sharp, (senior lecturer) software engineering design process, software engineering education, and pedagogical patterns; Stephanie Wilson (lecturer) user interface design methods and novel design tools, user participation in design, multimedia, designing for the Web and usability evaluation; Dr Julia Galliers, (lecturer) safety critical user interface engineering, decision support in safety critical domains and accessible user interfaces.

Some of the more recent achievements and research products are enumerated below.

Requirements Engineering Methods: Scenario-based Requirements Analysis (SCRAM) - Sutcliffe 1995, 1997; Scenario-based Requirements Validation (SAVRE) - Maiden et al 1998; Requirements Acquisition (ACRE) - Maiden and Rugg 1996; Process for product selection in RE (PORE) - Maiden and Ncube 1998.

Human Computer Interaction Design Methods: Task-based Information Analysis (TIM) - Sutcliffe 1997; Safety Critical User Interface Engineering - Sutcliffe 1997, Sutcliffe and Ryan 1997; Multimedia User Interface Design guidelines and method - Sutcliffe and Faraday 1994, 1977 (currently being incorporated into ISO standard 14915 Multimedia User Interface Design); Virtual Reality User Interface Design - Kaur et al 1997.

Software Tools Reusable library of generic models for Requirements Engineering and retrieval process (AIR) - Maiden 1997; Scenario-based requirements validation assistant (SAVRE) - Maiden et al 1997 Reusable class library for information retrieval applications (INTUITIVE) - Sutcliffe et al 1995; Web-based information searching tools (Multimedia Broker) Multimedia User Interface Design Advisor – Faraday and Sutcliffe 1997.

More details can be found on the Centre's web-site:

http://www.soi.city.ac.uk/research/hcid/index.htm

Author Index

Aczel, J. 3
Alem, L. 55
Anderson, A. 221
Anderson, T. 85
Atyeo, M. 223

Baber, C. 5, 17, 35
Bacigalupi, M. 105
Bates, R. 7
Benjamin, I. 209
Bernsen, N. 73
Bertus, E. 138
Bevan, N. 107, 109
Beyer, H. 125
Binsted, K. 77, 209
Blandford, A. 9
Boivie, I. 136
Borchers, J. 135
Bornat, R. 3
Borras, C. 145
Boud, A. 35
Boyle, T. 27
Brewster, S. 19, 21, 45, 67, 97, 133
Buchanan, G. 11
Butterworth, R. 9

Campbell, C. 93
Carey, T. 13
Clarke, I. 15
Cleal, B. 73
Cook, C. 53
Cooper, L. 17
Coventry, L. 151
Cox, M. 134
Crawford, A. 111
Crease, M. 19, 21
Crerar, A. 213
Cribbin, T. 23
Culwin, F. 113, 115
Cummaford, S. 25

Davenport, E. 211
de Vries, G. 215
del Galdo, E. 127
Dibben, M. 211
Dineen, F. 79
Dlay, S. 39
Dunlop, M. 133
Dybkjær, L. 73

Earthy, J. 117
Economou, D. 27
Eklund, J. 55
Emmott, S. 229
Esposito, C. 119

Faraday, P. 81
Fleischhauer, D. 191
Foster, R. 145
Foveau, F. 83
France, E. 29
Fung, P. 3

Ghosh, G. 157
Gillary, P. 47
Girgensohn, A. 121
Glendye, A. 97
Gonzalez-Abascal, J. 139
Good, J. 9
Göransson, B. 163
Graves Petersen, M. 185
Gray, P. 21
Grayson, D. 31
Gregor, P. 213, 225
Griffiths, R. 135
Gulliksen, J. 136
Gunn, K. 168

Halskov Madsen, K. 185
Halverson, C. 217
Hamilton, F. 33
Haniff, D. 35
Harrigan, K. 13
Harris, T. 5
Harrison, B. 5
HCRC 227
Healey, P. 140
Hewett, T. 123
Holland, S. 13
Holtzblatt, K. 125
Horita, M. 15
Hussam, A. 85
Hutchison, A. 87
Hynninen, T. 201

Ina, S. 37
indigo V 213

Jacobs, N. 85
Jensen, S. 89
Johansson, A. 91
Johnson, C. 137
Johnson, G. 17, 151, 229
Johnson, H. 33, 140
Johnson, P. 33, 140
Jokela, T. 174
Jones, C. 39
Jones, M. 47

Kaptelinin, V. 217
Karat, J. 217
Katz, L. 41
Kelley, J. 89
Kinnunen, T. 201
Kramer, J. 138
Kurosu, M. 43

Lambie, T. 141
Lantz, A. 136
Lee, A. 121
Leplâtre, G. 45
Linde, J. 91
Liukkonen-Olmiala, T. 201
Long, J. 25, 141
Luckin, R. 221
Lynch, P. 179, 215, 229

Mackaness, W. 15
Maglio, P. 93
Märker, O. 191
Marsden, G. 11, 47

Marsh, S. 211
Masoodian, M. 73
Matsuura, S. 43
May, K. 93
Mayes, J.T. 79
McKendree, J. 221
McKirdy, J. 49
Ménier, G. 51
Mitchell, W. 27
Modjeska, D. 95
Monk, A. 221
Montgomery Masters, M. 97
Morishima, S. 77
Moriya, S. 57
Moyse, R. 231

Newell, A. 225
Nicolle, C. 139
Nielsen, F. 77
Noirhomme-Fraiture, M. 139

O'Mahony, A. 89
O'Neill, E. 140
O'Shea, A. 53
Oakley, I. 97
Oestreicher, L. 134
Ormerod, T. 221

Peiris, D. 213
Pemberton, L. 135
Pettersen, T. 99
Pirkola, J. 174
Plowman, L. 209
Poirier, F. 51
Procter, R. 59

Quinn, C. 55, 134

Ramsay, J. 223
Rattle, J. 223
Rauterberg, M. 134
Ren, X. 57
Rose, T. 127

Sandbäck, T. 163
Schinzel, B. 213
Schmidt-Belz, B. 191
Shepherd, A. 217
Sherwood-Jones, B. 117
Smith, B. 93
Springel, S. 209
Stanyer, D. 59
Stewart, T. 196
Stoltze, M. 134
Stork, A. 141
Storøy, H. 99
Strand, C. 99
Strens, R. 61
Sutcliffe, A. 129, 233

Tarby, J.-C. 83
Thatcher, A. 41
Thimbleby, H. 11, 47, 211
Thomas, J. 209
Thomas, R. 63
Todd, S. 101
Trabak, A. 179
Treglown, M. 65
Trepess, D. 41
Turner, P. 61
Turner, S. 61

Walker, A. 67
Westerman, S. 23
Weston, J. 117
Wilson, S. 129
Wolf, C. 217
Wong, B. 69

Yotsukura, T. 77

Zhai, S. 93